BACK THEN — **"The most dangerous man in Western New York"** is how Emanuel Fried was publicly labeled **in the Time of the Toad, the 1950's**, by a Western New York corporation president, a prominent member of the Greater Buffalo Chamber of Commerce. This was followed by a major AFL-CIO union putting out a leaflet at factory gates, warning workers not to talk to Fried — followed by his expulsion from membership in another major AFL-CIO union.

AND NOW — **In 1991** the Greater Buffalo Chamber of Commerce joined the Arts Council in Buffalo and Erie County to publicly honor Emanuel Fried with **the Individual Artist Award for lifetime achievement in the arts.** And the Western New York Peace Center selected Fried as their **1991 honoree for his lifetime contribution to the cause of peace.** This followed the **1990** action on part of the Washington based Labor Heritage Foundation created by officers of national AFL-CIO, publicly honoring Fried with the **Joe Hill Award for lifetime contribution to advancement of the cause of labor through the arts.**

"He who has a WHY to live for
can bear almost any HOW."
            —*Nietzche*

WORKS OF EMANUEL FRIED

PREVIOUSLY PUBLISHED
Big Ben Hood, novel
Meshugah and Other Stories, fiction
Elegy for Stanley Gorski, play
Drop Hammer, play
The Dodo Bird, play

PLAYS PRODUCED
Brothers For A' That — Rochester, Pittsburgh, Buffalo
(Semi-finalist in Denver Center Theatre Play Contest and Beverly Hills Theatre
Guild — Julie Harris Award Play Contest. Honorable Mention in Perkins Play
Contest sponsored by International Society of Dramatists)
The Dodo Bird — New York, Toronto, Chicago, Pittsburgh, Cleveland,
Buffalo, Los Angeles, etc.
Drop Hammer — Los Angeles, Kansas City, Buffalo
The Second Beginning — New York, Pittsburgh, Kansas City, Buffalo
(Midwest Playwrights Program Selection, New York Writers Theatre Selection)
Elegy for Stanley Gorski — Buffalo
A Piece of Cake — Pittsburgh
David and Son — Buffalo
The Peddler — New York, University of Arkansas (Fayetteville)
Triangle — State University College at Buffalo
Brother Gorski — New York
The Judge — Pittsburgh, Buffalo
Rose — New York, Detroit, Buffalo
Mark of Success — Catawba College (Salisbury, N.C.)
(New American Playwrights Contest Winner)

PLAY: STAGED READING
Cocoon — Boston, Kansas City, Buffalo
(Playwrights Platform Selection in Boston)
Big Ben Hood (play) — Buffalo

NOT YET COMMERCIALLY AVAILABLE
(Circulating in manuscript form)
Lasting Out, novel
People Are Not Sheep, novella
Old Haunts, collection of short stories
Union Leader Stories, collection of labor short stories that appeared weekly in
Buffalo Union Leader
Pardon Me, Your Class is Showing, collection of essays

SCREENPLAYS FOR FEATURE FILMS
The Dodo Bird
(Optioned twice by Canadian film companies, but film never made; seed
money provided by Canadian Film Development Corporation)
Lasting Out

THE
UN-AMERICAN

Autobiographical
Non-Fiction Novel
by
Emanuel Fried

Springhouse Editions/Labor Arts Books

FIRST EDITION
PUBLISHED 1992

Copyright © 1992 by Emanuel Fried

Published by Springhouse Editions
in association with Labor Arts Books

SE ISBN: 1 - 877800 - 02 - 3
LAB ISBN: 0 - 9603888 - 6 - 9

Copies may be ordered from:

Labor Arts Books
1064 Amherst Street
Buffalo, N.Y. 14216

Printed in the United States of America

"That's me, Infantry 2nd Lieutenant, Army of the United States, World War II. Photo, 1944."

Have You Seen This Man?

HE is a **Communist**. His name is **MANNY FRIED.** HE has **red hair.** HE wears **glasses.** HE is a **COMMUNIST PARTY MEMBER.** HE has been identified by sworn testimony before Congressional Committees as a Communist.

HAS HE BEEN IN YOUR HOUSE? If he calls on you, remember, he is a **COMMUNIST,** an enemy of America.

He now tries to appear respectable because he works for the I.A.M. The I.A.M. is the other Union trying to organize you. If you should vote for the I.A.M. and pay dues to I.A.M. you would be paying wages to this **COMMUNIST, MANNY FRIED.**

Remember, the I.A.M. (called the Machinist Union) has **COMMUNISTS** on their payroll.

SO BE WISE. *organize* into I.U.E., the Union dedicated to drive the communists out of the labor movement.

Support I.U.E., the Union which has more G.E. employees as members than all other Unions combined!

DON'T PAY WAGES to America's enemies with your dues dollars.

This man is a Communist. He is on the **PAYROLL** of the I.A.M.

Issued by I.U.E.

502 Prudential Bldg.

28 Church St., Buffalo, N. Y.

JOIN I. U. E.

SIGN THE ATTACHED CARD

"Leaflet distributed to workers at main entrance to Fillmore Avenue GE plant, Buffalo, N.Y., when Machinists Union and International Union of Electrical Workers were competing for bargaining rights. This leaflet gave Machinists Union the reason to remove me from leadership of organizing drive. Those GE workers then voted for no union and I was subsequently charged with 'association with communist causes' and was fired and expelled from the union — blacklisted from 1956 to 1972 when, after I had several plays produced Off-Broadway in New York, I was hired at Buffalo State College to teach Creative Writing."

"Mr. and Mrs. Mandel Lurie of The Park Lane announce the forthcoming marriage of their daughter, Rhoda, will take place at The Park Lane on March 21, 1941. Photo, Buffalo Courier-Express, March 9, 1941."

"That's me, Edward Mann (my former stage name) far right, in party scene in Arthur Kober's *HAVING WONDERFUL TIME*, directed by Marc Connelly, at New York's Lyceum Theatre. Center are Jules (renamed John in Hollywood) Garfield and Sheldon Leonard, with Kathryn Locke between them. Photo, 1936."

"With Rhoda in living room in Gates Circle Apartments at time when, years later, Mindy's Brandeis University professor told her that when he was a student at University of Buffalo he thought of us as the 'Fred Astaire and Ginger Rogers of the Left.' Photo, Circa 1948."

"That's me, not in costume, while touring with WPA Federal Theatre production of Shakespeare's *TAMING OF THE SHREW*. Photo, circa 1934."

"Lorrie having her breakfast on enclosed porch of The Park Lane with her grandfather, Mandel Lurie, who died not long after that. Later, asked what she remembered about him, Lorrie said, 'He loved me.' Photo, 1946."

"Rhoda with our two redhaired daughters, baby Melinda Lurie Fried (Mindy) and Lorrie Elizabeth Mary Fried (just call me Lorrie) in our backyard at 125 Chatham Avenue, Buffalo, N.Y. — three years before I was subpoenaed to appear before House Committee on Un-American Activities."

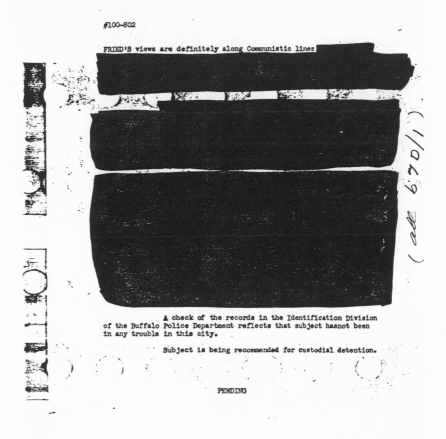

#100-802

FRIED'S views are definitely along Communistic lines

A check of the records in the Identification Division of the Buffalo Police Department reflects that subject hasnot been in any trouble in this city.

Subject is being recommended for custodial detention.

PENDING

"This is a typical blanked-out page from the FBI dossier on me, received under Freedom of Information Act. For years I have been trying to get such blanked-out information; my request is currently before the court. Note the phrase: 'Subject is being recommended for custodial detention.' There was much evidence back then that FBI already had set up the equivalent of concentration camps where they hoped to 'custodially detain' those whose political thoughts they considered dangerous."

"With presidential candidate Henry Wallace when I was American Labor Party candidate for Congress — at reception in Hotel Statler, Buffalo, N.Y., Dec. 11, 1947."

"Lorrie and Mindy. Photo, circa 1952."

"That's me, with 20th Infantry Regiment, Sixth Division, in Yosu, South Korea. There's a note on back of photo I sent to my wife: 'This rugged looking guy is awfully deceiving, isn't he? The extrovertive exterior doesn't seem to fit what goes on inside him, does it? Ugly brute!' — While I was in South Korea (over a year, 1945-46) I was told by a CIC officer (Counter Intelligence Corps) that on orders from the Commanding General he was required to turn in regular reports on what I said and did, the General apparently considering me suspect because my civilian job had been a union organizer for the United Electrical, Radio & Machine Workers (UE). The CIC Officer told me: 'The General sees everything through rose colored glasses.' Photo, March, 1946."

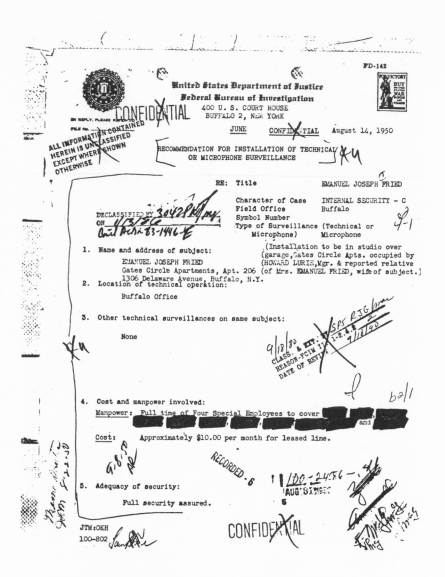

FD-142

United States Department of Justice
Federal Bureau of Investigation
400 U. S. COURT HOUSE
BUFFALO 2, NEW YORK

JUNE   CONFIDENTIAL   August 14, 1950

RECOMMENDATION FOR INSTALLATION OF TECHNICAL
OR MICROPHONE SURVEILLANCE

CONFIDENTIAL

ALL INFORMATION CONTAINED
HEREIN IS UNCLASSIFIED
EXCEPT WHERE SHOWN
OTHERWISE

RE: Title   EMANUEL JOSEPH FRIED

Character of Case   INTERNAL SECURITY - C
Field Office   Buffalo
Symbol Number
Type of Surveillance (Technical or
    Microphone)   Microphone

DECLASSIFIED

1. Name and address of subject: (Installation to be in studio over
                                      (garage, Gates Circle Apts. occupied by
   EMANUEL JOSEPH FRIED   (HOWARD LURIE, Mgr. & reported relative
   Gates Circle Apartments, Apt. 206 (of Mrs. EMANUEL FRIED, wife of subject.)
   1306 Delaware Avenue, Buffalo, N.Y.
2. Location of technical operation:

   Buffalo Office

3. Other technical surveillances on same subject:

   None

4. Cost and manpower involved:

   Manpower: Full time of Four Special Employees to cover

   Cost: Approximately $10.00 per month for leased line.

5. Adequacy of security:

   Full security assured.

JTM:OKH
100-802

CONFIDENTIAL

RECORDED-6

"FBI wanted to bug my wife's painting studio. (Her studio was over garage of Park Lane Apts owned by my wife's family, not over Gates Circle Apts garage.) The reason they gave is that they suspected that men and women who went into her studio went there to hold communist meetings. Actually, those were artist models coming to pose for her and a group of her painting friends. My wife was not political and generally disagreed with my political ideas, though the FBI stupidly states in my dossier that the only reason she is not a communist is because of fear of her father. That's ridiculous. She was her father's favorite and she adored him."

THE UN-AMERICAN

"Addressing outdoor rally in North Tonawanda, N.Y., when UE Strategy Committee
of Local Union presidents and chief stewards — to counter corporate refusal to
negotiate with our union because our officers followed lead of Mine Workers Union
President John L. Lewis to refuse to sign non-communist affidavits — shut down 13
plants in Western New York where we represented thousands of workers, to hold a
special meeting, showing we still had strength to compel continued recognition of
our legally secured bargaining rights. August 9, 1953."

"Buffalo contingent of Lurie family gathered around San Francisco tycoon Louie Lurie, with cigar, on porch of The Park Lane dining room. Rhoda and I are on the left. Her father, Mandel, and mother, Rae, are on either side of Uncle Louie. Standing over them is their famed maitre d', Peter Gust Economou. Louie and Mandel jointly owned The Park Lane managed by Mandel. Throughout Rhoda's life, her multimillionaire uncle promised her he was leaving her a million dollars in his will, but when he died he left his millions to son Robert, currently owner of San Francisco Giants baseball team, and Rhoda learned that she had been cut out of the will. Uncle Louie was good friend of FBI chief J. Edgar Hoover. I believe it was during this visit to Buffalo that Uncle Louie told me to give up my political ideas and my union organizer job and he would set me up in business with a string of taxicabs. I refused to do that, and I've since wondered if that was why he cut Rhoda out of his will. Photo, circa 1942."

Buffalo Girls Will See Real Matinee Idol On Gridiron Against Niagara Here Sunday

By ROBERT BURLINGHAM
Times Staff Writer

He plays some pretty good football for the Canisius College freshman team and when Jimmy Wilson's undefeated eleven meets the Purple Eagles of Niagara University, Sunday at the Villa, you're bound to see him.

He's not too big, given to the chunky side and topped by red hair. He's a back field man, second string quarterback to be exact, but besides being an athlete he's been a flock of other things, such as:

Actor, dishwasher, bus boy, chemist's assistant, carnival barker, grocery store supervisor, radio announcer, ager, garageman, counsellor at a boys' camp, candyman at the ball park.

His Name?—Well . . .

bellhop, salesman, writer, stage manager. Not bad. What's his name?

That's something else again. Born Emanuel Fried, son of Mr. and Mrs. Solomon Fried, 8 Linden Park, he's also Edward Mann, Broadway actor of considerable ability, and furthermore he's Edward Mann, who writes the Broadway stage column that appears bi-weekly in The Griffin, Canisius undergraduate news publication.

After graduating from Hutchinson-Central High School in 1930, he marked time with various odd jobs,

hanging around the Teck Theater stock players until he got a few bit and atmospheric parts.

Then three years ago he suddenly up and quit his job as a grocery clerk, hitch hiked to New York with two dollars in his pocket.

He was lucky enough to land a job right away with George Ford's summer theater. He played juvenile leads and served as stage manager. From there he obtained a part with the road company of "Sailor Beware," traveling through the East and Middle West.

His first Broadway part followed. It was the role of the reporter in the Theater Guild production, "They Shall Not Die."

Edward Mann romped on from one production to another, traveling to the left steadily and forming the friendship of many leading left-wing dramatists and actors, including Clifford Odets. Elmer Rice's "Judgment Day," "Sailors of Cattaro" and "Crime and Punishment" furnished him with minor roles and good experience.

He Becomes Star

Then he was selected to play the lead in "The Young Go First," becoming the youngest lead actor on Broadway.

The play only lasted six weeks but it was a darned good play for all that," he declared, kicking up a bit of turf with his cleats. (He was

taking time out during a practice session on the gridiron). "Variety said it was the best-acted play of the year, gave all the members of the cast, averaging 25 years old, an exceptionally high rating."

On the strength of his work in "The Young Go First," Mann was approached by Charlie Beahan, Hollywood agent and husband of Sidney Fox, with a tentative offer of a special movie contract for two pictures a year.

"I guess it was a little too tentative though, because nothing ever came of it," he remarked.

"The 'Matinee Idol' quarterback is what *BUFFALO TIMES*, now defunct, labeled me when, out of work following close of *THE YOUNG GO FIRST* in which I played the lead in New York, I returned home in 1935 to be part of undefeated Canisius College freshman football team — a team that included ringers like myself. (I had already played freshman football at University of Iowa.) When football season ended I returned to New York to continue my theatrical career, sadly learning that producers of Brecht's dramatization of Gorki's *MOTHER* had been looking for me to play male lead in that play, which had already closed."

"Rhoda, who turned down frequent requests to pose for fashion magazines, posing for our friend, amateur photographer Jim Tuttle, in backyard of his Frank Lloyd Wright house. Photo, circa 1948."

STANDARD FORM NO. 64

Office Memu   'um • UNITED S...... GOVERNMENT

Mr. Tolson
Mr. Nichols
Mr. Boardman
Mr. Harbo
Mr. Mohr
Mr. Parsons
Mr. Rosen
Mr. Tamm
Mr. Sizoo
Mr. Winterrowd
Tele. Room
Mr. Holloman
Miss Gandy

TO   :   DIRECTOR, FBI (100-24586)   DATE: 3/18/55

FROM :   SAC, BUFFALO   (100-802)

SUBJECT: EMANUEL J. FRIED, aka
         INTERNAL SECURITY - C   CALL INFORMATION CONTAINED
         00 - Buffalo   HEREIN IS UNCLASSIFIED
                        DATE 9/18/80   BY SP5 R364

               Buffalo, N.Y., telephonically advised the Buffalo Office he had received some literature through the mail which he believed to be of Communist nature.

                        was contacted at his place of business 3/10/55, at which time he furnished a mimeographed pamphlet entitled "The Un-American" by EMANUEL J. FRIED. Front page of this pamphlet contains the following notation:

            "This is a short chapter from a novel, The Un-American, on which the author is presently working. He hopes to have it ready for publication soon."

            Also typewritten on the front page of the pamphlet was:

            "Emanuel J. Fried   — U.E. organizer.
            125 Chatham Drive
            Buffalo 16, New York"

            This is the home address of the subject.

            Review of this pamphlet reveals the proposed novel is apparently a book to be based on subject's own experiences. The pamphlet appears to be a chapter dealing with the experience of the principal character while he is away from home, awaiting the time for him to appear before a Congressional Committee. This chapter deals with domestic difficulties caused by the activities of the principal character and hardship imposed on his wife and children. It further tells of the plan of the principal character to challenge the Committee and to decline to give it any information.

REGISTERED
KPG:RMM
(3)

17 MAR 21 1955

"Two pages from FBI dossier wherein FBI declares its interest in *THE UN-AMERICAN*, retaining a chapter in its Buffalo files and stating, 'This matter will be followed closely in an effort to obtain further information concerning the proposed book, especially in order to determine if there are any unfavorable references to the Bureau contained therein.'"

BU 100-802

"You have just read a short chapter from an uncompleted novel The Un-American.

This novel will be ready for publication soon. The author would like to know if you would be interested in reading the completed novel.

Sufficient expression of a desire to read the full completed novel may encourage some publisher to undertake its publication.

A note to the author would be appreciated

           Emanuel J. Fried
           125 Chatham Drive
           Buffalo 16, N.Y."

said he is not acquainted with subject FRIED, and that above mentioned pamphlet was not solicited.

advised he would contact the Buffalo Office if he receives any additional information regarding FRIED's proposed novel.

Above mentioned pamphlet is being retained in Buffalo files. This matter will be followed closely in an effort to obtain further information concerning the proposed book, especially in order to determine if there are any unfavorable references to the Bureau contained therein.

For my grandchildren Andy, Alison and Sasha, for whom I hope this will give a better understanding of what their mothers and grandmother experienced with me during the Time of the Toad in our country.

ABOUT THE AUTHOR. . .

Emanuel Fried conducts the Western New York Playwrights Workshop and is chairman of the Labor Arts Committee of the Greater Buffalo AFL-CIO Central Labor Council. Professor Emeritus in English following retirement from the full-time faculty at State University of New York College at Buffalo, he still teaches one writing course there. He has been a factory worker, a union organizer, a drama and film critic, a reporter, a candidate for Congress, an insurance broker, and with the stage name Edward Mann, an actor on Broadway who studied with Lee Strasburg, Benno Schneider, Elia Kazan, Harold Clurman, Morris Carnovsky, Bobby Lewis, Clifford Odets and others. He acted in New York in over a dozen plays, including the lead in **The Young Go First** directed by Kazan, a supporting role with John Garfield in **Having A Wonderful Time** directed by Marc Connolly and a smaller role in the short-lived production of **Dance Night** directed by Lee Strasburg, and he danced under the direction of Martha Graham in **Panic**, the verse play by Archibald MacLeish. Currently, he is in much demand by theatre companies in Western New York, accepting roles occasionally to keep the feel of performing on the stage — a sense of the dramatic scene — which he believes serves him well in writing both fiction and drama. Back in the Thirties in New York he was a member of the Theatre of Action and acted with the Theatre Union. More recently, he used his play **The Dodo Bird** to bring together the people who formed The New York Labor Theatre.

Born in Brooklyn, one of nine children, he was brought to Buffalo by his parents while he was a young child. He wrote his first play while he was in high school, about the prostitutes he met while working nights as a bellhop at a hotel — his discovery that they were human beings just like other people. When he graduated from high school he worked for several years in the DuPont Cellophane and Rayon factory before going off to the University of Iowa for one year and then on to New York City to become an actor. In 1939 he returned to Buffalo to direct the Buffalo Contemporary Theatre. The theatre company came apart in 1941 as its members went into the armed services during World War II. Fried went to work in the Curtiss Airplane factory where he became co-chairman of the union organizing drive of the United Auto Workers. Fired from Curtiss because of union activity, he was hired by the United Electrical, Radio and Machine Workers of America (UE) and headed up organizing drives at heavy industry factories during the period when that union swelled its ranks to represent 30,000 workers in Western New York.

Fried took time out from union activity to serve almost three years in the infantry, ending up a First Lieutenant, returning from Korea in 1946 to again head up the union's staff in Western New York, where he negotiated contracts and guided union members in many strike situations. In 1956, District 3 of his union voted to go into the Machinists Union to get out from under the heavy barrage of redbaiting being thrown at their members.

He had been summoned before the House Committee on Un-American Activities in 1954 and challenged them to indict him so he could make a court test of the Committee's right to exist under our U.S. Constitution. He was called again before the Committee in 1964 — because of what he was writing, the FBI told his new employer, Canada Life Assurance Company. Fried again refused to answer any questions, telling the Committee it was none of their business what he believed or with whom he associated.

However, in 1956 the Machinists Union Executive Board, by a one vote majority, surrendered to McCarthyism and fired Fried from the organizing staff. Blacklisted, with the FBI intervening to get him fired by every American employer who hired him, Fried finally hooked up with the Canadian insurance company, whose top officers rebuffed the FBI. While selling insurance, he continued writing both plays and novels and completed his college education — getting his BA in 1971, his MA in 1972 and his Ph.D. in 1974. As the result of getting several plays produced during his 16 years on the blacklist, Fried finally got hired in 1972 to teach Creative Writing at State University College at Buffalo.

Through it all, from the time he wrote that first play at the age of 15, he has been stubbornly writing, writing, writing — getting his experience down on paper, for future generations — if not the present generation — to know what it was really like to be on the inside of that turmoil in which he lived and survived.

AUTHOR'S NOTE

My wife Rhoda Lurie Fried — she's Helen Newman in this novel — died on March 17,1989 — and this finally made me feel fully free to publish this work and also to make clear that it is for real, an autobiographical non-fiction account, written with the technique of a novel. What happens in this novel happened to me and Rhoda and was a fundamental factor in our marriage the rest of our life together — from 1954 to 1989.

I decided to leave the names — Danny Newman for me, along with Helen for Rhoda, and all the other names as I'd changed them when I wrote the novel as "a work of fiction," though it never was other than an accurate report of what really happened to our lives before, during and after my appearance before the House Un-American Activities Committee in 1954.

However, I could not resist putting back the real name of what was at that time the most glamorous apartment house and restaurant and cocktail lounge in Buffalo, owned then by Rhoda and her family — The Park Lane — especially since as part and parcel of the local newspapers then declaring me a non-person, they also wiped out the name of the Lurie family as owners of The Park Lane, instead attributing ownership to an old-time employee.

While it appears that the problems connected with my appearance before HUAC in 1954 had been overcome by the end of the events reported in the novel — as I thought they were back then — the reality is that what the experience during that period did to Rhoda was never wiped away. My dossier secured under the Freedom of Information Act reveals that the FBI stupidly categorized Rhoda as a communist and they tried unsuccessfully to get a judge to give them authority to put a listening device in her painting studio in The Park Lane, mistakenly thinking her models were leftwing political activists meeting secretly with her. The truth is that Rhoda varied between being completely apolitical and being generally opposed to my political views.

But the FBI were not the only ones who got it all wrong. One of my daughters, who is now back in school to get her Ph.D., was recently told by her Brandeis University professor that when he was going to the University of Buffalo in the 60's he and his friends thought of Rhoda and me as the Fred Astaire and Ginger Rogers of the Left — (probably because of

Rhoda's tie to The Park Lane) — envying the glamorous life they thought this beautiful couple led.

But Rhoda never forgave me for what she went through because of my appearance before the Un-American Committee. We stayed together, but the rest of our life was troubled. Over the period of all those years we saw a string of psychiatrists and therapists and counselors, continuing right on up to her death from a stroke; in each instance, after several sessions it came down to Rhoda being unable to choke back tears as she accused me, referring back to the Un-American Committee experience, "I did nothing wrong and I got punished because of him."

But despite our differences — social, economic, political and yes, sexual — we remained good friends and supportive partners, which in a desperate scene one night in bed where both of us were trying to figure out why we were still together and if we should still stay together, I spontaneously summarized it, blurting out, "Look, I'll protect you and you protect me — and we'll both be safe." Rhoda never forgot that, quoting it back to me again and again as the factor that kept us together in our troubled relationship right up to the day of her death.

In the hospital, a moment before she died, I smoothed her tense brow and kissed her cheek and told her I loved her, which I did, and still do. A tear squeezed out of her right eye as she struggled to keep it open. And then she died.

I've been asked why I am now publishing this highly personal account. The answer is that I hope that the very fact that it is an "inside account" of what it was really like in that bad time will help to prevent it from happening again — to others, perhaps to you.

THE
UN-AMERICAN

Chapter 1

Spring, 1954
1:30 AM . . . Wednesday

He knew Helen wanted to talk to him about the subpoena and what would happen because of it.

They were sitting up in bed. He had switched off all the lights in the house except one light in the bathroom which they always left on because of the children.

Dreading the scene which was sure to come, Danny watched Helen as she puffed regularly on her cigarette, the burning end glowing each time she sucked in her breath — revealing her well-molded face, her dark brown eyes staring straight ahead into space and seeing nothing. There was a deep vertical furrow between her black eyebrows. Her brooding face receded into the darkness each time she took the cigarette away from her lips.

The silence became painful. As he saw Helen butt out the red end of one cigarette and then light up another one, his resentment mounted.

It had been past one o'clock when he had turned out the lights, and he had to get some decent sleep if he was going to be in condition to handle himself well when he got before that committee. The hell with her and her talk. He slid down under the covers. Helen's voice was sharp.

"You going to sleep?"

"No." Danny sat up again.

Helen's voice relented. "You better go to sleep — you have to get up so early."

"I can sleep on the train." He knew she would not quickly forgive him if he avoided the talk.

"You sure?"

"I'm sure."

Helen ground out the burning end of the second cigarette in the glass ash tray on the night table next to her pillow. In the darkness her voice sounded hollow and unreal. "I don't think you know how I feel about you." She waited for him to

1

say something.

"I think I do."

"How," she immediately challenged him, "*do* I feel?"

"Well" — it was difficult to answer without risking trouble. "It's hard to put something like that into words. — It probably is for you too, isn't it?"

She hesitated. "Yes. Very hard."

But he could tell that she was going to try.

"Danny, you're something special to me." The shaky huskiness in her voice surprised him since he expected that she was going to coldly tell him off before this talk ended. "Danny, you're like no one else I know. That's what makes me love you. And that's also what makes me hate you at times."

He watched the shadowy outline of her face in the darkness, wondering what direction she would take next.

"But," she continued, speaking slowly, seeming to try to think it out as she went along, "I know I love you more than I hate you — "

"Will you please put that in writing — for future reference," he suggested, with quiet sarcasm.

"Oh, Danny — "

She found his hand and held it tight. "I know our marriage started out terrible. But we stuck together for thirteen years and we both changed. You don't know the wonderful feeling I have when I watch you playing with the kids. You look so cute together. All redheads. You so big, and Linda always dancing with you, and gawky Ruth hanging on to your arm. The three of you — such cute redheads."

"What happens when my hair turns white? It's started to turn already." He meant it sarcastically, but Helen treated it as a straight question.

"Your hair has nothing to do with it. It's you! I know you're good for us. You handle Linda and Ruth with so much love. They know you love them. I know you love me."

She squeezed his hand. "And I know you're *good* for me. Without you I never would have stuck to my illustration work until now I'm finally beginning to get somewhere. Before I met you I was just a dilettante with my painting. Trying to show off and be a big shot. Wasting my life at lunches and cocktail parties and night club bars. Proud of my reputation as a drunk and a sexy dame. And miserably unhappy. — You gave my life direction."

She stopped and he sensed that she wanted him to say how good *she* had been for *him*. But from past talks of this kind, he knew that all the nice things said thus far merely preceded the sharp criticism which was sure to come. He said nothing, and Helen went on.

"Sometimes I wonder whether *I'm* immature because I get so upset about you and your union organizing work. Or is it *you* who's the immature one, sticking to your union work even though you know how much it bothers me — "

She interrupted herself to give him a chance to say something. He thought she was trying hard to draw him into a disagreement. This time she waited until he had to say something.

"Who knows?" he said, knowing he was in for enough trouble without saying anything more to make it worse.

Helen let go of his hand.

"Danny, I had already made up my mind" — later, in retrospect, it amazed him how calmly and quietly she said what followed — "that I was going to take the children and leave you." The slow waltz tempo of their bedroom talk suddenly zoomed up to a swiftly racing staccato rhythm and its terrible intensity made it hard for him to breathe. "I called Florida yesterday," Helen continued, appearing to him as unperturbed as if she were telling him about the groceries she had purchased at the store that afternoon, "and I spoke to Fran. I asked her if she had room there for me and the two girls." The tone of her voice changed as she switched off the main subject for a quick side comment. "Incidentally, Danny, she's your friend whether you realize it or not."

He knew she wanted him to ask why her sister was his friend, but the fear that this might really be the end of their marriage, that he might be left desperately alone again as he had been before he had become a union organizer — back during his years as an actor, the years of living alone in the furnished rooms in New York City during the depression Thirties before he had come back home to Buffalo and met Helen and went to work in the aircraft plant — that fear prevented him from talking. He could feel the cold sweat.

"Fran thinks I'll always regret it if I leave you — "

The darkness of their bedroom hid the surprise on his face as he thought how amazing it was that a woman could be preparing to leave her husband, making all the detailed arrangements to walk out on him, while he was completely unaware of what was going on — until, slap, he got hit in the face with the cold wet fish!

"But I'm going, Danny. Not right now. But as soon as Ruth is finished with school. The end of June. I'm going to take the children to Florida with me."

He tried to reassure himself that these nightmare talks had little relationship to reality, that next morning everything returns to what it was before.

But this was the toughest crisis they had ever faced. And this time he might be left all alone in this fifty-year-old three-storied barn of a house in this old respectable middle-class residential section of Buffalo. The fear of that great loneliness he had known once before for so many years in New York City kept him sweating, and he decided that if Helen left with the kids he would move out of the big house. Where? To an empty furnished room again?

Helen went on. "I don't want to leave you. I'd like you to come down to Florida with us. And we'll make a new life together with you out of the union and out of all union work forever."

Back to that again. He inwardly groaned.

"Forty-one. That's not too old to start over on something entirely new. My brother would be glad to take you into The Park Lane with him. I know he needs someone to help him run the restaurant and cocktail lounge. But with your reputation your name is mud here. I think Bob will be glad to advance you the money to go into some business in Florida where you can really make a good living for your family." She argued against his protest before he even had a chance to voice it. "I know you think that's running away. I don't think it is! I don't!"

"Helen — !"

She warned him to keep his voice down. But he had to let her know right away that there was no solution to their problem in that direction. There was no use creating any illusion that he was going to start to run at this crucial moment. No matter what the cost, he was not going to give up his basic convictions about his responsibility to his fellow man, and especially to the people who had stuck with him through all the hell thrown at them in the past four years.

"It's running away! Don't kid yourself — it's running away!"

"No, it isn't!"

"What *else* is it?"

She was silent.

That silence stretched out for what seemed like a long time and Danny thought that there should be wildly moaning offbeat music in the background, as part of the wholly unreal and nightmarish quality of the scene. He knew Helen had been piling up all these ideas inside her mind since Friday night when the U.S. marshall had served him with the subpoena.

"Danny, you must know I have very mixed feelings about you."

He kept quiet, forcing her to go on.

"Sometimes I feel so sorry for you. You're trying so hard to do what you think is right. And the whole world seems to be set against you — "

"Not the whole world!"

"My whole world. The people that I and the rest of my family know here in Buffalo. *They're* against you."

He could not contradict that. The group she was talking about had turned viciously against him when he had been smeared in the newspapers. Before that, many of them had considered it somewhat intriguing that one of their own number had married a union organizer, like the heroine of a strike novel written back in the depression Thirties. He felt Helen's hand touching his elbow, then moving down to his fingers.

"What do *they* know about you? They don't know how wonderful you are here at home with your family. "

"Thanks." He was unable to stifle the bitterness welling up in him.

"Oh, Danny, I mean it. That's what makes it so hard. You're such a sweet guy. If it weren't for *that*, I could walk away and never waste a minute's thought about it. You don't realize the hold you have on me, do you? I can't just walk away and leave you, much as I often would like to. Do you realize that? Do you know that's how I feel about you? You should be terribly flattered that someone loves you that much."

He suppressed a weary sigh. "I don't know what to think. I'm always aware — and it's bound to affect our entire relationship — that there's always the thought in your mind that some day you may just up and walk out on this marriage. — That's why I always feel so secure with you," he added quietly, with heavy sarcasm.

"Oh, Danny" — he felt her sharp fingernails cutting into the palm of his hand. — "I'm not explaining myself right if that's what you're thinking. I have a tremendous respect for you. But maybe I'm not up to living with someone who's willing to sacrifice himself for an ideal, for other people. Always getting yourself out there in front."

That put him on the defensive.

"Do you think I like the possibility of being arrested and jailed always hanging over my head? It scares hell out of me. I know myself well enough to know that my background didn't adequately fit me to be a working class hero."

"Danny, you could be such a successful person in business. People always instinctively trust you because you're so honest, even when it's going to hurt you. — We can go to Florida together and start a new life there."

"And one day a couple of FBI men will knock on the door and tell me I have to put the finger on all the people I knew or else they'll make it rough for me. And then what? Will it be easier to start fighting then, after I'm already running away?"

"My family know people with enough influence to fix it so you'll be left alone— *if only you'll promise to stay out of union and out of politics.*"

"No, Helen, no! That isn't it!"

His protest was louder than he had intended it to be. He hoped he had not awakened either of the children, and he wondered if Esther, the Buffalo State College freshman who lived with them during the school week, could overhear their conversation up in her room on the third floor.

He consciously dropped his voice down low.

"It isn't just a question of getting away from the hounding of the FBI. It's myself. What goes on inside me. I don't want to be the kind of person who runs away. I'd hate myself. Because I know the right thing to do is to stand and face it and fight it out."

"But why always you?"

"It isn't always me. But I can understand how it might seem that way to you. — Anyway, why argue about it if I've been subpoenaed? I can't turn and run."

"Why? Won't *they* let you?"

Her mysterious insinuation angered him.

"*They*? Who's *they*?"

"1 don't know who *they* are — "

He caught the note of terror in her voice. The wild nightmare seemed to be soaring way off the earth on a witch's broomstick, and he imagined that the eery offbeat background music should be rising to a screaming pitch at this point.

"Someone must have such a terrible hold on you! It scares me! What are they holding over you?" — Her fingernails clawed his hand. — "What have you done that you can't break with them? What is it? I'm your wife. Can't you tell *me*?"

"Nobody's holding anything over me! — Don't you understand? I haven't done anything wrong and no one is holding anything over my head. But I'm not going to turn around and run. I'm going to stand and fight for my rights. For myself. For you. For my kids. For the long-term good of everybody in our country."

He felt the headboard of the bed move as Helen shook her head from side to side.

"Why can't you let someone else stand and fight this time? Someone who's single? Someone with no children? Not you!"

He tried, not too successfully, to still keep his voice down and explain it very reasonably.

"Why do you think they subpoena someone like me — with my particular kind of background — to appear before the Committee? You can be sure they've investigated us thoroughly. They know that you, because of your family and

The Park Lane social group they belong to here in Buffalo, will exert terrific pressure on me. They think I'm ripe for the plucking. They know that right now you're putting the heat on me, and knowing the different pulls inherent in my own background, they know I'm arguing with myself as well as with you, and they figure I'll break."

"Oh, Danny, poor Danny — "

"It happened in Germany. One man runs, then the next runs — and then the next man, and the next man — until all the decent people are frightened and running hard. Helen, I'm not going to run. I'm scared to death but I'm not going to cooperate with the FBI or anyone else to fight against the rights of people, *including myself*, to think and speak as they please. — Believe me, I'm really scared by the thought of the hell it probably means for both of us and the kids. But if I run I know it'll be worse. — Do you think we could ever have a happy life together with me hating myself for running away?"

"1 don't know what to think — "

"I'm proud of what I've done — and I'm not going to act as though I'm ashamed of it. There's no reason to be ashamed!" He stopped. He could hear his own loud breathing. He sounded like he had been running. His throat felt dry. And he wondered what Helen was thinking now about going to Florida with the kids. It seemed like a very long time before Helen finally spoke.

"Danny" — her voice broke with dry huskiness — "Danny, sometimes I feel so sorry for you and I'm so full of love for you I want to take you in my arms and hug you and protect you from all the people in this town who are trying to hurt you."

He could tell that she was having a hard time holding back the tears and his own eyes became damp. They sat there in silence for a long while, motionless, in the darkness of their bedroom, holding hands.

Helen lit a cigarette, puffed several times and then spoke to him. "I really don't know what I want you to do. I can't seem to explain to you so you understand how I feel."

"I think I know."

She continued with her own train of thought. "My life has been so different from yours. Dad, when he was alive, kept all of us — mother and the three girls much more than the two boys — insulated from the outside world. He thought he was doing us a favor. — If he were alive now to know! — You'll never know how hard it was to come out of that warm cocoon, that sugar and cake world of The Park Lane, like I did when I married you."

He watched her put out the cigarette. His eyes had adjusted sufficiently to the darkness so that he could see her as she leaned back against the headboard of the bed and turned her face up towards the ceiling. He could hear her slow deep breathing.

"Danny — "

"Yes?"

"You have to be patient with me. — I know you *are* patient. Anyone else would have given up long ago and walked out. I don't know what I give you, why you don't get so fed up that you pack up and leave."

This wiped out whatever was left of his bitterness.

"Don't be silly. You're my wife. We're married. Marriages are made on earth, not in heaven — and you have to hammer out the differences to build a marriage. It's painful because we started so far apart and we're living in a difficult time. But we'll get there, kid."

She squeezed his hand.

There was one other very important thing he thought he could tell Helen some time, so she would know how much he really needed her — she seemed to have such a need herself to know that he needed her — but it was something not easy to talk about. She had been so very kind to him when he was a young man haunted with fear about his ability as a man with a woman, after another woman he loved very deeply many years ago, long before he met Helen, walked out on him because he was a Jew and because, she later inferred in a letter of explanation to him, he was not good in bed. Helen had restored his confidence in his manhood — and for that he was ever grateful. And he was still sweat-scared that the old doubts might return if their marriage ever broke up.

His thoughts were interrupted by the familiar sound of the deadened patter of small pajama-covered feet running across the hallway outside their bedroom door. He reached out and caught the door as it was flung open, before it slammed against the small night table on his side of the bed. Little Linda, cute little redhead in yellow pajamas which encased her feet, clambered into bed next to him without saying a word — it was her familiar place. Danny laughed out loud at the way she wriggled herself down under the covers.

"Hey," he cooed softly into her ear, "where do you think you're going?"

Not deigning to reply, Linda only cuddled her warm body even closer against his hip, and Helen said, "Let her stay a little while and then take her back to her own bed."

"Mommy says" — Danny whispered the message — "you'll stay here for a little while, honey, and then I'll take you back to your own bed where you can sleep the rest of the night like a big girl — "

"Take me to the bathroom, Daddy," ordered Linda, and Danny laughed with delight at the abrupt way she spoke to him. He carried the child to the bathroom, then back into their bed for a few minutes, then back to her own small bed. Linda did not complain. He tucked the covers in under the soft chin, kissed the warm cheeks, and returned to where Helen was waiting.

She waited for him to get settled.

"Danny. "

"Yep?"

"Here's what we'll do." Her definiteness put him on guard. "You do whatever you think is right when you appear before that Committee. Meanwhile, I'm going to Florida with the children as soon as Ruth gets out of school."

He winced and thought he should have known better than to have allowed himself to expect anything better than this.

She continued, "Once I'm in Florida, away from everything, I'll be able to think more clearly, and then I'll decide what I'm going to do permanently." He marveled at how coolly objective she was about the whole thing. She went on. "I'm going to start right now to put aside every penny I can save to finance the trip."

He rested the back of his neck against the top edge of the low headboard behind him and closed his eyes. There was no use trying to argue now. It would only make the situation more messy and solve nothing. He listened as she unfolded her plan.

"So, Danny, you do whatever you want to do. I'll make up my mind later about what I'll do. There's no reason why I have to make a final decision now, is there?"

She had asked a question and he answered it flatly without any coloring.

"No."

"I might as well wait until after I see what develops with you. Isn't that logical? I've got time because I don't want to take Ruth out of school anyway unless it's absolutely necessary. There's about six or seven more weeks before school ends." She was anxious to get his approval of her idea. "Doesn't it sound logical to you for me to wait and see what happens?"

He answered, "Yes."

He felt her hand patting the quilt over his thighs.

"You better get some sleep, baby" — she sounded so very solicitous — "or you'll get sick, getting up so early."

He thought about the extreme contradiction. With one breath she tore him apart by telling him she was going to walk out on him with the kids, and with the next breath she was concerned about his health.

"I'll sleep on the train tomorrow," he told her.

"You'll be leaving before I get up, won't you?" she said as she slid down under the covers.

"Yes." He wearily climbed out of bed and drew apart the drapes and opened a window to let in some fresh air and then returned to bed.

"Be sure," Helen reminded him, "to set the alarm for me so I'll wake up Ruth in time for school."

"I will."

Helen rolled over on her side, facing away from him. He slid down under the covers on his side of the bed. He noticed how careful she was to be far enough over on her side of the bed so no part of their bodies touched.

"Good-night," she said.

He resentfully noted how relaxed she sounded after having dumped the problem on him. The next move was his. Everything depended on how he handled himself at the hearing. He felt the bed move as Helen shifted position.

"Danny — " She sounded like she had just remembered something.

"What?"

"Good luck."

"Thanks."

"Will you call me from there? I'd like to know what happens."

"I'll call you."

He thought she had fallen asleep. She was still facing away from him. Then he heard her soft whisper.

"Poor Danny — "

He knew she was waiting for him to ask why, and he reluctantly asked the question.

"Why?" — a colorless murmur, as he feigned sleepiness.

"You should have married an entirely different kind of girl."

He gallantly but wearily replied, "The same goes for you."

"We're both stuck," said Helen.

He refused to contradict her. He remained silent, a mild way of getting even with her, but he knew he was being selfish. He felt a gentle pat on his behind.

"Good-night, baby."

"Good-night, kid," he replied with deliberate gruffness, but smiling to himself at how unpredictable she was.

The alarm rang. Danny leaped out of bed to shut it off. Six-thirty. Wow, did he feel exhausted! Completely drained! But he had to hurry.

He dressed quickly.

He kissed Helen on the forehead and she murmured something in her sleep but did not open her eyes. He went into Ruth's room to say goodbye to their tall seventh-grader and he kissed the sleeping girl's cheek. Ruth opened her eyes and held out her arms and sleepily embraced him and kissed him on the mouth. Linda was still asleep in her room when he kissed her fat pink cheek and she looked so innocently beautiful to him — she did not stir a muscle while he stood and gazed at that lovely pink and white creature, and tried to remember that face as it was at that time so he would always have that memory.

Esther, their college student helper around the house, came down from her third floor room wearing her pajamas and bathrobe and slippers. She told Danny she had heard him moving around and had come down to wish him good luck before he left.

"Thanks, Esther."

There was a close bond between Esther and himself. — He knew her mother and father. Both worked in shops represented by his union in the nearby industrial community of North Tonawanda. Danny knew he could usually count on Esther to be in his corner whenever he got into a tight spot on account of his political or economic beliefs. If only Helen had Esther's viewpoint! How often he had thought that. He heard a horn honking in front of the house, and he knew it was the taxi to take him to the railroad station.

As he closed the front door of the house, he melodramatically wondered if Helen would still be there with the kids when he got back.

Stepping into the taxi, he felt like a condemned man starting that last mile to the electric chair. It was a possibility, he knew, that there might be a very long time before he would see Helen and the kids again.

He tried to photograph each house with his eyes as they drove down the street, trying to freeze the memory of things as they were right then, to keep it all there to be remembered later, because nothing would look the same to him if he returned a marked man.

Chapter 2

Danny and the union's lawyer, Ed Murphy, were on the train from Buffalo to Albany. Sitting next to the window, Danny saw that it was a beautiful spring day.

He glanced at Murphy who was sitting in the seat behind, his legal books and papers spread out on his knees and on both sides of him. The lawyer had explained to Danny that he wanted to use this time on the train to refresh himself on what had been done at previous hearings — the arguments used and the procedures followed.

"Ed, how you doing?" Danny drew Murphy's attention by swinging his arm back over the rear of his seat.

Somewhat startled by the suddenness of the interruption, Ed Murphy looked up. A young man, younger than Danny, but looking older because of the pot belly he had already acquired. "Too much beer," he would explain, patting his stomach. — Danny had great respect for the lawyer because he had had enough belief in his principles to quit the staff of the National Labor Relations Board when he thought the Taft-Hartley Law transformed it into an agency strongly dominated by corporate capital. Danny could see that Murphy's thoughts were still tangled up in what he had been reading.

"Take a break, Ed."

Murphy grinned, "Do you think I earned one yet?"

"You've been grinding away for a couple of hours."

"Okay, but" — Murphy indicated the material spread out on his lap and on the seat — "I don't want to shift my papers too much."

The lawyer leaned back and waited for Danny to explain what was on his mind.

"Ed," began Danny, bending his head over the back of his own seat, and speaking low so he would not be overheard by the other passengers — "the more I think about it, the more convinced I am that Albert Einstein was right —"

"Why?"

There was a tolerant smile on the lawyer's round face, and

14

Danny noticed how he was keeping his index finger in his place in the thick legal book — the lawyer wanted to get back to his work in a few minutes. Danny tried to get right to the point.

"The more I think it over, Ed, the more I think the best thing I can do is refuse to answer any questions at all. Like Einstein said: 'Answer nothing!'"

Danny knew Murphy was familiar with the advice of Albert Einstein, given to those who asked him what they should do when summoned before the House Committee on Un-American Activities.

"Answering nothing is fine," Murphy agreed, "if everyone would do it that way. That would finish these inquisitions. Wipe them out like prohibition was wiped out. They couldn't possibly prosecute everyone if everyone refused to answer any questions. There would be too many people involved."

Danny nodded. "But someone has to start it — "

"He'll be risking a contempt citation," Murphy warned.

"What's the penalty?"

"One year. That's the maximum."

"One year?" Danny snapped his fingers over his head in a cynical mocking gesture. "What the hell is one year?"

"It's long enough if you're sitting in the can."

Danny noticed that a gray-haired woman sitting in the seat across the aisle was eavesdropping while she pretended to be engrossed in her magazine. He lowered his voice.

"Do they always hand out the maximum penalty?"

"Not necessarily. Especially if it's clear that the witness was consciously making a test case and if otherwise he conducted himself very properly. I doubt that he'd be sentenced to more than six months behind bars — "

"Could I count on time off for good behavior?" Danny grinned, trying to make the question seem like a joke, although he wasn't joking.

Ed Murphy shook his head. "The parole board hasn't been very lenient with political prisoners." He went on to explain to Danny that since political prisoners are put in jail to take them out of action they are usually kept in jail for their full term without any time off for good behavior. He went on to explain that parole boards were reluctant to stick out their necks when considering the case of a political prisoner.

Danny interrupted him. "Would I be completely safe if I use the Fifth Amendment to refuse to answer their questions?"

"About as safe as you can be. Thus far, the courts have time and again upheld the use of the Fifth Amendment, although they might rule differently in the future."

"And what about the First Amendment?"

"That's being tested in the courts right now. In the Julius Emspak appeal before the Supreme Court. But the court may duck that phase of the appeal." Murphy unconsciously assumed the voice of a pompous lawyer impressing a client. "For what worth the court may give it, the Julius Emspak brief cites the First Amendment, in addition to the Fifth Amendment. It also cites the separation of powers between legislative and judicial and executive bodies. Also, the angle that the legislation itself, the enabling resolution passed by the House of Representatives which established the Committee, is unconstitutional — "

"Is there any chance they'll rule on *that*?"

"On the constitutionality of the Committee itself?"

"Yes — "

Murphy made a sour face. "Not a chance. Not while there's any other grounds at all, however flimsy, on which the court can hang its hat to make their decision. That's too hot a potato, the constitutionality of the Committee itself. I doubt that the Supreme Court will ever face up to that one."

"Never?"

"Not unless every other door is closed to them and they have to go through that one door — "

"What do you mean?"

"Well " — Murphy wrinkled his forehead as he thought it out — "there's only one way as I see it, the *only* way you could compel the Supreme Court to rule on that one point."

Danny listened intently, his elbows over the back of his seat and his head cocked to one side.

"The only way to force a constitutional test on that one point," Murphy explained, "would be for a witness to refuse to answer any questions at all. He would have to tell the Committee he was refusing to answer any of their questions because the enabling resolution is unconstitutional. That would put the Supreme Court squarely on the spot. They would have only that one issue before them to decide, and they couldn't avoid it even though they're highly skilled experts at avoiding clean-cut decisions which finally decide something." Murphy kept nodding his head, and Danny could see that the possibilities intrigued the lawyer. "That would make a very interesting challenge!"

Danny posed a practical situation for Murphy. "Let's say that some guy like myself happens to be crazy enough to make that kind of challenge and he's cited for contempt of the House of Representatives and tried and convicted and sentenced to six months. Do you think the Supreme Court would rule favorably when the case finally reached them?"

The lawyer thought a moment and then shook his head.

"No, not the way things are now. Not in the present Cold War atmosphere. Not a chance, not a chance."

Murphy leaned forward so he could speak just above a whisper. "Of course, it's wrong to underestimate the intelligence of the people. They're probably more aware than we realize. There's always the possibility that such a challenge itself — with public opinion mobilized to support it once the challenge is made — might change the political atmosphere enough to persuade the Supreme Court to rule favorably. But even if such a challenge was not upheld by the Supreme Court, it could be a major contribution at this time towards the defense of civil liberties in our country."

Danny could not help his sarcastic grin as he listened to Murphy's enthusiastic explanation of the great contribution *someone* could make.

"All it would cost some poor idealistic sucker like myself, Ed, is about six months to a year in jail — "

Murphy raised his hand to stop Danny from treating the matter with such levity. "If someone decides that he wants to risk it he would be making a tremendous contribution. That kind of challenge would raise the sharpest kind of issues!"

The lawyer placed a hand on Danny's shoulder and there was a note of warning in his voice as he continued in a hushed confidential tone. "But I don't think anyone should go into something like that, Danny, without considering all the consequences. For example, you have to consider how Helen would feel about it."

The answer to how Helen would feel about it was so

immediately self-evident — they both laughed.

"She doesn't know what she wants me to do," Danny apologized for Helen.

"It's not an easy choice."

"All she wishes is that I was out of the whole thing. She doesn't want me to refuse to answer any questions. But at the same time she doesn't want me to be a stoolpigeon. She doesn't want me to use the Fifth Amendment. But at the same time she wouldn't want me to take any other position involving the risk of a jail sentence — "

Murphy opened the legal book in his lap to the place he had been holding with his finger. "If you want to play it safe, just yell out, 'Fifth Amendment!' any time you don't feel you can safely answer some question. It's like yelling, 'Home free!' when you played hide-go-seek. Unless the courts change their mind — the Committee members can try to bulldoze you and threaten you all they want after you take the Fifth for protection, but if you stick to your guns and keep repeating, 'Fifth Amendment, Fifth Amendment,' you'll be all right no matter what they threaten."

"Thanks" — Danny started to swing around in his seat to face front again — "sorry I interrupted your studies."

Murphy smiled. "That's what a lawyer is for." And he resumed his preparations for the appearance before the Committee.

Danny fixed his eyes on the things he saw through the train's picture window: trees with swollen buds ready to burst open, herds of cows, farmhouses, red barns, shacks in small dirty towns; but his main focus was still inward — as he tried to figure out what he should do.

He admitted he was scared but he was ashamed of himself for feeling that way. — What would Helen say if he told her he was thinking about challenging the Committee head-on? Could their marriage survive the consequences which would come with a contempt of Congress charge?

His stomach was churning — he headed for the toilet.

Chapter 3

A newspaper headline caught Danny's eye as he and Ed Murphy passed the newsstand in the Albany railroad station: **BRATER RENEWS RED HUNT**. The subhead: **PROBERS TO HEAR 30 WITNESSES FROM FOUR STATES**.

They stopped and bought two copies of the newspaper and stood there and read them, Danny scanning through the smaller print of the body of the story to see if he already had been mentioned in connection with the hearing. He looked up.

"It says here the hearings started already this morning."

Murphy nodded, without looking up from his copy of the newspaper. "They've had stoolpigeon number one spilling his guts — "

"But Ed" — a feeling of panic swept over Danny — "what about the postponement notice we got?"

Murphy did not appear disturbed. "Apparently only the people from our union had their appearances postponed for a day."

A feeling of being caught up in a swirling movement came over Danny, the way he had felt in years past when he had come in from a lazy summer in the country and stepped into a rushing crowd in Times Square and found himself being pushed along by the strong flow of pedestrians.

"You organizers can hold a union staff meeting," Ed Murphy quipped. "They've subpoenaed three of you — "

"Call the union office in Schenectady," Danny suggested. "Find out what's happening."

Murphy stepped into a telephone booth. While waiting, Danny read the news story several times. His name was mentioned among those subpoenaed. When Murphy returned he told Danny that the hearing had started at ten o'clock in the morning and had already been recessed for lunch and would resume at two o'clock.

"Let's grab a bite," Danny suggested. "I'm starving."

At that moment two husky deliverymen banged past

19

Danny and his lawyer, busting through the front swinging doors of the railroad station with a hand truck piled high with bundles of fresh newspapers. Danny followed them to the newsstand and tore open one of the bundles himself and took out two copies of the latest edition of the newspaper. Ed Murphy paid for the papers while Danny looked at the front page.

A two-inches high black headline: **FORTY IDENTIFIED AS LOCAL REDS**.

"The circus in on," he remarked to Murphy who carefully folded the newspaper and slipped it under his arm without even bothering to read it.

"Let's see if we can find a bar with a free lunch," he suggested.

Danny knew Murphy was kidding — free lunches were things of the past — but he resented his lawyer's good spirits. Ed Murphy was not the one who had been subpoenaed; he could afford to crack jokes.

Chapter 4

They ate roast beef sandwiches and drank beer at a bar across the street from the railroad station. While they ate they read the newspaper spread out on top of the bar. A picture of the first "cooperative witness" was there with the news item. He told the Committee he had become an undercover operative for the FBI after he joined the Communist Party. The face looked effeminate, and Danny wondered if the man was a homosexual and if that was used to blackmail him. The caption under the picture said the man was 33 years old. A fine start in life. A stoolpigeon at 33. With the bartender busy down at the other end of the bar, Ed Murphy whispered out of the corner of his mouth, " I don't smell any hysteria around here." Danny knew what Ed meant. When a real hysteria is whipped up in a small community you can usually feel it right away, especially around the bars in town. He had almost been run out of town by a mob when he was trying to organize a union among the workers at a small GE plant in nearby rural Brockport, where the company had whipped up a fever against "outside agitators who had come in to stir up trouble." He learned there what it feels like to walk down the main street in a village under the eyes of the very people who are preparing to run you out of town as soon as they can work up the necessary nerve to do it. It was *not* that way here in the State Capital.

"What's going on down at the courthouse?" Murphy asked the bartender.

"I don't know."

"I saw a crowd coming out of the building," said Murphy.

"There's always a crowd coming out of the courthouse around this time," said the bartender. "People going to lunch."

A man at the bar, near the door — Danny noted that he was dressed in working clothes — said, "A Congressional committee investigating communists. I heard it on the radio this morning."

21

Murphy thanked the man for his information. Danny noted that even though the bar was full of patrons nobody else said another word about the investigation.

Ed Murphy told Danny he wanted to go over to the hotel to check in; he had already reserved a room for himself and Ralph Kaufman, another one of the union lawyers, who was coming up from New York City to work with him. Danny knew that Kaufman was one of the most experienced lawyers in the country on handling appearances before this committee.

It was almost two o'clock, and Danny wanted to get over to the courthouse right away. He thought he might learn something about how to handle himself by watching others when they were called to testify.

"Ed, will you take my suitcase and reserve a room for me? I'll meet you later at the hotel."

"Right — I'll be in my room, working."

The courthouse was nearly empty when Danny arrived in the main floor lobby, and he wondered if he was late. The elevator operator told him the hearing was up on the third floor. When Danny stepped off the elevator he saw some people standing around in the corridor. He wondered if he would have difficulty getting into the courtroom. The wide and high corridor with concrete floor and marble-faced walls seemed cold and impersonal. He approached a uniformed guard standing near the elevator entrance.

"I'm looking for the courtroom where the Committee on Un-American Activities is holding its sessions — "

The guard, with an impassive face, pointed down the hallway.

"Has the afternoon session started yet?"

The guard took his watch out of his vest pocket and looked at it and put it away. "It should have started, but it hasn't." There was a critical note in his reply. Danny looked at his own wrist watch — ten minutes past two.

Danny stood in front of the two swinging doors. He peeked through a small glass window, a sort of square peephole in one of the tall doors. The courtroom was almost empty. That surprised him. He had expected to find the room jammed full with spectators.

The judge's bench up in front of the courtroom was empty

but a flock of reporters and photographers stood around the press tables off to the left of that bench.

Then he recognized one of the members of his union, from the big GE plant in Schenectady. Ray Foster stood alone, next to the wall inside the courtroom. Danny went in and circled behind the rows of benches which reminded him of church pews. Ray Foster saw him and came striding up the side aisle, his hand outstretched, a warm grin on his black face. They grasped hands.

"Ray" — Danny found it hard to believe — "have you been subpoenaed *again*?"

"Oh, no, no, no." Ray laughed out loud, the chuckle vibrating in his chest. "No, Danny, I'm just a spectator on this one. Twice is enough."

"I should think so," agreed Danny, recalling the national headlines when Ray accused a Senator of using Ku Klux Klan tactics at a similar hearing. Newspapers across the country carried photographs showing three husky guards dragging Ray out of the courtroom while he hurled defiance over his shoulder at the Senator. Danny remembered that there had been a threat of a contempt charge, but it never materialized because Ray gained too much public support by his bold counterattack. But later the GE people discharged him because he used the Fifth Amendment when he refused to answer the Senator's questions about his political beliefs.

"I'm sitting this dance out," Ray laughed.

"You here to lend moral support to us greenhorns who never appeared before one of these committees?"

Ray chuckled down in his throat.

"You don't need no moral encouragement from me, Danny. I'm waiting until you get up there in the witness chair. Don't be too hard on these Congressmen — they're miserable enough bastards as it is without you trying to make them any more miserable."

"They don't have to worry about me," said Danny. "This is strange territory for me — I've never been at one of these hearings before."

"You'll do all right, Danny."

The compliment made Danny grin with appreciation, but he wondered what Ray would think if he knew how frightened he was.

Danny became aware that a slight young man whose face was familiar was waiting to talk to him.

"Hello, Danny."

"Hi — "

"I'm one of the Mason boys — John Mason."

They shook hands, and Danny guessed that the young fellow carrying a pencil and some folded notepaper in his left hand was a reporter. He introduced Mason to Ray Foster. While the reporter shook hands with Ray, Danny tried to recall where he had met the man before. He looked like a recent graduate of some school of journalism — lean face, crew haircut, dark shell-rimmed glasses, loose sport coat, gray flannel slacks with cuffs not quite touching the toe tips of the highly polished tan shoes. Danny wondered where Mason had left his pork pie hat.

"You going to testify today, Danny?" The fresh young face glowed with friendly interest, and Danny guessed that the reporter knew him very well. But from where?

"Are you connected with the Buffalo newspapers, John?" Danny knew he had to be very wary — anything he said to the reporter, even in a friendly personal conversation, might be distorted and quoted against him back in Buffalo.

"No, I'm working for one of the wire services — "

"Oh," and Danny nodded as if that meant something to him.

"How's Helen?" the reporter asked — and Danny instantly remembered that this was the youngest of the five Mason boys who lived in a luxurious home across the street from The Park Lane where Helen lived before their marriage. Helen and her two brothers and her two sisters had grown up with the five Mason boys. They had played together and gone to school together.

"Helen's fine — "

Now Danny remembered more about John Mason. His father was one of the leading automobile dealers in Buffalo, a wealthy man, but a nice broad-minded person. The elder Mr. Mason had gone out of his way to act friendly toward Helen and himself when other people who were closer friends of Helen's family had stopped talking to him and Helen because of the notoriety he had received in the newspapers about the bitter strike at Markel Electric, a factory owned by

Joseph Markel, a good friend of Helen's family.

"You going to testify today?" young Mason asked.

"My subpoena is dated for today, but I received a wire telling me I wouldn't be called until tomorrow."

Young Mason did not ask anything further about the hearing. They talked about some mutual acquaintances in Buffalo, about Danny's two redheaded daughters — the spread between the older daughter who was in seventh grade and the three-year-old who was attending a nursery school.

Danny appreciated young Mason's talking to him this way. He had expected that he would be treated as a pariah by all the press at the hearing. John Mason coming to him and talking to him like this, in full view of the other reporters and press photographers, was bound to prompt some of them to ask John Mason about it later. Danny thought it took some nerve on young Mason's part to do something like that. He would have to tell his colleagues how he happened to know this witness, and that might make them consider the witness as a human being — it might soften up some of the rough stuff they might otherwise use in their stories.

"From my home town," Danny explained to Ray Foster, after John Mason went back to the press table up front.

"A reporter," said Ray.

"This one is a nice guy," said Danny.

"He can't write what he really thinks," said Ray.

A group of well-dressed men entered the courtroom through the small door that led from the judge's chambers. They filed into the jury box.

"Who's that gang?" Danny asked Ray. "There's no jury here. This is no trial."

Ray laughed.

"Those bums? — They're GE executives from the Schenectady plant — they got reserved seats for this ball game."

Danny found it hard to believe. "You'd think they'd be a little more subtle about revealing the direct link between the Committee and the corporation — "

Ray snickered. "What have they got to worry about? They got things pretty much under their control in this neck of the woods." One of the corporation executives glared back at him and Ray.

"Why is that guy giving us the fisheye?" he asked Ray.

"That's the chief of the company police at the plant in Schenectady — they got more cops on his force than they got on the city payroll in all Schenectady. When I was fired he personally walked me out of the plant."

The chief beckoned to the stately white-haired U.S. marshall who was in charge of maintaining order in the courtroom. They conferred and then turned to look back at Ray and Danny.

Ray said, "He's probably asking who *you* are."

"He's the least of my worries," said Danny. "Let's find a seat and sit down."

They slipped into the rear pew on the lefthand side of the courtroom to wait for the afternoon session to start.

Chapter 5

The courtroom was filling up and Danny guessed that the hearing was about to start. He felt two arms encircle his neck, a woman's arms, and he squirmed around so he could look up over his right shoulder. He recognized the woman and he jumped to his feet —

"Elsie!"

The woman kissed him and hugged him.

"Red, why didn't you let us know you were coming up here?" She kissed him again, and he laughed at the way she bubbled over as she told him, "You haven't changed at all, you redhead!"

"You're still as beautiful as ever," he laughed.

She stopped him with a wave of her hand. "Don't hand me any of that."

They both laughed — they were holding hands, laughing with the pleasure of seeing one another again after many years. He remembered Ray.

"Elsie, I'd like you to meet Ray Foster."

"Oh, I've known Ray — I know him as well as I know you — we're living here now, in Schenectady, Steve and myself."

"Is Steve here?"

"Over there — "

She pointed across the room; Danny saw Steve stand up and wave. Danny motioned for him to come over, and Steve slowly sauntered across the back of the courtroom to shake hands with Danny, with the usual sheepish smile on his face arousing a warm feeling of remembrance in Danny.

They sat down on the rear bench, Elsie squeezing next to Danny, and they gabbed rapidly about their children and about mutual friends they hadn't seen for so long, hurrying because they knew they didn't have much time before the hearing would start and they would have to be quiet.

"You haven't changed much," Danny told her, thinking it had been at least ten years since he had last seen her and Steve and their two daughters. She did seem a little heavier, but she still had the same nice face that exuded the warmth and understanding which had made her a mother confessor to so many bewildered young actors and writers.

Elsie told him that the two children were grown and married now, and Danny remembered that Lisa, the older daughter, had just finished first grade when he met the family at the summer resort up in the Adirondack Mountains where he was working as an actor in a stock company. Elsie was the cashier at the canteen, and her husband, Steve, was a bakery truck driver who delivered bread in the neighborhood.

"It's so good to see you again, Red." Elsie took his arm in her two hands and squeezed.

Danny guessed that she must be in her early fifties already even though she looked much younger.

After that season of summer stock ended he had gone back to New York City to make the rounds of the producers and agents, looking for a job in another play, and he had kept up a regular correspondence with Elsie and Steve. In his early twenties, living alone in the furnished-room jungle of mid-Manhattan, he had poured out his heart to Elsie. Steve treated him like something of a son or younger brother, though he was too old to be Steve's son. Elsie mothered him during the periods of hurt, but — thinking back — their relationship had not been a mother and son relationship. He had been the glamour of the live Broadway theatre to Elsie. Even though he had played only a few bit parts in several plays, he satisfied her need for something which she could not get in the raw mill town nestled up there in the Adirondack Mountains where she and Steve lived the year round. She was the sympathetic older woman who listened to his problems when the going got too rough to go on alone any longer.

He remembered how he had turned to Elsie for help when the frightened young socialite with whom he had been planning marriage turned on him and told him she found it too hard to adjust herself to living with a Jew. ("I love you so much, dear Danny, for the sensitivity you have which comes from you being a Jew in an antagonistic world. But you have some of the intense introvertive qualities which are the cause of the antagonism of the world against you people. And I can't help hating those qualities in you even though I know how wrong it is for me to feel that way. Oh, Danny, dear Danny, I'm so torn — help me!") And she left him to marry someone in her own class, someone completely acceptable to her family.

The days which followed were bitter ones — and the bitterness came back with the memory. He had not been able to go on living in his drab and lonely furnished room.

He wrote Elsie, asking if the invitation to visit them still stood, and he stayed through the whole winter with them in their small house in the little mill town up there in the Adirondack Mountains. Over his protests, Elsie moved the two young daughters into the living room, giving their bedroom to him. He remembered the good times he had had with the kids, especially with the older child, Lisa.

"Red, Lisa's working in your union office in Schenectady now."

So he would see Lisa again. Little Lisa had made him promise to wait until she would be old enough to marry him.

Elsie told him about Lisa's husband. Henry Michaels — "Hank" — was one of the GE employees who had been fired at the same time as Ray Foster. Like Ray, he had refused to answer questions concerning his political beliefs, using the Fifth Amendment, and the same chief of company police up there in the jury box in the courtroom, the man who escorted Ray Foster out of the plant, also escorted Lisa's husband out to the front gates, and that was when Lisa started to work at the union office in Schenectady.

"Hank's blacklisted, Red. So we moved down to Schenectady and we're living with them and we're helping to pay the rent. Steve's still driving a bakery truck and I usually take care of my two lovely grandchildren. We got a neighbor's kid watching them today while we're up here."

Elsie stopped to take a deep breath. Danny laughed with her. She took Danny's face between her hands, an impulsive gesture, and she squeezed.

"Oh, it's so good to touch you again, you redhead, you — "

Her husband reached over and tapped her on the shoulder. "Stop embarrassing the guy in public."

Elsie laughed.

"Don't bother us. We're just old friends, aren't we, Red?" She snuggled closer to Danny, enjoying his embarrassment.

"Look at him blush. He's the same old redhead we always loved."

Steve tried to help Danny by changing the subject.

"How's your wife?"

"Fine."

"You got two daughters yourself now."

"That's right — "

Elsie nudged Steve to shut him up so she could do the talking.

"What about your wife? How's she taking all this?"

"Oh — " Danny didn't want to be disloyal to Helen.

"Is she worried?"

"Well, she doesn't have a background like you." He tried to make a joke out of it. "I'm the first left-winger in her life."

"It must be very hard on her," Elsie was sympathetic.

"It is."

"This whole business must be confusing if she doesn't have some real political understanding. That must make it hard for you."

He shrugged it off.

Steve laughed. "That's what you get for not marrying a union girl."

"Steve!" Elsie punched her husband on the shoulder. "You mind your own damn business. And keep your big mouth shut."

"That's all right. Helen would be the first to agree with him."

"Would she?"

"Sure she would."

Elsie looked at Danny, not sure whether or not to believe him, and he nodded and laughed, enjoying her bewilderment.

Ray Foster reached across Steve and tapped Danny's arm and hissed, "Here they come."

Chapter 6

Three men dressed in ordinary business suits — Danny had almost expected them to wear judge's black robes — were taking their places in the chairs up on the platform behind the judge's bench. Flash bulbs were flaring one after another up in front of the courtroom as the photographers scurried around to get good action shots.

Danny watched the general movement down in front of the railing. Three more men connected with the operation of the Committee in some way or another were taking their seats at small tables down in front of the judge's bench, facing the spectators. One carried a bulging briefcase which he immediately emptied onto his table. A woman court reporter came in and set up a machine to type notes.

Another flurry of activity off to the right of the judge's bench caught Danny's attention. A skinny man dressed in a dark suit hurried in, flanked by two uniformed guards. Danny recognized that thin face from the picture he had seen in the newspaper. The man was still wearing a black leather bow tie. This was the friendly witness who had reeled off a long list of names at the morning session, and Danny wondered if he had been brought back to name more names.

The skinny witness sat down at a table in front of the judge's bench, facing the man who had emptied his bulging briefcase. Danny wondered if the witness was glad his back was to the audience.

"You testified this morning — "

Danny heard every word clearly. He noticed for the first time that there were microphones rigged up on the judge's bench, on the table of the "prosecuting attorney" and on the table of the witness. A real production number, he thought, as the hearing began again.

He concentrated every ounce of his attention on the performance up front. He wanted to penetrate to the inner mechanism, to find out what made each performer tick, so he could figure out the best way to handle himself when he stepped up there to become one of the unwilling performers

31

compelled to interact with those who had the advantage of having planned their performance in advance. He realized he would be matching wits with highly skilled men for very big stakes. Whatever happened when he was called up to the witness stand would decide his entire future with Helen and the children — and his relationship to the entire community back home in Buffalo.

He was fully aware of the great danger, and it made him sweat.

His years of experience as an actor in New York City, before he had come home again to Buffalo and ended up as a union organizer, came in handy. It took Danny only a few minutes to catch on to why the "stage director" of this performance in the federal courthouse had all the Committee members and their legal counsel and their investigator — (he furnished the spy reports to the legal counsel) — facing the audience, while the witness was permitted to show them only his back. *They* were upstaging him, and the audience was watching *them* instead of the witness, judging the witness by their reaction.

It reminded Danny of one of his early lessons in acting. What makes a man a king on the stage? The other actors treat him like a king, reacting to him as subjects would to a king. Therefore, he is a king!

That's what was going on here. The Committee's legal counsel and the investigator supplying him with the "dirt" and the three Congressmen up behind the judge's bench, all facing the spectators in the courtroom, were reacting dramatically to the witness, giving to the witness the character they wanted him to have. They treated the witness with the greatest consideration and respect, like he was a self-sacrificing, noble hero — what they wanted the audience to think of him.

This scene in the courtroom reminded Danny of an Elmer Rice play — *Judgement Day* — he had appeared in many years before, which dramatized the frame-up of the communists by Hitler with the German Reichstag fire.

The courtroom setting here was almost identical with that in the play, but there were some differences in the cast. In the stage play, the three judges were really judges, two of whom wanted to resist the orders of Der Fuhrer that they must bring in a conviction against the Bulgarian communist, Dimitrov, accused of setting fire to the Reichstag. Here, in this play in the courthouse, the "judges" were members of the House of Representatives of the United States and all favored a conviction of "unfriendly" or "uncooperative" witnesses.

While he had tried out for the role of the stoolpigeon in the stage play about the Nazis, he didn't get the part because he had not been able to comprehend the psychology of the man — how he had come to be a stoolpigeon. But now he could look back and see — while he watched this performance in the courthouse — that even the young actor who had finally played the role in the stage play about the Nazis had been all wrong in his conception of the part. In those days most people thought it required a dose of drugs to reduce a human being to the level where he would act as an informer against honest citizens, sometimes his best friends who had done no wrong except that they had thoughts and political beliefs disliked by those who were in power at the time; and the actor who played the part of the stoolpigeon in the play about the Nazis interpreted the character that way, as a man under the influence of drugs who said whatever he was told to say because he had been drugged.

But now Danny knew it was not that way. Not at all! The man here on the witness stand had not been drugged. He probably had been broken down, step by step, by pressure, by blackmail, conditioned by the FBI — Danny had seen it happen to some people he knew very well — rationalization is created, a sacrifice to expediency to save themselves from pressure in the community; he knew from his own experience the pressures exerted upon a man to make him give a public statement repudiating all left-wing ideologies, the pressures they exerted upon a man through his wife and children to force him to do something publicly to "cleanse himself" of all reddish political taint — this was part of the FBI formula for methodically capturing a man, he knew, part of the formula to lead a man, step by step, down the road to becoming a full-fledged stoolpigeon, while all along the way they talked to him, conditioned him and helped him to rationalize each additional step down the road. And since no man wants to be a despicable character in his own eyes, he accepts the rationalization which glorifies his role as a stoolpigeon, reassures him that he is a hero, a good American, and the stoolpigeon grabs at this glorification as a compensation to bury what he really thinks of himself. In Buffalo the evening newspaper had named a stoolpigeon as the "Man of the Year" because he "had the courage to expose his communist friends."

As he watched this performance in the U.S. Courthouse, Danny had the strange feeling that he was watching an American adaptation of that trial staged by the Nazis to arrive at a predetermined conviction, that the script was already written as it had been written in advance of the performance of that stage play about the trial conducted by the Nazis; and he knew that everything in the first and second acts was being made to conform with the predetermined conclusion of the third act of this staged play in the U.S. Courthouse — that final scene when Jean Dampier, the leader of the local union at the big GE plant in nearby Schenectady who was sparking the secession movement from "that communist-dominated union," would sweep into the courtroom and take the stand and answer all questions, the noble hero, in contrast to the despised union organizers named as communists by the FBI informers, who were compelled to grab the Fifth Amendment to save themselves from answering the $64 question about communist affiliation.

But Danny also remembered that Dimitrov, the accused Bulgarian communist, had upset the Nazi plans when he boldly defied his prosecutors by accusing them of setting fire to the Reichstag themselves in order to create a hysteria within which the freedom of all the people could be destroyed; and by his defiance and by his counterattack upon those who were trying to destroy the freedom of the people, he won the support of the people in Germany and throughout the world; and he won his own freedom in the process, while others arrested with him cracked under the pressure from the Nazi secret police and "cooperated" — and at least one, Danny recalled, committed suicide.

Danny thought about this, watching the performance in which he was soon to play an unrehearsed role, and he fought with himself over the interpretation he should give the character he was going to play when he got up to perform on that stage.

"You testified this morning" — the Committee's legal counsel pointed his pencil at the witness — "that you attended a series of Communist Party meetings at the home of Joseph Regelman in this city — ."

Danny noticed immediately how Denilworth, the fat legal counsel, kept his mouth open while he waited for the witness to confirm that statement — it was a trick to maintain suspense — and the mouth closed after the witness replied with an almost inaudible *yes.*

"Was Regelman a member of the Communist Party?"

That mouth in the fat face of the legal counsel was open again, while waiting to swallow the reply.

"Yes —"

The mouth closed.

Danny had heard of Denilworth — the Committee's legal counsel was a southern gentleman who rode with the hounds hunting the fox, a daily commuter to and from the city of Washington, and he had a soft drawl in his speech which was charming.

"Was Regelman" — Denilworth continued, while Danny watched and strained to hear every word — "also a member of the American Labor Party?" The mouth was open again, waiting to swallow the reply.

"Yes —"

The mouth closed.

Danny thought he detected Denilworth's purpose behind this line of questioning. The American Labor Party had been distributing leaflets in front of the building when Danny arrived, and this testimony was intended to discredit what was said in that leaflet and to teach the American Labor Party and anyone else who might be thinking of putting out similar material that they better keep their mouths shut or they were inviting trouble for themselves. That might explain why the stoolpigeon had been recalled to name more names on top of the long list he had given at the morning session.

"Here — " Danny slipped a folded leaflet out of his inside pocket and passed it to Elsie Brooks to read. She passed it back to him.

"I helped run it off on the mimeograph machine," she whispered, "up at the ALP headquarters."

Denilworth pushed right on, his chin jutting forward. "Did Regelman tell you to join the American Labor Party?" Mouth open.

"Yes — "

Mouth closed. "And the did you join the American Labor Party as he instructed you to do?" Mouth open.

"Yes — "

Mouth closed. "As an agent of the Communist Party — " Mouth open.

"Yes — "

Mouth closed.

Congressman Brater interrupted. Danny registered in his mind the pitted face, dark-rimmed glasses and sallow complexion of the man who was seated between the two other Congressmen up on the judge's bench. The Congressman leaned forward and spoke down to the witness —

"But you were reporting all your activities to the FBI, were you not? Like every honest and loyal citizen should be doing? Were you not?"

"Yes — " almost completely inaudible.

"The witness," prompted the Congressman sitting to the right of Brater, "will please speak up so that the spectators can hear him," and Danny watched the way this thin man squeezed his lips together in an expression of hard authority after he spoke. Ray Foster, who had identified Brater for Danny, whispered that this second Congressman was Holling, a notorious redbaiter from the mid-West — and Ray identified the third Congressman as Lester from one of the eastern mining states. Danny had heard of Lester; the Congressman had built his entire political reputation on the hunt for "Reds."

Denilworth dramatically repeated Brater's question.

"You were reporting your activities to the FBI?"

The witness's back moved, and over the loud speaker system Danny heard the clearing of the throat.

"Yes!"

The man's back was still bent forward, his head bent

down over the top of the table in front of him — he did not look up at any of the three Congressmen who looked down at him.

"You," Denilworth continued, "attended a meeting of a Communist Party cell at the home of Regelman, did you not?" and the mouth was held open awaiting the reply.

"Yes — "

The mouth closed.

"Several meetings?"

"Yes — "

"Did the members of the cell" — Danny noted how conspiratorial Denilworth made it sound — "discuss the American Labor Party at these meetings?"

"Yes — "

"Did they discuss the tactics to be employed in the American Labor Party?"

"Yes — "

"What did they say about the tactics to be employed in the American Labor Party?"

"They talked about what they should do to take over the American Labor Party."

Denilworth prompted: "How to infiltrate and maintain control of the American Labor Party?"

"How to take it over completely for the Communist Party," the witness dutifully murmured, his head still lowered.

Denilworth summed it up for the witness. "You attended meetings of a Communist Party cell where Communist Party members discussed how the Communist Party should infiltrate and take over the American Labor Party?"

Danny noticed how the fat legal counsel had again stopped his question on a high note, with that mouth open, holding the spectator's interest while he waited for the reply from the witness.

"Yes — "

The mouth gulped down the muted reply.

Danny couldn't help admiring Denilworth's technique: the way he asked a question, then held himself taut, his head tensed up in the air, cocked to one side, eyes gleaming, mouth wide open, his big body alive with excited expectancy — transferring his sense of excitement to the very ordinary reply which came from the very undramatic witness; Danny could see how the committee's legal counsel was making this dull, droning stoolpigeon appear to be a highly dramatic character who was revealing the most startling and shocking discoveries about a terrible spy underworld involving everyone's next door neighbor; Danny could almost feel the tremendous amount of energy the legal counsel poured into his performance — bringing corpses to life by the compelling force of his energy.

He could see that Denilworth had the situation under complete control. His was a conscious performance. He reminded Danny of a number of experienced stock actors he had known, the kind of stock actor who could give a highly energetic and emotional performance for the audience out front, with every gesture planned and controlled, while whispering unrelated comic deadpan asides to his fellow actors — never allowing himself to get involved emotionally as an individual with his performance, keeping his person and his performance as an actor separate and unrelated.

There was that mobile face with eyes buried in fat, eyes full of dramatic fire. Quick changes in expression to give variety to the part he was playing. Light and shadow. Speaking loud and then softly. Big gestures and then small gestures. A disarming smile to heighten the sudden switch to a face of terror, and then a sharp change to a face breathing great relief. Denilworth's face was not still for one moment. And his entire body kept moving, changing quickly from one highly charged emotional tableau, while awaiting an answer to a question, to another dramatic pose which lent another kind of drama to the answer which was to come from the witness.

Watching Denilworth was so interesting that Danny found himself forgetting that this was not a stage play and that soon he would be one of the actors performing in front of the courtroom, on the receiving end of the questions from this clever stock actor —

"Do you remember who attended those Communist Party meetings?"

"Yes — "

Elsie whispered apprehensively, "Here he goes again — "

Denilworth leaned forward with a smile of benevolent encouragement. "Will you please give us the names of the

Communist Party members who attended those meetings," he gently suggested, and he opened his mouth again, still smiling, listening for the names.

The witness bent his head down and rattled off one name after another. Danny finally noticed that the stoolpigeon was reading the names from a sheet of paper on the table in front of him. Denilworth interrupted several times to ask the witness to spell out long foreign-sounding names.

"The dirty rat," Steve Brooks muttered at one point, and Danny guessed that Steve knew someone who had just been named by the stoolpigeon.

Danny knew very well what was going to happen to those who were being named. He watched the reporters at the press table, rapidly scribbling away, and he knew that every name mentioned now would appear in the newspaper in the city where the victim lived, probably on the front page; and there would be a detailed story telling all about the occupation or profession or business of the man or woman named, and local "patriotic organizations" who were cooperating closely with the FBI would open up on the victim — to get him discharged if he was employed, or to boycott him if he owned his own business or had a profession where he was his own boss. No matter where he might run in an effort to escape persecution, no matter how he tried to earn a living, he would be tracked down and he would be marked wherever he went; his children would be marked; and his friends would be marked, if he had any friends left after the story appeared in the newspapers. He would be hounded out of any job he tried to get; and would be isolated in the community; he would be subjected to vicious personal abuse, and possibly physical abuse. His marriage relationship would become strained; his family would be tested on the torture rack and if the family broke under the strain the children would be separated, maybe forever, from the parent who had been named by the stoolpigeon. — No judge would award the children to a parent who had been named this way.

The stoolpigeon stopped. Denilworth prompted him to go on.

"In addition to these people you have named who attended those meetings where they discussed how to take over the American Labor Party, will you now give us the names of any other members of the Communist Party whom you know in this area?"

The question was an invitation for a wide scatter shot. The witness shifted several sheets of paper before him, reading aloud the next list of names. He droned on and on, one name after another, again spelling out foreign-sounding names upon request of the Committee's legal counsel.

Listening to see if he knew any of those named, Danny wondered how one could know so many people so well as to testify he knew their political beliefs. The answer, he knew, was that the lists had probably been given to him by someone working with the Committee.

"He must be reading from the telephone book," Elsie Brooks quipped into Danny's ear. "I know some of those people — and some of them wouldn't even know what the word *communist* means."

Danny noticed that the stoolpigeon's drone was picking up speed. He sensed that this was the grand finale of the man's performance — the Committee squeezing out the last wild scattered burst of bullets. And then the witness would be dismissed, squeezed completely dry, having served his purpose for the time being.

"He's finishing up," Ray Foster whispered.

"What happens next?"

Ray explained: "They'll dismiss him, and then they'll start calling some of the people he's fingered — starting with some people who are fairly well known openly as left-wingers, especially some who once were openly members of the Communist Party, people who pretty much have to take the Fifth Amendment to protect themselves, and they'll shove them around to make it look like they're dangerous characters. They'll leave the assumption that all the others named are in the same category and they'll invite anyone named here to come forward voluntarily to clear himself — if they're ready to help the Committee name more names."

During Ray Foster's explanation, Danny kept his eyes fixed on Denilworth who, like a true performer, was acting out his scene with the stoolpigeon right to the last drop he could squeeze from it, and then the legal counsel abruptly dismissed the witness —

"That's all, thank you."

As the witness stood up to go, Danny thought — with some sense of relief — at least the man had not named him. Apparently, someone else was going to have that dubious honor.

Congressman Brater stopped the witness from leaving, by stretching out his hand to catch his attention. And the Congressman's short speech convinced Danny that Brater felt it necessary to try to counteract the antipathy most people had against informers.

"I would like to convey to the witness," said the Congressman, "the tremendous gratitude and thanks of the United States Government — and I hope others will follow his example and come forward just as courageously as he has done to help expose the subversive foreign agents who are trying to undermine and destroy our dearly beloved American way of life for which so many of the flower of youth have bled and died on the battlefield. Young man, you have performed a service for your country, a service of which you can be proud!"

The man to whom he spoke stood perfectly still, staring down at the floor until he was sure the speech was finished. Then he walked out of the courtroom, leaving by way of the small door which led to the judge's chambers. Two uniformed guards were at the man's side as he left the room. The intent, Danny guessed, was to give the impression that the witness required police protection from those dangerous communists he had named.

As the door closed behind the stoolpigeon, Danny heard a quick muffled hissing sound coming from over on the far right side of the courtroom. The three Congressmen glared out into the courtroom, searching for the culprit. Brater angrily rapped his gavel. The U.S. marshal gracefully swept up and down the center aisle in regal fashion, examining faces in each pew, trying to unearth the guilty ones. He passed right by Danny without any special sign of recognition.

There was a conference between the three Congressmen and Denilworth and the clerk of the Committee, a short stout man wearing glasses and then the clerk announced a five minute recess.

Danny and his friends headed for the corridor outside the rear of the courtroom. For Danny this was a good chance to move around and relax from the tension of concentrated watching and listening. In a few minutes he would be able to start studying how witnesses fingered by the informer conducted themselves — how they did or did not use the Fifth Amendment, which questions they would answer and which questions they would not answer, how they were treated by Denilworth and the Committee, and how they handled themselves in this kind of a tight spot, the same kind of situation he would be in before the hearing ended.

Walking between Elsie Brooks and Ray Foster, with Steve Brooks following behind, Danny made an important decision. He decided that he had to figure out how to handle those Congressmen and Denilworth in a way which would permit him to retain his self-respect. Even though it might be a form of weakness, he had too much pride in himself as an individual to let them push him around.

Chapter 7

In the crowded corridor Danny met two fellow union organizers, Bill Kosciusko and Herb Kepler — both had been subpoenaed.

"Two to one it was you who did that hissing," Danny accused pint-sized Bill Kosciusko.

When their union was raided in North Tonawanda, Danny had seen Bill Kosciusko swing a punch at the biggest and toughest organizer of the rival outfit. The man had been razzing Bill about his war record of which Bill was very proud — he had been part of a combat infantry team attached to General Patton's tanks in the race across France into Germany. It was early morning, just after dawn; there was a National Labor Relations Board election scheduled for that morning inside the Remington Rand factories in Tonawanda and North Tonawanda to decide which union the workers wanted to represent them. A hot argument developed between the rival unionists at the gates of the plant in Tonawanda — about fifty or sixty volunteer and paid organizers of both unions were shouting at one another back and forth across the street — there was a lot of name-calling but there was nothing unusual about that. Then this organizer for the raiding union who was about six-foot-four walked up to Bill and sneered down into Bill's face — Bill being only about five-foot-six — "You're a lousy traitor to your country," he snarled down into Bill's face, "and you've been lying about your war record because they wouldn't have a lousy traitor like you in the army!" — Danny remembered the "clonk" as Bill's fist, swinging up almost from the sidewalk, connected with the giant's face, and the blood spurted out like a stream of water from a faucet. For about five minutes after that, a free-for-all raged in the street, until finally a majority of the men on both sides who had kept their heads broke up the battle. That incident accurately illustrated Bill Kosciusko's character, so far as Danny was concerned. Bill was very fortunate in his marriage in that he had married a woman who had also been

43

a union organizer and they had a wonderful relationship, which Danny envied.

Bill raised his right hand.

"I wouldn't hiss in a courtroom," he laughed, "but I've got a paper medal for the guy who did it."

"It was timed perfectly," said Herb Kepler, the other union organizer.

They all agreed that it had been done exactly at the right time.

"Herb, how's the new job?" asked Danny.

"Fine — negotiating like mad — wage and contract negotiations going on all over our district — "

Danny thought Herb Kepler looked very distinguished with his prematurely gray hair, much healthier and even younger than the last time Danny had seen him. He knew Herb's background well. The man had been fired from the organizing staff in the district where Danny still worked. The separation had been a friendly one. Herb had not been able to stay away from the whiskey bottle. He had been told he was being fired in order to make it clear to him that he couldn't go on any longer the way he was going — to force him to make some kind of decision regarding his wife who was openly sleeping around with other men, with Herb turning to the bottle for consolation. Getting fired that way seemed to have done Herb a lot of good. He split with his wife and stopped drinking and returned to work for the union in a different district. Now he appeared quite happy and self-assured, and Danny had heard that he had married again.

The three union organizers tried to figure out who might be called as a witness to put the finger on them. Danny was the only one of the three still working in the same district where they had once all worked, the district which included the State Capital. Bill and Herb had been transferred some time ago.

"Back in the early part of 1944 was the last time we were all together in this district," said Danny, trying to pinpoint who might name them. "Then you were drafted into the army, Bill, and after that you went off the staff for a while, Herb. Then I was stupid enough to volunteer to be drafted into the army."

"Sidney Raven," suggested Ray Foster who, together with Elsie and Steve Brooks, had been listening to the speculation of the three union organizers. "He's the man they used to name me and he was an organizer with you three guys, wasn't he?"

"He was," said Danny, "but why didn't he name us when he named you?"

Ray Foster laughed. "Maybe they didn't want to use up all their ammunition at once — saving him for this."

They all agreed that Sidney Raven was the most likely prospect to name them.

Danny tried to recall what Sidney Raven looked like. He hadn't known the man too well personally. They had never been assigned to the same city even though they had been working in the same district. Sid joined the union's organizing staff shortly after he, Danny, had been hired as an organizer, back in 1941; and about two years later Sid was discharged for not doing his work and deliberately lying to cover up his laziness. That might have been the time, Danny thought, when somebody got their hooks into Sid. The man was out of work, undoubtedly blacklisted. Former left-wing union organizers don't get new jobs quickly. That's when the FBI must have come to Sid, after they let him rot out of work for a while so Sid would know how it felt to be up against it without any prospect of getting work; and they probably sympathized with Sid about the lousy deal he had been given by the union. That was the approach the FBI had used unsuccessfully with two other former union organizers who told Danny about it. Maybe they had been able to make a deal with Sid, the deal they failed to make with the two other men. Anyway, Sid suddenly reappeared in Albany, working as a business agent for a small craft union, a soft job with good pay — a pie-card job, union people called it — and when the time came that the FBI needed their informer to name names, Sidney Raven appeared in front of a Congressional committee and did the finger-pointing at Ray Foster and several others who were members of the union.

"I can't understand Sid's wife," said Herb Kepler who had known both Sidney Raven and his wife very well. "Sid was never much of a guy, but his wife was a terrific person. I can't understand how she can still go along with this guy when he turns out to be such a rat."

"Who knows what's going on between them," said Danny. "They're both probably going through hell."

"No stoolpigeon gets any sympathy from me," said Bill Kosciusko.

"I'm sorry for his wife," said Elsie Brooks.

Her husband told her not to be sorry. "She asked for it when she married him, and she's probably got a lot to do with the kind of guy he is right now — "

"How do you know?" Elsie demanded.

Herb said he was going to phone Sid's wife and talk to her.

(The next day Danny would be told by Herb Kepler that Sid's wife said she was going to leave Sid, that she couldn't maintain her self-respect, married to a stoolpigeon who was informing against men who had been his friends. A month later Danny would hear that she left Sid shortly after the hearing here in Albany ended. And not long after that Danny would be told that she committed suicide. The same man who would tell him that would also tell him that the wife was the one most responsible for Sid becoming a stoolpigeon in the first place, because she lacked the guts to stick by him if he refused to cooperate with the FBI to cleanse himself. There was a contradiction there and Danny never would learn more than that.)

Elsie Brooks interrupted the bull session.

"The hearing's started again — "

They hurried back into the courtroom and sat in the last row. Danny took the seat next to the center aisle where, by leaning over to his right, he could get a clear view of what was happening in the front of the courtroom. Denilworth was already directing questions down at some man seated at the witness table with his attorney.

"Did you ever attend any meetings at the home of a man by the name of Regelman?"

Open-mouthed, bug-eyed, Denilworth waited for the answer. The witness attempted a brave reply, but over the public address system Danny could hear how the man's voice was shaking.

"Sir, I question your right to pry into my associations — "

Bang! — the sound of Congressman Brater's gavel smashing down on top of the judge's desk startled Danny.

"Enough of that!" the Congressman sternly ordered, with his head bent forward over the top of the desk so he could talk directly down at the head of the witness — "Let's understand one another right from the start!" He lifted his head and looked out over the audience. "This goes for this present witness. Or any other witness who is called up here to testify. When you are asked a question we expect you to answer that question. Or, if you feel it will incriminate you, then you may avail yourself of the Fifth Amendment privilege. *But we're not going to have any speeches. Let's understand that right now*!"

He glared at the spectators in the courtroom, letting that sink in. Then he returned his attention to the witness whose shoulders and head were hunched forward over the table as if withered by the angry blast. The Congressman spoke sharply.

"You've been asked if you attended any Communist Party meetings at the home of a man by the name of Regelmen, who has been identified here as a Communist Party organizer who directed the infiltration tactics by which the Communist Party took over and directed the operations of the American Labor Party in this district."

Congressman Brater stopped, folded his hands together, sternly set his face, and then proceeded, giving full weight to each word:

"*I direct the witness to answer that question.*"

Danny had heard enough about procedure in such hearings to know that when a Congressman formally directs a witness to answer a question, the stage is set for a citation for contempt of Congress. Denilworth opened his mouth wide and jutted his head forward to lend greater intensity to the hushed silence. There was not a sound as the courtroom audience waited. Danny wondered how the witness would extricate himself from this tight position into which he had so quickly been boxed. Would he use the Fifth Amendment?

After what seemed like a very long silence, the witness began his reply. "I don't agree with the right of this Committee — "

The man was still in trouble. The voice sounded weak,

almost plaintive, lacking steam, lacking fire.

Bang! — Brater's gavel cracked down again.

"Marshall, take this man out!"

The sternly outstretched arm and gavel pointed to the big doors in the rear of the courtroom.

Bewildered and frightened by the explosive command given by the Congressman, the witness hesitantly rose to his feet as the U.S. marshal and the two uniformed guards closed in on him. His lawyer frantically grabbed the arm of the witness and pulled him back down into his seat. There was a hurried whispering back and forth, a rapid shifting of heads, a frantic shuffling of mouths to ears that took only a few seconds. Then the witness nervously looked up into the stern face of Congressman Brater, while the U.S. marshall and the two guards hovered over him.

"Sir, I wish to cite the Fifth Amendment privilege as my reason for not — "

Bang! — the gavel cracked down again, cutting the witness short.

"Take him out!" the chairman ordered with a sweeping gesture, like a king ordering the summary execution of some vile subject who had dared thwart the wish and command of the noble exalted ruler.

The U.S. marshall gently nudged the elbow of the witness.

The witness stood up and meekly returned to his place in the third row of benches in the courtroom. He looked straight ahead, seeming to avoid all eyes looking at him, appearing to be a beaten man even though he had taken a principled position and held to it under pressure.

Danny's instinct as a union organizer told him that the witness should not have acted with such hesitancy, with such lack of self-assurance. The man had made observers think he was afraid, which undoubtedly he was. But he had acted as though he was guilty of having done something wrong. It was not the kind of performance which would generate public support.

Danny hoped other witnesses named by the stoolpigeon would put up more of a fight against the Committee — because they were establishing the atmosphere which would serve as a background for the questioning of the union organizers.

Even though he knew it required courage on their part to refuse to be "a cooperative witness" — Danny also knew that the frightened way they were refusing to answer the questions actually helped to increase the effectiveness of the Committee. He worried about it as he watched and listened. It was up to people like himself who had the experience to be able to do it — to take the offensive against the Committee.

But what about Helen and the kids?

The next friendly or cooperative witness was an interesting type. Denilworth's questions brought out his background. He had been studying labor relations at college when he went to work for a union during the summer vacation periods, doing public relations for them. He had joined the Communist Party, he testified, during the period of close cooperation between the United States and the Soviet Union to defeat the Nazis. He testified at length about the great sincerity of the people he had known as communists, what self-sacrificing good citizens they believed they were, devoting themselves to the cause of the working class. He was testifying only because he wanted to save these good people from themselves. They didn't realize how they were being duped. He would never do anything to hurt them. He hoped and prayed for the day when all the decent men and women he would name here would recognize that he named them now for their own good and that they would realize that, instead of harming them, he saved them from ruining their lives forever.

Then, reading from a sheet of paper, he recited the names of many union members he said were communists. After that he added the names of a number of college students and professors who, he said, had belonged to a Communist Party cell with him or had assisted in advancing communist ideas on the college campus, again assuring those he named that he was doing it for their own good.

That prompted Steve Brooks to swear at him, a hushed guttural grunt of four-letter words. The U.S. marshall gracefully swept back up the center aisle and stood next to Danny at the end of the bench, enforcing quiet by his presence. After a few minutes he drifted gracefully away again.

Danny wondered how this apparently decent guy could

rationalize himself into believing he was doing something which would help his friends. He had to know that each time he uttered a name he was crucifying that person with loss of job, blacklisting, crisis in the family, a life of hell.

(More than a year later Danny learned the answer from one of his cousins who came to visit in Buffalo. She said she knew the young man's father. The FBI had gone to the young man and asked him to become an informer and he had refused. Then the FBI went to his father, a wealthy real estate man. The father, after one heart attack, told the son he was dying. "You're killing me!" The young man agreed to "cooperate" with the FBI, provided he could temper his testimony with mercy. That explained the line he had followed in his testimony: how good the people whom he had known as communists were, how they don't realize what they're doing, how they're not to be too severely blamed since they think they're working for the good of the common people.)

Congressman Lester congratulated the young man for coming forward and naming names. He especially thanked him for revealing the communist influences he had encountered in the local union at the GE plant in Schenectady where he had worked during his summer vacations.

"This ought to be a warning to all members of this communist-dominated union," said Lester, "about how they are being used to advance the ideological line of the Communist Party. Every loyal American who belongs to this communist-dominated union owes it to himself and to his country to do something now to help clear up this situation.

It seemed to Danny that the Congressman had left himself vulnerable. His statement provided the link needed to prove on the very first day of the hearing that the primary purpose of the hearing was to help GE get rid of the union which was legally the bargaining agent for their employees at their Schenectady plant.

He made a mental note to call his boss, George Hernandez, in the Schenectady union office as soon as the hearing recessed for the day. The statement of Congressman Lester could serve as the handle for a solid blast against the interference of the Committee in the union situation in

Schenectady.

Two middle-aged men and a young woman who had been named by the cooperative witness were called to the witness chair and quickly disposed of, after each timorously gave the Fifth Amendment as their reason for not answering questions about their political beliefs and associations.

Then friendly witness number three was called to testify, another self-confessed ex-communist, and he gave the names of people he alleged were communists or communist sympathizers, and several of those he named were summoned immediately to the witness chair to testify. Their voices trembled as they used the Fifth Amendment when asked if they denied the accusations of the stoolpigeon.

The Committee was succeeding only too well, Danny realized, in establishing the pattern of fright. If only one witness would break the pattern, even just by boldly asserting the Fifth amendment as *a proud right*, not as a shameful, hesitant, defensive maneuver, and — added thought — if only someone would brazenly spit a big gob into Denilworth's mouth when the legal counsel leaned his head forward with his lips deliberately forming that big round opening to lend dramatic surprise to the coming reply of the witness —

Congressman Brater abruptly banged his gavel and announced that the hearing was recessed until the next morning.

Ray Foster offered to drive Danny and Herb and Bill to nearby Schenectady. Danny told Elsie and Steve Brooks he would be seeing Lisa, their daughter, at the union office. Elsie kissed him goodbye on the cheek, while Steve fondly patted him on the back.

At a drug store across the street from the courthouse, Danny telephoned George Hernandez at the union office in Schenectady and told him about the attack Congressman Lester had made against their union.

"Can you come out here?" George suggested. "It's not a good policy to say too much about this over the phone. It's tapped, sure as hell — "

"Ray Foster's driving us out there."

"Good. See you later."

The others were waiting for Danny in front of the drug

store. They stopped at the first newsstand and bought copies of all the newspapers. They compared headlines. The biggest headline read:

130 AREA RESIDENTS ATTENDED CELL MEETINGS, RED PROBE TOLD

All the names were listed.

Chapter 8

They stopped off to see Ed Murphy in his room in the Capital Hotel. The lawyer declined their invitation to go along to the Schenectady office. He was still working hard, digging out the different approaches which had been used by witnesses appearing before the Committee — his books and papers spread out on a small rickety desk. Ralph Kaufman, the other union lawyer, from the New York City office, had not arrived. Murphy wondered if he was still sick with the bad cold which had laid him up for the past two days.

"Murph, did you reserve a room for me?" Danny reminded him.

"There was nothing available. The clerk said you could check later to see if anything opens up."

Danny telephoned down to the desk. Still nothing available. The clerk said there wouldn't be anything open until the following day because of two conventions in town.

Bill Kosciusko and Herb Kepler were all set — they had already checked in at the Capital Hotel. Ray Foster lived in nearby Schenectady.

"You better find a room before you take off," Ed Murphy warned. " You don't want to come back late at night and find yourself without any place to sleep — unless you want to sleep in the tub in my bathroom."

"I don't sleep in tubs. That's where I usually take a bath. I'm eccentric that way."

"You don't know what you're missing," said Murphy.

Danny started to check through the list of hotels in the back of the telephone book. The phone rang. Danny answered. A man's voice asked if Herb Kepler was there. Danny handed the receiver to Herb. There was a short conversation, and Herb hung up.

"Two men from one of our locals," he explained. "They've been subpoenaed to come down and appear before the Committee tomorrow. They want to talk to me about it." He got up from where he had been sitting on the edge of one of the twin beds. "You fellas better go to Schenectady without

53

me. I've got to hold hands with these two guys. We got a Labor Board election coming up next week in their shop and they're so scared there's no telling what they might do when they get before the Committee." He put on his jacket. "Good-night, fellas." He seemed glad to get away.

Danny thought he knew why Herb Kepler welcomed this opportunity to avoid going along with him to Schenectady. They belonged to different schools of thought on how to deal with the key question: *Are you or are you not a member of the Communist Party?*"

One group in their union — Danny agreed with them — believed that no witness before the Committee should answer whether or not he is a communist, that to answer that question either yes or no in the existing Cold War atmosphere (Who would dare answer *yes*?) helped to fan the hysteria which was being used to stifle all dissent.

Another group in their union — to which Herb Kepler adhered — believed that because of the hysteria which had already been whipped up about communism, it was necessary, in order to still be effective as a union leader, to make a flat declaratory statement denying present membership in the Communist Party. After that you could try to hold the line and refuse to answer any further questions about political beliefs, thoughts and associations.

Danny believed that it was impossible to indulge in just a *little* self-cleansing this way. Once you start you'd be forced to go further to prove it was not merely a maneuver. Inevitably, if you want to satisfy those pressing you, the final end is to become a "cooperative witness," naming names — the only fully acceptable evidence that you have really cleansed yourself of all pro-communist taint, the only way you can get your pursuers off your back once they see that you have started to run.

Since both were fully aware of their differences on this, it had been a surprise to Danny that Herb had said he'd go with them to Schenectady. He had expected Herb to find some polite excuse to go off by himself, and the phone call from his two local union members provided him with the perfect reason for breaking away.

Bill Kosciusko went down to his room, two floors below in the hotel, to take a quick shower. Ray Foster went along. Ed

Murphy returned to his work while Danny telephoned several other hotels to locate a room where he could spend the night. The Regent had a room available.

"There's only a sink in the room. But there's a toilet and shower down the hall." When Danny hesitated, the clerk warned, "You better take this. Account of the two conventions in town there ain't another room available at any hotel in the city."

"How soon do I have to check in?"

"Right away, sir — we can't hold it open for you."

"What if I get there within a half hour?"

"All right, sir, but no later."

Danny hung up. Murphy was engrossed in his law books.

"Ed, who pays for your long distance phone calls?"

Murphy looked up.

"Who do you want to call?"

"I promised Helen I'd phone her."

Murphy laughed. "You got to report to mama every day?"

"I thought I'd let her know what's going on."

"There's nothing to tell, is there?"

"I guess not."

"You can call her. Ask the operator to put it on my bill."

"The hell with it. There's nothing to tell her."

Murphy returned his attention to his law books.

"Ed — "

Murphy looked up from his work — Danny could see that the lawyer was finding it hard to suppress his annoyance at the repeated interruptions.

"Sorry to bother you again but would you mind it I used your phone to call Art Manchester in Tonawanda? You can add the cost of the call to your bill for legal services when you submit it to our national office."

Ed laughed. "Think I won't?"

And they both laughed because they knew he would.

Art's wife answered the telephone and she called her husband. Danny heard the voice of the union organizer who worked with him in the western end of the state. He visualized the thin face, the gray hair, the rimless glasses, the ever-present cigarette — and the small pot belly Art Manchester had developed in the five years since he had come out of the Spaulding Fibre plant to become a part of the full-time organizing staff of the union.

"Hello, Danny. You still out of jail?"

"So far.

"Good."

"Did the Buffalo newspapers carry anything?" Danny knew that the residents of Tonawanda and North Tonawanda read the Buffalo newspapers even though they had a small local newspaper.

"Nothing today. Not a word."

"Good. Have you contacted all the local union presidents?"

"Every single one of them."

"Anything developing?"

"No excitement anywhere. Not a word about the hearing. All the shops are quiet."

"Good. Keep close contact so we're able to grab hold of anything that flares up before it gets too good a start."

"I will. Don't worry."

Danny was glad he had a competent union organizer like Art Manchester taking care of things back home. He had enough troubles without having a bonfire breaking out in his rear.

Art had a message for him.

"I don't know how much this means, but the chief steward down at the Westinghouse plant in Attica, Milt Reynolds, asked me to tell you that he phoned his Congressman in Washington, Representative Yates — his local union authorized him to make the call — and Yates promised he would contact Representative Brater today after the hearing to ask him to pass you up, not to call you to testify."

"Fat chance," Danny said quickly, but his heart started to beat faster at the thought of this unexpected break. He didn't want to appear too anxious to Art. "Oh, they'll never pass me up now. Too much involved."

Murphy, his curiosity aroused by what he overhead, stopped working. Danny made a face, signaling to Murphy that he would tell him about it later.

"It sounds far-fetched to me too," Art agreed. "But Milt's very optimistic. He's convinced they won't ask you to testify."

"Not a chance," said Danny, but hoping it would be true.

"I don't think so either, Danny. But Milt asked me to tell

you about it."

"Thanks. Art, I'm going over to Schenectady to see George Hernandez. I've got to be there right away and I don't have time to call Helen. Could you call my home and tell Helen everything's all right here? Tell her I probably won't be called to testify before Friday. — Don't tell her what Milt said. Let's not raise any false hopes. — Can you do that for me?"

"As soon as I hang up — "

But Danny had already changed his mind. Helen would resent it if he sent a message through Art. If he had time to telephone Art about union business, why didn't he have time to telephone her about their personal relationship?

"On second thought, don't bother — I'll call her later."

Ed Murphy was skeptical about any Congressman intervening on Danny's behalf, especially Yates who was no slouch himself when it came to red-baiting.

"Why should he stick his neck out for you?"

"To get the votes of our local union members who live in his district."

"That's easy. He tells your people he spoke to Brater, and then Brater is the bastard when you're still called to testify. Brater represents the Schenectady district and this area around Albany. He don't care how the people in Attica feel about him. Yates is still a good guy to the Attica voters because he says he spoke to Brater, but he doesn't even bother making the call."

Danny hoped Murphy was wrong.

The phone rang. Danny answered it.

"Where the hell are you?" Bill Kosciusko was down in the lobby with Ray Foster, waiting for him.

"I'll be right down."

Before leaving, Danny agreed to meet Murphy for a few quiet beers, a nightcap, after he got back from Schenectady. He took his suitcase when he left.

They stopped at The Regent so Danny could register. The desk clerk reminded him that his room did not have a shower or toilet. But it was still the only room available, and it cost only four dollars a day. Danny slipped the bellhop two quarters to take his suitcase up to the room and he went out and joined Bill Kosciusko and Ray Foster who were waiting in the car in front of the hotel.

They finally were on their way to Schenectady, all three sitting up in the front seat of the car, Ray Foster driving, Bill Kosciusko sitting in the middle.

"Bill, what are you planning to do when they ask you the $64 question?" Danny asked, trying to feel Bill out.

"Fifth Amendment," said Bill, without hesitation. "What about you?"

"I suppose I'll do the same. But I wish there was some safe way to tell them to go to hell. I'd rather do that if there was some way to get away with it."

Bill laughed. "Who wouldn't?"

"The only safe way," advised Ray, "is to use the Fifth Amendment."

"I know, I know," said Danny, thinking about Congressman Yates and wondering if there was any real possibility that his subpoena might be killed.

Chapter 9

George Hernandez, with bushy black mustache and fat cigar and his usual effusively loud and brash manner — which Helen had said she thought was a coverup for the man's deep feelings of insecurity — conducted Danny and Bill Kosciusko on a tour of the recently established Schenectady union office. He introduced them to the other organizers who had been brought in from all over the country for the election campaign at the big GE plant where local union president Jean Dampier was leading a secession movement out of the UE union, accused of being communist-dominated, into the IUE union, created with the help of the FBI to try to smash the UE organization. Ray Foster who came along knew everybody; this was his hometown.

"Red — "

The delighted shriek made Danny turn around.

"Lisa — "

She ran into his arms.

"Oh, Red." She squeezed him and then pulled back her head to get a better look. Her shiny young face crinkled with warm delight. "Oh, Red, George told me you were coming. You haven't changed a bit!"

They both laughed, and he saw that she still had a lot of freckles on her cheeks and on her nose. It had been many years since he had last seen her, not since she was still in grammar school. But those were the same soft and dreamy blue eyes with the bright twinkle. He remembered how, when she was still a child, he had told her that she had laughing eyes.

He flipped her pony tail up and down.

"Your pigtails are gone."

"I'm a grown woman now, Red." Lisa trilled, and her white teeth showed while she grinned up at him, proud of how she had developed into a ripe beauty since he had last seen her. He could feel her bosom rising and falling against his chest.

They had forgotten the others, but George Hernandez

reminded them that they were not alone.

"I don't think," said George with dry hoarseness, "I have to bother introducing you two. You seem to have met in some saloon or cathouse before."

Danny and Lisa pulled apart, both flustered, flushing pink.

"George," protested Lisa, "Red and I have known each other for years. He used to come and visit us when I was only a little girl."

"A likely story," said George, before he stuffed the end of his cigar into his mouth and chewed at it.

It's true, George." Danny rushed to corroborate what Lisa said. "I used to visit her mother and father when she was still only a kid."

George laughed, enjoying the game.

"She's still quite a kid now if you ask me." He took the cigar out of his mouth and tapped off the ashes, letting them drop to the floor. "She never kissed me like that — and I'm her boss. What the hell have you got that I ain't got?"

He was playing to his audience, to Bill Kosciusko and Ray Foster and the rest of the organizers who were standing around and enjoying the scene. He looked around, making believe he was checking to see if anyone was listening. "Danny, if I were you, I'd be careful." He lowered his voice and spoke out of the corner of his mouth. "This babe is married, with two children. It's all right to fool around, but be a little more careful when you're out in public like this."

"Oh, go to hell, George!"

The entire group laughed at Danny's embarrassment.

"Don't mind him, Red," said Lisa, putting her arm around his waist in a protective gesture. "He's jealous."

"I sure am," laughed George, letting out a roar. "Here I've been trying for weeks to make time with this gorgeous babe. Look how she's stacked up — "

Lisa interrupted, laughing with embarrassment of her own, "Oh, shut up, George!"

" — And this guy, Danny Newman, walks in cold and in one minute the guy's in like Flynn. What's he got that I ain't got? That's all I want to know. As one good friend to another, Lisa, tell me — "

"Oh, you!"

She lunged at George. Roaring with laughter, George fled from the room, with Lisa chasing after him, thumping his back with her fists. Danny and the others followed after the pair. They watched Lisa chase George around the desks in the main office. The organizers shouted encouragement to her. George finally let her catch up with him. She rained weak blows on his head. George, still laughing, shielded his face with uplifted arms.

And then the excitement subsided as quickly as it had flared up.

The group broke up to go out and eat.

"We'll talk over what happened at the hearing after we eat," George, now completely serious, suggested to Danny. "Right now everybody's hungry."

"Okay."

Lisa said she had to wait for her husband.

"You eat with them," George suggested to Danny, "and we'll get together later."

George Hernandez went along with all the others, leaving Lisa and Danny to wait for her husband.

Alone with Lisa, Danny felt very ill-at-ease. She had grown into such a ripe young woman from the freckle-faced child he had known. Lisa tried to make him feel more comfortable.

"I think you'll like Hank," she said, in order to provide a subject for conversation.

"Your husband?"

"He's a strong union guy."

"Good — "

How different his life would have been, Danny thought, if he had married someone like Lisa.

"How's your wife?"

"Okay," he said, wondering if she guessed what he was thinking. Feeling self-conscious, he awkwardly moved around behind the desk and sat down in the swivel chair. Lisa perched herself on the edge of the desk, looking down at him.

Helen's okay," Danny said, hesitantly, guiltily conscious that he was inviting further questions.

"This bothers her — your subpoena?"

He silently nodded, and they sat there for a while without saying anything. She made him feel like a bashful youngster.

She smiled down at him and he grinned in appreciation of her springy freshness: the dark brown hair swept back into the thick pony tail, the shiny scrubbed face, the bright red lips and the sparkling blue eyes. Her eager intensity brought back to him nostalgic memories of the years he had lived in Greenwich Village in New York City. She reminded him of the young ballet dancers and students of the modern dance he had known in those long ago days which, when he thought of them, seemed to belong to some young redheaded stranger who had lived many years ago in an entirely different world from the world he lived in now.

Lisa took a pack of cigarettes out of her purse.

She offered him a cigarette.

"No, thanks."

"Don't you smoke anymore?"

"I quit. Used to burn my throat out chain smoking during contract negotiations."

He took the book of matches out of her hand and struck a match for her. She puffed until she was sure of the light. Then she took the matches back from him and put them away in her purse.

While she smoked they silently watched each other, grinning with remembrance of the nice days they had spent together when she was still a very young girl, liking one another for the memories they brought back to each other. He began to feel awkward again and he had to think of something to say.

"How's married life? You happy?"

"Very!"

"Good."

"And you?"

Her red lips were pursed open, waiting for his reply.

"Oh, all right, although I've got some problems. Nothing tremendous."

He realized he had deliberately invited her curiosity and sympathy, and he didn't like what he had done. He was being disloyal to Helen and it could lead to nothing worthwhile.

"Your wife?" Lisa prompted.

"We get along all right," he said, trying to make up for what he had already intimated.

"She doesn't like you being a union organizer?"

He shrugged. "Her whole background has been on the other side of the fence."

"That must be hard for you."

"Oh, it'll work out all right. In time." And then he couldn't resist adding, "Anyway, I hope so."

Lisa smiled encouragement, then switched away to a subject which was less personal and less dangerous. "George says you're doing a wonderful job up there in Buffalo."

"I'm doing my best," he said, trying to appear modest.

"Who would have thought" — Lisa directed a thin stream of bluish smoke up at the ceiling while she directed a coquettish smile at him — "that you would end up as a union organizer after all those years you were acting in New York City?"

"No one," he said, and the old nostalgia bubbled up in him, "especially not me."

"Do you miss it?"

"What?" he stalled.

"The stage — the theater."

"Yes and no. Not the acting. But sometimes I wish I had time to write for the theater — plays — and do some directing again. Some day, maybe when I retire or get kicked out. The pace on this job is so fast you can't keep it up after you're fifty, not the way a younger man does.

"He could see she was eyeing him curiously.

"You," she said, warily, "must have a long time to go before you're fifty."

"Not so long. Less than ten years. — Surprised?"

"Oh, you're kidding — "

"No."

"Was it so long ago when you were staying with us?"

"Centuries ago."

"But you still look so young!"

"White hairs mixed with red hairs produce reddish blonde, not gray. Very misleading."

"How old?"

"Forty-one."

"Oh, no!"

"Oh, yes!"

"I'd never believe you were that old — never!"

And suddenly he did feel bitterly ancient, worn-out in spirit, a stodgy adult talking to an emotionally immature young woman. He impatiently glanced at his wrist watch, and she noticed the gesture.

"Hank should be here any minute. He stopped to speak to a minister about a community campaign they're working up in defense of those who use the Fifth Amendment."

"I'm not too hungry. I can wait." He nervously glanced at his watch again. "I ought to call my wife now."

"Haven't you called your wife yet?" She seemed surprised.

"Not yet."

"You ought to call her. She's probably very worried."

"Probably," he agreed, suppressing an impulse to be very dramatic by replying that he didn't think Helen was concerned so much about him as she was about herself.

Lisa handed him the telephone. "Here, use this and it'll go on our office bill."

"That's the membership's dues money you're spending so freely," he laughed up at her.

"They won't mind. Even organizers are supposed to call their wives."

He lifted the receiver. While he gave the Buffalo number to the operator, he watched Lisa checking her face in a small mirror she took from her purse. She carefully smeared fresh lipstick on her lips. It was like watching a delightful child at play.

His older daughter, Ruth, answered the phone in Buffalo — he recognized her voice when she said hello.

"Hi, honey, is your mother there?"

"Daddy?"

"Yes."

"Where you calling from?"

"Our union office in Schenectady — it's only a few miles from Albany."

"Is it all over, Daddy?"

Caught off guard by the intense anxiety in her voice he tried to sound cheerful.

"Not yet, honey, but don't worry — everything will be all

right."

Her silence revealed her disappointment. He had tried to explain it to her the day before he left, warning her that he might be smeared in the newspapers again, and that her friends might be cool to her again. He tried to explain why it was so important that he should do his share to defend the country's Constitution, what had happened with the Nazis in Germany where so many people had not faced up to their responsibilities — what happened to the Jews. He asked if she understood that what he was trying to do would help her in the long run, not hurt her. And she turned to him — they were sitting in the front seat of the car: "I know you would never do anything to hurt me," and then, very simply: "You're my daddy!" He kissed her and fought back the tears. How wonderful to be loved so simply, so completely.

"Ruth, honey — "

"What, Daddy?"

"Is your mother there?" Lisa was watching him, a serious look on her face. He smiled at her and she smiled back, encouragement.

"Mommy went over to see Grandma." That was Helen's mother. Helen rarely went to visit his own mother unless he brought her there.

"Tell her I called, honey!" He was glad she was not home. "Tell her everything's all right and I'll call her tomorrow night."

"Okay, Daddy."

He covered the mouthpiece for a hurried aside to Lisa. "She'll be twelve years old next month. The baby is only three and a half." He took his hand away from the mouthpiece. "Where's Linda, honey?"

"Esther's upstairs with her, putting her to bed. Do you want to say good-night to her?"

"She'll only get overexcited. Kiss her good-night for me. And say hello to Esther for me." His hand over the mouthpiece again, he added another aside for Lisa's benefit — "Esther's a college freshman who rooms with us during the week and goes home weekends." He heard Ruth say she would give Esther the message. He took his hand off the mouthpiece.

"Good-night, honey."

A young man walked into the office. Lisa jumped off the desk and kissed him. Danny heard her whisper, "It's about time," and he guessed that this was Hank, her husband.

"Good-night, Daddy," Ruth said at the other end of the telephone line, and Danny heard her make the sound of a smacking kiss. She was waiting for him to reply in kind.

"Good-night, honey." He self-consciously made the sound of the kiss Ruth expected, but he was aware that Lisa's young husband was eyeing him very suspiciously. He was glad the phone conversation was finished.

Lisa introduced her husband as Danny rose and stretched out his hand.

"One of my kids," Danny explained, nodding toward the telephone.

"I've heard all about you from Lisa," said the young husband. Danny wondered how much Lisa had told Hank about his personal problems when he had taken refuge for a whole winter with her family up in the Adirondack Mountains.

"Why don't you two kids take me to some nice spot to eat?" he suggested. "My treat."

Lisa's husband protested, but Danny brushed aside any argument.

"Look, I'm still working and I'm getting that paycheck every week. Let me be a bigshot for a few bucks."

They went to a restaurant nearby where there was a bar and they had a few drinks before sitting down to eat. While eating, they talked about the problems Lisa's husband was encountering now that he was blacklisted, and Hank told Danny about the support he had received in certain sections of the community, especially from a group of ministers to whom he had gone for help after he had found it impossible to get a job.

"I'm really surprised at the number of people in all sections of the community who are signing our petitions supporting our demand that GE reinstate those of us they fired for using the Fifth Amendment — "

"But meanwhile," Danny wanted to know, "how are you getting along? You still got to eat."

Lisa answered for her husband, smiling, showing her white teeth. She pointed to herself.

"Remember me? I'm his wife."

The simplicity of her explanation struck Danny, and he wondered how long his own marriage would last if it happened to him — if he ended up out of work and blacklisted. The thought depressed him.

"It's getting late, kids," he said, looking at his wrist watch. "I gotta get back to the office to meet George Hernandez. You two stay here and take your time. I'll take care of the check on the way out."

They urged him to have another cup of coffee before he went, but he felt that he had to get away from them as quickly as he could. He stood up and put on his coat. He shook hands with Lisa's husband, and then with Lisa.

"Goodbye, kids, and good luck. The best."

He paid the check and hurried out into the street without looking back at their table.

Chapter 10

George Hernandez had been joined by Sanford Wilkins, the international union's public relations man, and Julius Emspak, its secretary-treasurer.

"This," said Sanford Wilkins, hanging onto Danny's hand as he addressed George Hernandez and Julius Emspak — (Emspak had been a tool and die maker at the Schenectady GE plant before he moved up to the top in the union.) — "This Danny," said Wilkins, "is the redheaded guy I met the first time at our national convention up in Boston. I couldn't figure him out. He talked like a college professor who had gone to work in a shop, and like a shop guy who got a job teaching college — I couldn't figure out which it was. His mixture of profundity and vulgarity confused me."

The four men, gathered in the union's office in Schenectady, laughed. They were exchanging a few pleasantries before getting down to the business of deciding what to do about the attack Congressman Lester had leveled against their union at the hearing in the courthouse. They found seats around the desk.

"How," Emspak asked Danny, "do you like being a guinea pig for the modern version of the Spanish inquisition?"

I'm not in your class yet, Julius," said Danny, remarking to himself how tired the other man looked. Emspak had been carrying that six months jail sentence around on his back at least three years — four years! — since he had been convicted on a charge of contempt of Congress because of his refusal to name names in front of the Committee. What a strain it must be, knowing that any day, any hour, any minute — you might be plucked out of your outside world to serve a six months sentence in jail!

"You may not be in my class yet," Emspak said very dryly, "but give yourself a chance, wait until they get you up there on the witness stand — you'll be given full opportunity to join me."

"No, thanks," said Danny, "the honor is all yours."

Their conference was a short one. Danny told how Congressman Lester had complimented the witness who identified members of their UE union as communists and how the Congressman made an appeal to the workers in the Schenectady GE plant to oust their union, while Wilkins took notes.

George Hernandez took the cigar out of his mouth. "Was that the only reference to our union at the hearing today?"

"The only one I heard."

"That's enough, isn't it?" Emspak impatiently demanded, tossing his gray head. "Doesn't that reveal where these bastards are heading with this hearing? What more do we need?"

"Take it easy, Julius" — George Hernandez motioned for Emspak to relax — "all I wanted to find out was whether or not there was anything else we had to consider before we worked out some kind of statement of our own."

"We don't need anything else, do we? That exposes their purpose clearly enough, doesn't it? What more do we need?"

"Nothing more," said George Hernandez, and he calmly puffed at his cigar before addressing the publicity man, Wilkins. "Sandy, do we need anything more to go on?"

"This should do. In our last shop paper we predicted that the purpose of the hearing would be to help the company destroy our bargaining rights here, and now Congressman Lester's statement confirms that prediction. We can bring it to the attention of all the people in the shop."

Danny tried to listen to the discussion about the form the union statement should take.

"A telegram from Julius Emspak here to Congressman Lester," Wilkins suggested to George Hernandez, "blasting the pants off the guy for interfering in this situation in Schenectady — "

George reminded him, "We need something that will get the message to the people in the shop." He showed his cigar stub while he waited for the publicity man to come up with an answer to that.

"Release the telegram to the newspapers," suggested Wilkins.

Emspak spat, "They'd never print it," — and Danny saw the look of disgust in the deep wrinkles in that face which had become so cynical in the past few years.

Danny couldn't keep his eyes off Julius Emspak.

He had known Emspak for many years before the man was hauled in front of the Un-American Activities Committee and was cited for contempt of Congress, and was tried and convicted and sentenced to six month in jail. It was easy to see how much the man had aged in the few years since the six months jail sentence had been loaded on his shoulders, since he had begun the long series of appeals which finally brought the case up to be placed on hold on the docket of the United States Supreme Court. Emspak's hair had turned all gray, and his face had become seamed with a bitter weariness, and he was always irritable and angry.

Even though Emspak had been appointed by Franklin Delano Roosevelt to serve on the National War Labor Board, representing all labor during World War II, his fellow labor leaders and the majority of the middle-class liberal leaders now pointedly disassociated themselves from his case, leaving him all alone with the Sword of Damocles hanging over his head tied to a frayed piece of grocer's string. Danny tried to imagine how he himself would feel if he were in Julius Emspak's shoes. Would be begin to think that maybe he had been a damn fool to sacrifice himself? Could he carry a six months jail sentence on his back for as many years as Julius had carried it? Could he do that without cracking up? Could he repel the pressure being used on Julius to force him to surrender and name names. Danny reminded himself that he didn't have much time left before he would have to make that decision.

"What do you think, Danny?"

He apologized to George Hernandez for not listening to the discussion, and George asked Wilkins, the publicity man, to sum up what they were planning to do about Congressman Lester's statement.

"We'll send a telegram to him, signed by Julius, attacking the Congressman for his interference in the union situation here, accusing him of assisting the company in its effort to destroy our union. We'll give copies to all the newspapers, without any illusions that they might print it in any recognizable form. And then, to really make sure all the people at the shop get the information, we'll reproduce the telegram on leaflets which our organizers will distribute to all the people at the shop gates tomorrow morning — "

George Hernandez took the cigar out of his mouth.

"Sound all right, Danny?"

"Sounds okay."

The publicity man started working on the telegram while Julius Emspak called Congressman Lester every filthy word he could summon up from his excellent vocabulary of swear words.

George Hernandez took out a fresh cigar and bit off the end.

"Danny," he suggested, "why don't you find a typewriter that's not being used — and draw up whatever kind of personal statement you want to kick together to give to the Committee?"

Emspak made a face. "Don't waste your time with any statement — "

"Why not?" asked Danny.

"Do you think they're going to let you enter any kind of statement into the record? Don't forget — this whole circus is only meant to be a set-up for you organizers to affect the election here. They may be polite with some of those other poor suckers they're dragging in ahead of you guys — they may let them enter statements into the record — but wait until they get to you organizers! That's when they take off the kid gloves and turn on the red hot heat. They'll be rough as hell with you guys. After all, that's what this whole show is building up to — you're going to find out when they call you up there to testify."

"You still better write a statement," quietly advised George Hernandez in his rasping voice. "Even if they don't let you read it into the record here" — he stopped to light his cigar — "you can distribute it to the membership when you get back home . . . and you can tell them this is the statement you tried to present to the Committee, but the Committee wouldn't take it from you. — In that statement you can forcefully expose the true purpose of the Committee hearing being held now — to affect the union situation here — and you can state why you refuse to answer any questions concerning your thoughts, your political beliefs, or your associations — why you're going to exercise your constitutional rights. — So the membership will understand why you use the Fifth Amendment. — A statement like that can be put to very good use when you get back home after the hearing."

"Okay," said Danny.

"Find a typewriter in one of the empty offices."

"You'll be wasting your time," insisted Emspak.

George Hernandez took the cigar out of his mouth. "There's a good typewriter in my office down at the end of the hall — "

Danny went off in search of the typewriter.

He tore up the third rough draft he had written. His mind was too agitated. He could not concentrate enough to draw up a logical intelligent statement. He had to talk to someone about Helen. Maybe Murphy. There was no use trying to write a statement while he was so disturbed that he couldn't even think rationally. He went to look for Ray Foster and Bill Kosciusko to see if they were ready to drive back to the State Capital — he hoped Ed Murphy was still waiting for him so they could have a few beers and talk it over.

Chapter 11

No one answered when he phoned up to Ed Murphy's room from the lobby of the Capital Hotel.

Danny was alone. Ray Foster had driven back to Schenectady after discharging his passengers in front of the hotel. Bill Kosciusko had gone up to his room to write a letter to his wife and go to sleep. Danny wondered if Murphy was down in the bar waiting for him.

A bellhop told him there were two bars in the hotel — one off the main lobby, a fancy cocktail lounge with an orchestra for your dancing pleasure, the other in the basement, a plain ordinary bar for drinking. Danny knew where to look for Murphy.

A wide marble staircase led to the basement level. Men were lined up all around the bar. Edging his way into a small opening at the bar, Danny checked the faces around the inside of the circle, passing from one face to the other. Halfway around the circle, he found the lawyer. Murphy smiled a friendly recognition when he saw that it was Danny who quietly slipped into the narrow space at his left elbow.

"What the hell are you so happy about?" Danny asked.

"I've finished my research and now I'm relaxing like a stinking rich plutocrat," Murphy grinned.

Danny gave a cold nod at the four full bottles of beer lined up in front of Murphy. "You trying to buy up all the beer in the joint in advance. Or are you just plain thirsty?"

"This beer dispensing emporium is so damn busy," Murphy confidentially explained, "you have to make an appointment in advance to speak to the bartender. The only thing an intelligent man can do is to stock up ahead when he has the opportunity to make a purchase. Otherwise, you are likely to find yourself caught high and dry in the burning desert with your tongue hanging out, gasping for one little drop of this piss-water to save your life."

"I thought you decided to go into business for yourself."

"A logical but incorrect assumption." Murphy offered Danny a bottle of his private stock. "Sir, do me the honor of being my guest."

"Ed, I don't want to take the beer right out of your mouth."

"I insist."

"Your generous hospitality overwhelms my simple, crude — but honest! — workingman's soul," said Danny, accepting the bottle.

Murphy impishly grinned. "Something tells me that you are under the extremely erroneous impression that I am a trifle under the weather."

"Oh, never. How could you possibly think that I could possibly ever think anything like that about you?"

"Methinks I detect a bit of delicate sarcasm."

"Delicate, hell. I think you're polluted."

Danny was laughing, but Murphy feigned a wounded look.

"Sir," he protested, "that is absolutely the grossest slander," and then a grin spread over his round face and he laughed appreciatively at the game Danny played with him. He thought of something and he rapped his knuckles loudly on the bar to draw the attention of the bartender.

"A clean glass, sir, for my friend," he cried, "and two more bottles of beer to replenish our ailing stock of refreshment."

The bartender brought a glass and two bottles of beer. Danny insisted on paying for the beer. "I can't steal the stuff right out of your mouth, Ed. Not without replacing it. My conscience won't allow it."

Murphy started off on a hunt for two empty bar stools, and Danny watched that ludicrous figure, hunched forward, circling the bar, the wild game hunter stepping high through the underbrush as he intently follows the trail of his prey. The bartender reached over and tapped the game hunter on the shoulder and guided him to two empty stools to get him to come quietly back to his place at the bar.

"Did you see George Hernandez?" Murphy asked, after they got settled on the bar stools.

Danny nodded.

"I assume," continued Murphy, "everything is under control in Schenectady since the situation is in such capable hands."

"As good as can — "

Murphy interrupted, waving a pointed finger with the excitement of recalling something he wanted to remember to tell him.

"I almost forgot. Ralph Kaufman phoned from New York City. He's coming up tomorrow instead of tonight. You can move in with me if you want to. Ralph wants a separate room so we can both be holding sessions with our people if we're pressed for time."

Murphy's voice dropped and he leaned over so his lips were close to Danny's face — so the men at the bar on each side of them could not hear what he was going to say.

"Ralph said he would like to represent you, Danny — after I told him about your thoughts concerning a constitutional test of the right of the Committee to exist. As a matter of fact, it wasn't until after I told him what you were considering that he made up his mind definitely to come up here. Otherwise, he was going to skip it on account of his rotten cold and let me handle the whole works. Meanwhile, I'm going to have that empty bed in my room, Danny, if you want to switch back to this hotel."

"Too much bother to move now, Ed."

Once Ed Murphy started on a beer-drinking jag like this Danny knew he wouldn't stop until the supply was shut off sometime in the wee hours of the morning when the bar closed. He himself was exhausted as the result of having had so little sleep the night before because of the long talk with Helen.

"Ralph's coming up mainly on account of you," Murphy confidentially repeated.

"Really?" Danny worried about getting himself in so deep since he hadn't made up his mind yet about what to do.

Murphy explained.

"I told Ralph your thinking on the subject and he said it would be wonderful — *if* you knew fully what you're doing and *if* you're ready to take the risk." With a pointed finger, Murphy started to carefully draw an imaginary diagram on top of the bar. "Incidentally, Ralph doesn't think the risk is as great as I thought it was" — he looked up from his diagram — "because Ralph doesn't think the Committee will risk going completely out of business. That's the risk they'll be taking if they cite you for contempt after you refuse to answer any questions and present them with the challenge that they have no constitutional right to exist as a Committee and question anyone." Murphy held up his drawing finger. "Of course, all this conjecture is predicated on you making the challenge *if* you decide to go through with something like that."

"*If*," Danny hissed emphatically into Murphy's ear, making it unmistakably known to the lawyer that he had not yet committed himself.

"*If*," said Murphy, and he nodded, conceding that it was all in the realm of hypothetical discussion at that point.

Murphy poured more beer into Danny's half empty glass.

"Anyway, Danny, *if* you decide to do it it'll be a very exciting test of the powers of the Committee."

Danny could tell that Murphy was beginning to feel absolutely no pain. But from past experience he knew Murphy would be able to keep on talking with a fair degree of lucidity and logic the rest of the night, no matter how much more beer he might drink, no matter how glazed his eyes might become, no matter how much his speech might thicken, no matter how much his words might drag as he formed them with clumsy recalcitrant lips. But Danny knew that if he wanted to discuss anything important with Murphy he better do it before it became too exasperating to drag out those slow and involved and labored replies from the man.

"Ed — "

Murphy shoved his fixed smile into Danny's face.

"What?"

"How long do you think this case would drag out in the courts if we make this fancy college try?"

Murphy mobilized his senses together, trying to be very professional in his manner.

"With appeals?"

"With appeals."

"Well" — Murphy distorted his face with the great effort it required of him to think it through — "let's say two; no, at least three; or maybe four — who knows, maybe even four years."

Danny winked comically at Murphy, but he thought of Julius Emspak and his jail sentence — what it had done to

Emspak to walk around with that sword pointed at his head every day, twenty-four hours a day. He thought of a vulture perched on his own shoulder, dripping poison from its beak, the poison dripping steadily, every minute, every hour, every day, for three or four years.

Murphy was eyeing him curiously. "Why do you want to know?"

"Oh, no special reason."

Murphy lifted his glass — a toast — and they drank. The lawyer very deliberately set his glass down on the bar.

"I understand that you haven't definitely made up your mind to challenge the constitutionality of the Committee. But you're still considering it, aren't you?"

"I don't know, Ed."

"Well, if that's the case — I wouldn't hesitate to change my mind. Don't hesitate."

Thinking that Murphy was more alert and possessed of his faculties than his halting thickened speech indicated, Danny toyed with his glass, wondering how much he could discuss with the lawyer in his present condition.

"You say Ralph's coming up here primarily because of the possibility that I'll make the challenge?"

"That doesn't mean anything."

"Well — "

"You've got to make up your own mind."

"I know."

"If I were in your shoes" — Murphy's head bobbed around in small circles as he concentrated to think and speak clearly — "I wouldn't hesitate to change my mind. Ralph will understand if you tell him you'd rather not take any chances, that you'd rather use the conventional approach of the Fifth Amendment."

"That's a long trip for him" — Danny wondered if Murphy could see how afraid he was — "coming all the way up here for nothing."

"He can use this trip as a vacation. He needs a rest after being so sick with a cold." Murphy peered directly into Danny's face, the personification of sincerity. "It would be wrong for you to feel you must challenge the Committee because Ralph is coming here — *if you decide you don't want to challenge the Committee!*"

"I haven't decided yet — "

Danny filled the two glasses, pouring the beer from one of the bottles of reserve stock. A toast to nothing, and they both drank, bottoms up. Murphy refilled the glasses.

"You worried about Helen?"

The question made Danny grin slightly, recognizing Murphy's astuteness, full of beer or not full of beer. He nodded in reply to the question, and Murphy tried to reassure him.

"I don't think you have to worry about Helen."

"She's talking about taking the kids off to Florida to her sister's."

"Temporarily or permanently?"

"Maybe permanently." Danny laughed at himself and put his arm around Murphy's shoulder. "Next week we play East Lynne. The week after that we got the bloodhounds chasing Eliza across the ice — Uncle Tom's Cabin."

Murphy jauntily waved away the dire possibilities. "I don't believe that about Helen. She's too intelligent. Underneath that snap judgement exterior where she says the first thing that comes to her mouth, she's too level-headed to walk out on you. It's true" — and Murphy had a silly grin on his face, his cupped hand hiding part of it — " she may swing out on a lot of wild detours along the way, but she's stuck to you through some fairly bitter difficulties."

"Never anything like this, not the possibility of jail."

"Oh, sure. You were arrested and socked in the can for passing out leaflets without a license up in North Tonawanda."

"A lot different from this. That licensing law was unconstitutional. We tested it and it was thrown out. You can't require a license to give out leaflets."

"How does that differ from this situation?"

"No comparison."

"The law setting up the Committee on Un-American Activities is unconstitutional. That's our contention. No more and no less unconstitutional than a law requiring you to get a license before you can distribute leaflets in North Tonawanda. What's the difference?"

"A big difference."

"What?"

"The penalty for distributing leaflets without a license was a lousy ten dollar fine!"

Danny didn't have to remind the lawyer what the penalty was for a conviction of contempt of Congress. Murphy's smile was nice and round again.

"Use the Fifth Amendment and the hell with it!"

"It isn't that easy — "

"Why not?"

"If I use the Fifth I'll be smeared all over the Buffalo newspapers as 'a Fifth Amendment commie' — Helen will have more hurt with that than if I take the offensive and tell the bastards to go screw themselves!"

"Then take the offensive — "

"But that could mean six months or a year in the can. I dunno."

Despising himself for the weakness which kept him from making up his mind definitely one way or the other, Danny swore under his breath, a long string of oaths, directed at himself more than anyone else.

Murphy patted Danny on the back.

"Let us relax," he lectured sonorously, "and let us not talk any more about anything to do with the Committee. Let us just sit here and listen to the delightful rhythms emanating from the many-colored jukebox — and let us steadily suck up all the beer we can pour into our dry, withered bellies."

The corners of the lawyer's mouth pulled upward at both ends, an infectious half-circle smile of a circus clown, forcing Danny to smile in return.

"Okay, Ed."

Danny lifted his glass, and they clinked their glasses together.

"Down with the bastards," said Murphy.

Chapter 12

The Regent was the kind of place — "A flea bag," George Hernandez called it — where couples registering at the hotel desk after midnight got the fish eye from the stout hotel detective who always firmly planted himself at a good vantage point a few yards away from the desk; but no couples were ever turned away because of any squeamish concern about their marital status.

This kind of hotel was very familiar to Danny. During his last three high school years before graduation and for a year during the big depression, after he had been laid off at the chemical plant, he had worked at one of these cheap drummer and tourist hotels in Buffalo — it had been his first close contact with the cheap and seamy side of life.

The lobby of The Regent was deserted except for the clerk behind the desk, the attendant behind the cigar stand and the house detective — Danny placed his occupation at one glance — who was sitting in a big leather upholstered armchair, keeping his weight off his sore feet. Danny got his key from the clerk. He bought copies of the local newspapers at the cigar stand — all headlined the Committee hearings.

He looked for the stairway up to the second floor where his room was located but found the elevator entrance first. The wasted old man who took him up to the second floor pointed out the men's room — next to the elevator entrance. Danny stopped there before going down the hall to find his room. Beer always ran right through him. The men's room was fitted out with a complete bathroom, including tub and shower. A gloomy joint. He resolved that he would take all his showers in Murphy's room at the Capital Hotel.

His room was the last door at the farthest end of the dark hallway. He switched on the overhead light as he entered. The room was so small it gave him a trapped-in feeling. No desk. Two windows, one in each of the two walls on the outer corner of the building. He poked an opening between several slats of the Venetian blinds on one of the windows and peered through it — a full parking lot, probably cars of the hotel guests. When he looked through the slats of the Venetian blind covering the other window he saw the side of a brick office building, all dark, across a narrow alley. There was a modernistic pipe-stemmed table lamp on the dresser; he switched it on and went back to the door and flipped the button which shut off the bright overhead ceiling light. His eyes felt better with only the indirect lighting from the lamp. A small sink was attached to the inner wall, with a mirror above it. At least he could shave and wash without walking all the way down the hall to that gloomy men's room.

He pulled the chain which operated the bare bulb above the mirror and stared at his face — tired, the usual coloring drained out of his cheeks. The red-lidded blue eyes sullenly stared back at him.

"Who do you think you're looking at?" he asked, aloud.

And then he was startled by the sound of someone clearing his throat. He noticed the door on the left of the wash basin, connecting with the next room. It was bolted on his side, and he assumed that it was also bolted on the other side.

The throat cleared again.

Danny froze.

Someone was standing smack up against the other side of the door.

Was it someone assigned to trail him or was it just some character who thought his next door neighbor might be interested in getting together with him? Again, that same sound, an ugly phlegmy sound.

Danny crossed to the telephone on the dresser. The operator answered. "Call me," Danny gruffly growled, loud enough for his next door neighbor to hear, "at eight o'clock in the morning, please."

He put down the phone and listened. No further sound from the other side of that connecting door.

He wanted to get to bed right away but he didn't want to have to get up during the night to take that long walk down the hallway to the men's room. He still had a lot of beer inside him to be gotten rid of. Of course, there was the sink, but that didn't appeal to him. Some of his buddies had used their steel helmets in similar emergencies when he was in the army. With some amusement he thought how Helen would grimace and act revolted if she ever learned he had even entertained such an idea.

His suitcase was at the foot of the bed. He got out his electric razor and stripped down to his waist. He washed and shaved and dressed again, and then sat down to read all the newspapers, consciously planning to keep his mind so occupied with other things that he would stay away from the problem of what he was going to do when he stepped in front of Denilworth in the courtroom. He was not going to think about that until he caught up on his sleep.

When he put down the last newspaper, his wrist watch showed twenty minutes to three. He had been reading everything including the advertisements to make the time pass away. He started on his third trip — the last for the night, he hoped — to the men's room. The carpeted narrow hallway was dark and silent, and Danny assumed that each room behind each door was tenanted with people sound asleep in bed. As he passed some doors he heard loud snoring.

He wished Helen had come with him, that she were there to keep him company. He was afraid of this feeling of loneliness, knowing it too well from the years he had lived alone in the furnished rooms in New York City when he had been an actor. What if Helen took the kids and left him?

He awoke. The room was dark. He reached up and pulled the chain, lighting the reading lamp attached to the headboard of the bed. Twenty-five minutes past five, his wrist watch showed. He pulled the chain. Darkness. He tried to fall asleep again, but his bladder needed emptying again and he could not fall asleep because of the uncomfortable bloated feeling. For what seemed like hours he debated with himself. Should it be the sink or the men's room way down the hall?

He pulled the light chain again. Five minutes past six.

He got out of bed and put on his shirt and trousers over his pajamas, then shoes without socks, and took the lonely walk through the long dark and narrow hallway.

In bed again, he was back to thinking about what he

should do when he appeared before the Committee and what would happen with Helen and the kids. His wrist watch showed seven-thirty when he finally gave up and got out of bed. He could see light through the narrow space where he had opened the window looking out on the narrow alley and the office building. A dirty gray morning light. But the room itself was still quite dark.

The telephone rang. "Good morning, sir, eight o'clock!"

He mumbled his thanks and asked the switchboard operator to connect him with the Capital Hotel. He asked for Ed Murphy, and after a long wait he heard Ed croaking a sleepy hello.

"Get up, you drunken barfly — "

"I'm up," Ed croaked.

"Don't go back to bed."

"I won't."

They arranged to meet for breakfast.

"You feeling okay, Ed?"

"I could say I feel fresh as a daisy but that would be stretching the truth slightly. What about you? Feeling better about everything after a good night's sleep?"

"Oh, I feel fine."

"Good. I was worried about you last night."

"I'm all right — "

"Good. I'm really glad to hear that."

While he washed and dressed, Danny wondered if he would be named this day. Or would he have to wait until tomorrow, Friday? The sooner the better.

He looked into the mirror above the wash basin. "*If 'tis done when 'tis done then 'twere well 'twere done quickly!*" He wasn't sure the words were in exactly the same place where Shakespeare originally put them. But the blue eyes staring coldly back at him from above the high cheekbones of the long face reflected in the mirror knew what he meant. Tiny rivulets of nervous sweat ran down his sides from underneath his armpits. He forced a grin onto the redhead's face reflected in the mirror, trying to pick up his depressed spirit.

Chapter 13

Holling was the only Congressman sitting up on the judge's throne on this second day of the hearing. He pontifically explained into the microphone that Representative Lester had been compelled by the press of other business to return to Washington and that Representative Brater had unfortunately become ill during the night with the recurrence of a chronic stomach ailment and had been ordered into a hospital by his doctor for an immediate checkup.

"Every time a politician wants to hide, "Danny whispered to Bill Kosciusko, "he heads for the hospital."

Holling announced that he had asked the chairman of the parent Committee in Washington to designate another member of the Committee to join the subcommittee in place of Lester. He surveyed the audience in the courtroom and waited for absolute silence.

"Meanwhile," he resumed, squeezing his mouth into a wide, mirthless smile, "I shall continue to hear witnesses this morning. Our important work of investigating subversive activity in this vital area must go on."

He straightened up and tapped his gavel. Denilworth, the Committee's legal counsel, rose and shuffled his papers, preparing to call the first witness for the day.

A few minutes earlier Ed Murphy and Danny had huddled in the corridor outside the courtroom with Bill Kosciusko and Herb Kepler and Herb's two local union leaders who had arrived the night before with subpoenas in their pockets. Murphy set up a schedule of conferences to take place in his hotel room where he could talk to each man alone and familiarize him with the kind of questions he might be asked and with the rights he had under the Constitution — including such things as when the Fifth Amendment privilege of refusing to answer a question could be asserted, or when answering one question or a series of questions might prevent a witness from legally availing himself of the

Fifth Amendment privilege in regard to related questions because he, as the lawyer described it, "had already opened the door to that line of questions."

Herb Kepler volunteered to be the first to go off with Murphy.

Bill Kosciusko and Danny found seats in their favorite spot, next to the center aisle on the rear bench on the left hand side of the courtroom; but Herb Kepler's two local union leaders hurriedly slipped away the moment they entered the courtroom. Danny wondered if Herb had warned his men to stay away from him because of the difference of opinion about answering or not answering the big question about Communist Party membership.

Danny left the courtroom and phoned George Hernandez at the office in Schenectady to tell him about the disappearance of Congressmen Lester and Brater from the hearing. George attributed their departure to the leaflet blast the union had issued against Lester about his interference in the union situation in Schenectady.

"They decided the issue was getting too hot."

"Think so, George?"

"Sure, what else?"

"Maybe Brater's really sick."

"Oh, sure." George laughed, and then he became serious. "This must mean the deal Brater made with Jean Dampier is off." Danny had heard that Brater had promised Dampier he would be granted immunity if he flatly denied any communist or pro-communist leanings or associations in front of the Committee in order to create the sharp contrast with the answers the Committee expected to get from the union organizers."

George explained:

"When Brater headed for the hospital that meant the end of the deal. He put Jean on the spot."

"You think so?"

"You can be sure Brater didn't go into any hospital just to get a checkup at this particular time."

George had an uncanny sense for sniffing out dirty deals, double-crosses and double double-crosses which were a normal part of the turbulence underneath most surface-smooth political situations. He had learned the hard way with the Loyalists in the Civil War in Spain and with the cloak-and-dagger O.S.S. in the U.S. Armed Forces during World War II, dropping behind enemy lines in Europe to contact the underground partisan guerrilla forces. He was probably right about Jean Dampier — the double-crosser was being maneuvered into a double double-cross.

"Wait and see," George predicted.

"I'm not going anywhere," said Danny.

"It's come quicker than I thought it would," added George, "but I'll bet this is where they hang Jean up by his thumbs — they'll keep him hanging there, where they can make him scream whenever they want him to make a move. From now on he'll have to kiss their ass or they'll castrate him. You watch the way they put the noose around his neck today — the deal's off — Jean's been double-crossed — that's why Brater stepped out of the picture!"

Danny promised George he would call again with any further important developments at the hearing.

He heard the names of Lisa and Henry Michaels mentioned by the witness as he returned to his seat next to Bill Kosciusko.

"What's up?" he whispered.

"They called back one of the 'pigeons' from yesterday," Bill explained. "He says he rented a room from a couple in Schenectady who later recruited him into the Communist Party . . . and he reported them to the FBI."

"I know the couple," Danny whispered. "That's the girl I was speaking to yesterday in the office in Schenectady — she and her husband."

He wondered if Lisa would be subpoenaed — he quickly glanced around the courtroom to see if her father and mother had arrived while he was down on the first floor calling George Hernandez. He didn't see them but he saw a good-looking blonde woman bending over, talking earnestly to the two local union leaders from Herb Kepler's district while she was taking notes. A reporter. A photographer snapped a picture of her talking to the two men. The explosion of the flash bulb drew the eyes of the courtroom spectators. The two men uneasily glanced around and

Danny could see that they were worried about the attention they were attracting. He wondered if the photograph had been taken for use in connection with the Labor Board election coming up in the shop where the two local union men worked, maybe to be printed in the newspaper there with a phony witch-hunting caption intended to whip up an atmosphere of hysteria. The blonde reporter returned to the front of the courtroom where she checked her notes with several other reporters. Danny glanced back at the two men she had interviewed and caught the eye of one of them. He motioned with his head and the man came over. Danny pushed over to make room for him to sit down.

"What did she want?" he asked, while noticing that the U.S. marshall and the GE chief of police were staring back at him from the front of the courtroom.

"She's a reporter from our hometown newspaper." The man sensed that Danny disapproved. "She's not too bad. She's given us some fair breaks in the past."

"I'd be careful," Danny warned. "Remember, you've been subpoenaed to provide propaganda against your union in the Labor Board election back in your shop."

"I know."

The man was apologetic. He nodded agreement as Danny continued, but kept his eyes averted.

"The less you say to reporters the better. It's just that much less for them to twist around."

Suddenly, startling both men, a press photographer stepped out from behind their bench into the middle of the center aisle, standing right above them, his camera aimed down at their faces, catching them in a position which Danny knew would look very conspiratorial. The thought flashed through his mind that there would be some dirty caption on the picture about union organizer accused of communist affiliation whips wavering local union leader back into line. His instinct told him to do something which would stop the photographer from snapping the picture.

His hand shot up and he thumbed his nose at the photographer. The flash bulb exploded! The photographer grinned as he walked away, leaving Danny sadly wishing he had not been so impulsive. That picture would not look good when it was printed in the newspapers. It made him look like a wise guy who was too damn smart for his own good. And the picture might be sent out over the wires to the Buffalo newspapers where Helen would see it.

The photographer looked back and laughed. Danny's cheeks felt hot and his armpits became soaked with sweat again. The local union officer fled back to his seat on the other side of the aisle.

Danny nudged Bill Kosciusko.

"We better split up. These guys are trying to make us look like a bunch of conspiring mugs. Any time we lean our heads together we're liable to get our pictures taken."

Bill Kosciusko moved to a seat down in the first row. Danny saw the U.S. marshall and the GE corporation's chief of police with their heads together, both smiling, probably at the way the organizers had been forced to split themselves up in the courtroom.

Danny swore at himself for having acted so stupidly.

The performance up in front of the railing moved ahead rapidly, while Danny watched and listened and evaluated, trying to learn from the experience of others. The friendly witness was dismissed and in quick succession three men he named were called and asked whether they were members of the Communist Party — and they asserted their right under the Fifth Amendment not to answer the question — and were dismissed.

Denilworth seemed to be in a hurry, asking the questions without taking time to create the mood as he had done on the previous day. Was the Committee going to jump directly to the union organizers now that Representative Lester had revealed the primary purpose of the hearing?

Another cooperative witness revealed that he had been asked by the FBI to join the Communist Party — and he read off a long list of names he had brought with him on a sheet of paper. The reporters scribbled furiously.

Several people named by the cooperative witness were called. The first one, a young woman with no make-up on her face or lips, replied that she was twenty-four years old to the question asked by Denilworth. She looked much younger and quite defenseless, reminding Danny of his older daughter, Ruth. All arms and legs, awkward and scared, her voice quivering when she spoke into the microphone on the table in front of her. Like other witnesses, she sat with her back to the audience in the courtroom.

"Are you a member of the Communist Party?" Denilworth asked her, like a loving father chiding a wayward young daughter. His kindly, forgiving manner and tone of voice told the audience he was letting this witness know that she was a nice young girl who probably did not know what she was doing when she got mixed up with that wrong crowd, and if she would only admit the error of her ways all would be forgiven.

"Under the Constitution of our great country" — she struck out bravely, the bravest speech of any of the witnesses thus far, her voice shaking so much she sounded ready to break into tears — "we have freedom of political belief, and you are trying to destroy the protection guaranteed — "

The insistent rapping of Representative Holling's gavel brought her brave statement to a halt. He waited for absolute silence.

"Young lady" — Holling was careful to smile at her; he knew she had the sympathy of the spectators in the courtroom — "answer the question," he gently admonished, "and if you want to assert the Fifth Amendment privilege to refuse to answer the question you know you can do that." He raised a warning finger and shook it at her, "But no speeches!"

The young woman was silent, apparently too nervous and disconcerted to know what to say to the Congressman.

"Do you," Holling prompted in a firmer voice than he had used thus far, "wish to claim the Fifth Amendment privilege?"

"You know," she argued, her voice still shaking, "that if I claim the Fifth Amendment privilege I'll lose my job," and Danny realized that she must be employed by some firm which, like GE, had established a policy of discharging employees who exercised their constitutional right to refuse to answer questions directed at them by a Congressional investigating committee.

"Then, young lady," Holling suggested with a grim politeness, "why don't you answer the question and tell us whether or not you are a member of the Communist Party?"

"And have your paid stoolpigeons frame me for perjury?" She was getting control of herself now, forgetting the fear in the excitement of expressing a deepfelt conviction. "Is that what you want to do?" she demanded. "Do you want to frame me with your paid stoolpigeons?"

It was the first real fight-back that any witness had attempted thus far in the hearing and there was a murmur of admiration out in the audience.

"You're excused," said Holling, aware of the growing sympathy among the spectators. He tapped his gavel, a signal for Denilworth to get on to more important things. "Let's move on" — he was very business-like — "and call the next witness."

This had been the first witness who had forced the Committee to back away. Danny wondered if she would be fired by her employer for her refusal to cooperate, as he watched the second "unfriendly witness" walking up the aisle, a skinny and wizen-faced elderly man wearing ill-fitting clothes, followed by his lawyer, a short man with thick-lensed glasses.

In reply to Denilworth's piercing questions — he was attacking the witness sharply, apparently to make up for what had happened with the previous witness — the elderly man stated with a thick accent into the microphone that he had been born in Sweden and was a carpenter by trade, and with a great deal of worry evident in his voice he admitted that he had gone to Russia.

"During the depression in 1931," he explained, as though that would make his visit to the communist country less of a heinous act.

This was the perfect target for Denilworth. He seemed to enjoy himself while he used his bag of tricks on the witness, repeating that open mouth stunt again and again to create an atmosphere of intense suspense while he awaited the stuttering replies.

The witness tried to explain what had prompted him to take the trip to a communist country but Denilworth got him so mixed up that his lawyer intervened.

"If you'll permit me," he politely objected to Denilworth, "the witness has answered your questions and you are trying to distort what he has said — "

Representative Holling tapped his gavel lightly, disdainfully, to bring the attorney to order.

"Let the witness speak for himself, counsel!"

Holling leaned forward over the judge's desk and looked down at the head of the witness who turned his face upward a soon as the Congressman spoke to him.

"You, Mr. Witness — you speak English, don't you?"

"Yes, sir."

"Do you need an interpreter?"

"No, sir."

Holling instructed Denilworth to proceed.

The witness got himself into hot water trying to answer Denilworth's questions, Danny noted. Instead of citing the Fifth Amendment and refusing to answer questions on a subject which by its very nature tended to incriminate him in the existing anti-Soviet atmosphere, the skinny carpenter tried to explain that he happened to take a trip to the Soviet Union during the big depression in the United States because he had heard so much about the communist experiment and he was curious to find out for himself if they had found an answer to unemployment and poverty at a time when there was so much unemployment and poverty in the United States. The Committee had a whipping boy to get their hearing back on the right track after it had been jarred slightly off its course by the boldness of the previous witness. Denilworth hammered away at the man about his visit to the Soviet Union and built it into something diabolical with overtones of espionage and sabotage. At this point the witness's common sense seemed to reassert itself. He shook his head like a shaggy wet dog flinging the moisture from his body.

"Fifth Amendment" he muttered, and then — apparently with growing panic — he repeated it over and over, "Fifth Amendment — Fifth Amendment — Fifth Amendment — ."

Denilworth couldn't break him loose from that. Nor could Representative Holling who reminded the witness that he was a naturalized citizen whose citizenship could be taken away — and he could be deported.

"Fifth Amendment."

"The witness is dismissed!" Holling angrily declared.

And as the bowed carpenter stepped away from the witness chair, the Congressman pointed the gavel, halting his departure.

"Mr. Witness, this committee is turning your name over to the immigration authorities with a recommendation that denaturalization and deportation proceedings be started immediately to get you out of this country."

The elderly carpenter, probably in his late sixties or early seventies, somberly nodded, acknowledging that he had registered the threat. Holling dismissed him, and the carpenter walked through the center aisle, looking down at his feet, avoiding the eyes of the spectators in the courtroom.

The fear evident in the man's face had a profound affect on Danny. Right then and there he made up his mind that he would rather be stood up against a wall and shot than have his personal dignity and self-respect slobbered up and spit upon by that bastard of a Congressman up there on the judge's bench and his bastard of a Lord Executioner, Denilworth.

Congressman Holling tapped his gavel to secure the attention of the spectators.

"I have here a sworn statement — " Holling went on to explain that he himself had secured this statement from a witness now living in the mid-West. "He was unable to come here because of a heart condition."

Holling handed the statement to Denilworth.

The Committee's legal counsel seated himself in front of a microphone. He dramatically took his time putting on his dark-rimmed reading glasses and then picked up the statement and read aloud:

"'*Congressman Holling*: What is your name?'

"'*Pearl*: Julius Pearl.'

"'*Congressman Holling*: Are you a member of the Communist Party?'

"'*Pearl*: Not now.'

"'*Congressman Holling*: Were you a member of the Communist Party?'

"'*Pearl*: Yes, I was.'

"'*Congressman Holling*: Were you a paid functionary, an organizer for the Communist Party?'

"'*Pearl*: Yes.'

"'*Congressman Holling:* Where did you work as a paid functionary, as a paid organizer for the Communist Party?'

"'*Pearl*: In the State Capital area including Schenectady.'"

Denilworth stopped and looked up at his audience, the courtroom spectators. His face urged everyone to pay the closest possible attention to the subsequent testimony he was about to read into the record. Then he looked down at the statement in his hands and he began to read, slowly, his voice loaded with dramatic portent.

"'*Congressman Holling*: Did you personally recruit any members into the Communist Party while you were assigned as a paid functionary of the Communist Party to the area around the State Capital including Schenectady?'

"'*Pearl*: Yes.'

"'*Congressman Holling*: Who was the most prominent, the most outstanding person in that area whom you personally recruited into the Communist Party?'"

Danny noticed how Denilworth dramatically bobbed his head up to look at his audience, to keep them coming along with him, and then he looked down at the statement in his hand to read the reply to that question. By now Danny had guessed what was coming. This was the double-cross of the double-crosser, as George Hernandez had predicted it. Denilworth read the reply slowly:

"'*Pearl*: The most prominent person I recruited into the Communist Party in that area was — Jean Dampier who at the time was president of the local union at the GE plant — '"

Reporters did not wait for the rest of the testimony. They rushed to call in the news. There was a noisy stirring and shifting in the courtroom. Danny noted that Holling was not making any effort to stop it. He seemed to want this kind of excited reaction to take place and to develop without restriction.

Danny saw Bill Kosciusko in the front row, looking back, stretching his head as high as he could. They waved quickly to one another. Bill made a funny face, a grotesque horse-laugh, ridiculing Dampier who had thought he could purify himself so easily by a back-door deal with a reactionary petty politician. Danny nodded, indicating that he understood the message contained in that pantomime.

But, surprising even himself, Danny felt sorry for Jean Dampier even though the man had deliberately stabbed their union and his close friends in the back with the secession movement he had prompted. Jean had put himself on the record publicly that he was going to appear before the Committee and flatly deny any and all connections with the Communist Party, past or present. Now, with Pearl's sworn statement entered into the record of the hearing, Jean would be deliberately sticking his neck into the noose if he followed the course he had charted for himself — but the man was too far committed publicly to retreat now from the policy of answering all questions as opposed to what he had labeled as the "Fifth Amendment equivocation" of the organizers. Jean was trapped. The FBI had fitted the ring into his nose and they could lead him wherever they wanted him to go.

Denilworth was still droning the rest of Pearl's question-and-answer statement into the record. Danny left the courtroom to telephone the latest developments to George Hernandez at the office in Schenectady.

Hernandez was not surprised.

"I predicted it, didn't I?" he smugly chuckled. "That ought to teach us a lesson that you can't make a deal to save your hide by agreeing to be just a little bit of a lousy stoolpigeon. They'll make you go whole hog or hang you once they get their claws into you and have you backing off. Jean's over a barrel. If he uses the Fifth Amendment he blows sky-high the whole stunt he's worked out with the Committee to make himself a patriotic hero compared to you dirty subversive organizers, the stunt they figured out to clinch the Labor Board election" — George laughed; it sounded to Danny like the grating of sandpaper against wood — "and if Jean doesn't use the Fifth Amendment they can send him up for perjury any time they want to jerk the rug out from under him."

"He'll *have* to use the Fifth, won't he, George?"

"He can't! He's too far committed. They've got enough into the record right now to hang him — and they won't let him back off!".

"Then he'll get sent up for perjury!"

"Oh, no, not yet. They don't want him in jail. They want him right where they got him. Now they got another guy in a key position in the labor movement to help them destroy it from within. They can tighten up on that noose any time he doesn't cooperate. That perjury charge is always there — and when the statute of limitations has almost run out they can charge up the battery again by putting him in the same tight box before some kind of committee where he has to answer exactly the same way."

Danny shivered his voice in mock fright. "I'd hate to be in Jean's shoes."

"So would I," George agreed with a hearty laugh, and then that must have reminded him. "When do you think you're going to be named?"

The thought immediately sobered Danny.

"I don't know."

"This afternoon," George confidently predicted.

"Maybe not until tomorrow — "

"No, this afternoon now that they've pinpointed Jean. You fellas will be named early enough this afternoon so there can be a big buildup in the newspapers today for the big showdown tomorrow. You fellas have to testify first to set up the big scene for Jean where he beats his breast and publicly declares *he is not and never has been.* After he gets through — the show's over — anything else would be an anti-climax."

"Sounds logical."

"That'll be a real show tomorrow!"

George seemed to have forgotten that one of the unwilling performers who would probably be held up to public ridicule was talking to him on the telephone.

"Why don't you get the ticket concession?" Danny sarcastically suggested.

George Hernandez tried to make a joke out of it. "This time it's you. Next time it might be me. They're not playing favorites."

"I know."

"But if I did have the ticket concession," George added, unable to resist the opening for a clever wisecrack, "I'd tour the country with this monkey show and make some real money with it."

"Go to hell," said Danny, and he slammed down the receiver, cutting off the rasping laughter of George Hernandez.

Chapter 14

At lunch Ed Murphy told Danny and Bill Kosciusko that he had warned Herb Kepler that a categorical denial of present Communist Party membership would undoubtedly be followed up by a series of questions to pin him down.

"They'll ask if he was a Communist ten years ago; five years ago; one year ago; one month ago; a week ago; yesterday; this morning before you entered the courtroom —"

Danny broke in.

"Ed, he's sticking his neck into a noose, isn't he, just like Jean Dampier?"

"No, this is different — Jean apparently is going to give a categorical denial of present *and past* membership, while Herb intends to say 'No' only to present membership."

"Won't they zero in on him until they establish the exact breaking point where he has to use the Fifth Amendment?"

"Herb thinks he has a way out. He's going to try to provoke them into tossing him out of the courtroom after he flatly denies present membership — "

"Can he pull that off?"

"We'll see."

Back at the courthouse Danny and the lawyer stopped off at a window alcove in the corridor to talk to Herb Kepler and his two local union officers, while Bill Kosciusko walked on into the courtroom.

"You ready to meet with me now?" Murphy asked the two local union officials.

They looked to Herb for their reply. He told them to go with Ed Murphy and he'd meet them later, either in the courtroom or back at his room in the hotel. They went off with Murphy.

Danny noticed how quickly — and without a word — Herb Kepler slipped away from him as soon as they entered the courtroom.

The show had already begun. Danny took his usual seat in the last row on the left side of the center aisle. Denilworth was holding some papers as he read aloud a continuation of the question-and-answer statement between Holling and Pearl.

"Danny — "

Bill Kosciusko bent over him from behind. Danny glanced around quickly to make sure there were no press photographers within striking distance.

"Danny, I heard the reporters talking up there — Jean Dampier has already issued a statement to the press calling Julius Pearl a liar. He's asked to appear before the Committee to clear himself. He's set to testify tomorrow morning."

"That means they'll call us this afternoon. Before Jean."

"Maybe first thing in the morning."

"First they have to call somebody to name us."

"This afternoon," said Bill. "He's next."

"Watch out!" Danny gave Bill a shove.

The U.S. marshall ambled slowley back up the middle aisle as Bill circled around behind the last bench and walked down the side aisle back to his place up front. The gray-haired marshall, with the faintest trace of an indulgent smile on his face, followed Bill back to his seat and then returned to the rear and came around the back of the bench and stood next to Danny for a minute or so — and then he returned to the place where he had started from, the spot in front of the jury box, next to where the GE chief of police was seated.

Denilworth droned on with the question-and-answer statement, all further proof that Jean Dampier had been a member of the Communist Party. It sounded so dull that Danny had to concentrate to listen — but he knew that these were the sticks of dynamite being placed under Jean Dampier who must be sweating.

A familiar name mentioned in the statement abruptly jerked Danny back to full attention.

"Sidney Raven — "

Denilworth droned on with the statement, Holling asking the questions, Pearl answering:

"'Question: Did you know Sidney Raven?'

"'Answer: Yes.'

"'Question: How did you know Sidney Raven?'

"'Answer: As a member of the Communist Party, active in

the trade union movement in the area around Albany and Schenectady.'"

Denilworth put aside the papers. A long silence for dramatic purposes while he sternly looked out over the audience. Then his voice vibrated from way down deep in his barrel chest, the sound going out through the loudspeakers in the courtroom and reverberating as it bounced back and forth between the smoothly plastered walls.

"Will Mr. Sidney Raven take the stand please?"

Danny stretched his head, trying to see where Raven was coming from. Then he saw him hurrying across the front of the courtroom to the witness chair. He had slipped in through the entrance from the judge's chambers. Danny caught only a quick glimpse of Raven's face and then the U.S. marshall and several court attendants blocked the view. Press photographers milled around the witness, their flash bulbs popping one after another as they aimed cameras and snapped pictures.

As Danny recalled Sidney Raven, the man had always been stocky, a little on the heavy side for someone of less than medium height. From that quick glimpse it did not appear that he had changed any in size and he still wore dark-rimmed glasses.

Raven stood there, waiting to be sworn in. The photographers kept moving around, trying to get dramatic shots of the key witness.

Congressman Holling administered the oath and Raven dropped his right arm to his side and slid into the witness chair. The press photographers stopped moving.

Denilworth waited for absolute silence before he spoke, his voice very low to dramatize the replies.

"What is your name?"

"Sidney Raven."

Danny was surprised by the bold tone of the reply, and he craned his neck out into the middle aisle, trying to get a better view of the witness and of Denilworth's face, while he unconsciously turned his left ear slightly toward the front of the courtroom to catch the delicate shadings of tone in the answers of the witness. He listened intently while Denilworth led Raven through a series of questions establishing that he had been an organizer employed by the same GE union to which Jean Dampier belonged.

"What difference was there between the policy of that union and the policy of the Communist Party?"

"None," Raven firmly replied.

"Did the union's organizers carry out the policies of the Communist Party?"

"Yes, sir."

In reply to further leading questions from Denilworth, the witness went on to testify that these policies of the union were carried out by a staff of organizers, all of whom — and he stated this most emphatically — were either communists or followed Communist Party instructions.

"They regularly attended meetings where a leader of the Communist Party explained the latest policy of the Communist Party and subjected each of the union organizers to criticism about the way he was or was not carrying out the Communist Party line."

"You mean — if he was not satisfactorily carrying out the Communist Party line, the Communist Party instructions, he was criticized?"

"Yes, he was criticized if he was not satisfactorily carrying out the Communist Party line, the Communist Party instructions," Raven parroted with the simplicity of a school child.

Danny wished he could sit down alone with Sidney Raven, without any possibility of anyone else knowing what they said to one another, so Raven could speak freely and tell how he rationalized what he was doing up there on the witness stand, winding a noose around the necks of the men he had worked with and the necks of their families.

Denilworth asked for the names of organizers who were members of the Communist Party. Danny began to sweat as he strained to hear.

"William Kosciusko and Herbert Kepler — "

In reply to the leading questions from Denilworth, Raven testified that these were two union organizers with whom he had worked and who had attended Communist Party meetings — that he had had many conversations with them and knew they were taking orders from the Communist Party just as he had done until he saw the light. Danny marveled at the bland manner in which Raven named the two men whom he described in his testimony as good friends of his for whom he still had a great regard.

Then, unexpectedly, it was over, and Danny realized that Sidney Raven had not named him.

Denilworth glanced at his wrist watch and then arbitrarily cut off the testimony with the announcement that the hearing would be recessed until the next morning because the Committee was going into executive session where they would continue with the questioning of the witness —

"And we will resume the questioning of this same witness publicly tomorrow morning at ten o'clock."

Congressman Holling rapped his gavel as a signal that the hearing was officially recessed.

Danny waited for Bill Kosciusko out in the corridor. There were a lot of people milling around there, not quite ready to go home, surprised by the unexpected announcement of a recess until the next morning.

Herb Kepler came out of the courtroom, and Danny saw that his face was pale.

"What," asked Herb, "do you think of that bastard . . . my buddy!"

Danny gripped Herb's arm, trying to show sympathy.

"How did I rate, I wonder?" he asked, apologizing for the omission of his own name.

"He'll probably get to you tomorrow," said Herb.

Bill Kosciusko came out of the courtroom. He didn't seem nervous except that he was too boisterous. He slapped Danny on the back.

"Where do you get the drag?"

Bill was obviously only joking, but Danny felt a pang of guilt as he thought about Congressman Yates and the effort Milt Reynolds of the Attica Westinghouse local union had made to kill the subpoena. He tried to laugh it off.

"I wrote a letter to my Congressman."

"Write one for me," suggested Bill, still trying to joke about it.

"Include me in that," said Herb, starting down the corridor, and he called back over his shoulder — "I'm going to meet my men over in Ed Murphy's room. We have to put in a call back home to tell them about this before they read about it in the newspapers."

Danny and Bill started slowly down the corridor toward the elevator entrance. They said nothing to each other in the crowded elevator. And they were silent until they left the first floor lobby of the building.

"Danny," said Bill — they were descending the front steps of the courthouse — "do you think you'll be named tomorrow morning?"

"Probably. Most probably."

He wondered how much the Buffalo newspapers were printing about the hearing. How much Helen was reading. He hoped the Buffalo newspapers did not print the photo of him thumbing his nose at the photographer. That would shake her.

Chapter 15

Back at the hotel Danny phoned Ed Murphy from the lobby and learned that he was in conference with Ralph Kaufman who had arrived from New York City. Murphy suggested that Danny and Bill wait down at the bar. An hour later Danny phoned up to Murphy's room again. The conference was still on.

"George Hernandez just arrived, Danny. We'll be through soon."

Danny wondered what was so important that George Hernandez had rushed in from the Schenectady office. "We'll be out in front of the hotel or in the lobby when you get through — "

"Don't get lost," cautioned Murphy. "We're discussing you — "

"Oh?"

"Ralph and George want to talk to you as soon as we get through with a few other things."

"What about?"

"What we've been talking about."

"What?"

"Challenging the Committee."

"Oh."

Danny's mouth suddenly felt very dry. He promised that he would stay either in front of the hotel or in the lobby where he could be found easily.

Out in front of the hotel a news truck pulled up to near where Danny and Bill Kosciusko were standing. The driver and his assistant tossed several bundles of newspapers out onto the sidewalk and then jumped down from their truck and carried them into the lobby. The two union organizers followed to the newsstand.

DAMPIER SUBPOENAED was spread across the top of the front page.

"Hey, Danny" — Bill Kosciusko thrust another newspaper before Danny's face — " you made front page on this one!"

"Oh, no!"

It was an involuntary exclamation from Danny as he grabbed the newspaper from Bill Kosciusko. "Oh, brother," he groaned. There he was, thumbing his nose directly back at himself and at every other newspaper reader.

"That's a nice picture," said Bill, unable to stop laughing at Danny's horrified reaction. "You'll get a Hollywood contract."

Danny tried to join in the joking.

"You mean I got sex appeal in my fingers?"

"He caught you just right," said Bill, and Danny saw that the photographer had done exactly that — the picture showed the thumb exactly in place against the tip of the nose, with the fingers spread out like an opened fan. The wise-guy expression on the face bothered Danny most. If Helen saw it —

"*Mis*-ter Daniel Newman! . . . *Mis*-ter Daniel Newman!"

He was being paged. A call on the house phone. It was Ed Murphy.

"Danny, we've moved over to Ralph's room. Can you come up now?"

"What about Bill?"

"Tell him to go and eat without waiting for the rest of us. We'll meet with him back here at eight o'clock."

As he got into the elevator Danny reminded himself that he had only a few minutes left before he had to make a definite decision. He wiped his palms of his hands dry on his topcoat.

Ed Murphy opened the door.

"Entrez," he said with a mocking bow.

"Danke," said Danny, adding as he entered, "my German is as good as your French."

Ed closed the door behind him. They were in the small anteroom of a big suite. On his left Danny could see the bedroom. Off to his right at the end of a narrow hallway was a large sitting room. Ralph Kaufman stood there, his hand outstretched.

"Danny."

"Hi, Ralph."

They squeezed hands hard. Danny had a tremendous respect and liking for Ralph Kaufman, knowing the man's reputation as one of the most brilliant labor lawyers in the country and also knowing that Ralph could have easily amassed a fortune by using his skill on behalf of employers instead of unions, or even by placing himself at the service of some conservative labor outfit instead of their UE union which was continually under heavy fire.

"How's the situation up in Buffalo?"

"Fine, Ralph, fine."

"You're looking young as ever. Younger every time I see you."

"It's the quiet uneventful life I lead, Ralph."

"I'm sure it is."

They both laughed.

With his shiny bald head, his thin face, and his slightly hooked nose above the neatly trimmed dark mustache, Ralph reminded Danny of an imperious eagle. The older man's brown eyes had a piercing quality which, Danny knew, tied in with an alert mind capable of penetrating immediately to the essential core of very difficult and confusing problems. — But, unlike the imperious eagle, Ralph also radiated a disarmingly gentle warmth, a quality he was exuding all over the place as he welcomed Danny.

"Come in, come in."

Ralph made a sweeping gesture with his left hand which held his ever-present pipe with its curved stem and big bowl, as his right hand guided Danny into the sitting room. There was George Hernandez, grinning in his usual cocky way. Tongue in cheek, Ralph introduced the two organizers.

"Here's your Simon Legree boss — *Captain Hernandez!*"

Danny knew that even though Ralph Kaufman was poking fun at George Hernandez, the older man had a tremendous admiration and respect for Hernandez who as a former army officer had been repeatedly commended and decorated during World War II for his bravery in parachuting behind enemy lines many times to make contact with partisan underground forces — George's army record included letters of commendation from General Dwight D. Eisenhower and General Omar Bradley, plus citations by most of the allied governments.

Playing the game, George Hernandez straightened up and barked out an order.

"*Ten*-shun!"

Danny snapped to attention.

The two men briskly saluted one another.

"At ease, Lieutenant."

"Yes, Captain!"

"Be seated, Lieutenant."

"Fuck you, Captain!"

The two lawyers and the two union organizers laughed at the little act and Ralph Kaufman took Danny's topcoat and draped it over his arm.

"I understand you and George have some things to say to one another. So if you'll excuse us — "

The two lawyers silently disappeared into the bedroom. Danny wondered why they were leaving him alone with George. Without a word George Hernandez walked across the room to the radio. Danny watched. George switched on the radio and twirled the dial until he tuned in on some news commentator, adjusting the volume down so low that it was hard to make out exactly what the broadcaster was saying.

"In case this room is tapped," he explained as he returned to Danny — they both knew that the drone of the radio commentator's voice in the background would jumble up and make unintelligible any recording made of their conversation.

They both sat down on the long sofa and Danny apprehensively waited. George Hernandez took his time importantly biting the end off a fresh cigar and spitting out the piece of tobacco into the ash tray. With a great show of calm and unconcern, he lit the cigar, inhaled deeply and blew a thick column of bluish gray smoke up at the ceiling. Knowing how much George Hernandez liked to dramatize everything he did, Danny could not help grinning.

"What's up, George?"

Still obviously enjoying the dramatics, George Hernandez looked over at Danny without moving his head.

"I'm talking to you alone," he began, very mysteriously, "because our lawyers don't want to get involved yet, not until after you've made up your mind by yourself. — There's some technicality involved here about what a lawyer can tell his client in these congressional investigations which is beyond the comprehension of an ignorant layman like myself" — he shrugged and made a face — "some legal nonsense which makes it better that you and I talk this thing out first by ourselves. . . . Apparently, some way, I don't know exactly why or how, it would create some sort of problem in their lawyer-client relationship with you if the lawyers were to involve themselves at this stage of the game — "

His cigar was clutched between his teeth while he talked. Now he grandly removed it from his mouth and tapped the gray ash into the plastic tray which bore the name of the hotel in gold letters.

Danny impatiently nodded for George to go on and get to the point. But George sniffed and brushed down the bristly ends of his bushy mustache, several short strokes on each side with the back of his hand. Danny wondered why George was so nervous.

"I understand," George resumed, and then he stopped to stick the cigar back into his mouth and to inhale and then puff out a cloud of smoke toward the ceiling.

He began again:

"I understand you're thinking of trying to become a hero — "

He stopped and sniffed and nervously laughed out loud before Danny could say anything, using his infectious laughter to make Danny join with him. They laughed as though there was some big joke.

"Murphy tell you?"

George Hernandez did not reply to that question. Instead he took the cigar out of his mouth and asked his own question.

"You still planning on going through with that kind of a challenge?"

Both men were smiling. A musical recording replaced the news commentator on the radio. A hot jumpy number. George was waiting. Danny knew he had to make up his mind.

"I'm thinking about it."

"Of course," George quickly assured him, "it's all your own decision to make."

"I know."

"I don't want to sway you" — George stuck the cigar back into his mouth — "but — "

He stopped there, waiting for Danny to prod him to go on.
"But what?"

"It would be a great thing if you did *that* . . . . I wish I were in your shoes right now. Here's a real chance to serve the cause of freedom in our country. . . . If they subpoenaed me and gave me the same opportunity you have right now — "

"Cut the shit, George! — Hand out the shovels when you start piling the crap that high. — I'll need hip boots to walk out of this place — "

George Hernandez burst into loud peals of laughter and slapped his thigh, enjoying the way the organizer who worked under him had pricked the high-flown appeal he was making. Still laughing, he put his hand on Danny's shoulder.

"Seriously, Danny, I wish I were in your place."

"Don't shit me, George. You're tickled to death you weren't subpoenaed. I don't blame you. I'd feel the same way."

"Okay, okay, okay." George Hernandez bubbled with laughter, conceding the point. He exuberantly poked Danny's knee. "Okay, nobody asks for trouble. We get enough without looking for it, don't we?"

His infectious manner had Danny laughing along with him.

"Danny, let's put it this way." He became serious. "If I was subpoenaed I would rather take the Committee head on and refuse to answer any questions — rather than get all mixed up and involved in answering some questions and refusing to answer others. I think that's a much better position to be in, don't you?"

Danny carefully nodded agreement.

"I've reached that conclusion myself, George, but I hate to pin myself down to that course of action — "

George puffed his cigar silently, and Danny knew that his fellow organizer was evaluating the full meaning of that. George thoughtfully rolled his tongue around over his gums and teeth, while he held his cigar between the thumb and forefinger of his right hand. He turned to face Danny.

"What about Helen?"

"What about her?" Danny asked as if it had never occurred to him that there might be any problem in that direction, and he consciously relaxed his arms, trying to stop the nervous twitching of his fingers.

"Have you spoken to her about this?"

"Not about this specifically."

George Hernandez lifted his eyebrows and rolled his eyes.

"She'll raise hell, won't she?"

Danny didn't want to think about that now. If he started to worry about Helen again, he would never arrive at any decision. Anything he did in this situation would be wrong to Helen.

"George" — he tried to sound very objective and calm and undisturbed — "I agree that Helen will be better off in the long run — both Helen and the kids — if I attack instead of defend."

The definiteness of his position was a surprise even to himself. He realized that despite the hesitations which had plagued him, he had arrived at a clear concept of what he wanted to do and why he wanted to do it. Attacking instead of defending, he would be arguing that the Committee is in the wrong instead of defending his use of the Fifth Amendment or whatever.

"You've made up your mind?" George Hernandez asked for a clear commitment. He waited for the reply, with his cigar poised in mid-air, stopped in its path to his open mouth.

Danny nodded.

The other man put the cigar into his mouth and puffed several times. For some reason or other he still did not seem to be completely satisfied. Danny nervously made conversation.

"I'll need a lot of help from the lawyers so I'll know all the exact details of the arguments I can use to back up my position in front of the Committee."

George Hernandez jerked his thumb toward the bedroom door.

"The best lawyer in the country on this kind of stuff is waiting in there to hear what you've decided." He paused significantly and took the cigar out of his mouth. *"Should I tell him you've made up your mind?"*

Now Danny knew what George wanted — a straight unequivocal commitment expressed in words so there could be no confusion about it later, no backing out later. He took a deep breath and noisily exhaled between pursed lips.

George Hernandez waited and grinned sympathetically.

Danny weakly returned the grin.

"Okay, George. — Okay."

He had committed himself, finally and without reservation of any kind.

George Hernandez got up to his feet, and Danny rose with him.

They very solemnly shook hands.

"You can be sure of support from some of the best minds in the country," George assured him. "You're bound to pick up support from all sections of society throughout the entire country. This is directly in line with what Albert Einstein has been urging, and a lot of people have been waiting and praying for someone with the courage to start it off. Others are sure to follow."

Danny hoped George was right. It would be awful lonesome to be all alone there in left field.

George stood there, hesitating, and Danny wondered what was still bothering him. Ralph Kaufman and Ed Murphy were waiting in the bedroom.

"Danny," George reminded him, very quietly, very seriously, "there *is* a risk — "

"I know there is, George."

"Six months to a year in the can."

"I know."

George Hernandez laughed, seeming relieved to know that Danny knew the risk he was taking.

"This is the kind of a thing, Danny, you can tell your grandchildren — "

"Oh, yeah," Danny caustically cut him off.

"Well, it *is* something big."

"I know," said Danny, letting the other man know that he didn't want to talk about it any more. George didn't have to kid him about there being brass bands greeting him if he challenged the Committee. There would be a lot of heat and it would be difficult to maintain the calm and peaceful serenity that is supposed to go with the long view, especially for a guy with his domestic problems.

"George," he laughingly complained, scratching the side of his hand like a bewildered yokel, "I don't know how the hell I always do it, but somehow or other — " He broke off. "Why do guys like us have to stick out our necks? What need do we have? Why do we do it?"

"I don't know why," George Hernandez laughed. He stuck the cigar back into his mouth and put his hand consolingly on Danny's shoulder. "But we certainly do it, don't we?"

George called Ralph Kaufman and Ed Murphy back into the sitting room. Danny saw that George was enjoying the opportunity to build suspense. The two lawyers stood there, awkwardly waiting to hear what had been decided. And then, timing it perfectly to make it dramatic, George made his announcement.

"He's decided to be a hero!"

Embarrassed, Danny awkwardly cursed the other union organizer, "This guy Hernandez is so full of shit that it's pouring out of his ears!" But he said it in a way that confirmed that he had committed himself to challenge the constitutionality of the Committee.

The two lawyers soberly congratulated Danny.

"I don't know of anyone," said Ralph Kaufman, "whom I consider more ideally suited than either one of the two of you to take this kind of position in front of the Committee. You're both very capable of thinking fast on your feet under pressure — and that's what this will require." He gestured with his curved stem pipe. "I couldn't have any better person to represent than either of you two guys in a situation like this. And since you, Danny, are the only one of the two who's been subpoenaed, it's a great honor to be your attorney and represent you. It'll be a very historic moment when you challenge the Committee."

Danny shrugged, dismissing that idea.

"Oh, yes," argued Ralph Kaufman, "it's very possible that history may look back some day and record this as marking one of the major turning points in the development of the resistance to the forces of fascism in our country. This will place the whole fight for the protection of civil liberties in the posture of an offensive, taking it off the defensive, and it will serve as an inspiration to the liberal and progressive forces throughout the country."

The lawyer's enthusiasm affected Danny, counteracting some of the fear which had begun to bother him again. There was a freshness and honesty in the way Ralph Kaufman said things which had been lacking in George Hernandez's somewhat cynical, though well-meaning, attempts to build up what a great thing it would be to challenge the Committee.

"I'll need a lot of advice," he reminded Ralph.

Ralph patted his arm. "We'll provide plenty of legal advice. That's easy. Lawyers are a dime a dozen in situations like this. But guys like you and George are not so plentiful!"

"Oh, nuts!" Danny felt his cheeks getting warm. He added a string of swear words to cover his embarrassment.

"I'm serious," insisted Ralph Kaufman, "very serious."

"Okay," said Danny. "But I'm starved. Let's go eat before I drop dead of hunger and spoil our whole case."

They ate at an Italian restaurant and while they waited for the dessert George Hernandez scanned the newspapers to see what Jean Dampier had to say for himself.

"Danny, you stupid shit!" George suddenly exploded, and he went on to call Danny every obscenity he could remember.

He pointed to the nose-thumbing photograph on the front page. Danny tried to appear unbothered by the outburst, but he felt like a high school kid who had been caught drawing "feelthy" pictures of the young well-stacked teacher. George silently passed the newspaper to the two lawyers. They shook their heads. It took a few minutes for George to calm down enough to stop swearing blindly at the redheaded union organizer.

"Danny" — you could tell that George was still boiling — "that's not so smart, especially with this highly principled position you're planning to take before the Committee tomorrow."

"I know," said Danny, now beginning to get angry at the way George was taking off on him.

Ralph Kaufman gently explained, "It's not very dignified."

"I'm sorry," Danny remorsefully apologized. "I did it automatically, not thinking."

"Can't you see all the newspapers," said George, "reprinting this smart aleck puss of yours when you get up there tomorrow morning and try to exercise some dignity in challenging the constitutionality of the Committee?"

"It's done, George, and I'm sorry. What the hell more do

you want?"

Ralph Kaufman intervened to gently suggest that Danny should speak to the press photographer who had snapped the picture. "It's important to be on good terms with these photographers. You can tell him in the morning that you were only fooling around when you thumbed your nose at him — and now he can take all the pictures he wants of you."

"I'll speak to him first thing tomorrow morning," Danny contritely promised.

"And make an effort to act dignified!" snapped George Hernandez, and then he burst out laughing.

"Okay, Captain," Danny snapped back.

"As you were, Lieutenant."

"Fuck you, Captain."

They had finished dinner. Ralph Kaufman suggested that Danny get some sleep up in Ed Murphy's room while he and Ed met with Bill Kosciusko in his suite back at the hotel.

"We'll probably be up all night," Ralph warned, "getting ready for tomorrow. I'll be sitting with you when you're in the witness chair, but we better not plan on them allowing me to give you any advice once we're before the Committee. They might very well toss me out on my ear, leaving you up there alone. We have to be ready for that possibility — "

On their way back to the hotel, Danny told Ralph about the telephone call the union's Chief Steward in Attica had made to his Congressman in Washington. He thought it only fair to let the attorney know there was a possibility, however slight, that the subpoena might be killed or ignored by the Committee.

"Don't build up any illusions," the lawyer replied without hesitation. "Tomorrow morning you'll be named by Sidney Raven, you'll be called, you'll be questioned. It'll take someone much more important than an obscure Congressman to stop this Committee from proceeding with its master plan to create conditions for fascism in our country. Real mass pressure is the only thing which blocks or deters them. They're afraid of votes. Nothing else."

"I didn't think there was much chance," said Danny, "but I thought I ought to tell you — "

"Fine," said Ralph. "If the miracle happens and you're not

called, we've lost nothing but a little sleep. But I'm quite certain you'll be called to testify, Danny."

"I'm sure you're right," Danny hurried to agree, ashamed that he might have given the impression that he was anxious to get off easier than the other organizers who had been subpoenaed with him.

"We'll see in the morning," said Ralph, and he calmly puffed his pipe.

They continued their walk back to the hotel, with George Hernandez and Ed Murphy up ahead of them. Danny reminded himself that he had to telephone Helen to tell her what he was planning to do — before he did it. Just the thought of how she probably would react made him shiver inside.

"Don't you think that was a wonderful dinner?" said Ralph, trying to make polite talk.

"Oh, yes," agreed Danny. "Wonderful."

But he was thinking about Helen, dreading the talk he would have with her within a matter of a few minutes.

Chapter 16

Danny switched on the light and closed the door after letting himself into the hotel room with Ed Murphy's key. The glaring light shed by three bare frosted bulbs in the ceiling fixture depressed him. He looked around and saw a lamp on the dark mahogany dresser. He turned it on and crossed back to the door and switched off the overhead lights.

Through the right window — there were two windows, both on the same wall, one on each side of the dresser — he could see across the inner court. Lights were on in most of the rooms in the other wing of the hotel. Danny looked at his wrist watch: a minute or so before half-past eight. For a few minutes he watched the physical activity in the rooms across the court — people walking around in their rooms, people sitting, people unpacking, people reading — and then he pulled down the green shades on both windows.

The room shrank.

Feeling hemmed in, he sat down on the edge of one of the twin beds. Helen and the children had already eaten by now. With his mind's eye he could see the activity going on in their house — Ruth doing her homework on the dining room table, Helen relaxing on their bed after having given Linda her bath, their college student helper Esther substituting for him, telling Linda her bedtime story.

This was the best time to be sure to catch Helen at home.

He reached for the telephone on the night table between the twin beds. She would never forgive him if he didn't tell her in advance what he planned to do when he would be called to testify before the Committee.

Helen would be leaving the house if he waited too long. She always was restless when he went out of town on union business — as soon as she got the kids straightened away for the evening, with Esther there as the sitter, she would be going over to The Park Lane to see her mother, or she would be driving out to visit his sister-in-law Hilda and his youngest brother Joe — or she might even go back to her basement room over in The Park Lane to work on her children's book illustrations, trying very hard to do something which would get her illustration work from the book publishers. If he wanted to be certain to catch Helen at home this was the best time to call her. But he deliberately put off making the call. He needed more time to prepare himself for the emotional scene which would be sure to develop.

A shower would pep him up, he decided. He bolted the outer door shut and went into the bathroom and quickly undressed and stepped under the shower. Standing still under the prickling water spray, he slowly turned the faucet lever to make the water gradually hotter and hotter until the heat was almost unbearable, and then he manipulated the faucet lever slowly in the opposite direction, carefully making the water colder and colder until he began to shiver and his skin became stippled with goose pimples. Then — all the way over with the lever!

Ice cold water!

"Wow-w-w — "

He let out an involuntary war whoop.

Continuing to yowl at the top of his lungs, he jumped up and down while he pounded his fists against his stomach muscles and slapped his chest and his face and then grabbed desperately at the lever and jammed it all the way over to the "OFF" position.

Still shivering after the water had stopped flowing, he rubbed and kneaded his arms and legs to increase the blood circulation and to warm up his body. He pushed the shower curtain aside and stepped out of the porcelain tub and got the bath towel, grabbing it at both ends and pulling it back and forth across his back and shoulders, vigorously drying himself until the friction made his skin tingle with warmth. He scrubbed his face with the rough towel and looked into the mirror of the medicine cabinet. His skin was a shiny pink, he saw, after he wiped the steam off the mirror. He started to jog up and down on the damp floor. Ever since his days as a high school athlete when he had won several letters as a cross-country long-distance runner and as a hurdler in the shorter distances he had kept up his daily jogging exercise, either running in place in one spot like he was doing now or moving around from room to room, like he usually did at home in Buffalo, or sometimes taking a slow trip around the block where he lived or through the nearby park, jogging slowly, just fast enough to stimulate all the muscles and speed up the blood circulation.

The physical feeling of well-being made the problem of speaking to Helen seem easier. There was no reason why Helen shouldn't understand everything if he explained it right. It was only logical that they would be better off if he took the offensive against the Committee instead of permitting himself to be shoved into a defensive position. She wouldn't want him to be a coward when a little courage would pay off so much better in the long run.

He tied the towel around his waist and looked into the mirror above the wash basin. He made a funny face to go with his disheveled red hair. He had left his comb over in his own room at the other hotel. He used his hands to part his hair on the left side and then to plaster down the hair on both sides of the part.

His shorts and undershirt were hanging on a hook behind the bathroom door. He put them on and went out into the other room to look at his wrist watch which he had left on the dresser.

A few minutes past nine o'clock already.

He had to call Helen right away or she would be sure to be gone.

He stretched himself out on the twin bed alongside the inner wall of the room. The bathroom door below the foot of the bed was open, with a glaring shaft of light pouring from the bathroom into the main room, the only light in that room — he had switched off the lamp on the dresser.

The pillow did not feel comfortable. He pulled it out from under the bedspread and propped it up against the headboard behind his back. He closed his eyes and half-dozed for about five minutes, letting his jaw hang limp, relaxing the muscles in his face, and then he decided that that was enough — he opened his eyes wide and flexed his arms and kicked his feet up into the air several times, bringing his body to full wakefulness again.

"Stop stalling," he said aloud, quietly, and he lifted the telephone receiver and put it to his ear. He heard a voice.

"Number please?"

The hotel switchboard operator gave him long distance, and the long distance operator took the Buffalo number and the name of the party he was calling. The Buffalo operator repeated his home phone number. The telephone at his home in Buffalo was ringing. Someone answered the phone.

Helen.

He wondered if she picked up the phone in the breakfast nook or was she on the extension upstairs in their den? He heard the operator talking to Helen.

"I have a long distance call for Mrs. Daniel Newman — is she there?"

"Speaking."

"Is *this* Mrs. Daniel Newman?"

"Yes."

"Here's your party, sir,"

He thanked the operator and then tried to sound cheerful.

"Hiya, Helen — "

He was aware of an ominous pause before Helen replied.

"Danny?"

"Yes. How are the kids?"

Before she replied he was aware of that heavy pause again.

"Fine."

So subdued, it seemed to him.

"Linda in bed already?"

"She's asleep."

"And Ruth" — he worked hard to sound cheerful — "is Ruth around?"

"She's upstairs" — that meant Helen was talking from the breakfast nook — "doing homework."

"And you?"

There was a deadly long wait before she gave a very noncommittal reply.

"I'm all right."

Silence again, and it was hard to keep up the pretense of cheerfulness. But he had to tell her what he planned to do.

"Oh, they still haven't called me to testify." He said it quickly, in a very offhand manner.

"No?"

"Not yet." He waited for some comment, but she said

nothing and he was forced to continue. "I'll probably be called tomorrow."

He waited again, but still only silence from the other end of the line. He sensed that the long silences and clipped replies were loaded with repressed fury and their conversation was sure to end in catastrophe. He had a panicky impulse to hang up the receiver. He would explain after he got back to Buffalo that the connection had been broken. But she would not forgive him his cowardice if he let her read about it in the newspapers.

"Hello" — he realized he was nervously combing his left hand through his damp hair, and he stopped doing it. "Helen — "

"I'm still here," she impatiently answered.

He lamely apologized. "I thought the connection was broken."

"No, I'm here."

He didn't know how to start. Helen spoke and this time he thought he detected a touch of concern for him in her voice.

"How is it going?" she asked.

He quickly responded with an effort to sound optimistic, trying to haul the whole conversation up out of the pit of somber melancholy into which it had fallen.

"Fine, Helen!" — He thought he sounded very cheerful. — "Everything's going fine!"

He realized immediately that he had overdone it.

"*It may be going fine with you*" — the naked hate revealed in her voice made him shudder — "*but it's not going so fine here with us!*"

"Oh-h-h, Helen," he involuntarily groaned, and he became aware that his body was shivering from head to foot, in nervous waves.

There was a long silence while he exerted all his energy to stop the involuntary nervous jerking of his muscles. Not a breath of sound from Helen, though he strained intensely to hear anything from her end of the line. He imagined her face, lips pressed firmly together as she also strained with similar intensity to hear any further sound from him.

He fought down an impulse to hang up the receiver. He couldn't hang up. Not yet. Not until after he told her what was going to happen the next day when the Committee called him to testify. With a touch of grim humor, he thought that then she would probably hang up on him.

"Helen — "

"What?"

"Helen, I'm doing my best. — I'm handling this the best way I can for you and the kids — "

"And *yourself!*" she accused, her voice quiet, loaded, weary. "For yourself *first!*"

"That's not true. You're not being fair to put — "

She broke in.

"Oh, what's the use?"

"Helen, I'm trying to do what's right!"

He stopped. Another long silence while she refused to comment. He decided that there was nothing left for him to do but to cut through to the reason for the phone call and get it over with.

"Helen" — in a matter-or-fact voice he proceeded to tell her, quickly — "the best thing for me to do is to take on the Committee head-on, to go on the offense. That's the best thing for me to do — "

"And what," she interrupted, quietly, her voice so fraught with pent-up emotion that it bled away his attempt at brave resolve, "is the best thing for *me* to do?"

"Helen — "

"Oh, never mind!" she angrily cut him short. "You live your life as you please and we'll live our lives as we please, myself and the kids, and " — with a threatening note — "we'll see what happens!"

"That's no way to look at it."

"Isn't it?"

"I'm only trying to do what's right. I've thought it through, and it's best if I just politely tell the Committee to go to hell instead of using the Fifth Amendment — "

"Don't you understand? I can't take it any more." The tragic quality in her voice tore away what little was left of his courage. He felt like he was being swallowed up in a morass of quicksand which had already reached his neck and was making it hard for him to breathe. The pain in her voice was frightening. "Don't you understand? I can't take it any more! I can't! I just can't take it any more! I can't! I can't! I just can't!"

It took him a long while before he was able to say anything.

"I'm sorry."

It sounded very weak, totally inadequate, and he knew he would have done better to keep his mouth shut.

"It doesn't do any good to be sorry," she snapped, rejecting his offer of sympathy. "That doesn't help those of us who are back here, taking all this punishment because of you. Even though we ourselves have done absolutely nothing wrong."

"Helen, I've done nothing wrong either, nothing to be ashamed of."

He could feel a pencil-thin stream of cold sweat running out from under his right arm, coursing its way down his side. No use arguing. Anything he said would only aggravate the situation. The hell with it.

The silence became unbearable as it dragged on . . . and on . . . and on . . . and on —

It seemed to Danny that the silence would never be broken as they both stubbornly waited for the other to speak first. He wondered if Helen had quietly hung up the receiver at her end of the line. Then she spoke.

"Are you still there?"

"I'm still here."

"You do whatever you please" — she spoke quite calmly and logically, and again sounded like she had relented — "whatever happens will happen."

"Okay — I'll see you soon."

"Maybe," said Helen, "not quite as soon as you think — "

He knew what she meant but he had to have her confirm it for him. It took a great effort, the sweat oozing out on his face, to make himself ask her the question he knew she wanted him to ask. The word came out of his mouth with great difficulty and he felt like a pitcher in a baseball game, with three men on base, who has pitched three bad balls in a row to the fourth batter and then cuts the fourth ball straight across the center of the home plate, a perfect setup, knowing the batter will probably clout the ball right out of the ball park —

"Why?" he croaked.

And, as he expected, Helen clouted the ball out over the

right field fence, a home run.

"I've got a call in," she said, "to my sister Frances in Florida," and then she stopped and waited for him to prompt her to go on.

"So?" he prompted her, like a hypnotized subject sticking pins into his own flesh to see if it will hurt.

"I'm taking the kids and we're going down to Florida as quickly as I can get things arranged — "

"Helen," he began, thinking maybe he ought to gather together what was left of his energy and make a determined effort to explain why he had to do it this way, why it was really best for all of them. But there was no use bucking his head against a stone wall.

Helen resumed.

"I don't know how long we'll stay in Florida." She sounded like she had thought it through and very definitely made up her mind. "I'll have time to think things over — and you'll have plenty of time to do the same — and we'll see what happens."

She stopped and waited for him to say something. Danny swallowed to lubricate his dry throat. He could think of nothing to say that would not aggravate the situation further. He had the strange feeling that he was standing aside and watching a movie about a telephone conversation between Helen Stack Newman of the Stack family of The Park Lane and her husband, Danny Newman, a union organizer who was to be questioned by the Un-American Activities Committee the next morning, and he was not the least bit involved in the complex emotional situation.

But Helen's voice brought him back to an awareness of reality.

"Are you still there?" she finally asked with some impatience.

"I'm here."

She went on, seeming calm, almost disinterested.

"You do what you think is right, and I'll phone Frannie — I can't make up my mind whether to go down there right now or to wait until Ruth's school term ends in June." She appeared to be talking out loud to herself as much as to him. "I'll wait and see how much nastiness there is in the newspapers after tomorrow, and then I can decide whether to leave right away or to wait until June."

"Helen" — he started a last feeble attempt, one more try, not to let their marriage collapse by default for lack of trying to hold it together — "there'll be less nastiness if I attack the Committee tomorrow morning and tell them in a polite way to go to hell. I'm thoroughly convinced, Helen, that this is the best way — *the most right way in the long run* — to handle this situation."

"Danny! I don't know what's right or wrong any more," she irritable interrupted. "I don't know and I don't care! *I only want peace, that's all! I only want peace!* — I don't want a life of turmoil any longer — I can't take it any longer. Don't you understand, I can't take it any longer, I can't, I can't, I can't — !"

She couldn't go on. He knew she was quietly crying. But no crying sounds. Helen was too proud to let out any crying sounds if she could possibly suppress them.

"Helen — " What could he say? "Helen, I honestly and sincerely think I'm doing the right thing, the best thing for all of us. If I didn't, I wouldn't be doing it."

"I know — "

She sounded so weary she made him feel loaded down with guilt.

"I know," she repeated, quietly.

He still had a vivid picture of her in his mind, sponging her eyes and nose and cheeks with a flimsy piece of cleansing tissue she fished out of her purse. He imagined that she was using one hand to slip on her dark shell-rimmed reading glasses to hide her red eyelids and the puffiness underneath her eyes.

"I'm sorry," she said, and he could tell that she was trying to sound more cheerful. "I know I shouldn't be talking to you this way right now when you need someone to encourage you — to keep up your morale."

"That's okay, kid. Forget it."

"We never should have married. We're all wrong for each other. All wrong."

"Helen" — he had to say something — "we're *not* all wrong!"

But she wearily brushed aside his pious protest.

"Oh, let's not argue about it. We're way past that. I'm

going to Florida to think things through. Meanwhile, you do whatever you think is right. You know your field much better than I do. All I know" — she sounded sad and lost — "is that I'm miserable and unhappy, and I can't keep going on this way."

"I'm sorry." He wanted to say more but there was nothing more he could say. "I'm really sorry."

She accepted his apology with a quiet kindness which revealed to him how much soul-searching she must have gone through.

"It's my fault as much as yours. I'm just as responsible for this marriage as you are. I was a spoiled brat who wanted everything I thought would amuse me, and then counted on my father and the prestige and influence and financial position of The Park Lane to get me out of my predicament later when I tired of the toy I was playing with. But Dad's gone now, and I'm in too deep to get out without being hurt and without the children being hurt. And you too. — Without the children it might be a lot easier, but this way we're both horribly trapped."

"Oh, it'll turn out all right, Helen," he said, trying to encourage her, but he felt like a damn fool as soon as he said it, especially since she immediately reacted with a quiet bitter laugh.

"You mean you think I'll forget all about it again, like I've forgotten all the other times, and you can keep right on going the way you've been going. Isn't that what you mean?" Her voice dropped and became hard. "Not this time, not this time. I'm really going to Florida with the kids this time — "

She stopped herself, and he knew she was waiting for him to express his opinion. But he decided it was best to say nothing. Helen finally sighed, signaling she was about to bring their conversation to a close.

"I'm sorry. I haven't been much help to you, have I?"

"That's all right."

"I wish I could be."

"Forget it"

"Good luck."

"Thanks."

"Goodbye — "

"Goodbye — "

He heard the phone click as she hung up.

Danny reached over and carefully put down the receiver. It was done. He had made the call. He leaned back against the headboard of the bed in the darkness of the small hotel room, with the light shining through the open door of the bathroom. He closed his eyes and he felt dizzy.

The physical and emotional strain of the conversation with Helen had left him thoroughly exhausted. He dozed off and had a series of quick dreams that took him back to his high school and college days, exhausting himself in a hurdle race, then a cross country race, then a football game, and then he was in uniform in the army again, struggling up a long muddy slope, straining uphill, his rifle clutched with both his hands up high in front of his chest, a heavy pack strapped on his back, his chest ready to burst, half-crying with the desperate noisy effort to breathe, his feet refusing to move, every muscle in his entire body screaming its protest, refusing to budge further — he collapsed flat on his face in the mud, arms and legs sprawled wide, chest heaving, body and clothes drenched with sweat from head to foot, mouth wide open, tongue tasting the wet earth, half-sobbing, the will to live squeezed absolutely dry —

Chapter 17

Once, years before, Danny went home from New York City — he was still an actor then — and his parents wanted him to stay there, in Buffalo! "Acting on the stage? That's for sons of rich men who can provide a steady income."

He was a lost person then, uprooted, feeling friendless, and fearful of drowning his individuality in lower middle-class sameness and emptiness. It was a shallow viewpoint, he realized later, but an understandable one in a young person still searching for himself.

He often recalled that late Sunday afternoon when he got on the train in Buffalo after saying goodbye to his father and mother and his sisters and brothers, starting back to the uncertainties of the stage in New York City, practically penniless, with no job waiting.   A chicken bone got caught in his throat while he was eating in the dining car and he was taken off the train for emergency treatment at the hospital in Schenectady. He was not choking, but he was extremely uncomfortable. His throat pained every time he swallowed. The hospital could not get any specialist to come in and look at him Sunday night. Since he could not afford a private room, he was placed in a ward to wait until morning. He was unable to sleep. The nurse gave him a shot of some drug with a hypodermic needle. It put his body to sleep but it jolted his mind into furious activity, racing from one idea to another as he sifted through each of his problems, building tiny worries into major problems and major problems into suicide-worthy situations. He had only a few dollars in his pocket. How would he get out of the hospital? Would they take the few dollars he had? If they did, what would he do when he got back to the big city again? There was no job waiting for him. He would have to start making the rounds of the producers and agents. He might go through the whole season without finding work. — And the hospital ward itself was a nightmare. He would always remember that old man who was out of his head: the old man had urinated in bed and cried that he was drowning and won't anyone please save me; the nurse told Danny — when she saw him with his eyes wide open and she stopped to give him another hypodermic injection which only made his thoughts wilder — she didn't want to touch the old man because he was laced up in a straitjacket, his insides rotted out, and absolutely nothing could be done for him except to let him die; and the poor old man moaned and wept all through the night that he was drowning and won't someone please, please, please take pity on a poor old man and save me from drowning — it was a dragged-out horrible nightmare, and Danny went through a similar agony after his phone conversation with Helen, after hearing that she had definitely made up her mind to leave him and take the kids to live with her sister Frances in Florida.

For hours after he said goodbye to Helen, until almost midnight, waiting for Ralph Kaufman to call, he lay there on top of the bed in Ed Murphy's room, clad only in shorts and undershirt — he hadn't moved from that position since talking to Helen — dozing for short spells, dreaming, waking, brooding, torturing himself with the wildest kind of pictures in his mind about what was going to happen with his life after he appeared before the Committee.

Several times he tried to gather together enough energy to get up and turn off the light in the bathroom and come back and climb under the covers to really sleep, but he couldn't pull himself together enough to make it. His body seemed paralyzed even though his mind was wide awake and his imagination was acting up with amazing sharpness.

Again and again he wished that it was all over and he was back in Buffalo to face whatever might come after the hearing — to face it and get it done with.

He believed — with every single fibre of his body, he believed — that his best move would be to make a frontal challenge against the Committee, even if it meant a citation for contempt of Congress, even if he were tried and found guilty, even if he were sent to jail for six months or a year.

It would be better for Helen and the kids to be in a position where they could truthfully say he was in jail for defending a principle — the right to preserve one's thoughts from invasion by a tyrannical and unconstitutional Committee — than it would be for them to have to say that he was being smeared because he had answered questions or because he had used the Fifth Amendment not to answer questions, even though he would be out of jail that way.

Although Helen might wish that he would answer all questions — even she would not carry that so far, he believed, as to want him to be a stoolpigeon, an informer. Anyway, he would never be a stoolpigeon, no matter what the cost of the refusal.

So, obviously, answering all questions was impossible, and there was no use wasting time even thinking about that.

What about answering *some* questions? Just enough to take off some of the pressure? Could he walk a tight rope, answering just enough to lighten the load a little on Helen and the kids, without getting so embroiled that he would still face the choice between becoming a stoolpigeon and naming names or going to jail for contempt of Congress because he refused to name names? He doubted it.

And truthful answers to dangerous questions concerning his known left-wing economic and political beliefs and associations might draw added fire on Helen and the kids. Could he hold back and answer only a few of those questions? Could he answer such questions very carefully, drawing the line where he would want to draw it?

No. To satisfy Helen's family and the small circle of professional and business people who constituted that influential splinter of the Buffalo community in which she grew up, he had to answer enough questions with flat-footed denials of belief, or membership, or association, to be certain to leave himself wide open for a perjury charge. Anything less would merely open up the subject and stir it to a boil, leaving it in a worse state than if he left it alone.

Would Helen stick with him through that kind of mess, especially if he was charged, tried and convicted of perjury? Would she stick with him while he served a term in jail? He doubted it.

Could he take it, six months to a year in jail? Maybe longer, for perjury. Could he retain his mental and emotional balance through that kind of devastating loneliness in a prison cell away from all contact with a woman? It was bad enough the long year he was stationed at an isolated outpost in Korea right after World War II ended; and he still became filled with apprehension whenever he thought about the years of loneliness he spent in a drab furnished room in Manhattan when he was an actor — but several years in jail, or even only a year, or only six months, knowing he was alone, abandoned on the outside by Helen and the kids!

But what about his responsibility to the people in the labor movement? To the people in the progressive movement? To Bill Kosciusko? To the people in their local unions back in Buffalo and Tonawanda and North Tonawanda, the people he represented and who trusted him not to fail their belief in his courage and integrity?

From his experience as a union organizer he knew too much about the relationship of forces in the whole country to make believe that he didn't know better than to cooperate in this dirty business by answering the questions of the Committee.

Perhaps it would be best to invoke the Fifth Amendment privilege and not answer any of the dangerous questions, like Bill Kosciusko was going to do. No one could hate him for handling it that way, and he would be fairly certain that way to avoid going to jail.

But then he reminded himself that using the Fifth Amendment would not solve his particular problem because he would still be smeared in the newspapers and the pressure would still be increased in that section of the Buffalo community about which Helen was most concerned, and Helen would still feel that she and the children had been subjected to this additional stigma because of him.

Could she endure that additional stigma easier than she could endure the kind of reaction there would be in that section of the community if he went to jail for six months or a year for refusing to answer any questions, challenging the constitutionality of the Committee?

What would he do if there were no Helen and there were no children: no Ruth and no Linda? Would be proceed, without all this agonizing hesitation, to challenge the constitutionality of the Committee?

"Undoubtedly," he whispered aloud, answering himself, "knowing what I know, believing what I believe, it's the only course of action that makes sense: attack instead of defend."

And with Helen and the children?

"It's still the best thing to do," he whispered aloud, "even for them!"

But he knew that Helen would never believe he had done it because it was better for *her* as well as because it was better for the labor movement and the liberal and progressive movement and would advance the whole cause of defense of freedom in their country. She would always believe he had sacrificed her personal welfare for the good of others — for what, she would say, he had selfishly rationalized as being for the good of the country as a whole.

It seemed that no matter what he would do he would still be doomed to the terrible loneliness of living the rest of his life without Helen and the kids. If he used the Fifth Amendment he opened himself up to all sorts of snide attacks in the community back home in Buffalo, and Helen would be placed in a bad position in relation to the Stack family and her few remaining friends in that old group she had known before their marriage; inevitably, she would still reach the same conclusion — that her only way to avoid all the unpleasantness would be to take the children and go to live with her sister in Florida. Once she was in Florida with the children, she might find it such a relief to be away from him she might never want to return to live with that source of her difficulties. The end of that road was also divorce, separation for life from Helen and the kids.

It was easy to resolve to still keep in close touch with the kids after a separation or divorce, but he recalled in detail all the people he knew who were children of broken marriages, specific cases where the fathers were compelled, by the need to earn a living and to build a tolerable life of their own, to make the break wider and wider, gradually seeing less and less of their children until the love of the children for the father was destroyed. His guts ached at the thought of losing his kids.

Round and round he wrestled the argument with himself. If he didn't use the Fifth Amendment, if he challenged the constitutionality of the Committee, there was a good possibility he would be cited for contempt of Congress, possibly go to jail for six months or a year. Helen undoubtedly would take the children to Florida and he would face exactly the same threat of losing them that he faced if he used the Fifth Amendment.

If the same disaster would befall him whether he used the Fifth Amendment or challenged the constitutionality of the Committee — wouldn't it be better to challenge the constitutionality of the Committee, going on the offense? Wouldn't that be better than inviting the sneaky-sounding title of "Fifth Amendment Communist" in the Buffalo newspapers?

Were Ralph Kaufman and Ed Murphy telling Bill Kosciusko all about how he — Danny Newman — was going to challenge the constitutionality of the Committee? What if he changed his mind now? How could he tell that to Ralph Kaufman and Ed Murphy and George Hernandez and Bill Kosciusko? What if word got around to the rank-and-file union membership back home that he had planned to challenge the constitutionality of the Committee, but that after phoning his wife he lost his nerve? What would the membership back home think of the coward?

And, more important, what would he himself think of the coward?

The telephone rang. It was Ralph Kaufman. Danny welcomed the call. Now he had to make a decision and get it over with.

"Did I wake you up?" Ralph Kaufman asked with some concern, and Danny realized that he must sound sleepy.

"Oh, I just dozed off for a while, Ralph. I'm wide awake now."

"Rested?"

"A little."

"We're through with Bill. Are you ready to start?"

Danny hesitated, and then answered, "Yes."

"Murphy's gone down to the bar with Bill to have a beer. I'd like to get something myself before we start our session. I'd prefer coffee, but if you want beer — "

"Coffee, Ralph. I'd like coffee too."

That way he would be alone with Ralph, away from the others, and he could tell Ralph about the difficulty that had come up with Helen.

"Do you want to come up to my room or shall we meet in the lobby?"

"I'm not dressed yet, Ralph. I just woke up."

"Good! I was afraid you might be too highly pitched up to get any rest before we got started on our all-night session."

"I slept fairly well," Danny lied.

"Good. Shall we meet in the lobby in about five minutes?"

"I'll throw on my clothes and be right down, Ralph."

"Take your time." The lawyer spoke very soothingly, like a fight trainer taking care of his up-and-coming boxing boy before a big match. "There's no hurry. We have all night. Though we should try to get through in time for you to get at least a few more hours of sleep so you're not all worn out when you go up on the stand."

"I'll meet you in the lobby right away, Ralph."

Danny sat on the edge of the bed for a few minutes, squeezing his face as hard as he could between both hands, trying to pull himself together. He started the circle of arguments again but was too disgusted with himself to keep at it. Ralph was waiting. He quickly dressed and got out of the hotel room.

Chapter 18

12:03 AM . . . Friday morning —

Ralph Kaufman was waiting in front of the elevator entrances on the main floor. The lawyer smiled warmly, and Danny saw that he had his Sherlock Holmes curved-stem pipe with him, characteristically holding the bowl cupped in his right hand while his teeth gripped the flat end of the stem. Ralph took the pipe out of his mouth when he spoke.

"Let's take a short walk," he suggested, "and see if we can find a coffee shop close by. I'd like a little fresh air."

Without a word Danny fell in beside the lawyer, walking much slower than his normal rapid pace, to keep from getting ahead of the shorter man. At the revolving doors Danny stepped aside to let the lawyer pass through ahead of him.

"Age before beauty," bowed Ralph, without taking the end of his pipe out of his mouth as he guided Danny to precede him.

A stiff breeze hit them as they stepped out under the hotel marquee.

"Windy," commented Danny, as he turned up the collar of his topcoat.

Ralph nodded agreement. He took his pipe out of his mouth and tapped the bowl against the palm of his left hand. The wind whisked away the dead ash and burning tobacco with a quick swirl of sparks. Ralph slipped the pipe into his right hand coat pocket and turned up his collar against the wind.

"I think," he suggested, "I saw some restaurants on this other street when the taxi brought me to the hotel from the railroad station." He led the way around the corner where they could see electric signs, colored bulbs flashing off and on, as they walked by a line of lighted store windows.

Danny glanced at his wrist watch. Past midnight already. They walked on without talking until the silence made Danny feel too self-conscious to remain quiet any longer.

"We'll have trouble," he said, "finding anything open at this hour."

"Oh" — Ralph's voice was muffled by his upturned coat collar — "there must be some small all-night coffee shops where cab drivers hang out. How about that cafeteria over there?" He pointed to a brightly lit corner.

They crossed the street. Gusts of wind blew the dust around in circles at their feet and tugged at their topcoats as they bent their heads and hurried toward the protection of the cafeteria entrance. It was a relief to escape from the rising wind.

Ralph Kaufman jerked two checks from the dispensing machine in front of the watchful eyes of the bald cashier.

"It isn't often," he said with a wry smile, "I can afford to treat one of you organizers to anything," and he pushed away the hand Danny extended for one of the checks. "Next time it'll be your turn."

They stopped at the pastry counter next to the coffee urn. The only counterman on the job at this hour was waiting there for them, the inquiring look on his pale night-worker face asking what they wanted. Ralph politely gave his guest the first chance to order.

"What will you have?"

Danny faced the counterman.

"Do you have a baked apple?"

Without wasting the energy it would take to reply, the counterman barked the order for one baked apple into a microphone attached to the end of a long stainless steel pipe extending down from the ceiling over his head.

"Make it two," said Ralph.

The counterman barked the order into the microphone.

"Coffee," said Danny.

"Milk for me," said Ralph.

Danny changed his mind. "Make mine milk too."

The stare of the counterman's tired blue eyes let him know how stupid he was for changing his mind. The man wearily put down the cup and saucer he had already picked up to serve coffee. He picked up two waxed cardboard cartons of milk and placed one on each tray, and then a glass on each tray.

"Sorry," said Danny, apologizing for his stupidity.

The counterman put a baked apple on each tray.

"Cream with your apple?" he asked, his pale face still expressionless while he held aloft two small glass containers of cream — one in each hand — poised in mid-air, ready for serving.

"No," said Ralph.

"Yes," said Danny, to show the counterman he had a mind of his own.

His face still expressionless, the counterman placed a small container of cream on Danny's tray.

"Do you want anything else?" Ralph asked, and the counterman did not move a muscle as he impatiently waited for them to make up their minds.

"Are you going to have anything else?" — Why did he ask Ralph that? Why couldn't he make up his own mind without consulting Ralph?

Ralph said he didn't want anything else. Neither did Danny. He followed Ralph to a spot near the window where they transferred their food from their trays to the table. The busboy, a thin little man, quite old, took away the empty trays. The two men draped their topcoats over an empty chair and sat down.

Danny had not forgotten his problem for one moment — how to tell Ralph about Helen. Still thinking about that, he concentrated on carefully pouring the cream over the sugared baked apple. He could feel that Ralph was examining him closely.

"It looks like a good baked apple," said Ralph, obviously making talk to ease the situation. "I usually don't eat anything as rich as this at night. I intended to get a small bowl of porridge, but you lured me on to this special delicacy."

A polite smile from Danny. So Ralph had copied him in ordering the baked apple. That gave him a slight feeling of satisfaction. Maybe this indecision is normal. His failure to make up his mind once and for all with unshakable finality regarding how to handle himself at the hearing had shaken his confidence in his ability to make up his mind about anything, even about an inconsequential matter such as what kind of midnight snack to order in a cafeteria.

Ralph was digging into the baked apple with his spoon,

breaking off a sugary chunk. He did the same. They both were quiet while they chewed and swallowed the first bites. Then Danny felt he had to tell Ralph. It was probably very obvious that something was bothering him.

"Tastes good," he said, to break the ice.

"It certainly does," Ralph agreed.

They were silent again while they continued to break off big chunks of baked apple with their spoons and chewed and swallowed, concentrating on the food, avoiding looking at each other. Danny was sure that Ralph must know that he wanted to talk to him about something it was very hard to talk about.

Their eyes met and Ralph gave Danny an encouraging smile and kept right on eating. Danny put down his spoon.

"Ralph — I called my wife tonight — on the telephone — up in Murphy's room —"

"How is she?" Ralph pleasantly suggested.

Danny mutely moved his head forward in several false starts before words came out of his opened mouth.

"She blew her top."

"Oh?"

"She doesn't understand, Ralph. She comes from an anti-labor background. And she's scared to death."

"Can you blame her?"

"Hell, no — I'm scared too — I'm supposed to be a pretty tough guy with a lot of experience in tight spots like this."

"I'm scared too," said Ralph. "Who isn't — with what's happening these days?" A quick smile, and then he became very serious. "The pressures we're forced to live with constantly these days are not very conducive to a feeling of lightheartedness. I'd say there's absolutely nothing wrong with feeling scared. What counts is — *what are we doing about it?*"

"That's right, Ralph," Danny readily agreed. He toyed with his spoon for a moment. "Well, Helen — she finds it very hard, Ralph."

"I'm sure she does. After all, it isn't an everyday occurrence for a wife to have her husband dragged before this kind of committee where he can be subjected to all kinds of humiliation which usually redounds upon her and upon her children."

He was so understanding it was embarrassing. Danny made sugary mush out of his baked apple, squeezing the pulp with the flat of his spoon and mixing it with the cream. He knew Ralph was waiting. But it was hard to say what he had decided to tell him.

"Ralph — I tried to explain to her."

The lawyer nodded encouragement to keep him going.

" — I felt I had to tell her before I went ahead with it."

"Of course you had to tell her. It would have been unthinkable for you to proceed without telling her."

Danny took a paper napkin from the metal container on the table and wiped his sticky fingers, keeping his attention fixed on his fingers.

"She's leaving me — with the kids — going to Florida to visit her sister — to decide whether or not our marriage is finished."

Ralph reacted at once with great sympathy. "I'm very sorry to hear that." Then he gently added, "Is it because of this position you're going to take before the Committee?"

Danny noted how Ralph still phrased the sentence in such a way as to indicate that he still assumed they were going through with the challenge. Or is he trying to sound me out?

"Is that why?" Ralph softly prompted.

"I guess so — though, to be realistic about it, I don't know if it will make any difference at this stage of the game whether I do or don't go through with what we planned."

"Don't you think it might help some if you didn't challenge the constitutionality of the Committee, if you used the Fifth Amendment?"

"I don't know. Maybe. Who can be sure?"

"Well, if it might — "

He stopped and waited to hear from Danny.

"It might," said Danny, after a long pause. "It might."

"Then — " Ralph shrugged. That ended it. There was no argument from him.

"Funny thing" — Danny laughed weakly — "is that I'm not sure it would make it any easier if I used the Fifth Amendment. Probably, in the long run, it will be easier if I challenge the Committee and answer no questions at all.

Ralph looked puzzled. He fished his pipe out of his

topcoat pocket and then sat back, the pipe in his hand, staring at Danny, half-smiling in a kindly way.

"Only you can decide for yourself."

"I know — "

"But don't feel the slightest bit of hesitancy about changing your mind. Not at all. There's no reason why you must go ahead and challenge the constitutionality of the Committee tomorrow. There should be no feeling of compulsion on your part." He put the pipe into his mouth, gripping the stem with his teeth. Danny noted that the bowl of the pipe was empty. "It would be wrong," continued Ralph, "for you to go ahead with the challenge if you're not absolutely certain you want to do it."

At least a full minute of silence went by, both men sitting perfectly still, before Danny answered the question implicit in what the lawyer had said.

"I'm *not* certain."

"Then don't do it."

"I feel like a shit."

"There's no reason why you should."

"I'm letting everybody down."

"Nonsense." Ralph took the pipe out of his mouth. "Someone else will come along in more favorable circumstances who will decide to make the same constitutional test. None of us are indispensable. If you don't make the test this time, someone else eventually will come along who will."

The matter-or-fact way in which the lawyer explained it only fanned Danny's feeling of remorse over his failure to carry through what they had planned, and there was added to the remorse a tinge of regret at missing this great opportunity which someone else would take to be recognized as having struck an important blow in defense of civil liberties.

Ralph tried to make it easier for him.

"Don't worry about it — the only other people who know you were contemplating this constitutional test are Ed Murphy and George Hernandez, and I'll explain to them in the morning. I'm certain they'll understand."

"I feel really lousy about it," said Danny, fearing that he did not sound convincing.

"There's absolutely no reason why you should castigate yourself. You're making sufficient contribution to the cause of the common man in this country with your activities as a union organizer."

"Oh, yeah — "

"You're making the good fight every day."

"Oh, sure — "

"There's no reason why you should feel so terrible because personal circumstances make it impossible for you to do this one particular thing."

"But I should go through with it." He was arguing with himself, not with the other man. "I know it's the right thing to do."

Ralph played with his pipe, tapping the empty bowl against the palm of his hand as he spoke precisely, like a corporation lawyer giving a weighty opinion to the full board of directors.

"Danny, I don't know your circumstances at home well enough to advise you on that matter any further than to say — that you have a perfect right to consider your personal situation in making any decision. After all, we are human beings, and we are carrying on this struggle for what is right with the specific purpose in mind of making life happier for human beings, including our families and ourselves along with all the rest of humanity."

The lawyer put the stem of his pipe back between his teeth, smiling gently to indicate that he had finished and now it was Danny's turn.

"I don't think" — Danny managed a grin — "I'm going to be happy no matter what decision I make. I'm damned if I do, and I'm damned if I don't."

"Oh, it's not that terrible." The attorney laughed, trying to stir Danny out of his welter of self-pity, but Danny was reluctant to be so stirred. This was his only way to let Ralph know how badly he really felt about losing his guts, not going through with what he had told them he would do. "You're sitting right on top of it this minute," argued Ralph, "and that makes it seem worse than it really is. You're over-excited and nervous and that makes you exaggerate the effect of everything right now."

"Maybe — "

"Try to forget the whole thing and get a good night's sleep. Tomorrow I'll still go along with you as your lawyer — you can use the Fifth Amendment on the dangerous questions. I'm sure you'll know what to do when you're up in the witness chair. You'll have no trouble. You can take care of yourself. I know that."

"Thanks," murmured Danny, hating himself.

They talked about the weather and cafeterias and other odds and ends while they gulped down their milk and the rest of their baked apples, staying away from any further mention about what was going to happen the next day. As soon as they finished eating, they got out of the cafeteria.

The sky overhead was still cloudy when Danny looked up to see if the moon and stars were out. He saw that a few drops of rain had fallen. The sidewalk was splattered with big wet blotches. There was a gusty wind which caught at their coats and made them clutch their collars tightly around their necks while they bent forward to protect their faces.

Danny's hotel was several blocks beyond the Capital Hotel where Ralph was staying. The two men were silent until they stopped and faced one another under the dark marquee in front of the revolving doors where Ralph was going to leave.

They shook hands.

"Get some sleep tonight," shouted Ralph above the noise of the wind.

"Thanks," Danny yelled back, while gusts of wind flew dust and old newspapers in small whirlpools around their feet. "See you in the morning."

"Don't worry!"

"I won't!"

Danny watched the lawyer go into the hotel, shoving his way through the revolving doors. Ralph waved goodnight back at him from inside the lobby. A wave in return, and then Danny started back to his own hotel, bending forward into the strong wind which noisily tried to shove him backward. His mind was furiously active while he walked several blocks — he was thinking and thinking and thinking — and then he was pushing up the steep slope of the last block, and he could see the small canvas marquee of The Regent.

"The hell with it!"

He whipped around and started rushing back to Ralph's hotel. He would go through with it! He couldn't stand hating himself!

The wind was at his back, pushing him — he was running!

He was stopped by the red signal at the corner near Ralph's hotel. It took forever to change to green, and by the time it had turned green Danny's impulsive burst of courage had been just as abruptly washed away by the vivid picture his mind created of Helen and the children on their way to Florida, going out of his life forever while he rotted away behind iron bars in a small lonely prison cell, the kind of small cell he had seen in Sing Sing prison when he had performed there in the Thirties with a WPA Federal Theatre troupe, in Shakespeare's Taming of the Shrew.

The signal turned to red again while he stood on the corner, unable to move in either direction, momentarily completely paralyzed.

And then he slowly turned around and started fighting his way back uphill against the wind toward his hotel, head down, chin pressed against his chest, his shoulders hunched forward to protect his face from the sharp gusts of wind and he blamed the dust blowing into his eyes for the wetness that blurred his vision.

Chapter 19

The clerk at the desk handed Danny his key. He noticed the husky hotel detective giving him the once over as he started back through the main lobby. There was a white cloth banner hanging from an overhead balcony with a proclamation in red block printing announcing that teachers were welcome to a regional educational conference. He recalled seeing a lot of women milling around in the lobby when he left the hotel that morning. Now there were only the house detective and the desk clerk and a cleaning woman and a man behind the newsstand and himself.

He bought copies of all the newspapers, even the ones he had read earlier in the day. He could show the local union membership back home how the newspapers in the State Capital had tried to whip up a witch-hunting hysteria with lurid banner headlines.

The night watchman, his time clock resting in his lap, sat in an armchair across from the entrance to the elevator in the small back lobby. Holding the room key so the watchman could see it in his hand and know that he was a hotel guest, Danny pressed the button to ring for the elevator — the arrowed pointer showed that the elevator cage was up on the eighth floor.

"He's taking coffee up to one of the rooms," the night watchman volunteered — "he'll be right down."

Danny turned to face the watchman. "My room is on the second floor. Any way to walk up?"

The watchman pointed to a short flight of stairs which climbed steeply up to a door half-way up the side of the blank wall of the high-ceilinged back lobby. At the top step Danny turned and curtly nodded (thank you); and the watchman nodded in return (you're welcome).

The heavy metal fire door clanged shut behind Danny and he was all alone in the hall. He looked around, trying to figure out the direction to his room. The elevator was on his right. Then he saw the men's room between himself and the elevator entrance. He decided to stop off there before going on to his room at the end of the narrow corridor.

When he came out of the men's room and started down the dim hallway he wondered if he would run into any of the teachers. It sounded like there were several late parties in progress. He could hear women's voices, laughing and talking loud. He heard music, a dance orchestra on the radio. The women sounded like they were having a good time, and he envied them, wishing he were with them instead of marching down a dimly lit hallway to a boxy hotel room where he would be all alone.

At the end of the hallway — his room was the last door on the left — he stood and listened. There was a party directly across the hall from his room. He heard shrieks of laughter. He put the key into the lock and stood there, not turning the key, listening. There were no men's voices in the room across the hall. Only women. Teachers attending the convention, he guessed. They sounded like they were really enjoying themselves. What would they say if he knocked on their door and asked to join them? He hated to go into that small empty room. He needed people to talk to and to laugh with — to help him step out of his skin and stop arguing with himself. But if there were only women in the room across the hall, they might be frightened if he tried to intrude at that late hour — they might complain to the management. He could imagine that burly house detective coming up from the lobby to make a big scene. Wouldn't that make a fine story for the late edition of the morning newspaper? **UNION ORGANIZER THROWN OUT OF HOTEL AFTER ATTEMPTING TO MOLEST TEACHERS!** What a nice background for a follow-up later in the day about the same organizer using the Fifth Amendment privilege to avoid answering questions about his political beliefs and associations!

Danny turned the key in the lock and opened the door of his hotel room. He reached his hand in and switched on the overhead light. He stepped in and softly closed the door behind him. The overhead light was too bright — he turned on the lamp on the dresser and switched off the other glaring light.

What if he telephoned the teachers across the hall? If they were not receptive that would be the end of it. The telephone was on the dresser. He rested his hand tentatively on the receiver. He heard several more shrieks of laughter. They were really having a lot of fun over there. A long peal of laughter brought him to his senses. No use trying to fool himself — it would take a lot more than a party to pull him out of this depressed mood.

He heard the sound of the man in the adjoining room clearing his throat. He flared up and hurled a curse at the flimsy door which separated the two rooms.

"Oh, go to sleep you dirty — "

Absolute silence.

Annoyed at the childishness of his outburst, Danny's anger turned back on himself. He impatiently hoisted his feet, shoes and all, up on top of the bedspread and stretched himself out flat on his back and stared morosely up at the low ceiling.

"Coward!"

Brooding would solve nothing. He swung his feet down to the floor and sat up on the edge of the bed again. There was nothing to do but to get undressed and go to sleep — nothing to do but go through all the motions, as if nothing had happened to disturb him.

A problem. The inner fires of nervous tension were burning furiously. His body was throwing off a liquid waste, creating an intense need to empty the fluid out of his system. In plain English, as Danny vulgarly phrased it to himself, he had to piss so bad he could almost taste it.

When he returned from the men's room he almost obeyed the impulse to knock on the door across the hall — they were laughing in there behind that door and they sounded a little drunk and very carefree. But he suppressed the dangerous impulse and quietly entered his room, relieved that he hadn't knocked on that door.

It was too hot in his room. The radiator almost burned his hand when he touched it. He checked the Venetian blinds to make sure they were shut tight. Then he undressed. He stood in front of the dresser, looking at his reflection in the big mirror, proud of the way he had kept his body in good physical shape. That was one worthwhile thing he had learned as an officer in the infantry — to always keep himself in good physical shape by regular exercise. Despite his forty-one years, he knew he looked like he had the physique of a young college athlete. There was no loose fat. All the bunchy abdominal muscles were clearly defined beneath the tight skin on his stomach, with a hollow dividing line running vertically through the flat mid-section.

A woman in the room across the hall let out a long shrill peal of laughter — she sounded rich with the warm enjoyment of living.

Danny stared into the deepset blue eyes which defiantly stared back at him from the dresser mirror — and he stared deeper into them — and deeper into them — until the strain of staring became painful and his eyes watered.

"You coward!" he taunted the redhead in the mirror. "Cut it off! You got no use for it any more! You're no man! You're a coward! *A lousy coward!*"

He saw the redhead in the mirror slowly shaking himself from side to side like a wrestler painfully trying to wrench himself free from an opponent's choking grip, and the long face contorted itself into deep lines of loathing and disgust for himself. He covered his face with his hands to blot out the face in the mirror and he forced himself to turn away.

Standing hunched over that way for what seemed like a long while, his back to the mirror, grinding his fingertips into his tightly shut eyelids, the strong wave of self-hate which had surged up in him subsided. He took his hands away from his face and turned around and looked at himself again in the mirror.

The redhead sullenly stared back at him.

"Go to hell" he mumbled. A woman's shrill laugh prompted him to add, in the direction of the room across the hall, "You too." Remembering the stranger in the adjoining room, he growled in the direction of the connecting door, "And you too. All of you. Everybody. Go to hell!"

A wild idea suddenly hit him.

Could this next door neighbor who never seemed to go to sleep be an FBI man assigned to keep an eye on him? Or was that too fantastic to be real?

He decided it was possible, though not necessarily probable.

But how would they know he had checked into this particular room? He had checked in at the hotel desk on the previous day, on his way out to Schenectady. If all the hotels in the State Capital were given a list of names with instructions to report to the FBI as soon as any of those individuals registered at the desk it would be easy to plant this character next door to him. His neighbor might be an FBI man. While it would make no difference in how he would answer the Committee it added to the fear and nervous tension to think that there might be an FBI man planted on the other side of that flimsy connecting door, listening to every sound he made, keeping track of when he came in and when he went out, possible recording his telephone conversations. It was very unlikely that this actually was an FBI man next door, Danny told himself, trying to dismiss the disturbing thought — he was letting his imagination run away with himself. He relaxed and stopped straining to hear any sound from the next room. He had heard nothing since the one time the man had cleared his throat.

The speculation about the possibility of an FBI man being in the next room brought Danny out of himself for a little while. That was an outside danger, easire to cope with than the inner conflict, the doubts and indecision. He opened his suitcase and took out his pajamas. No sound from the adjoining room. But the party noises across the hall were still there. Preparing to go to sleep, for lack of anything better to do to help him forget himself, he pulled back the bedspread and turned off the lamp on top of the dresser. The room seemed to be pitch black for a few moments, until his eyes adapted themselves to the sudden darkness. Then he could see a horizontal slit of light, about a quarter of an inch wide, between the rug and the bottom edge of the connecting door. But still not a sound from that room.

He turned on the lamp again and looked at his wrist watch. Twenty minutes past one. He telephoned down to the switchboard operator and put in a call for eight o'clock in the morning, wondering if his next door neighbor had his ear pressed up against the connecting door, listening to every word.

The room seemed very stuffy. He shut off the steam in the radiators and opened one window a few inches at the bottom. A cold breeze hit his thighs, and he gingerly backed away. He switched off the lamp. Pitch darkness again until his eyes adjusted, and then he sat down on the edge of the bed. No sound from the next room, but there was a babble of laughing women's voices across the hall.

He was still too disturbed to lie down and try to sleep or even to remain seated in one position. He got up and methodically padded with his bare feet back and forth in the small space between the dresser and the door to the hall.

While he kept moving he went over the possibilities again. What would happen if he *tried to answer all questions*; or if he *refused to answer only certain dangerous questions* by using the Fifth Amendment privilege; or if he *refused to answer any questions*, challenging the constitutionality of the Committee? What could happen if he went to jail? If he *didn't go to jail*? Would Helen really leave, taking the kids? Would the parting be permanent? Would he ever see the kids again? What kind of relationship would he have with them? Would the local union leaders and the rank-and-file back home stick with him when the heat went on, stronger than ever before, hotter than ever before? Or would they be afraid of drawing fire on themselves and their families if they publicly showed their support for him? How badly would he be smeared in the Buffalo newspapers? What would be the attitude of Helen's mother and her brothers and sisters? What would be the attitude of his own mother and father and his own brothers and sisters? What about the neighbors on the block where they lived? The people who knew only Helen? The people who knew only him? The people who knew both of them?

He minutely analyzed each possibility — weighed and dissected and juggled and tore apart and reassembled into different combinations and tore apart and reassembled again into further combinations —

The intense emotional mental activity and the cold air pouring into the room through the opening where he had raised the window produced a peculiar effect on him — he had to relieve himself again so badly it was painful. Instead of bothering to get dressed again to walk all the way down the long narrow hallway to the men's room, he used the wash basin. He thought about how revolted Helen would be if she knew what he was doing. But at the same time he felt that by this act he was defying her effort to dominate and criticize, from her viewpoint, everything he ever did. He grinned as he thought that it was a form of declaration of independence. Anyhow, it didn't matter that much any more. He had already destroyed his respect for himself as a person by backing down on the decision to challenge the Committee. Then he realized that he was acting like a petulant child.

"If you really want to challenge the constitutionality of the Committee, you'd do it, Helen or no Helen. How much respect do you think she is going to have for you if you don't do what you *know* is the right thing to do?" And he silently answered his own question, "No respect. None. None at all."

His hands still clung to his face and he dug his nails into the skin covering his high cheekbones, while he conjured up a vision of Helen in his mind — tall and slender and very attractive in a haughty way, with contemptuous brown eyes.

"If you were so sure," she sneered, *"that it was the right thing to do, why didn't you do it? You didn't listen to me on many other things. If you really wanted to do that, you would have done it no matter what I said or did."*

There was a telephone only a few feet away on the dresser, and he could call Ralph Kaufman and tell the lawyer he had changed his mind. But the thought sent a chill through him, and the vivid frightening picture flashed through his mind again — the picture of Helen taking the children off to Florida while he sat in a lonely prison cell — alone as he was this night in the hotel room in the darkness, alone this same way for six months or a year.

His bare feet felt icy cold. He slipped under the blanket and lay there on his back.

"I've done it. I've castrated myself. Destroyed my pride in my manhood. I'll never respect myself again."

He pulled the blanket up over his face but he couldn't shut out the female shrieks of laughter which came from the room across the hall. Then he heard the man in the adjoining room loudly clearing the phlegm out of his throat. He rolled over and buried his hot face in the wet pillow.

Chapter 20

Sleep was impossible.

Scenes from the past and the future raced through his head as he lay in bed, staring up at the ceiling in the semi-darkness. Not since his youth had tears involuntarily started down his cheeks the way they had flowed a few minutes ago, and he was still ashamed for having given in to his emotions like that.

Puzzled and deeply perplexed, he searched back through his life trying to find out what was the right thing to do. He started as far back as he could remember in his working life, trying to trace the process by which he had gradually accumulated a progressive working class viewpoint — to advance by advancing the interests of the whole group — as opposed to the individualist beat-the-other guy values — climb, climb, climb out of this group to the next higher group and the next higher group.

While in grammar school he worked as newsboy, candy butcher at the ball park, balloon vendor at the city zoo, carwasher's helper and delivery boy at a grocery store.

While in high school he worked, after school and during summer vacations, as a garage boy at the hotel in downtown Buffalo, as a movie house usher and as a shoe clerk.

After he left high school he went to work in the factory, his first job in a factory, the job his high school chemistry teacher got for him so he could earn good money quickly to save enough for a college education — working in a chemical plant, with all the danger and excitement of hopping between boiling tanks of dangerous chemicals, handling poisonous and explosive materials. Working rotating shifts, a different shift each week, prevented him from seeing his middle class friends, his high school fraternity brothers. That was when he broke with the "old gang" he grew up with.

Then, in 1931, came depression, and he was laid off. He went back to high school for a post graduate course to fill in the empty jobless days while he worked nights as an elevator operator and bellhop at the same hotel where he had been a garage boy. Then he was back to work at the chemical plant.

Next year — escape! He quit the job at the factory, fleeing to a course in theatre at the University of Iowa, far from everything and everyone connected with the middle class shopkeeper background which had been his home, far from everything and everyone connected with the factory where he had worked. Escape!

A year at the university and then not enough money to go back for the second year, even with free tuition in return for playing football. His goals were not clear enough to give the incentive to put up a real fight for a college education. The depression had left its mark on him.

Home again in Buffalo, he went to work as a clerk in a chain grocery store. After a year of hard work he was promoted to assistant supervisor of green goods — fruits and vegetables — for all stores of the chain in the entire Buffalo area. But he was dissatisfied with his life, and a year later he was demoted because of his surly attitude. He didn't give a damn whether or not he sold an extra dozen oranges or another bunch of carrots. He couldn't whip himself up into a state of excitement about selling fruits or vegetables.

Disgusted with the pointlessness of everything, he quit the clerk's job and hitch-hiked to New York City to become an actor on the stage. Each day he made the rounds of the producers' and agents' offices — and during the next few years he acted bit parts and walk-ons in several plays on Broadway and on the road, and one lead role Off-Broadway; then back to the street and out of work and lonesome and hungry — he hitch-hiked back to Buffalo where he picked up a football scholarship at Canisius College to while the time away. After the football season ended he fled back to the big city and the glamour of the theatre.

He studied hard — acting, voice and dance — through the years of lonely search in the big city for a meaning to life, a philosophy to fill the emptiness of existence, gravitating more and more toward left-wing cooperative acting groups who performed before working class and progressive middle class audiences.

Thinking about it now, lying in bed in the hotel room, much of it came back to him, much which he had not thought about for many years. Looking back at it from his new vantage point, it seemed very different from what he thought of it when those things actually were happening.

It momentarily amused him as he recognized that he had acted the role of a union organizer in short plays and sketches before union and progressive audiences in New York City at least six or seven years before he became a real-life union organizer. The truth was — and it came to him for the first time while he lay there in the hotel bed digging into his mind for a solid perspective — he gained respect for the importance of the role of a union organizer in society from the research he had done as an actor to bring such a character to life on the stage.

Through the contacts he made while working with the left-wing theatrical groups in New York City, he received an offer to go back to Buffalo as director for The Buffalo Contemporary Theatre, an amateur theatrical group which was trying to present productions dealing realistically with current life problems. Unemployed at the time — between engagements — penniless, he returned home to Buffalo, intending to stay there just long enough to get on his feet again.

That was when he met Helen. Her liberal-thinking older sister Eleanor brought Helen to the first public performance of the first production he directed for the Buffalo group: a variety show in which he acted. After the performance Helen boldly introduced herself. "I decided I had to meet you." Shortly after that Eleanor and the other liberal-thinking member of the Stack family, the younger brother Nat, fled from Buffalo to live in Greenwich Village in Manhattan. The contradictions in Buffalo, where they saw too clearly how their income came from the labor of others by way of a system of which they were theoretically critical but practically wished to maintain because of the benefits they derived from it, became too great for them to be able to remain in Buffalo.

The amateur theatrical group in Buffalo folded very quickly due to lack of funds. Helen refused to go to New York City with him and he went to work at the airplane factory as a template maker, making tools to make airplane parts. He joined the company union and became involved in fighting its corrupt leadership.

Married to Helen!

Then — and how well he remembered the detailed events of the day when it happened — he was discharged from the airplane plant because of union activity on behalf of the United Automobile Workers of America, given the phony excuse (later rescinded) that the local Army Air Corps representative at the plant had termed him "undesirable" for employment there.

Blacklisted!

Out of work for almost a year!

Then a temporary job, an "extra," filling in, selling in a chain shoe store several evenings a week and on Saturdays.

He continued the fight to win reinstatement to his job at the airplane plant, using every bit of his skill and energy to win over the support of the unions in the area, to get their backing in his fight. As a result, he was offered a job as a union organizer with the United Electrical Radio and Machine Workers of America (UE) and continued with that job even after he won the right to return to work at the airplane plant with back pay for the money he lost as a result of his unjust discharge.

Reviewing the history of his work life, he lay there in bed in the hotel room, staring up at the ceiling, trying to understand himself — how had he come to be so indecisive, vacillating on this matter of deciding what was the right thing to do when he would testify before the Committee in the morning.

Looking back, all the transitions and developments seemed very logical. One thing led to the next thing and he realized for the first time that in their family of eleven, nine children and his parents, there had always been the conflict between loyalty to the working class and the drives of the lower middle class. He remembered what he had long forgotten: how, as a small child, he had heard his father speak about his experiences as a young man when he had been an active member of the cigar makers union and had known Socialist Labor Party leader Daniel DeLeon. Then his father had operated a dress factory in a loft in New York City, only to be wiped out by a fire — a relative pocketed the insurance premium. After that, his father traveled all over the country as a salesman, finally settling in Buffalo, establishing himself there as a small shopkeeper with a dry goods and notions store. In a small country village such a store would have been called "a general store." By this time his father had become a shopkeeper in his thinking, unsympathetic to strikes except when he happened to know some of the strikers personally. As a shopkeeper, he always saw strikes as a *bad* thing, not as a declaration by working people of their strength and their belief in their dignity and their right to a better life. Danny remembered the big street car strike in Buffalo. He was in grammar school then. His father and mother, knowing many of the strikers who lived in their neighborhood, sided with them, especially when the Governor sent in the National Guard to break the strike by providing protection to imported professional strikebreakers who were operating the streetcars. Danny remembered how, along with other kids in the neighborhood, he threw rocks at the windows of the scab-operated streetcars and screamed, "Scab! Dirty scab!" But his parents' great sympathy with the strikers they knew did not prevent them from sending one of his older brothers — he grew up to become a college professor — to high school on scab-operated trolley cars, until one day several young South Buffalo toughs met the older brother as he dismounted from the street car on his way to school and beat him so badly that he had to have his bruises treated and he was put to bed when he got home.

Still staring up at the ceiling, in the same position in which he had been lying all the while he had been furiously digging into his mind for the solution to his dilemma, Danny thought about his own attitude toward strikers, how his thinking had changed so quickly!

He recalled the long strike at the Remington Rand plants in the Tonawandas back in 1936, at a time when he was home from New York City on a short visit — he remembered the uproar in the newspapers about the pitched battles fought between the Remington Rand strikers and the imported professional strikebreakers, the scabs, especially that memorable skirmish, still frequently discussed at the bars in the gin mills of North Tonawanda, the famous Battle of the Rock Pile where the strikers used only rocks to drive a busload of imported gun-armed professional strikebreakers out of town — he recalled the newspaper headlines and the pages of photographs of strikebreakers with bloodied heads and faces, and he remembered how terrible he thought it was that the strikers had done such a thing to the strikebreakers.

That, he thought, as he lay there in bed in the hotel room, thinking and thinking and thinking, was the viewpoint which had resulted from the pull of his middle class environment.

And then he saw in his mind again what happened in 1947, only eleven years after the 1936 strike — he saw himself standing on the running board of a sound truck in front of the same Remington Rand Company plant where the Battle of the Rock Pile had been fought; he saw himself and the rest of the army and navy veterans on the picket line that morning in 1947, wearing their army and navy uniforms; they had been warned there would be a company-sponsored back-to-work move that morning under the protection of a swarm of sheriff's deputies and local police, and they had held a meeting and had decided that if the deputies and police were going to club their way through the picket line that morning they were going to be forced to manhandle pickets wearing the very same uniforms they had worn when they defended their country in World War II — he was wearing his GI suntans, standing on the running board of the sound truck, a microphone in his hand, fervently appealing to the crowd of office workers who had been shaped up by the company's supervisors on the corner across the street from the plant in preparation for the massed assault on the picket lines. His appeal to the office workers was successful — they dispersed and went home — but then a sobbing messenger brought word that police swinging nightsticks had clubbed a path through the picket lines at the other plant across the canal, on the north side — a small group of scabs had gotten through into the plant. —Danny felt the excitement again as he saw with his mind's eye, the line of automobiles racing reinforcements through town and across the bridge to the besieged plant on the north side of the canal — he helped to set up the sound truck in the midst of the milling crowd of furious strikers who had seen one of their men, a young veteran wearing his bemedalled World War II uniform, taken to the hospital with blood pouring all over him from a cracked skull; the word spread over the grapevine to the nearby plants, and sympathetic workers poured into the streets, mushrooming the crowd into an angry army of several thousand men and women surrounding the factory, ready to fight to right the wrong which had been done — Danny saw himself standing there with the microphone in his hand, appealing to the scabs in the plant, begging them to come out of the plant under their own steam, before the aroused workers — who were already scuffling in the streets with the police and overwhelming them by sheer force of numbers — went into the plant to forcibly evict those who had gone in; he remembered how he had pleaded with the people in the streets to stop their fighting before someone would be killed, and how the fighting had stopped, and how the strike committee had negotiated a truce with the police and with the scabs, permitting the scabs to evacuate the plant immediately without any harm. . .

He desperately raked through the ashes of the memories about the strikes at Remington Rand, searching for the key to his current situation. He thought about the dead leader of the union at that plant, Charlie Cooper. What would Charlie do in his situation? What would Charlie advise him to do?

He knew the answer.

More important, he recognized that in turning to Charlie for advice he was trying to convince himself to challenge the constitutionality of the Committee. Charlie would have pleaded and begged and argued and cursed to convince him to challenge the Committee.

Danny visualized the hard-bitten face of the veteran one-legged leader of the 1936 Remington Rand strike who was the man who later trained him as a union organizer. There was a working class hero if there ever was one!

And Danny remembered how — in 1946, a few weeks after he had come home from the army — he went to see Charlie in the hospital, seeking advice on what to do with his life now that he was a civilian again. The scene came back to him, in clear detail.

Charlie lay in bed in a crowded ward. The surgeon had cut off another piece of his leg, almost all the way back to the groin. Charlie said he was nearing the end of the road.

"One more slice by that meat cutter," he bitterly laughed, "and that's all the butcher can cut. It's all over."

But the end was nearer than that. The next morning a blood clot broke loose inside Charlie and hit some vulnerable spot in his heart. He died.

Danny went over what happened the day before Charlie died.

Charlie asked him when he was coming back to work for the union now that he was out of the army.

He told Charlie he hadn't made up his mind —

He was discharged from the army at Fort Dix, and Helen met him in New York City. Before starting back to Buffalo, they stopped off to see a good friend who had won recognition as one of the top stage and screen directors in the country, Elia Kazan, who had directed him in the lead role in *The Young Go First* when his (Danny's) stage name was Edward Mann. Kazan asked what he intended to do now that he was a civilian again. He told Kazan he didn't know what he wanted to do. Helen didn't want him to go back to work with the union. Kazan offered him a small role in *Boomerang*, a movie the director was shooting up in Connecticut. But he couldn't decide immediately whether or not he wanted to go back to acting. Kazan suggested that he take a little time off and rest a while and think it over and then decide whether he wanted to go back into union work or back into the theatre. If he decided to go back into theatre, Kazan said he would help him. Helen strongly favored returning to the theatre, though she wondered if it might not be too impractical, not as sound as going into some kind of business with financial help from her family. He was not sure he wanted to give up union work. It was the most satisfying work he had ever known, and he wondered if he would ever be satisfied with anything else.

When he told Charlie Cooper about his dilemma Charlie gripped his arm with a powerful hand which had become so strong from handling his weight when he walked with his crutches.

"Danny, don't abandon us, you sonofabitch," he belligerently pleaded, keeping his voice down so patients in beds on either side of him in the hospital ward would not overhear. "We need you, Danny. Don't you abandon us, you redheaded sonofabitch!"

Charlie made it very hard to leave when he put it that way. It would be like walking out on a sacred trust, a sacred responsibility, if he left the union and went back to the theatre in New York City. Danny again felt those strong fingers gripping his arm. With his mind's eye he saw Charlie's unshaven face, the sunken cheeks, and the intensity of those deepset eyes as the older man sat up in bed and argued with him.

"You're a smart guy, Danny. You got brains. Education. You can talk. You can write. You can organize. And most important, on top of all that you're honest and you got a conscience. We don't have crowds of people like that around this neck of the woods, not on our side, not as developed as you are. We need you — so don't you dare walk out on us, you redheaded sonofabitch, don't you dare even think of it — "

"Charlie — "

"What the hell do they need you in the theatre for? Do they need another handsome face? They don't need you there to act in the theatre like we need you here in the union. You mean something important here. What difference will it make to them if you don't go back there to act?"

"None — "

"But it'll make a great difference if you walk out on us, you redheaded sonofabitch! We need you!"

"Charlie, no one is indispensable."

"But it takes time to develop, and until we develop someone else, until we find someone else to take your place — "

"You got along without me while I was in the army, for two and a half years."

"But we missed you, you sonofabitch! We missed you, we missed you! I've been waiting for you to come back so we could start moving ahead again. I'm telling you, Danny, we need you. Don't walk out on us! Don't walk out on us!"

Charlie made him feel like he would be a traitor if he left the union and went back to the theatre.

"I don't know, Charlie. I don't know what to do."

"I know how ungrateful this work is, Danny" — Charlie did not let up for a moment, fiercely arguing his point — "I know that again and again the very people you're trying to help are the ones who give you the hardest time — "

"That isn't it, Charlie."

"You've got to understand," Charlie rushed on, "that these people have been sold out so often in the past they still don't trust anyone completely, not until you've proved yourself over a long period of time. They'll learn to trust you, Danny, when they get to know you as well as I know you. But you've got to trust them too. Keep faith with them. Don't walk out on them just because the going gets a little rough at times."

"That's not it, Charlie. It's me — myself — something inside of me — "

Charlie still gripped his arm. "Believe me, Danny, you'll destroy yourself if you run out on us. You'll never forgive yourself. You're that kind, like me. Do something like that and you'll destroy yourself!"

Danny tried to explain to Charlie about Helen and her family and The Park Lane. "I have to find a way of life into which the both of us, my wife and myself, can fit — "

"You don't belong with them in that kind of life. You belong with us. You'd never get us out of your system, no matter how hard you try. You're a man with a strong conscience, like me, and you can't get away from it." Charlie pulled down his voice because he noticed that other patients in the ward were listening. "Danny, I don't blame you for getting disgusted with some of us stupid bastards — "

"No — "

Charlie brushed aside his protest. "Sure, it's aggravating when they don't back you up. You get disgusted. So do I! But you can't walk out! You can't even if you want to! *You'll never get over it! You'll destroy yourself!*"

With his mind's eye and his mind's ear, Danny saw Charlie and he heard Charlie's voice. He could feel the iron grip of Charlie's fingers digging into his arm: —

"You can't even if you want to! You'll never get over it! You'll destroy yourself!"

Danny tossed back the covers and bounced out of bed and switched on the lamp on the dresser. He looked at his watch — two minutes to three. Ralph Kaufman would understand if he telephoned him, even though it was so late. Charlie was right. He had to go through with it. If he walked out now, he would destroy himself. He'd be no good for Helen or the kids or anybody, no good for anything except to continue degenerating under the added pressure he would invite on himself by retreating.

Ralph Kaufman sounded very sleepy when he answered the phone but he immediately became very wide awake and extremely solicitous after Danny excitedly blurted out who was calling.

"Yes, Danny. What is it?"

"Let's go through with it, Ralph. I know it's very late, and I'm sorry I didn't call sooner — I hope you'll forgive me — but I've just made up my mind to go through with it."

Ralph Kaufman sounded very sober, as he questioned Danny. "Are you very sure you want to do this?"

I'm sure, Ralph. I'm scared to death about it but I know now what I want to do. I *have* to do it, Ralph, if I want to live with myself."

"All right, Danny. Do you want to come over here now and get started?"

"We better get at it right away, Ralph," Danny nervously laughed. "Before I change my mind back and forth a few more times and drive myself completely crazy."

The lawyer laughed sympathetically. "Give me a few minutes, Danny, to take a quick shower to wake up completely. — How long will it take you to come over here to my room?"

"Oh, maybe five or ten minutes — "

"Take your time and make it a good ten minutes."

"Okay, Ralph."

No sooner did he put down the receiver than he wanted to pick it up and call the lawyer back to say he had to think it over a little while longer before he definitely made up his mind. The vision of Helen and the children leaving him, a lonely redheaded figure in a tiny barred prison cell, gnawed at him. But he was too ashamed to call Ralph back again. What kind of moron would Ralph think he was dealing with?

He slowly dressed, feeling like he was preparing to attend his own funeral.

Chapter 21

"This," Ralph Kaufman explained to Danny, opening a paperback book to the place he had previously marked with a torn piece of paper, "is the brief we've submitted to the United States Supreme Court in the Julius Emspak case."

Danny nodded as he kept his eyes fixed on the skinny figure sitting erect and alert in the overstuffed easy chair, the lawyer's slippered feet resting on the gray rug, his maroon dressing gown tightly drawn over his blue and white striped pajamas — Ralph Kaufman looked like a sharp-eyed elf.

With his pencil held in readiness to jot down notes, Danny intently waited for Ralph to explain about the brief. The lawyer had given him a pad of lined yellow paper, and Danny was sitting in a straight-backed chair at the other end of the room, resting the writing pad on the edge of the small table which belonged to the big sofa.

Ralph held the book out to Danny in his left hand, pointing with the index finger of his right hand at the passage he wanted Danny to read.

"This," he explained, "is the enabling resolution passed by the House of Representatives extablishing the Un-American Activities Committee — it's blatantly unconstitutional, as you'll see for yourself."

With a nervous bounce Danny crossed the room and took the brief and returned to his seat.

"Read it over carefully," advised Ralph, "and see if you can pick out the main flaw in its wording."

Danny read the stilted language of the resolution slowly, word by word, searching for the flaw, but it escaped him. He finally looked up at the lawyer. "I must be stupid, Ralph." He read the resolution again, even more slowly, but he still couldn't find anything wrong. When he looked up at the lawyer and made a face indicating that he gave up and wanted to hear what the flaw was, Ralph Kaufman smiled and forgave his ignorance.

"What do you think," he slyly suggested, "of the use of the words — 'un-American' and 'subversive'?" Danny realized he must have looked blank because Ralph added another hint. Exactly what do those words mean — *'un-American'* and *'subversive'*?"

A light dawned in Danny's brain. "They don't have any specific meaning by themselves, do they?"

Ralph Kaufman smiled. "That's it, or at least part of it. The vagueness of those two words, those two terms, their lack of meaning." The lawyer pointed at the book Danny still held. "That resolution sets up a committee to investigate *'un-American'* and *'subversive'* activity. But exactly what is meant by *'un-American'* activity? Exactly what is meant by *'subversive'* activity? Examine that resolution carefully again and you'll see that the House of Representatives neglected to define the meaning of those two words — *'un-American'* and *'subversive'*."

A quick check by Danny confirmed what Ralph said. "It can mean anything at all. Anything the Committee wants it to mean. It that it?"

"Exactly!"

Ralph resumed his lecture.

At the outset he had explained to Danny that he would ramble on, projecting a number of reasons a witness might give to justify a refusal to testify before the Committee. It would be up to Danny to decide which of these reasons he wanted to use.

It was understood between them that Danny would *not* use the "fear of self-incrimination" portion of the Fifth Amendment as a reason for refusing to testify, since that would weaken the constitutional challenge by allowing the Supreme Court to duck the question of whether or not the Committee had a constitutional right to exist. The Court might rule he had the right under that provision of the Fifth Amendment to refuse to answer any questions but might not disturb the existence of the Committee itself.

Ralph cautioned him not to undermine those who did avail themselves of the Fifth Amendment privilege as part of their constitutional rights, and Danny assured his lawyer that he would tell the Committee that although he was not claiming the Fifth Amendment privilege, he "believes that those who do avail themselves of that constitutional privilege are performing a real patriotic service to their country by helping to preserve for all citizens the protections afforded them in the Bill of Rights."

Now that he was involved in the actual preparation of the arguments he would use later that morning, Danny no longer debated with himself about whether or not he should make the challenge. All his attention and energy was concentrated on scribbling notes on the lined yellow paper to remind him later of what he wanted to say at the hearing.

"After we're through here," Ralph warned, "you'll still have work to do. I doubt very much that you'll get any sleep tonight. You'll have to study your notes and fill them out with flesh and blood from your own thoughts and your own concepts and your own experience."

This alarmed Danny.

"Can't I take my notes with me when I go up to the witness chair. Can't I refer to them when I'm being questioned?"

"Oh, you certainly can," Ralph assured him. "But there's bound to be a lot of excitement created when you spring this new approach on the Committee in the courtroom, and you better be ready for all kinds of surprises and maneuvers — and the more thoroughly familiar you are with all the arguments you want to use, the less chance there is that anything they say or do will get you flustered or twisted up. Also, obviously, the notes you're taking down here will necessarily be of a very sketchy nature. You'll have to fill them out later with explanations and illustrations from your own experience. I'm merely indicating to you, very generally, the different approaches or arguments you could use. It's up to you to study these and decide which you want to use and how you want to expand them."

Danny nodded.

"Another thing," Ralph continued while Danny nervously strained to remember the details of what he was being told now, since he was not taking notes on them, "you must remember, Danny, that they may not give you much time when you're in the witness chair. They may try to cut you off quickly, especially when they realize where you're heading. So you must organize your arguments in advance to be able to get them across in a very few words before they stop you."

"Okay."

"They may try to trick you into answering a question or two — to get you away from the important constitutional challenge flowing from a refusal to answer *any* questions on the grounds that the very existence of the Committee is illegal. They may try to provoke you — so you can be charged with use of *contemptuous* language or of employing a *contemptuous* manner or having a *contemptuous* attitude —"

"I'll be very careful, Ralph."

"No matter what they say or do" — the lawyer pointed a finger sternly at Danny but smiled to take the sting out of the harsh gesture — "you must rigidly control that fine redheaded temper of yours."

"I will."

"The more angry they get, the more excited they get, the more provocative they get, you must become just that much more restrained and respectful. The wilder their provocations, the more polite and respectful you must act towards them — no matter how you may really feel about them. Remember: you respect the *office* the man holds, even though you may not respect the *man* who holds the office."

That struck a familiar chord in Danny. The army had taught him that about saluting officers.

The lawyer continued. "And you continue to show your respect for that *office* no matter what the *man* holding office does and no matter how little respect you have for him as an individual." Ralph wagged a warning finger. "That's most important, Danny. If you want to make a highly principled challenge against this Committee and leave them trapped without an easy out, you musn't let them destroy the effectiveness of your challenge by allowing them to provoke you into getting loud or unruly or disrespectful!"

The lawyer stopped and gave an emphatic nod, putting a period on the lesson. He straightened up and laughed. "That's the end of that phase of the lecture."

Danny also relaxed for the moment. "You mean I shouldn't thumb my nose at any of them?" he asked, keeping a straight face while he reminded Ralph of his stupid brush with the photographer.

"That," said Ralph, nodding his bald eagle's head, "is exactly what I mean. You keep that fine redheaded temper of yours under control all the time you're up there before the

Committee."

"It'll be hard to restrain myself" — keeping a straight face — "but I'll try my best."

The lawyer pulled his chair a little closer to Danny.

"Seriously," he said, "I know you have the ability to make a tremendously valuable contribution towards the preservation of civil liberties in our country. What you're going to do may even get into the history books some day when they write about how this Committee, which was trying to pave the way for fascism, was stopped." He smiled. "It's important enough to warrant mention in some graduate student's thesis right now — "

Embarrassed, Danny cut Ralph short.

"Okay." He was conscious again of the sweat wetting his shirt under his arms while he nervously tapped his forefinger on the notes he had already taken. "Let's get going, Ralph. Daylight is sneaking up on us fast, and I still don't know exactly what I'm going to say."

Ralph was not disturbed.

"Take it easy," he calmly advised. "Let's review what you've got there so far. Using your own words, you tell me why you refuse to answer their questions. — Ready?"

"Ready."

The lawyer sat up straight and folded his arms across his chest.

"We'll start from the beginning, Danny. — Your name is called. You're sitting there in the courtroom with the rest of the interested spectators. And so am I. You hear your name called out. You rise and proceed up to the witness table where I join you. We stand there, side by side, while you raise your hand and take the oath — "

"What about the photographers — and the floodlights?"

"Will they distract you?"

"I think so."

"Then you politely ask the chairman to tell the photographers to take all their pictures before you are asked any questions and to desist from taking any photographs during your testimony."

"What about television and newsreels — the floodlights?"

Ralph calmly reassured him. "If you state your objection I'm sure the chairman will tell them not to shoot anything while you're testifying. That's been firmly established by precedent."

"On second thought, Ralph" — Danny scratched his scalp with the eraser end of the pencil — "it might be a good idea to keep all that show going on there if it'll give wider publicity to our challenge."

"Fine," said Ralph, ready to agree to whatever Danny wanted, "if it won't disturb you or get you nervous to have all the bright lights shining into your eyes."

"Well" — Danny pictured the spotlights glaring into his face — "maybe we better ask them to shoot all their pictures before any fireworks start over my refusal to answer questions."

"All right. — Now we're standing up in front of the witness table. You've asked the chairman to tell the press photographers to take their pictures and get that over with. You've asked him to shut off the newsreel and television cameras because their floodlights might disturb you. Now the Committee's legal counsel, Mr. Denilworth, asks you to identify yourself— "

"I refuse," declaimed Danny, recognizing his cue, "to answer your question, sir, because — "

Ralph interrupted, laughing quietly. "Oh, yes, you answer *that*, Danny. You have to answer *that* much. You've got to identify yourself."

"Won't that prejudice the case we're trying to make — of refusing to answer any questions at all because this Committee has no right to conduct these investigations?"

"No, you must identify yourself for the record," Ralph insisted. "You do that first. Then they'll ask if you have legal counsel with you — "

"You'll be right there with me, won't you?"

"Standing right beside you. And you'll tell them you do have legal counsel with you, and then I'll identify myself for the record — "

"And that's all!" said Danny, emphatically, but he waited for his lawyer to confirm that.

With a big nod, Ralph agreed, "And that's all!"

They nodded at one another, silently.

"On the very next question," said Danny, "I tell them to go to hell — right?"

"Respectfully and politely," Ralph reminded him.

Danny bent forward stiffly, a slight mocking bow. "*Very* respectfully, *very* politely." His flippant manner, however, was only a mask to hide his fear. Inside, he felt like a man with only several more hours to live before facing the firing squad at dawn. The skin on his face felt drawn and stretched thin. As he went on, he became aware again and again that he was rubbing his fingertips over his cheekbones, trying to relax the pulling sensation he felt there.

"Don't forget," Ralph reminded him, "try to get *them* to define the area of their investigation. Try to get *them* to quote the enabling resolution at you. But, if necessary, quote it yourself."

"Right."

The lawyer said he would not interrupt again. He folded his arms across his chest. At times he pretended that he was Congressman Holling, the chairman of the subcommittee, and he also pretended at other times that he was the Committee's legal counsel, Denilworth, both trying to compel Danny to testify.

Danny stumbled through his notes, fumbling for the right words to express his thoughts, carefully filling out each idea, building long sentences around the few skeleton words he had jotted down on the yellow sheets of paper. He saw that whenever he hesitated Ralph nodded approvingly to encourage him to continue, and he haltingly went on, looking to the lawyer for comment as he wove his way through the arguments he thought would be most appropriate in the courtroom later that morning.

When he finished going over the notes he had already accumulated, Ralph Kaufman suggested that they discuss further reasons he could use to justify refusing to answer the questions of the Committee, and Danny prepared to jot down more notes.

"I doubt," the lawyer cautioned him, with his chin resting on his manicured fingertips, "if the Committee will permit you to say even as much as you've got there already. But we should be prepared, I think, for the unexpected. You might by some stroke of luck just happen to catch them so flatfooted and so far off balance that they may let you go on. In that case you ought to be ready to give them every good reason we can think of for refusing to answer their questions."

Ralph Kaufman meticulously folded his hands in his lap and pursed his lips and vacantly directed his gaze up at the ceiling. Danny wondered what was coming now.

"There's some question as to how much I'm permitted — as your attorney — to tell you in advance about what to say in this kind of Congressional hearing." He dropped his eyes, and they met Danny's questioning stare. "But there's no doubt about this. I can tell you all the things I think *could* be said in such a situation, and then it's up to you to pick out whatever you think is most appropriate." A long meaningful pause, while they stared at each other. "I think we understand one another, don't we?"

"I think so — "

Danny noticed how carefully Ralph chose his words, as if he knew his words might be recorded by some device planted in the room, each word to be pored over later by someone in search of a loophole with which to hang both of them.

Ralph talked on, carefully, and Danny accumulated several more pages of scribbling, then they took time out while Danny sifted through the notes, picking out the best arguments, rearranging them to put them into order of importance, packing the thoughts into capsule phrases for easy memorizing. He counted on his memory to enable him to expand the capsules again when he faced the Committee later in the morning. Ralph brought him a drink of ice water from the bathroom and the coldness of it tasted wonderful.

Then Danny talked his way through all the notes while Ralph at times interrupted to make him think some points through more completely. At other times Danny stopped to ask the lawyer to clear up a cloudy point.

Then he finally gave up. He was too exhausted to think any more.

"That's it, isn't it, Ralph?"

There, on the lined yellow paper, was the third rough draft of the arguments he intended to use, written carefully so he would be able to read the points quickly when he would be under pressure, the arguments listed in order of importance and their degree of relevance to the type of constitutional test he would try to make — so he would be sure to get the most important arguments into the record in the event he was cut off anywhere along the line. Danny could see that Ralph Kaufman was also ready to call it quits and go to sleep for a few hours before they would have to get up again. He appreciated how the older man's patient kindly manner never seemed to leave him.

Ralph got up out of his chair. "Danny, study it over again when you get back to your room. There isn't any more for me to do. You've got everything you need there, and more."

"Maybe we ought to go through it once more, Ralph, to make sure I've really got it down pat."

"Fine." Ralph tightened the belt around the waist of his robe and sat down again and folded his arms across his chest and leaned back in the easy chair, tipping his bald eagle's head toward his left shoulder as he assumed the listening pose of an alert spectator.

Danny picked up his notes and facetiously announced:

"Lights out — curtain going up — *final dress rehearsal!*"

Ralph smiled.

"I'm sitting in the courtroom," began Danny, abruptly dropping the facetious manner, every muscle tense as he prepared to weave his way carefully through from the beginning to the end of the arguments which would constitute the foundation for the challenge he would be making within a matter of only a few hours. "My name is called — I stand up and walk down the aisle to the witness table in front of Denilworth — you join me on the way, coming up there with me. —I'm carrying these notes — and I'm carrying this copy of the Emspak case brief so I can refer to the enabling resolution if I have to — "

His shirt felt wet again, as the sweat poured out under his arms. Ralph solemnly nodded approval. The performance had begun satisfactorily. Danny went on —

"Next, the oath — I hold up my right hand — I say, 'I do' — I sit down — you sit down beside me — then Denilworth or Congressman Holling asks me if I've brought along legal counsel — I say, 'Yes' — you identify yourself — " He threw up his hands to put the brakes on his own glib discourse. "Wait, wait, wait!"

"What's wrong?" asked Ralph.

"The photographers — the cameras — the floodlights." Danny saw that Ralph was pleased that he had caught his own omission. "As soon as we sit down, I tell them — no pictures — no cameras — no floodlights — while I'm being questioned." He hurriedly added, "I make the request *politely* and *respectfully* — I lean over backward and kiss their respective asses with utmost respect and politeness — correct?"

"Correct!"

They both wearily grinned. Danny immediately became serious again. There was no time to waste.

"At the first opportunity — *I state for the record that I have had nothing to do with any sabotage, espionage, or spying of any kind* — I get that into record as quickly as I can — so the bastards can't deliberately twist my refusal to answer questions to give it that kind of vicious implication — "

"You have to look for any opening," Ralph reminded him.

"I *make* an opening" — and then he realized that sounded too cocky, and he added, "if I can possibly make one."

"But always respectful and polite," the lawyer gently cautioned.

"Always — I tell them to go to hell in the most disgustingly polite and respectful manner I can possibly manufacture."

"That," warned Ralph, "is the *only* way you can do it and get away with it."

Remembering that he had said he would not interrupt, the lawyer smiled and motioned for Danny to go on, with a gesture indicating he would not interfere with his comments again.

"The preliminaries, " resumed Danny, "are out of the way. We're seated. Denilworth asks me to identify myself. I do — *'My name is Daniel Newman.'* — and then comes the showdown. — They ask me another question — maybe, *'Where were you born?'* or *'Where do you live?'* — and I refuse to answer that question — that's where I throw the challenge at them!"

"Respectfully," Ralph urgently reminded — and Danny realized that because of the great act of bravado he was staging for the lawyer's benefit Ralph was overestimating his courage. He was too scared inside to fly off the handle at anyone in the courtroom.

"Right!" he brightly agreed with the lawyer. "Respectfully! I *most* respectfully throw the challenge at the Committee — I ask them *why* they're conducting the investigation — what they're investigating — and I try to lead them on, to get *them* to discuss the enabling resolution itself — "

"Good," said Ralph.

"Gentlemen" — Danny addressed the imaginary subcommittee, seated up there on the judge's bench up over Ralph Kaufman's head — "I refuse to answer your question — on the grounds that the enabling resolution passed by the House of Representatives, establishing the Committee on Un-American Activities, is *unconstitutional* — because it violates the First Amendment to the Constitution of the United States — by permitting this Committee to declare that certain categories of ideas are — *verboten!*" — (On an unexpected impulse, without having thought about it before, he used the German word *verboten*, instead of the English word, forbidden; the German word neatly tied together what the House Committee on Un-American Activities was trying to do with what had been done by the Nazis in Germany.) — "The enabling resolution permits this Committee to establish certain ideas as *verboten* — and these ideas — when embodied in the written or spoken word — are still *verboten*; — and ideas — whether written or spoken — become associated with certain people, become embodied in the person of certain individual human beings, and therefore it becomes also *verboten* for other people to associate with those individuals or groups of individuals who have become identified as embodying in their person these *verboten* ideas — "

He was vigorously pounding the points home, with a feeling that he was getting control of the arguments, and he could see a big smile on the lawyer's face.

"And thus — people are made fearful to associate with those who embody such *verboten* ideas in their person — resulting in interference with the right of association — and interference with the right of assembly."

Stopping to take a deep breath, he saw that Ralph was beaming. With rising confidence Danny went on to sum up the first argument.

"In this fashion, gentlemen" — he was still addressing the

imaginary subcommittee seated above Ralph Kaufman's head — "this enabling resolution passed by the House of Representatives gives this Committee on Un-American Activities the power to destroy freedom of thought, freedom of speech, freedom of the press, freedom of association and freedom of assembly — freedoms guaranteed to every citizen of our United States of America by the First Amendment to our Constitution. — That, gentlemen, is why this enabling resolution passed by the House of Representatives of our Congress of the United States is flagrantly unconstitutional — that, gentlemen, is my *first* reason for refusing to answer your question!"

"Bravo!" Ralph quietly exclaimed, noiselessly clapping his hands together, laughing softly. "Let's assume," he added, still smiling approval, "they haven't thrown you out after that. But even if they do stop you after you've said only this much, exactly as you've stated it now, you can still be proud of the contribution you will have made to the fight to preserve civil liberties in our country."

With a wooden bow of only his head and shoulders, Danny unsmilingly thanked the lawyer. He might be acclaimed a hero, and he could be proud of what he had done. But he would be alone again. Goodbye, Helen and the kids.

His lips felt dry, even though he kept wetting them with his tongue. The wave of elated confidence which had momentarily risen in him passed away, and he found it painful to keep his eyelids from closing together. — He had to exert himself to stay awake. The feeling of exhaustion permeated his entire body, depressing him so thoroughly that he wondered if he should try to go on through the rest of the arguments. Ralph was waiting.

He glanced down at the second phrase he had marked down in his notes — *Un-American and subversive too vague* — and he forced himself to begin.

"Gentlemen" — a loud weary sigh escaped him, drawing a quick smile of sympathy from Ralph Kaufman — "I refuse to answer your questions on the grounds that the enabling resolution passed by the House of Representatives under which this Committee functions is unconstitutional because" — he slowed down as he spelled out the reason — "it is so vague that no person can tell what are supposed to be the *boundaries of the Committee's power* to investigate — no person can tell what are supposed to be the *boundaries of the area* which this Committee is directed to investigate, particularly because of the meaning — or *lack* of meaning — of the words *'un-American'* and *'subversive'*. — Gentlemen, what's *'un-American'*? What's *'subversive'*? — Who defines it? — The House of Representatives has *not* defined it — nowhere in this enabling resolution can you find it defined. — You, gentlemen, you who are the Committee set up by this resolution, you are the only ones who define what you are investigating! And *how* do you define it? You define it as anything at all that this Committee is against. Anything that this Committee opposes. Anything this Committee doesn't like! That's *'un-American'*! That's *'subversive'*!"

"Respectfully," cautioned Ralph, and Danny dropped his voice.

"Gentlemen, this Committee has not been given any definite boundaries to outline the area it is to investigate — no boundaries to guide it. Therefore, gentlemen, in the hands of unscrupulous men" — he quickly corrected himself — "*or* in the hands of well-meaning but mistaken men, since none of us are perfect in our judgements, these words, *'un-American'* and *'subversive'*, can be interpreted to mean anything that the members of this Committee oppose. — For example, as you know, a prominent official in Washington recently spoke of the long period of New Deal and Fair Deal administrations under Presidents Franklin D. Roosevelt and Harry S. Truman as *'twenty years of treason'*. Thus, gentlemen," he summed up, "it can readily be seen that — because of the very vagueness of these words, *'un-American'* and *'subversive'* — they can be interpreted to mean whatever the members of this Committee want them to mean — "

He stopped unable to think of what else to say. He looked at Ralph Kaufman and shrugged. The essential point had already been made several times. He was repeating himself, going around in circles. He awkwardly scratched his scalp with the eraser end of the pencil.

"That's it, I guess, Ralph."

He waited for the lawyer's opinion.

"Fine" — Ralph was satisfied — "that's enough on that

point."

"I'm not using the best English," Danny wearily apologized, while he rubbed his fingertips hard against the skin over his cheekbones, trying to relieve the drawn feeling — his skin felt like it was stretched drum-tight over the bone structure of his face.

"You're getting it across," Ralph assured him, "in your own words — in understandable language — and that's what counts."

The lawyer leaned back and waited for Danny to proceed with the next argument.

"Reason number three" — a loud tired sigh, after a noisy deep breath, and Danny glanced down at his notes before plodding on — "why I refuse to answer your question is that this enabling resolution passed by the House of Representatives is unconstitutional" — another deep breath and another deep sigh before going on — "because it has been used and can be used — for inquisitions into personal and private affairs — where Congress doesn't have the right to stick its nose in — "

"Careful," Ralph gently corrected him, with upraised forefinger, "I wouldn't use that kind of language — "

"Okay, Ralph."

They both laughed.

"I wouldn't," Danny explained, "say it that crude way at the hearing — I was trying to pin down the thought in my own mind." He re-phrased the argument: "I refuse to answer because the enabling resolution has been used and can be used for — *inquisitions?*" He looked at Ralph who nodded approval of that word, and Danny went on with — "for *inquisitions* into personal and private affairs, something Congress cannot authorize — since Congress does not have the right to inquire into private affairs unrelated to a valid legislative purpose."

"Better," said Ralph Kaufman, "much better — more dignified."

"Gentlemen" — Danny quickly glanced down at the next phrase in his notes — "the fourth reason why I refuse to answer your question is — because I cannot be compelled to testify since there is *no legislative purpose* either in the enabling resolution itself or in this inquiry which is being conducted as the result of the enactment of that enabling resolution. — On the contrary, gentlemen! Rather than for the purpose of legislation, this Committee's primary purpose — as often publicly admitted by members of this Committee — is to *expose* individuals for beliefs which are not popular with the members of this Committee!" He thought he should say something more on that point. His one-man audience was patiently waiting. "I didn't phrase that very well, did I, Ralph?"

"Well — "

"It gets the idea across, doesn't it?" Danny was too tired to go back and think through that argument again.

Ralph was very flexible. "Danny," he suggested, smiling in his usual kind way, "you might go into the matter of the reason for this hearing in the State Capital now, its relation to the inter-union and intra-union conflict in Schenectady, the attempt to expose certain individual members of the union as holding unpopular beliefs in order to affect the outcome of this conflict — between the unions in Schenectady — certainly not a *legislative purpose.* — And I'm sure you'll think of other examples later — but if you don't think of anything else, well, what you said will do very nicely, especially since, as I've said, I doubt very much that they'll let you get even this far. — But we better be ready in case they do let you go on. Anyway, you'll probably be able to file a statement later with the Committee, giving all the reasons you *would* have given if they allowed you to give them." He leaned back, the signal for Danny to resume. "You're doing fine."

Danny apologized. "My method of phrasing is not the best, I guess — "

"You're getting it across, Danny." He was very nice about it. "They're your own thoughts expressed in your own words, and that's what is important — you're not supposed to be a lawyer. If you express yourself as fluently as this when you appear before the Committee, you'll be doing fine."

"Let's hope," said Danny, "I don't get stage fright," and he rubbed his hands together to warm them up — they felt like ice.

"I'm sure you won't get stage fright."

"I hope not, Ralph."

"You'll do very well. Don't worry."

Danny looked down at his notes and silently read the next capsulated phrase he had written on the lined yellow paper: *Due process provisions of Fifth Amendment violated — illegal assumption by legislative branch of powers of judicial branch.*

He looked up. His audience was waiting. The lawyer's dark eyes sparkled encouragement. Danny grinned.

"Gentlemen!" he barked, and they both laughed. Danny shook the tenseness out of his shoulders with a quick movement, getting ready to start this next, a very complicated, point. "Gentlemen, the next reason why I refuse to answer your question is" — he proceeded very slowly, carefully weaving his words together to form the exact shape of what he wanted to say — "because the procedures followed by this Committee violate my rights under the due process provisions of the Fifth Amendment. — *Gentlemen, I am being tried, illegally, without due process of law!"*

His notes were spread out on the small table beside his chair, and he kept glancing down at them as he ticked off the specific violations which constituted deprivation of his rights under due process of law, counting them one by one on the fingers of his left hand.

"*One* — I have not been given any copy of the charges against me, and so far as I know, no other witness summoned here has been given a copy of such charges — "

"*Two* — I don't have the full right to legal counsel the way I would have it in a legitimate judicial proceeding — "

"*Three* — I don't have the right to cross-examine witnesses — "

"*Four* — the evidence against me has not been sifted by a grand jury to determine whether or not any charges should be filed against me, with the result that I'm on trial and tried and even convicted and sentenced without any charges ever being placed legally against me — "

The big smile on Ralph Kaufman's face encouraged him to run on more freely, and Danny leaned forward, extending his hands, with fingers tensed, as though he was appealing to a jury.

"Gentlemen, this Committee is acting *illegally!* — it is acting illegally as a judicial body, without giving me or any of the other subpoenaed witnesses the judicial safeguards provided by law by our United States Constitution." He was aware that he was waxing too eloquent, and he pulled himself back. "In other words, gentlemen, this Committee, acting for the legislative branch of our government, is unlawfully assuming the powers of the judicial branch of our government — by these investigations, by these hearings, and most specifically and especially *by the consequent penalties illegally dealt out by this Committee!*"

His voice had run away with him again, and Ralph Kaufman motioned for him to keep it down. "Shhh — "

The interruption threw Danny off, and he had to glance down at his notes again to remind himself of the types of penalties dealt out illegally by the Committee: *ostracism — blacklist — thought control —*

"Gentlemen," he resumed looking up, ready to proceed very deliberately to expand his notes, "what do I mean by penalties illegally dealt out by this Committee?" — Like an actor who knows when he has his audience in his grasp, Danny knew he could handle what he was going to say — the underlying concepts and the overall design of his approach to the Committee on this phase of the argument was very clear to him. — "I wish to say right now, gentlemen, that I speak not only for myself, but for hundreds, thousands, possibly even millions of people in our country, who have directly or indirectly been punished by you — *without any judicial trial! — without any judicial proceedings! — without the protections of due process of law as provided by the Bill of Rights in the Constitution of our country!*"

A long dramatic pause.

"Now what do I mean by illegal penalties, gentlemen?"

He allowed time for his rhetorical question to sink in before answering.

"*First* — I refer to the awful punishment of ostracism in the community! — Gentlemen, the right to be free from an ostracism illegally imposed by this Committee is just as much a basic right of every citizen as is the property right of a corporation to be free from slanderous and illegal boycott imposed by any Congressional Committee without recourse to due process of law!"

"Good!" exlaimed Ralph Kaufman who seemed to be enjoying the performance despite the early morning hour.

The interruption broke the spell. Danny, in a normal tone of voice, quickly explained. "At this point, Ralph, I'll draw on my own personal experience to tell something about the ostracism which has been directed against my wife and children in the community, as well as against myself. I'm so thoroughly familiar with that — there's no use wasting time at this hour to go over it in detail. Using our experience as the example, I'll make the point that this same kind of illegal penalty of ostracism has been applied in similar fashion to people in all walks of life — without these people being given their right, under due process of law, to be tried and convicted and sentenced legally before penalties are applied."

"Cor-*rect!*"

"Now — *the blacklist!*" Danny resumed his eloquent address to the imaginary group up on the imaginary judge's bench. He consciously tried to keep the volume of his voice down. "Gentlemen! Another one of the penalties illegally handed out by your Committee is loss of job: *the blacklist!* — Undoubtedly, I've been summoned before your Committee with the intent of helping certain people, both inside and outside our union organization, develop a movement to destroy my union and wipe out my job, or to drive me out of the union and wipe out my means of livelihood. — Once that job is destroyed and I look elsewhere for work, I'll find that I'm on a permanent and perpetual blacklist established by this Committee through its method of 'listing' and so-called 'exposure'. — Gentlemen! Without any trial whatsoever, you are trying to sentence me — and my family — to economic hardship. If you could, you would starve us into submission. That is your aim, your purpose — you are trying to deprive me of my means of livelihood and to keep me so deprived for the rest of my life, or as long as I refuse to conform to your way of thinking. — And you do all this, gentlemen, without legal trial, without judicial proceedings, without due process of law! — And not me alone, gentlemen! If it were me alone, that would be a comparatively unimportant matter to anyone else but me and my immediate family. But you have already done the same thing to workers in industry, to teachers, to scientists, to professors, to actors, to writers — yes, even to some clergymen — even to some business people who disagree with you and your particular definition of patriotism!"

He dropped his voice to normal again. "Ralph, I could expand that further very easily. Should I?"

"If you're permitted to get into the record even one-tenth of what you're saying right here now, you'll have accomplished a miracle."

"What about the third penalty?"

"What's that?"

"The establishment of thought control by the Committee — censorship — by taking away my right and the right of others to dissent or disagree."

"If you get the chance — give that one too."

"Okay."

Danny laid down his pencil and took a deep breath, filling his chest to its utmost capacity, straining to expand his ribs, and then he let the air rush out through his mouth with a noisy sigh.

"That's it, Ralph."

"Excellent, Danny, excellent."

Feeling completely worn out, Danny silently folded up his notes and slipped them into his pocket. He tucked the Julius Emspak case brief under his right arm. He looked at Ralph Kaufman.

"Class dismissed?"

"Discussion ended," the lawyer corrected him, rising and tightening the belt of his robe. Danny also got up on his feet.

They shook hands, saying good-night, and each promised to call the other in the morning to make sure neither of them overslept.

Alone in the hallway outside Ralph Kaufman's room, Danny looked at his wrist watch — three minutes past five o'clock. Only three more hours before the switchboard operator at The Regent would be waking him. He wondered if he would get any sleep — he still had to study his notes. His feet dragged as he walked down the hallway towards the elevator. His eyes were so tired that they were every sensitive to light and they kept closing on him. His head felt so heavy and his arms and legs were so weary — he thought he could drop to the cold green carpet right there where he was walking and be sound asleep before his body hit the floor. He rang for the elevator and leaned his head against the wall

and closed his eyes.
 The elevator operator woke him up.

Chapter 22

Back at The Regent.

The teachers' party in the room across the hall was over — no more female shrieks of laughter. Danny stepped into the darkness of his hotel room and locked the door behind him. He stood there until his eyes became accustomed to the darkness. There was a crack of light still shining under the connecting door. Was Agent X waiting up for him?

He switched on the light. Sitting on the edge of the bed, he went over his notes several times from start to finish, trying to grasp firmly the skeleton outline he had made of the arguments he intended to use at the hearing. He assumed that the details would take care of themselves if he could only remember the overall design — the capsulated phrases he worked out to summarize each major argument.

After about an hour of intensive study he gave up. It was past six o'clock in the morning and he was too tired to concentrate further. He needed sleep more than anything else, even though there wasn't time for that before the switchboard operator would be ringing the telephone in his room. He took a trip down the lonely hallway to the men's room, then back to his room where he undressed and put on his pajamas.

Lights out, and into bed.

Each minute dragged on slowly, his wrist watch madly ticking off each second, the sound so loud that he finally buried his left arm under the thickness of two fat pillows to blot it out.

The turmoil in his mind about Helen and the kids and what would happen if he challenged the constitutionality of the Committee in the courtroom that morning did not let up until the telephone rang in his room at eight o'clock. It was a relief to get out of bed, released from the obsession which had prevented any sleep.

He looked at the mirror over the wash basin. He had heard a story about a Buffalo truck driver whose hair turned

179

white when he spent a whole night alone in the middle of a desert with the corpse of his murdered brother. Looking into the mirror over the wash basin he saw that his hair was the same blondish red it had been the night before. But his eyelids were red and his eyes were bloodshot.

He telephoned the Capital Hotel and spoke to Ralph Kaufman.

"How do you feel, Danny?" the lawyer asked.

"Fine."

Ralph said he would wake Ed Murphy and the three of them would meet in the lobby of the Capital Hotel in twenty minutes and go to eat breakfast together. Danny hurried to wash and shave and dress in time.

Chapter 23

Danny saw that the corridor outside the courtroom on the fourth floor was crowded and there was a general hubbub, an excitement, a feeling of expectancy, as there is in the lobby of a theatre on opening night of a big production. Bill Kosciusko waved to him. Ralph Kaufman and Ed Murphy followed Danny across the corridor. The two organizers shook hands.

"Hi, Bill. Looks like the show hasn't started yet."

"Not yet. They're waiting for the producers and the money angels to show up."

They stood out in the corridor and talked. Danny listened to the others but did not say anything. His mind was back in Buffalo. At this time in the morning Ruth was already in school and Helen was eating breakfast with Linda. Or were they all packing their things into suitcases, getting ready to leave for Florida?

Then he saw the photographer.

"Ralph," he whispered into the lawyer's ear, "there's the guy I thumbed my nose at yesterday."

The lawyer took a quick look and whispered back, "Tell him you were only kidding around. No use antagonizing him."

Danny stepped out to intercept the photographer who immediately recognized him. They both grinned.

"I'm sorry about yesterday," said Danny. "I was only kidding."

The photographer chewed his gum. "That's all right. It turned out to be a darn good shot, didn't it?"

"A good shot, but it made me look like a snotty wiseguy — a real horse's ass."

The photographer laughed out loud. "It had character!" That's what made it an interesting shot. Put it on the front page."

"Next time you take any pictures I won't make a monkey out of myself like I did yesterday."

The photographer seemed to consider that an invitation.

He shifted some of his equipment from his shoulder down to the smooth concrete floor. "You testifying today?"

"I don't know for sure yet."

The photographer hoisted his equipment back up to his shoulder. "If you're called to testify" — still chewing his big wad of gum — "I'll shoot what I want while you're up there in the hot seat. Okay?"

"Okay."

"Good luck."

The photographer went into the courtroom.

Danny turned to rejoin Ralph Kaufman and Ed Murphy and Bill Kosciusko, but they had disappeared. He saw Herb Kepler and his two rank-and-filers approaching.

"Hey, Herb, did you see Bill Kosciusko or Ed Murphy or Ralph Kaufman? They were here a minute ago."

"They must have gone inside," said Herb, and he hurried past, going into the courtroom with his two rank-and-filers.

Catching one of the swinging doors and holding it open, Danny looked into the courtroom. About half the space on the benches was already filled with spectators. The gray-haired U.S. marshall glided back toward him on cat feet. Danny quickly slipped into the courtroom and let the door swing closed behind him. He was sure the eyes of the U.S. marshall were following him until he sat down in the left-hand corner of the rear bench, the seat farthest away from the witness chair up front.

It was evident that there was much more going on up in front of the railing this morning than on any of the previous days. Batteries of floodlights had been rigged up in the front left corner of the courtroom to light up the entire area surrounding the judge's bench, the witness chair and the table where the Committee's legal counsel would be spreading out his papers. Danny watched as workmen tested a powerful spotlight focused on the witness chair, and he imagined himself sitting where a workman in overalls was squinting up into that glaring light. Television cameras with a conglomeration of supporting technical equipment were already in place and the cameramen were ready to start them rolling. There seemed to be an extra large contingent of reporters and press photographers milling around up there.

Danny felt a hand on his shoulder and looked up. It was

John Mason, the young reporter who had lived across the street from Helen in Buffalo.

"You testifying today, Danny?"

"I haven't been named yet." He smiled, trying to appear very much at ease.

Young Mason bent over and whispered confidentially into his ear, "Sidney Raven is starting off on the witness stand again this morning. They're calling him back." The young reporter straightened up. Danny didn't allow the half-smile on his face to change. Young Mason asked, "Do you think he'll name you?"

Danny shrugged. *That* could not be misquoted in the Buffalo newspapers. Young Mason smiled and nodded goodbye and continued on up to the front of the courtroom to join his colleagues at the press table.

Danny stood up and looked around for Ralph Kaufman and Ed Murphy. He finally saw them, down in the front row where they could easily step up and join any of the organizers as they passed by on their way to the witness chair. He sat down, feeling more secure.

Flash bulbs flared in front of the railing as a group of men came into the courtroom from the judge's chambers. A man wearing a black string tie joined Congressman Holling up on the judge's bench, and Danny wondered if he was also a member of the House of Representatives. The GE executives had come in with Congressman Holling and the red-faced newcomer on the bench. Danny watched them file into their reserved grandstand seats in the jury box. The clerk and the court reporter took their posts, and Denilworth and his assistant sat down at their table and opened their leather briefcases and began to unload their documents, setting up shop for another day's business. Danny heard Congressman Holling rap the gavel, and then he watched the U.S. marshall slowly float up and down the center aisle, looking over the heads of the spectators, making sure everyone was quiet. Another sharp rap of the gavel.

The hearing was officially in session.

Holling started off by reading a telegram into the record, announcing that Congressman Sackville had been appointed as a substitute for Congressman Lester who had been summoned back to Washington on extremely urgent business. The same telegram still listed Congressman Brater as an active member of the subcommittee, which tickled Danny, since it was general knowledge that Brater was snugly bedded in the local hospital with his convenient undefined stomach ailment.

The Committee's counsel called the first witness.

"Mr. Raven, will you return to the stand?"

And there was Sidney Raven again. He must have been part of the group which came in with the two Congressmen a minute or so earlier and he must have very unobtrusively slipped into that seat at the small table directly in front of the jury box. Raven rose from his seat and hurriedly crossed to the witness chair where he stood facing Denilworth who was in his usual spot on the raised platform directly in front of the witness. Danny could not hear any other sound in the courtroom outside the voices of Holling and the witness as Raven was sworn in again.

Raven sat down.

Danny could feel his heart pounding — he was certain now that he would be called to testify this morning!

Denilworth began the questioning.

"In the early part of your testimony, Mr. Raven, you referred to staff meetings of union organizers which were held from time to time — " He stopped and waited for confirmation.

"That is right," said Raven, in a firm voice.

"Were those staff meetings held in any particular place or at designated intervals? Or what were the arrangements?"

"They were not held at any particular place or at designated intervals," Raven replied. "They were held on call. In most cases staff meetings would be held at the same time as district conventions were held; and those were held frequently during the year."

"How often?"

"Sometimes as many as six times a year. And in most cases when the district convention was held all the organizers on the staff of the district were called for a meeting."

Denilworth continued to question the witness as reporters scribbled away. Danny assumed that John Mason would make sure the whole thing got into the Buffalo newspapers.

He heard Sidney Raven, in reply to a question from Denilworth, name two former union organizers who were in charge of the union's staff in the district where he now worked under George Hernandez.

"Yesterday," Denilworth reminded the witness, "you named both these persons as members of the Communist Party, did you not?"

"Yes," said Raven, "definitely!"

"Now," said Denilworth, "will you tell the Committee who constituted the staff that met at these staff meetings? I'm not asking the names of individuals yet. But will you tell us which officials comprised the staff?" He nodded very importantly and tilted his head to one side while he waited for this revelation.

"The staff," said Raven, "was comprised of all the organizers who were working for the national union, and at these staff meetings there were also some organizers from time to time who may have been working for that particular district. They were organizers on the district payroll. There were also other individuals, such as a director of women's activities or an educational director, who were also part of the staff."

A crazy thought came into Danny's head. How often, he wondered, had the FBI or the Committee's legal counsel or his assistant gone over this material with Sidney Raven before he was summoned to appear here on the witness stand? An amusing thought: had Raven gone over his notes more often then he had gone over his? Of course, Raven had the advantage in having Denilworth there to guide him with leading questions.

"You told us in the earlier part of your testimony," Denilworth said to the witness as Danny strained to catch each word, "you told us that staff meetings were held — and the business of the union was discussed at these meetings — and then there were other meetings held by the same people, if I understood you correctly." He waited to have that confirmed.

"That is right," said Raven.

"What was the nature of the meetings that were held?"

"In some cases," Raven explained, "the staff meetings would be held in the afternoon or in the morning, and in the evening there would be another meeting, and almost all the staff members — there may have been some who didn't attend — but almost all attended another meeting at which time the Communist Party functionary was present."

"Was this Communist Party functionary or these functionaries to which you refer employed in anyway by the union?"

"No."

"What was the purpose of these meetings which were held, at which functionaries of the Communist Party were present?"

"The purpose of the meetings?" Raven echoed before answering. "Of course, to start out with, all of the members of the organizing staff in the districts that I worked in were members of the Communist Party, and so the party functionary was brought in in order to lead the meeting, in order to give leadership to the meeting."

The latest addition to the subcommittee, Congressman Sackville, interrupted with a measured soft drawl. "Were all the members there who attended those meetings — *communists*?" He sounded as though he found that hard to believe.

"Definitely yes, sir," asserted Raven. "They wouldn't be allowed to attend unless they belonged to the Communist Party and were members of the union's staff or both."

"How many," Sackville continued, "on the average would be in attendance?"

"Well, it would depend on how many people were on the staff at the particular time, because it fluctuated. I would say as many as from twelve to twenty."

"Have you named all twelve — or twenty?"

"No, I haven't named them all."

Now Danny was certain he would be named.

Congressman Sackville leaned over the bench and looked down at the Committee's legal counsel. "You *are* going to ask that, Mr. Denilworth?"

"Yes, sir," said Denilworth, bobbing his heavily joweled face up and down, "and I may as well do that at this point. Mr. Raven, you gave us the names yesterday of numerous officials of the union, most of them being organizers, who were members of the staff at the various places that you worked. But you have told us this morning that, in addition to ones who were regularly working in those areas, that organizers from places where you were not working attended the meetings."

"That is right."

"So that list that you gave us yesterday did not include all the union's organizers who were in attendance at those meetings."

"That is correct."

"Will you tell the Committee, please — or *give* the Committee the names of all other persons in this district of the union who were officially connected with the union, whether as organizers or in any other capacity, who attended the staff meetings which were devoted to Communist Party purposes."

There was not another sound in the courtroom as Raven began to list the names, and Danny strained to catch every word the witness said. He hardly breathed while he cocked his left ear toward the witness table to hear better. Raven listed names of people Danny had never heard mentioned before. But they might be people who worked for the union before he was hired. Then he began to recognize the names he heard — Raven wasn't missing anyone — and Danny guessed that Raven started way back at the beginning, when he himself first joined the staff of the union, and was working his way up to the present, mentioning every organizer who ever worked in that district of the union. Danny strained to hear each name. And then he heard the name he was waiting for —

"*Daniel Newman.*"

If anyone was watching to see how he reacted, Danny was determined not to show any fear. There wasn't going to be anything for John Mason or anyone else to read in the stiff mask with which he covered his face. Mason would have to write: "*When Newman's name was mentioned by Raven, the Buffalo labor official did not show any emotion.*" — Trying to appear completely undisturbed, Danny slipped his handkerchief out of his back pocket and wiped the palms of his hands, and then he dabbed at the two moist spots his palms imprinted on the covers of the Julius Emspak case brief. He became aware that Raven was still giving names to the Committee — and he tried to concentrate on that, forcing himself to listen. But his attention kept straying back to what he had to remember to say when he would be called up there to testify, perhaps in only a matter of minutes. He grabbed his notes out of his inside pocket, unfolded the yellow sheets of paper on his lap and anxiously scanned through the pencilled phrases to refresh his memory.

The sound of scuffling of many feet in the rear of the courtroom caught his attention. Heads all around him were turning. Danny looked to see what was happening behind him. A crowd of men, some still wearing dirty work clothes were filing rapidly into the courtroom. He recognized some of the faces — these were officers and executive board members and stewards of Jean Dampier's local union at the GE plant in Schenectady, the secessionists who had pulled out of his union.

Congressman Holling called a halt to the testimony of Raven, waiting until the new arrivals found seats. Danny noted that the Congressman acted as though he expected this interruption.

Several of the Schenectady local union officials whom Danny knew very well saw him and recognized him — and quickly moved away, either too afraid to say hello to him or too ashamed to talk to him after what they had done to help pull their local union out of the national organization —

The eyes of the thickset chief steward Sam D'Amico met Danny's eyes before Sam quickly looked away. Danny remembered when they ate lunch together and Sam confided that the FBI was visiting him regularly in his home, pressuring him to turn against the UE union, and Sam said he would never surrender to their blackmail. Now he had surrendered.

There was Dave Russo, the president of the local union. He publicly pledged that he would never give into redbaiting. Now he looked the other way as he passed by Danny.

Dave's younger brother Joe stopped still when he saw Danny, shocked by the unexpected, and then he whirled around and walked over to the middle aisle. Danny remembered when he and Helen had given Joe a lift after a district council meeting, driving him to Buffalo to visit his relatives, and on that trip Joe had told Helen how much he admired Danny's integrity and that was why he liked their union — because the organizers had such deep-seated principles and worked their heads off for the membership — and Joe said that he would always back the union organizers against any kind of redbaiting — he didn't care what their politics were. Now Joe looked the other way, walking down the middle aisle in the courtroom.

And then he saw Hank Mansfield and Les Smith, two executive board members of the local union. The very first time he saw them operate as a team at a union meeting he whispered to George Hernandez that he was willing to bet his life that they were undercover agents who had been infiltrated into the Schenectady GE local union to wreck its militancy. George Hernandez, an experienced hand at the cloak-and-dagger business in the OSS during World War II, whispered back that he didn't think there was any danger of losing the bet. Hank and Les wouldn't look Danny in the eye as they passed. They had seen him, he knew, and they looked the other way.

It was an embittering experience for Danny — to be shunned this way, like one of the lepers he had seen wandering through the streets of villages in Korea when he was there with the 20th Infantry of the Sixth Division in 1945, World War II.

Several of the new arrivals — he didn't know them and they, apparently, didn't know him — filled up the bench where he was sitting. But then someone must have slipped them a warning about the dangerous man sitting on the end of their bench. A wide gap suddenly developed on Danny's right between him and the next man seated on the bench. The group squeezed themselves away from him. Out of the corner of his eye, Danny could see that the man nearest him was red in the face as he stared straight ahead. The poor fellow was probably wondering what might be said by the others to him later because of where he happened to seat himself.

The U.S. marshall glided noiselessly up and down the aisle, restoring order merely by the magic of his handsome gray-haired presence. Without a word, only a graceful nod here and there, he indicated that it was all right for the latecomers to stand along the sidewalls of the courtroom

since there were no more seats available to accommodate all
those who had come to see the star attraction of the big
show.

Danny wondered where Jean Dampier was. Then he
realized how stupid he was to expect to see Jean take a place
out in the audience. Only "unfriendly" witnesses came up to
the witness chair from the audience, and Jean had made it
clear in his statements to the press that he did not intend to
be an "unfriendly" witness. He was going to answer all
questions and under oath he was going to flatly deny that he
had ever had any communist affiliations. That must be why
he brought along his entire political machine from the shop
— so they could give eyewitness reports to the workers back
in the GE shop in Schenectady — that they saw and heard
Jean Dampier take the oath with his right hand upraised
and then heard him catagorically deny any present or past
communist affiliations —

Congressman Holling rapped the gavel.

The courtroom became quiet.

Holling nodded to Denilworth to go on.

The Committee's legal counsel, expert showman that he
was, immediately jumped his line of questioning to the
subject he knew would hypnotically grab the attention of the
men from the GE shop in Schenectady. He spoke very slowly,
with great dramatic import, as he resumed his quizzing of
the witness.

"Mr. Raven, you have stated earlier in your testimony that
you were recommended for the position of organizer by Mr.
Dampier?" Denilworth stopped, his head stretched forward,
awaiting confirmation. His mouth was round and open, a
fish in the act of gulping for air.

"By Mr. Dampier," said Raven. "That is right."

Denilworth closed his mouth around the reply and
repeated for emphasis: "*Jean* Dampier?"

"*Jean* Dampier," confirmed Raven. "That is right."

"You also told us" — Denilworth leaned forward, screwing
up his face with the intensity of his search for the answer —
"you told us that you did not know whether Mr. Dampier
knew at that time that you were a member of the Communist
Party." He hesitated, waiting for confirmation from the
witness.

"That is right," said Raven, his voice hollowly reverberating throughout the courtroom.

A long pause.

Danny guessed that Denilworth was dragging it out in order to heighten the suspense. Now that he was juggling the name of Jean Dampier in one hand and the Communist Party in the other Denilworth knew he had the attention of every member of Dampier's political machine from the GE shop in Schenectady. A real showman, Danny reluctantly admitted.

"Mr. Raven," Denilworth blandly resumed, "do you know whether Mr. Dampier knew Mr. Pearl — Julius Pearl — the Communist Party organizer in the Schenectady area?"

"Well," Raven replied, speaking in the manner of man-to-man, just between friends, "I don't know whether or not he palled around with him or anything like that. But I did see them at a dinner that was held in honor of Mr. Pearl. I did see Mr. Dampier present at that dinner."

The double-cross!

This, Danny immediately guessed, was the beginning of it. By linking Jean Dampier even loosely with a Communist Party organizer at a dinner in honor of Pearl, the Committee's counsel had cunningly tightened a noose arond Jean's neck in front of his political machine of local union officers and executive board members and stewards. Even if the Committee pressed no further, they had already fixed the ring through Jean's nose and they could lead him around as they pleased. He would always know they could hang him any time they wanted to.

Denilworth went on to ask several questions about the dinner and Raven testified that it was a farewell dinner for Julius Pearl who was leaving the area and it was attended by many Communist Party members. Then the Committee's legal counsel shifted to a slightly different tack, and Danny tried to puzzle out the reason for the shift.

"You have testified in some detail, Mr. Raven," Denilworth began, allowing his gaze to wander out over the courtroom, "regarding Communist Party activities within the national UE organization with which you were once connected. Now can you tell me" — he fixed his eyes on Raven again — "at the time when you were an organizer for that union — did any facts come to your attention. . . within your own knowledge — *regarding Communist Party activities within the local union at the GE plant in Schenectady?*"

The purpose of the question seemed clear to Danny. The Committee was deliberately driving the wedge in further between the local union and the national union organization. Their theme, as they appeared to be developing it, was to be that the local union was politically pure, but the national union was contaminated with communists on its organizing staff. Therefore, the local union should make final its breakaway from the contaminated national organization in an election to be conducted by the National Labor Relations Board. But what about the contradiction they were developing by linking Jean Dampier, the business agent of the local union, with Pearl, the Communist Party organizer — especially since Dampier was leading the secession movement?

Meanwhile, Raven answered Denilworth's question about Communist Party activities within the local union as Danny had expected he would.

"No!" the witness exclaimed, so emphatically Danny wondered if he had been over-rehearsed on that point. "I would say, *No!*"

And Denilworth quickly followed up: "You had no knowledge that Mr. Dampier was a member of the Communist Party —" It seemed as much a statement as it was a question.

"Oh, *no!*" exclaimed Raven.

Oh, perish the thought, Danny silently said to himself, cynically mimicking the witness.

"No more questions," said Denilworth.

Congressman Holling immediately took over, leaning forward, looking down at the witness from his place up on the judge's bench. "Mr. Raven, this concludes your testimony." The chairman sounded very important. "And again the Committee wishes to express its thanks for your cooperation and assistance in giving the Committee the valuable information you have given. You are discharged."

Danny imagined how relieved Raven must feel as he escaped from the courtroom, hurrying without a backward glance to get through the door leading to the judge's chambers.

Now Danny knew it was *his* turn — his and Herb Kepler's and Bill Kosciusko's, the subpeonaed union organizers who had been named by Raven. That had been the pattern on the two previous days: first, a "friendly" witness was called by the Committee to name names; then some of those so named, "unfriendly" witnesses, were summoned from the audience to be worked over by the Committee.

Who would be called first?

Someone else, he hoped — he needed more time. It would help him to see how it went with one of the other organizers before he was called up there. Bill Kosciusko had a lot of guts — he would be a good man to kick off for their side. It wouldn't be too bad following after Bill.

Danny saw that Denilworth was taking some papers from his assistant. The Committee's legal counsel looked down at the papers, silently reading something there, and then he looked up —

"Mr. Herbert Kepler, will you come forward please?"

Chapter 24

It took Danny a moment or two to locate the other organizer over on the right side of the center aisle, about four or five benches back from the railing which separated the courtroom spectators from the performing area up front.

On the surface Herb appeared quite cool but Danny was sure that beneath that calm surface Herb must be as extremely agitated as he himself would be if he were in the other man's shoes. Herb's movements seemed to be *too* well controlled.

Trying to guess the other organizer's thoughts and emotions, Danny watched Herb carefully smooth out his topcoat and gently deposit it on the bench to hold his place until he returned. Then with all eyes in the courtroom on him Herb straightened up and stepped out into the center aisle and walked steadily forward, tall and slim, head high, shoulders back and rigid, like a toy soldier marching on parade. His firm control stirred Danny's admiration.

Studying Herb's face with its regular features softened by the neatly trimmed crop of prematurely gray, almost white, hair — the handsome face and the stiff tall way Herb held himself made Danny think of the stock company matinee idol type of leading man he had met years ago while working with several theatrical companies. He thought he saw a slight sneer on the other organizer's lips. But then he wondered if he only imagined the sneer was there because that was the way he thought Herb must be feeling inside about Denilworth and Congressman Holling and the newcomer, Congressman Sackville, because Herb was smart enough to know that they were going to try to make him hop through the hoop at the crack of their whip, like a trained animal in a circus performance. A very proud person, extremely touchy about his personal dignity, Herb must hate them for that.

He felt the same way Herb did.

While his eyes followed Herb, walking stiffly down the aisle, Danny thought it was no accident that Herb Kepler was the first of the "unfriendly" organizers to be called to testify. The Committee's investigators, assisted by the FBI, must have dug out the information that Herb intended to deny categorically present membership in the Communist Party before following up with the Fifth Amendment privilege as a reason for refusing to answer concerning past membership. They were undoubtedly all set for Herb. They would zero in on him like a mortar squad zeros in on an enemy machine gun emplacement: a shell aimed *over* the target, a shell aimed *short* of the target, and then aiming between the two previous shells, *on target* and *fire for effect*, dropping shells on the target as fast as you can pump them into the mortar tube!

They would let Herb deny present membership in the Communist Party, and then they would ask him: "Mr. Kepler, were you a communist last year — last month — last week — yesterday — this morning — one hour ago — when you were sitting in this courtroom exactly five minutes ago — when you walked up here to take the oath? — And after Herb cited the Fifth Amendment privilege to refuse to answer those questions, they would start back at the beginning again, asking him again if he is a member of the Communist Party *now*, and Herb would have to be consistent and say no again, the same way he answered that question the first time they asked it, and then they would start zeroing in on the target all over again — and they would go over that same ground again and again, rubbing in the fact that he was denying *present* Communist Party membership but was refusing to deny *past* Communist Party membership even as of the moment he walked up to the witness stand to take the oath.

And then they would apply the same technique to the question of possible future membership: Mr. Kepler, will you be a member of the Communist Party *again* — next year — next month — next week — tonight — as soon as we dismiss you from the witness chair? They'd really work him over. And the job they would do on Herb would be linked by the newspapers to the two union organizers who would follow him to the witness chair, no matter how they handled the questions of the Committee.

But Danny knew that Herb was aware of the trap the

Committee would try to set for him after he answered that he is not presently a member of the Communist Party, and Herb had his plan to break out of that trap. But could he provoke them into tossing him out of the hearing? And if he was tossed out as a result of a very messy scene — couldn't that be just as damaging, propaganda-wise, as if he was publicly subjected to the full zeroing-in treatment by the Committee?

Ed Murphy, leather brief case in hand, rose from his seat in the front row, and Danny saw him follow Herb Kepler up to the witness table. They stood, side by side, in full glare of batteries of spotlights rigged up for the newsreel and television cameras, their backs to the audience.

Reporters and photographers closed in around them.

Flash bulbs flared while Herb lifted his right hand and took the oath.

His hands dropped.

He sat down.

Ed Murphy, on Herb's left, also sat down, and he zipped open his briefcase and took out some papers and distributed them on the table.

Danny strained his head higher to see what was going on. The press photographers did not let up — flash bulbs flared one after another, back and forth and all around the two men seated at the witness table, the rapid succession of explosions pulling Danny's eyes from one side to the other. Only the back of Herb's neck and head was visible above heads of intervening rows of spectators who jammed the courtroom. From the stiff way Herb was holding the upper part of his body, Danny visualized the cold disdainful expression on the other organizer's matinee idol face. Imagining how he himself would feel if he were in Herb's place, Danny's heart went out to the other organizer. Underneath that tightly controlled surface the poor bastard must be scared shitless.

The Committee's legal counsel idly leafed his way through some papers given him by his assistant, probably an investigator's report on Herb, while he patiently waited for activity of the photographers and reporters to subside. Then, ready for business, he looked down at the witness from his vantage post up on the platform. Pursing his fat lips and half-smiling in a professional meaningless way, he spoke briskly.

"What is your name, please, sir?"

"Herbert Kepler."

Herb's voice sounded strong and Danny thought Herb deliberately intended it that way as a declaration to the Committee that he was not buckling under to them. Several more flash bulbs exploded as Herb spoke, some photographers apparently poised with cameras to snap him in the act of answering.

"Are you accompanied by counsel?" Denilworth asked, with precise politeness.

"I am, sir."

Danny heard Ed Murphy clearing his throat as he leaned his head forward to bring his mouth closer to the microphone on the witness table. Ed identified himself for the record and then asked if the Committee would please have the bright lights extinguished and if they would stop the photographers from interrupting the proceedings with their exploding flash bulbs. Congressman Holling interrupted and asked if that was the way the witness wanted it.

"I would appreciate it, sir," Herb frigidly replied, in a way that made Danny smile with admiration at the man's coolness, "if they would finish *their* job, and then I will get on with *mine*."

Holling seemed to ignore Herb's barbed sarcasm. "Your request is granted. The press will take their pictures and desist during the taking of testimony. You may proceed, Mr. Denilworth."

The newsreel and television technicians switched off their batteries of spotlights and the area in front of the railing seemed to become dark by contrast with the previous intense glare. But Danny noticed that the press photographers were not retreating from the vantage points they held — they crouched down on their haunches, cameras and flash bulbs ready to pounce into action again.

Denilworth resumed.

"When and where were you born, Mr. Kepler?"

Herb answered without hesitation, and when he named a small town in the Midwest and year 1912, a year before Danny was born — Danny reminded himself that when *he* would be sitting where Herb was sitting, he would *not* answer that question. While he was thinking about what that would provoke from the Committee, he half heard Denilworth go on to ask Herb by whom he was employed, and when Herb answered that he was employed by their union, the UE, Denilworth asked how long he had been employed by them.

"Well, my employment with the union has been intermittent," Herb explained, still maintaining an air of defiant pride, "but I first went to work for the union back in 1937."

"In what capacity?"

"As a field organizer. And then my employment by them was interrupted — " Herb told Denilworth that during this period when he was off the union's organizing staff he held various machine shop jobs. This was the period, Danny recalled, when Herb was dropped from the staff because he couldn't stay away from the whiskey bottle, and Danny wondered if the Committee would mercilessly delve into Herb's marital situation at that time. But Denilworth went right on, without touching on anything relating to that period, and Danny guessed that the Committee knew all about Herb's problems during that period but had decided to leave it alone because an attack of that kind might create sympathy for the witness.

"Will you tell the Committee, please, what your educational training has been?"

Denilworth was working harder now, really turning on the energy — with open mouth and all the other hammy gestures calculated to arouse in the courtroom spectators the kind of emotional reaction he wanted them to have to answers of the witness.

Herb answered, "I completed high school."

"Prior to 1937," said Denilworth, "in what work were you engaged?"

"Various work," curtly replied Herb. "When I graduated from high school I went to work as a photostat operator and general helper around the photographic laboratory in a steel plant. Then I went to work for a gas company — I worked in various capacities for them, clerk and one thing and another."

Denilworth jutted his chin forward and his next question was an accusation. "You were an organizer for United Electrical Radio and Machine Workers, the UE, your present employer, were you, in 1948?" His sharp tone alerted everyone in the courtroom for some impending startling disclosure.

"Well" — trying to maintain his suavely disdainful manner, Herb fenced off Denilworth's sharp thrust by very leisurely explaining that he had been on the payroll of the district office in 1948 but had actually been performing work for the national organization. "It was only a question of who paid me, and otherwise it made no difference in the work I was assigned to do — "

"Did you," Denilworth impatiently shot at Herb, trying to keep up a state of excitement, "become acquainted with a young man by the name of Temple?"

Herb did not answer right away.

That name sounded familiar to Danny. Temple? Then he remembered. Temple was one of the "friendly" witnesses who testified the day before — the one who said he lived with Lisa and Henry Michaels in Schenectady. Herb probably knew Temple, but apparently he wasn't sure of the best way to handle Denilworth's question. He was silent, while Denilworth waited, perfectly still, his head jutted forward with mouth open to gulp down Herb's reply.

"Yes," Herb answered, guardedly — Danny could tell that he was afraid of what his answer might lead to. "Yes," he repeated, a little more confidently, "I know Ray Temple."

It was a mistake, Danny thought, a bad mistake. That was when Herb should have used the Fifth Amendment privilege to refuse to answer. He had let the Committee link him by his own testimony directly to the stoolpigeon. Once you cross testimony with a stoolpigeon where it's only your word against his word, you've got a good chance to get jugged for perjury, even though every word you say is the truth, the whole truth and nothing but the truth, so help you, God. The Committee had Herb trapped — so quickly! — and Danny was not surprised by the follow-up question which Denilworth very quietly asked Herb.

"Did you know Raymond Temple as a member of the Communist Party?"

How could Herb answer that one without putting a lynch rope around his own neck? The Committee's legal counsel curved his fat lips into a big round dramatic circle and raised his eyebrows as he waited for the reply from the delicate thrust into the heart of the witness. Herb was silent, and Danny imagined how frantically he was trying to figure his way out of the tight box into which he had been so quickly maneuvered.

If Herb replied *No*, Temple would say Herb lied, and Herb would be judged guilty of perjury and sent to jail. If Herb answered *Yes*, he admitted associating with a man he knew to be a member of the Communist Party, with all this could be made to imply — including substantiation of any allegations Temple might subsequently make about Herb.

Danny hoped Herb would use the Fifth Amendment privilege to refuse to answer, though he realized it might already be too late to invoke that privilege since there was a legal question as to whether or not Herb could use the Fifth Amendment after he himself had opened the door to this whole line of questioning by admitting he knew Ray Temple.

Herb ducked a direct reply. "I knew Ray Temple," he said somewhat scornfully, "as a brash young man who went to work for the local union at the General Electric — GE — plant in Schenectady."

Danny surmised that Herb was taking this slap at Temple in order to discredit, in advance, any harmful testimony Temple might give against him later.

But Denilworth had no intention of letting the witness sidestep the crucial question that easily, not after he had already secured the damaging admission from the witness that he knew Temple, a man who had already voluntarily testified under oath that he had been a member of the Communist Party when he was working in Schenectady. Denilworth pressed his advantage.

"Aside from that," he said quickly, not relaxing his tense posture, *"did you know Raymond Temple as a member of the Communist Party?"*

"I would like to say," began Herb, obviously still trying to get away from the dangerous line of questioning into which he had been lured, "with respect to this question, and also with respect to any other questions that you may ask along the same line — "

The loud whack of the gavel startled Danny! Congressman Holling angrily demanded that the witness answer the question he had been asked. "Not with respect to any *other* questions, Mr. Kepler!" he spat down at Herb. "There is only *one* question before you now! Will you answer that question!" It was a command.

Absolute silence in the courtroom.

Danny saw that all heads in front of him were motionless. Everyone seemed hypnotized by the Congressman's sudden attack. Their natural inclination must be to sympathize with the underdog as the wolf pack fiercely closes in. But at the same time Danny sensed a wave of fear passing through spectators in the courtroom — any one of them could easily be put in the same position if he openly opposed what the Committee was doing.

Poor Herb. The Committee hadn't asked the question he wanted them to ask first, the question which would have permitted him to give a pointblank denial of *present* Communist Party membership, and he had blundered by not using the Fifth Amendment privilege to refuse to answer the question about knowing Temple. His anxiety to avoid using the Fifth Amendment until *after* he had denied present Communist Party membership had trapped him. Danny guessed that Herb had been afraid the Committee might dismiss him immediately if he invoked the Fifth Amendment about knowing Temple. With him not given the chance to deny present Communist Party membership, they would be able to say he was dismissed because he used the Fifth Amendment to avoid revealing his link to an admitted member of the Communist Party. Danny watched the reporters rapidly scribbling away. Danny sweated along with Herb who must be frantically ransacking his brain for a way out of the trap. He should take time out to consult with Ed Murphy. But maybe he's too excited to think of that —

Herb's face was turned upward as he looked directly at Congressman Holling whose countenance was the picture of sternness, the tightened muscles around his mouth insisting that Herb answer *this* one question.

"All right, Congressman," Herb resolutely struck out, and Danny hoped the sudden boldness meant that Herb had found a way out of the trap, "I will answer this question — I want to say that" — Herb hesitated, and then before he could be stopped, rushed on — *"I am NOT a member of the Communist Party."*

Congressman Holling fiercely thwacked his gavel down on the judge's desk, but he was too late. Danny grinned as he realized that Herb had turned the tables, getting into the record the pointblank statement he wanted to get there first — that he is not now a member of the Communist Party. Now, even though there was still some risk since he had admitted knowing Temple, he could offer the Fifth Amendment as his reason for refusing to answer any further questions about his past or future relations with the Communist Party or any admitted former Communist Party members such as Temple, and he could try to get the Committee to throw him out before they again zeroed in too closely on him.

Holling's complexion flushed cherry red. "That is not a response to the question!" he viciously snapped at Herb.

"Congressman," said Herb, seeming completely at ease now, his voice dripping with acid, "I am doing my best here to bring you the information which you are looking for."

Holling must have realized he was not playing it right by letting the spectators see him lose his temper while the witness remained calm. The Congressman's voice became quiet but his face remained crimson as he tried to regain the initiative.

"Mr. Denilworth most likely will ask some additional questions," he firmly informed Herb Kepler, leaning forward to speak down at him, "and after you have answered those questions, if there is any explanation you want to make, you will have an opportunity to make such an explanation. But there is this question before you, and that is: *Whether you knew Raymond Temple as a member of the Communist Party?"*

"Well, as to that." Herb seemed quite confident now that he had gotten into the record the denial of *present* membership in the Communist Party. "I must say that I invoke the Fifth Amendment of the Constitution. I will not testify against myself."

"You refuse to answer on the grounds of the Fifth

Amendment of the Constitution?" the Congressman asked Herb, and Danny wondered if Holling would insist that the witness answer on grounds that he had already opened the door to this line of questioning when he admitted he knew Temple.

"That I do," Herb firmly replied.

"Very well," said the Congressman. "Proceed, Mr. Denilworth."

Holling had apparently decided he had what was needed for the inter-union conflict at Schenectady: the use of the Fifth Amendment by the organizer so he could be tagged a "Fifth Amendment communist" while Jean Dampier had publicly committed himself not to use the Fifth Amendment. The comparison between their answers would be there to be milked for all its propaganda value.

But the newcomer on the bench, Congressman Sackville, quietly interrupted before Denilworth could put another question to the witness. "You say," he slowly drawled, "you are *not* a member of the Communist Party?"

"Are you asking me that question?" Herb countered, and Danny guessed that, like himself, Herb was trying to puzzle out the purpose of the southern Congressman's question.

"Yes," said Sackville, nodding as he fingered his black string tie, "I think you are entitled to make that statement."

Danny was suspicious — the newcomer was trying to be too helpful.

"I am not *now* a member of the Communist Party," said Herb, and then he quickly added, *"nor, Congressman, have I ever engaged in espionage, sabotage or anything of that nature."*

Inwardly, Danny applauded as he recognized that Herb had found exactly the right kind of opening to get in the important statement which he himself would have to get into the record somehow, even though he himself did not intend to answer any of the Committee's questions. Congressman Sackville intently eyed Herb, and Danny wondered if the Congressman was going to object to Herb's additional statement as not being responsive to his question.

But then, as though he had forgotten all else which had gone before, Sackville innocently asked Herb an apparently offhand question.

"What was the name of the man you mentioned?"

Herb did not answer immediately, and Danny imagined that the other organizer was wondering what was the purpose of that simple question.

"Raymond Temple," he answered.

"Do you," Sackville continued with the same disarming offhand approach, "have personal knowledge of his affiliation or association with the Communist Party activities in any manner, in which you yourself were *not* connected?"

It was a deliberately confusing question and it seemed to Danny that *any* answer would seriously entangle Herb. How could he have personal knowledge of Temple's affiliation or association with the Communist Party activities without thus establishing, by his own testimony, an association with such activities on his own part? And if he said he had no such knowledge Temple could say he *did* have such knowledge and Herb would be defending himself against a perjury charge.

"Congressman," began Herb, still looking up at the impassive face above him. — Herb's voice began to rise, and as its intensity rapidly increased Danny concluded that Herb had decided to start the build-up toward a head-on emotional clash with the Committee, hoping to end the inquisition by provoking them to toss him out. "I am perfectly willing here to answer any and all questions dealing with my employment, my activities, and my association in my union, but when it comes to this Committee or any other committee inquiring into my personal beliefs, my past associations, my habits, my thoughts, I say, sir, that it is not only wrong, it is actually illegal for this Committee or any other committee to do so. I say that the First Amendment of the Constitution of this country guarantees me freedom of speech and thought and association, and I say, sir, it is not only wrong, but it is actually illegal for your Committee or any other committee to inquire into those matters — "

Sackville interrupted, retreating, "I was merely asking you a question which I thought would be limited, so it would not be necessary for you to invoke the Fifth Amendment in your response to Mr. Denilworth's question concerning Mr. Temple — if you had any personal knowledge concerning any communistic activities on Mr. Temple's part with which you were *not* personally connected."

"Well," retorted Herb, "I have already testified I am willing to say what I know about Raymond Temple in connection with the union, but I am not going to be dragged into *this* line of inquiry."

Sackville nodded his head, apparently indicating he would abandon that line of inquiry to which the witness objected. But then he came back at once with another loaded question. "Do you," he very innocently asked, "have any personal knowledge of any espionage activities on the part of Mr. Temple which you yourself were *not* connected with?"

Danny recognized the skill of Sackville in concealing the fish hook with a juicy worm, trying to make it appear like he was trying to help the witness clear himself. Sackville was more skilled and more dangerous then Congressman Holling whose antagonism to all "unfriendly" witnesses was too apparent.

"I would be delighted to answer that question," said Herb, not sounding delighted but like he was stalling, trying to think his way out of the trap.

Sackville quietly but very firmly interrupted. "You have further stated," he drawled, "that you have never been guilty of espionage or disloyalty to the country. As a patriotic citizen, you of course would reveal such activities on the part of any other person, would you not?"

"Congressman," said Herb, right back up into that cunning face poised above him, "I am delighted you asked me that question," and this time he really sounded happy about it. "I know of no instances of espionage on *anyone's* part. And had I found out of any you wouldn't have to drag me before any congressional committee — *I would have reported it!*"

Danny felt like applauding. Herb had successfully shaken Sackville off his back.

But as Sackville settled back into his seat, for the time being giving up his attack, Congressman Holling leaned forward and resumed *his* attack, speaking firmly down at the uplifted face of the witness.

"All we asked you was whether you knew Mr. Temple was a member of the Communist Party. When you invoke the Fifth Amendment, we proceed no further on that. — But now the question I want to ask you is: Were you *ever* a member of the Communist Party?"

Danny was sure Herb must know what would follow this. Here is where they would zero in on him. Like a mortar squad zeros in on an enemy machine gun position. One shot *over* the target. One shot *short* of the target. Then *on target* and *fire for effect!* — They started now with: *Were you ever a member of the Communist Party?* If Herb replies: *Fifth Amendment*, the next question will be: *Were you a member a year ago?* Then: *A month ago?* Then: *A week ago?* — *Yesterday?* — *An hour ago?* — *When you walked up here to be sworn in?* He had put himself on the defensive by trying to cleanse himself with a direct denial of *present* Communist Party membership instead of citing the Fifth Amendment privilege on that question along with all other questions relating to the matter of Communist Party membership. The Committee had him cornered, like a third baseman and a catcher in a baseball game ready to close in on a runner caught between them, tossing the ball back and forth until they run the runner down between them and tag him out. But if Herb gets tagged here they can hang a perjury charge around his neck with a penalty of several years in jail and maybe the end of his second marriage.

Herb Kepler finally spoke up, but his answer sounded weak and defensive, even though he was obviously trying to be very forceful. "As to that, sir," he replied, "I have the following answer to make. I refuse to answer this question on the following grounds. Number one, I consider it beyond the province of this Committee, illegal and wrong and against the First Amendment of the Constitution for you to pry into my past associations, beliefs and thoughts — "

"So far," Congressman Holling blandly interrupted him, "the courts have disagreed with you. We do have that right. But if you want to invoke the *Fifth* Amendment on this question, you have the right to do so."

"I want to answer your question," insisted Herb, his anxious manner convincing Danny that he was fully aware that this was only the beginning of the zeroing-in process and that he was searching for a way out of it.

"But so far," Congressman Holling angrily snapped back at him, "you haven't answered it!"

Herb smacked the flat of his hand down on the table — it made a loud angry noise — and Danny knew immediately that Herb had decided that this was the moment to break it up. Before the Committee had a chance to zero in on him he had to make the Committee toss him out. "*Sir,*" he belligerently yelled at the Congressman who glared down at him, "*are you trying to impersonate Hitler and Mussolini?*"

The suddenness of this attack caught Holling off guard. The Congressman flared bright red and screamed, "*I just want you to answer the question!*"

The hot eruption of tempers brought the press photographers to their feet. Ignoring the previous order not to take pictures during the testimony, they snapped one shot after another, milling around for better vantage points while flash bulbs exploded on all sides of the witness, contributing a quality of increasing excitement and confusion. Newsreel and television cameramen switched on batteries of bright floodlights, bringing into sharp focus the two angry men confronting one another, one up on the judge's bench glaring angrily down at the witness whose head was turned upward in a tense challenging pose, both seeming to be ready to trade punches if they could get at one another. The tension was terrific, and Danny wondered what the Congressman would do now.

Whack!

Congressman Holling's gavel pounded down on top of the desk in front of him with the loud crack of finality. "Mr. Marshall," he called out in a harsh but piercing tone of command, "you will remove the witness from the courtroom. We will have no more of this contempt!"

The Congressman had apparently decided that this was the perfect climax to close out the testimony of this uncooperative witness. But Danny knew this was exactly what Herb wanted to happen.

Two court attendants took Herb Kepler by the arm and shoulders as he rose to his feet. They wheeled him around and started up the center aisle, with the gray-haired U.S. marshall gliding ahead of the trio, assuring them a clear path through the courtroom to the rear exit. Several photographers and reporters moved along close behind the small group. There was no struggle. Herb walked willingly, trying to hide his triumphant smile. All heads in the courtroom turned as the spectators watched Herb move up the aisle. There was not a sound except for the scuffling of the feet of the small group moving toward the exit. No boos. No cheers. No murmurs of criticism. No indications of approval. Only a sullen quiet. *Fear*, concluded Danny, fear so thick you could almost reach out and feel it with your fingers.

"Let the record show," the Congressman declared, as Herb was escorted through the swinging doors out into the corridor, "it is the opinion of the Chair, at least, that the witness is clearly in contempt of the Congress!"

Holling whacked his gavel. He had the show rolling and apparently wanted to keep it swiftly rolling. He sharply directed Denilworth to proceed with the next witness.

Danny's thoughts were still tangled up with Herb Kepler's situation when the next name was called. Though he had expected it, it still caught him by surprise.

"Mr. Daniel Newman — "

Chapter 25

He saw heads around him turn to look for the next victim as he rose and started around back of the rear bench toward the center aisle.

The U.S. marshall came to meet him as he proceeded down the aisle. The marshall stepped in front of him and bent over to look at the brief on the Julius Emspak case which he had under his left arm. Danny realized — a slight shock — that the marshall was looking to see if he was carrying a weapon of some kind. He grinned reassuringly at the marshall as the gray-haired man straightened up. The marshall smiled in return, giving Danny a feeling he hadn't had before — that the man wasn't a bad sort of guy and he was actually sympathetic to the emotional strain of the witness.

As he followed the marshal he was conscious of all eyes staring at him from both sides of the aisle. He was surprised to find himself able to pick out faces of a few individuals from the mass as he looked for friendly ones from which to draw strength. — Elsie and Steve Brooks and Ray Foster and Bill Kosciusko. Instinctively, he winked at each of them and they winked in return, each wishing him good luck.

His notes? He reached into the inside pocket of his jacket and felt the folded sheets of paper and transferred them to his left side pocket where he could get at them more easily. With everybody watching every move it was awkward to do all that transferring and still hang on to the Julius Emspak brief under his arm.

Following behind the U.S. marshall he recalled the advice of Benno Schneider, his acting teacher in New York City who had since journeyed out to Hollywood to work as a coach for one of the motion picture studios. That short intense man with the foreign accent, holding his hands out in front of him, palms up, fingers cupped together, had preached to him about double attention:

"At all times on stage you must be the actor who is *acting* out your role in the play — and at the same time you must be the actor who is *watching* how the actor acts out the role in the play. With one self you portray the character and with the other self you constantly check the appearance of the body movements of the actor, his voice, his control of the emotion, his expenditure of energy — "

Walking down the aisle now, he exercised *double attention*, as a witness going up there to testify and at the same time as Danny Newman checking the witness from the outside to make sure he looked like someone who intended to make a serious constitutional challenge against the Committee.

He walked straight and tall, head high, chin in, chest out, shoulders relaxed, smiling just a little to appear like a nice person, not a wiseacre. He touched the middle button of his dark brown single-breasted jacket — it was buttoned. A quick downward glance reassured him that his quiet tie was tucked inside the jacket.

And then he thought: where is my lawyer? Where's Ralph Kaufman? Why hasn't he appeared yet?

For a frightening moment he lost control. Faces on both sides of the aisle blurred into a mass of unrecognizable features about to sweep over him and drown him.

He tripped and the U.S. marshall dropped back to take his arm and steady him. Danny stood there, his face sweating as he searched the audience for his lawyer.

The U.S. marshall gently nudged his elbow, to get him to move towards the Committee waiting up there for him.

"My lawyer," Danny hoarsely whispered and then tried to make it a joke. "I lost my lawyer. He got drowned in the crowd."

He searched frantically for Ralph's bald head and then saw that eagle face looking back to him. Ralph was waiting up front. In all the excitement Danny had forgotten that Ralph was already down there in the first row with Ed Murphy. There was Ralph, a slight figure with his imperious eagle face, smiling encouragement. They met at the gateway through the railing in front of the spectators, and Ralph gently patted Danny's back.

Flash bulbs exploded on all sides of them as photographers climbed on chairs or crouched down to shoot upward angle shots.

Danny, blinded by the glare, involuntarily winced as he stepped into the bright fire from rows of spotlights strung high up in the front corner of the courtroom.

While the two men stood still in front of the witness table the newsreel and television cameramen moved in their equipment for close-ups. Danny tried to look like the quiet and serious and very purposeful young man, with his shell-rimmed glasses and his blondish red hair which, he knew, made him look years younger than his actual age of forty-one. He wondered if any newspaper readers with preconceived antagonistic notions about the appearance of union organizers would be disarmed by his presenting an appearance different from what they expected. He consciously tried to keep a touch of a friendly smile on his face while he waited for the oath to be administered.

The photographs taken of him standing there would look good. But he was convinced that most of the newspapers wanted photos more exciting than any taken thus far. They preferred a photograph of him being forcibly conducted out of the courtroom by the U.S. marshall's assistants. Or a photograph of him with his mouth wide open, his arms wildly extended, caught in the act of flailing them in the air to the accompaniment of some denunciation against the Committee. Or a snapshot of his face reflecting great fear or anger or some such desperately strong emotion which would make it worthy of a quote from one of the members of the Committee, terming him a "Fifth Amendment Commie."

No matter what happened he was determined that at all times there would be only one picture they would be able to take of him while he was up there in the witness chair, and that would be a photograph of a very serious, respectable, self-contained, earnest person who was doing his best to avoid loud argument and who was doing his best to explain most respectfully why, on highly principled grounds, he would not answer any of the Committee's questions.

"Do you solemnly swear that the testimony you are about to give will be the truth, the whole truth, nothing but the truth, so help you, God?"

"I do, sir."

Trying to give a good impression, he made his reply crisp,

serious, direct.

There was the flash of photo bulbs exploding as several photographers caught him in the act of affirming the oath and then Ralph Kaufman touched his arm, signaling that now it was all right to sit down. Sitting, Danny carefully placed the Julius Emspak brief on the table in front of him and slipped the notes out of his side pocket and put them down on the table, without as yet unfolding the yellow sheets of paper. Meanwhile, he kept his eyes fixed on the Committee's legal counsel, Denilworth, who was reading over some papers he had taken from his assistant.

Denilworth looked up and smiled that same toothy, mirthless, professional smile Danny had seen him use with previous witnesses.

"What," Denilworth asked, very politely, "is your name, please, sir?"

"Daniel Newman. — May I ask that if these gentlemen" — a finger pointed at the photographers on his right — "want to take pictures, they take all they want right now and during my testimony I not be bothered by that?"

Although he addressed his request to Denilworth, it was Holling who answered. "Your request is granted." Danny looked up at the thin face above him while the Congressman continued. "The press will take its pictures and then desist from taking any during the testimony."

One of the photographers asked Danny to repeat the peremptory gesture he had unconsciously made when he asked that the photographers be told to take their pictures and then not bother him during his testimony. Danny readily smiled for the photographer while he repeated the gesture as best as he could remember it. Flash bulbs exploded while he held on to that half-serious smile and was careful about how he moved his hands or any part of his body which showed above the table.

There were just so many pictures the photographers could take of that one particular pose, and then they backed away, some kneeling and some sitting down on their haunches. Danny noticed that most of them were keeping their equipment ready to jump into action if there was some unexpected development like that which had resulted in Congressman Holling ejecting Herb Kepler.

The overhead batteries of lights were turned off, and Danny no longer felt like he was staring into a row of blinding footlights on a theatre stage. Denilworth smiled at him. Danny smiled back. It was an exchange of professional courtesy. Two very proper swordsmen, thought Danny, delicately touching the tips of their swords together before slashing away at one another in a to-the-death duel.

He remembered what Ralph Kaufman had told him about the Committee's legal counsel: "You'll find Denilworth is not as bad as the Congressmen on the Committee. True, he'll try to hang you just as they will, but he'll perform the operation with full attention to all the proper niceties prescribed by polite society. When he rides after the fox he gives the fox every chance it is entitled to receive from a proper gentleman of sporting blood. He always figures he'll get the fox eventually even if it escapes once or twice, or even more often than that."

"Are you accompanied by counsel, Mr. Newman?"

"Yes, sir, I am."

While Ralph Kaufman identified himself for the record, Danny wondered if Denilworth guessed that Ralph's presence meant they were preparing an unusual challenge. He noticed the friendly way Denilworth nodded to his lawyer, a friendly acknowledgment of a powerful opponent. Then the Committee's legal counsel quickly glanced down at his papers and back up again at the witness.

Having already given his name to identify himself for the record, Danny knew this next question would be the one he would challenge.

He waited — his heart pounding — and kept up the faint smile, matching the remains of a smile which flickered over Denilworth's florid features.

Denilworth leaned toward him.

The question was coming, and so far as Danny was concerned, this was to be *the* question.

Denilworth's eyes gleamed with professional friendliness as he delivered the question so easily that Danny was certain that the Committee's legal counsel was not prepared for what was to come.

"When and where were you born, Mr. Newman?"

Denilworth cocked his head to one side, his mouth open

ready to swallow the reply. Danny took a deep breath to steady himself and reminded himself to be polite so the Committee could not use anything about his voice or his manner as the excuse to throw him out of the courtroom before he got his arguments into the record for the constitutional test.

He spoke slowly and clearly, trying to select the right words to make sure his response properly prepared the way for the test and that he spoke loud enough to be heard all the way back to the rear of the courtroom. He aimed his precise reply above the round fat face of Denilworth, speaking directly to the chairman sitting up there on the judge's bench, Congressman Holling.

Politely, he again cautioned himself.

"Before I reply to that question, sir, I respectfully — with the *utmost* respect — ask this committee of Congress to advise me — ." He stopped and took a deep breath to clear the shakiness out of his voice. And then he came out with it, strong and definite:

"What — is the nature — of this inquiry?"

"You will answer the question asked," Holling snapped right back.

Danny recognized it as a warning that the chairman wanted him to know that the Committee was not going to tolerate any monkey business from the witness.

"With reference to your name and address," added Holling.

Firmly — to let the Congressman know he was not backing off, but politely and quietly, Danny corrected Holling.

"I was not asked about my residence."

"Whatever question was asked!" snapped the Congressman.

Denilworth amiably clarified the situation.

"My question was: *when and where was the witness born?"*

Congressman Holling glared down from the judge's elevated position.

"The witness will answer the question!"

Danny saw Denilworth sink back into his seat. The legal counsel might have already guessed what was coming — the collapsed, almost uninterested look on his face and the relaxed posture of his body reminded Danny of a baseball pitcher standing on the mound, watching the last batter lazily trotting around the bases after he had hit the ball thrown by the pitcher way out over the left field fence for a home run — it was an attitude of resigned helplessness, as though he knew he had pitched the ball across the plate with his question and could do nothing about what happened after he pitched it.

"The witness will answer the question!" Holling again insisted with increasing exasperation.

"With the utmost respect, sir — " Danny addressed the angry face above him, keeping his voice as quiet and calm as he could to prevent a premature explosion which might get him tossed out. "I repeat again, sir — I would like to know the nature of this inquiry, so I may know whether or not this question lies within the purview, or context, of the power of this Committee."

Holling's face flushed a deeper red.

"The witness will answer the question!" he commanded between clenched teeth.

Turning away from that angry face, Danny went through the motions of conferring with his attorney — a breathing space to gather himself together for the big showdown. He hid his nervousness with a touch of bravado, whispering into the lawyer's ear, "Ralph, this is where I'm going to tell this bastard to go fuck himself." He turned his head around so the lawyer could whisper a reply into his ear.

"Good luck," Ralph whispered.

Still trying to slow down the action so he would have a calmer situation confronting him when he turned to Congressman Holling, Danny nodded his head several times as though he was weighing the sage advice his lawyer was whispering into his ear. Then he turned around and faced the Committee.

Denilworth was putting away his papers as if he knew there would be no more questions required of him for this witness. Danny saw two heads above him now. Congressman Sackville joined Congressman Holling in the front lines, both Congressmen leaning forward, alert and ready to tangle with the witness.

In the excitement of the immediate situation Danny forgot all the problems relating to Helen. Out of the corner of his eye he took split second notice of the photographers getting their cameras ready for the blow-up which seemed sure to come, while reporters rapidly scribbled. Behind him in the crowded courtroom there was absolute silence. He felt that he had good control of the situation.

The first thing to do, he reminded himself, was to make it unmistakably clear to the Committee — get it into the record that he was *not* citing the Fifth Amendment privilege, the refusal to answer because of fear of self-incrimination. It was necessary to establish at the very start that this was to be a head-on challenge against the Committee's right to *exist* under the Constitution of the United States.

"Sir," he began, speaking over the top of the head of Denilworth directly to the two Congressmen. He fumbled awkwardly, trying to find the best words to express exactly what he wanted to say. "With the utmost respect, I would like to state at the very outset — I would like to make it clear — that one of my reasons for not answering your question is *NOT* the Fifth Amendment privilege. — At the same time, I would also like to make it clear, sir, that I believe that those who have cited the Fifth Amendment privilege are making their contribution toward the defense of our United States Constitution — "

"Mr. Witness!" Congressman Holling sharply interrupted, and Danny thought the Congressman seemed to be disconcerted by the statement that the witness did not intend to cite the Fifth Amendment privilege. There was a moment of hesitation and then the Congressman slapped the flat of his hand down on top of the bench. "There is only one question before you! And you are not going to make a speech!"

"Sir," Danny quickly responded, in the most soothing and apologetic tone of voice he could produce, trying to placate the irritated man and make it difficult to put an end to his testimony before he could state the constitutional basis for his challenge. "I am not intending to make a speech."

It was hard for Holling to continue to speak so angrily to the witness in front of all the people in the courtroom, especially with the witness groveling before him to demonstrate his respect for the Congressman's authority as chairman of the Committee.

"If you will testify," Holling tautly responded, checking his temper and sounding quite reasonable, "we will give you an opportunity to explain any answer you want to make."

But Danny knew that if he answered even only one question — how desperately Holling wanted him to answer it! — the basic character of his challenge, that the Committee itself was unconstitutional and *did not have the right to ask anyone any questions*, would be destroyed. In response to the first question he had to insist, politely but firmly, at this crucial point that he was not going to answer that question or *any other* question. Then the Committee would be compelled to let him state for the record his reasons for refusing to answer.

"Sir, I am going to give you the reasons why I am declining to answer this question, *and why I am declining to answer any of your questions.* The reasons are as follows — " But then he remembered that he hadn't put into the record the statement about no espionage, sabotage or spying. Now was the time to do it — quickly! "Let me say before I begin, to keep the record clear I would like to state I have never engaged in any espionage or sabotage or spying activities — "

Whack!

Congressman Holling smashed down his wooden gavel. Shaking his head, he seemed so furious he could hardly speak.

"The answer of the witness," he finally shrilled, "will be stricken from the record as not responsive."

Before the Congressman could follow this up with an order to the U.S. marshall's assistants to conduct the witness out of the courtroom, Danny started to speak quickly in a hushed placating tone, but with an intense energy to capture the attention of the audience and to prevent Holling from breaking in. He spoke softly, trying to avoid anything which could be construed as provocation, keeping his voice down so he could not be accused of making an inflammatory speech, as he explained why he would not answer any questions — explaining factually and quietly and respectfully, just hallowed all over with sincerity and humbleness in the presence of this august and oh-so-important congressional body.

"The first reason why I refuse to answer your question, sir, is that the resolution under which this Committee functions is unconstitutional, because it violates the First Amendment to the Constitution under which citizens are guaranteed freedom of speech, freedom of thought, freedom of association." — Still talking rapidly he picked up his notes and held them in his hand. "This Committee, by its form of inquiry, its questions concerning thoughts and beliefs and associations, is establishing a category of thoughts which are considered to be disapproved thoughts, *verboten* thoughts, and by establishing this category of disapproved or *verboten* thoughts is interfering with the right of freedom of speech, is interfering with the right to express such *verboten* thoughts in spoken words, or in written words — interference with freedom of the press — and, also, since thoughts become identified with people who possess those thoughts, this Committee is interfering with the right of freedom of association."

His notes were still gripped in his left hand, but he was too excited now even to unfold the yellow sheets of paper. Although his words had not been the best, he had the good feeling inside that he was getting across the heart of the idea.

"The second reason why I refuse to answer your questions, gentlemen — "

Still talking fast, he laid aside the notes and picked up the printed legal brief which had been submitted to the United States Supreme Court in the case of Julius Emspak. There was a torn piece of paper marking the place he wanted in the book, and he flipped open the brief to this page — on which was printed the enabling resolution passed by the House of Representatives establishing this Committee on Un-American Activities.

" — and again I assure you I am speaking only after great consideration."

He saw that Congressman Holling wanted to interrupt — the angry man was rocking the upper part of his body back and forth, impatiently seeking an opening to bust in. Danny knew he had the full legal right to give his reasons for not answering the Committee's question, but he wondered how soon the Congressman would angrily lower the boom on him. Legal or not legal, it didn't look like Holling was going to let him go on much longer, not the way the red-faced Congressman was shaking his head up there. Danny talked as fast as he could, piling his words on top of one another with no space between, no gap where the Congressman could pry his way in and block him from going on.

"I am taking this position here only because I feel it is for the good of our country." He kept the words flowing until he found what he was looking for in the brief. "The second reason is that the resolution under which this Committee functions is unconstitutional because it is so vague that no person can ascertain the boundaries of the Committee's powers, and I am speaking particularly in reference to the words 'un-American' and 'subversive' which are included in this enabling resolution — "

Mouth open, trembling with the anxiety to rush on with his thoughts, Danny hesitated, faltering, as he glanced down at the resolution and hurriedly scanned down the page to find the particular paragraph which contained the two vague words — the paragraph he wanted to read into the record.

"May I pose this observation?"

With a sinking sensation in his stomach, Danny looked up at Congressman Sackville. That moment of hesitation had given the cunning southern gentleman with the black string tie the opportunity to break in. Respectfully looking up from the brief, too busy to berate himself for permitting an opening for this interruption, Danny kept his eyes fixed on Sackville, alert for a clever trap, like the trap Sackville had tried to weave around Herb Kepler. He still held the brief in his hands.

"In the beginning," drawled Sackville in his softly pretentious voice, "you asked the Committee the purpose of this inquiry —"

"That is correct, sir."

"It appears you have considerable knowledge concerning the purpose, and I wonder why you asked the question since you are so well equipped there with all the information you have." It was a masterpiece of delicate sarcasm.

Sackville waited for an explanation. Thinking quickly, Danny was sure he had been thrown a curved ball even though he didn't have time to figure out all the barbed hooks in it. He framed his reply cautiously, thinking while he was talking, feeling his way.

"I asked the question, sir — to find out — if this Committee — was trying to carry out the purpose designated by Congress — vague and undefined as it was — " He stopped but knew that his answer was unclear. Should he clarify it?

He didn't get the chance, Congressman Holling could contain himself no longer. "Just a minute. Let's have no more of this." He glared down at Danny and demanded, "Are you going to answer the question or not?"

"I would like to give the reasons why I will not answer the questions."

"I understand you are *not* invoking the Fifth Amendment."

"That is true."

"The witness is dismissed."

The abrupt dismissal shocked Danny. The Congressman rapped his gavel and summarily motioned to the U.S. marshall to conduct the witness from the stand. Danny became aware of flash bulbs exploding all around him as the press photographers jumped into action. The batteries of overhead lights glared into his eyes again as newsreel and television cameramen started their equipment operating. He remained seated, stunned by the speed with which he had been cut off and reluctant to leave the witness chair before he had given more reasons for refusing to answer the Committee's question. He did not want to create a disturbance which would contradict the quiet and respectful impression he wanted to convey, but he began to argue in a subdued way for the right to give the rest of his reasons for refusing to answer the question.

"Sir," he pleaded with Holling, "I just want to — "

A sharp prod into his right shoulder stopped him. He looked up. There was the U.S. marshall standing over him. He threw an appealing look at the marshall to let him know he was not going to resist but wanted only a few seconds longer to straighten out this misunderstanding. The marshall's finger tips pressed into his shoulder. Despite the mounting excitement around him, Danny was determined not to give the photographers a shot of him getting hauled out of the courtroom by the marshall and his assistants, or a shot of him storming out of the courtroom and shouting back over his shoulder at the Committee. In that short moment he had to decide what to do and concluded it would not fit in with the rest of his characterization as a very respectful and polite witness if he got into a loud argument with the members of the Committee. He turned to Ralph Kaufman, the look on his face appealing for help.

Ralph immediately rose to his feet. "The witness," he politely explained to the Committee, "had not concluded his answer to your question."

But Congressman Holling was fuming. "The witness is dismissed. He says he is not invoking the Fifth Amendment."

"The witness has the right to indicate the reasons — "

Danny knew that Ralph was risking a contempt citation for himself by arguing this way with the chairman of the subcommittee. As the rules stood — there was a movement under way in Congress to modify them because they were so generally considered to be unfair — his attorney did not have the right to address the Committee. All he can legally do is advise the witness as to the possible consequences if he answered one way or the other when the witness seeks his advice on some specific question.

"You understand the rules as counsel," warned Holling.

"These are only the reasons," Ralph earnestly pleased. "He should be entitled to give the reasons, to tell you why he is declining — "

Holling rapped his gavel. "I warned you now," he threatened.

"Very well," said Ralph, "there is nothing more I can do." The resignation in the lawyer's usually self-assured voice surprised Danny. But Ralph made one more try as he prepared to leave. "The witness," he told Holling, "will submit to you in writing the reasons why he is refusing — "

But Holling sharply interrupted. "The witness is dismissed, counsel."

At this point Ralph nodded to Danny to leave. Danny quietly rose to his feet, still determined that the photographers would not get one of those wild shots they wanted. Any picture they took of him at that time was going to show him self-possessed and serious and sincere and respectful and completely under control *on the surface* — no matter how great the turmoil going on inside him. He gave a slight smile to the U.S. marshall, thanking him for his cooperation. The marshall gave the faint touch of a smile in return, thanking Danny for thanking him. They started up the aisle, side by side, walking toward the rear of the courtroom.

Ralph Kaufman stopped off at his place in the first row. The photographers gave up after following Danny part way up the aisle, returning to their posts in the front of the courtroom. There was nothing dramatic in his orderly retreat to his seat in the rear left-hand corner of the courtroom where he had left his topcoat. The marshall dropped behind. When Danny sat down he could feel that the atmosphere around was more friendly than when he had gone up to testify. The man nearest him on the bench, the same man who had sidled away before, sat close to him, and he and others on the bench made no effort to shift away again when Danny returned.

But the fear was still there. None of the men on the bench looked at him when he returned to his seat, although he knew they were very much aware of him, just as he was aware of them.

Bill Kosciusko was called to the witness chair, joined there by Ed Murphy. A terrific feeling of exhilaration came over Danny. For the time being he didn't want to think about the problem of Helen and the kids and the consequences which might flow from his defiance of the Committee. He was part of the group of union organizers who were fighting back, and they were doing a good job of exposing the Committee so the people could see the iron heel behind the false face of "legality." His friend was up there in the witness chair, picking up the ball where he had left off — and knowing Bill's courage, Danny was confident his friend would do well.

At the very outset Bill Kosciusko launched into a sharp clash with Congressman Holling by calling Sidney Raven, "A fink and a liar!" Raven had testified that Bill attended a communist meeting at a time when — Bill proved — he was already serving in the army in World War II and was miles away from where the meeting was supposedly held. Denilworth asked Bill if he had attended a communist meeting at any other time than the time named by Raven. Bill slammed right back, saying that he refused to permit a Committee to judge him and his past when a member of that Committee was the co-author of an Immigration Act which used measuring sticks similar to those used by German Nazis he had fought against in World War II, and he said he was invoking the protection afforded him by the First and Fifth Amendments to refuse to answer Denilworth's question, telling the Committee he thought it was his duty to defend the freedoms guaranteed in the Constitution because he had fought for this privilege in combat, up in the front lines where the fighting was the toughest, telling the Committee that he had bled for this privilege and that every morning in combat he died a thousand deaths. Danny's spine tingled the way Bill said it. And Bill told the Committee he was ready to lay his life on the line again to protect these privileges for which he had already fought in combat.

But Congressman Sackville must have thought Bill was spreading it on too thick about his combat record. He asked Bill — somewhat sarcastically — if he had really seen so much combat service, and Bill reeled off his combat record, telling how he had been in active combat as an infantryman, fighting through northern France and on into Belgium during the desperate Battle of the Bulge, and on into Germany, fighting through the Nazi Siegfried line, and he told — Danny's spine tingled again — how he was wounded — "My blood poured out on top of a concrete bunker in the Siegfried line" — and he told how he still went on, fighting alongside his comrades, fighting on into the heart of Nazi Germany — " doing my share to defeat those lousy Nazis who did what this pro-fascist Committee is trying to do now!"

As soon as he could break in, Sackville quickly changed the subject by asking Bill for a definition of a stoolpigeon, referring back to Bill's vehement characterization of Sidney Raven as "a lousy stoolpigeon," and Bill told him a stoolpigeon "is a fink, a trained seal who will say anything anybody tells him to say, particularly for money" — Sackville tried to correct him, saying that a stoolpigeon is a man who betrays a confidence by giving truthful information, particularly about the person who calls him a stoolpigeon, and Bill told Sackville that this might be Sackville's definition of a stoolpigeon but that his own definition of a stoolpigeon "is a rat who would do anything for money, even sell his soul for the green bucks — "

Holling abruptly interrupted and asked Bill if he was a communist while he was in the army, and Bill told him that he refused "to let a bunch of small-minded men here, for a few green bucks, destroy the Constitution of the United States for which I fought and bled" — and then he invoked the Fifth Amendment "for which our forefathers fought and bled."

"The witness is excused," said Holling, obviously glad to get rid of that slightly built man who tossed back a hand grenade every time a question was thrown at him.

Next the Committee summoned to the witness chair one of the two rank-and-filers from Herb Kepler's district, and he very quickly revealed that he was not as adept as Herb had been in handling himself before the Committee. He invoked the Fifth Amendment privilege to refuse to answer when he was asked whether or not he had ever been a member of the Communist Party, and then he awkwardly interjected that he wanted the record to show he is not a member of the Communist Party, as Herb had done; but then, unlike Herb, he didn't know how to handle the Committee when they zeroed in on him. Danny felt sorry for the poor guy as he weakly repeated, "Fifth Amendment," completely on the defensive, not knowing how to turn the attack back on the Committee, as he was asked: *"Were you a member of the Communist Party yesterday?"* — *"When did you resign?"* — *"When you came into the hearing room this morning were you a member of the Communist Party?"* — And the Committee worked him over until they tired of the sport, making up for the unpleasant resistance they had received from the three previous witnesses; and then they excused him — he was visibly relieved to escape from their clutches, wiping the sweat from his brow with his crumpled handkerchief as he retreated up the aisle back to his seat.

Holling, Sackville and Denilworth held a quick conference, and then Holling rapped his gavel to quiet the courtroom and announced a ten minute recess.

Danny glanced at his wrist watch. Exactly ten o'clock.

A recess? This early in the morning? It must mean that

the Committee is preparing for the grand finale with Jean Dampier taking the stand. The preliminary acts were out of the way — the other rank-and-filer from Herb's district would probably be skipped to make room for the star, Jean Dampier, to appear.

Spectators streamed out of the courtroom to grab a quick smoke in the corridor and stretch their legs. Danny joined the exodus, taking his topcoat with him.

He wondered if he should telephone Helen to tell her what had happened before she read about it in the newspapers. He could use the pay phone in the lobby on the first floor.

Someone patted him on the back. It was Mason, the young reporter who knew Helen. Mason smiled in a friendly way, without saying anything, and then he pushed on through the moving crowd. Danny saw the notes in the reporter's hand and guessed that Mason was going to phone in the story of the morning's hearings, the story which would appear in the Buffalo newspapers.

Following the reporter out into the crowded corridor, Danny wondered how badly Helen would react to the news story — if she had not already fled to her sister's place in Florida, taking Ruth and Linda with her.

Chapter 26

Ray Foster and Elsie and Steve Brooks and a group of their friends, local people whom Danny didn't know, gathered around him in the noisy corridor, shaking his hand, patting him on the back, congratulating him. He saw Bill Kosciusko come out of the courtroom and he waved to Bill to come over and join him — they gripped hands.

"You did a good job, Bill."

"So did you."

"Thanks — I really enjoyed the way you told off Sackville."

"When you first got started," said Bill, "I didn't know where you were heading — you were too polite to them, too quiet, not your usual self."

"Did you think I'd turned 'pigeon'?"

"No, I knew right away you were trying something different."

The rest of the group gathered around Bill and shook his hand and congratulated him. Danny, standing on the edge of the group, saw a woman coming toward him. She reached out and embraced him — he was so surprised he didn't know what to do. She was wearing a fur wrap which tickled his chin; her highly scented perfume engulfed him; she kissed him on the cheek, and he wondered if she had smeared her lipstick on him.

"At last," she breathed into his ear, "at last someone really told them." Her big bosoms pressed against him. He was very embarrassed. She let him go.

"Thank you," he stammered, his cheeks getting hot as he noticed people nearby watching them, "thank you — "

The woman — stylishly dressed, she seemed to be in her late forties — took his hand and squeezed it. Her voice sounded smooth and husky, and her diction was perfect, like a character in a drawing room comedy. "You were just wonderful," she said, and then she took Bill's hand and kissed him on the cheek. "You were *both* wonderful," she said. Then the attention she was getting from the people nearby must have made her feel self-conscious — she adjusted her fur wrap, smiled goodbye to the two union organizers, turned and slipped back into the courtroom.

When Ralph Kaufman and Ed Murphy joined the two organizers a few moments later Danny apologized. "They stopped me before I got a chance to say very much — I thought of arguing with them, but I was afraid they might call an argumentative attitude 'contemptuous' and that way destroy any cleancut constitutional test we might be able to make with what I did say before they stopped me."

"You did fine, Danny" — Ralph patted his arm — "and you did right not to argue with them."

"Did I get enough into the record to make a decent test case on the constitutionality question — if they cite me for contempt?"

"I think so," said Ralph, and then interrupted himself to light his pipe before adding, "you got in the main point about the enabling resolution itself being unconstitutional."

Ed Murphy shook Danny's hand, congratulating him, while at the same time reminding him about the problem he was going to have later. "I'm sure if Helen were here and saw the restrained and intelligent fashion in which you conducted yourself she would be proud of you."

"Thanks."

But Danny knew that Helen's background and her fear of the disapproval of that group which included her mother and her brother Bob would prevent her from seeing his performance in the same light that Murphy saw it.

He wondered if he should hurry down to the main floor and call Helen on the pay phone down there. Would it help to tell her right away? Or would that only aggravate the situation? He only half-heard the conversation of the others — talking about Jean Dampier and what he might be expected to say when he went up to the witness chair to testify after the intermission. Wouldn't it be smarter to leave Helen alone until he got back to Buffalo and could talk to her in person? Of course, he assumed she would still be in Buffalo when he got home —

A short man wearing thick-lensed glasses took Danny by the arm and drew him and Ralph and Ed aside. Danny recognized him as a lawyer who had represented some of the earlier "unfriendly" witnesses. The newcomer kept his voice hushed so he would not be heard by any of the people milling around nearby in the crowded corridor.

"I think you're in the clear," he said.

"What do you mean?" Danny was puzzled.

"The chairman got so flustered he forgot to *direct* you to answer the question, and unless he specifically *directs* you to answer the question after you've refused to answer it — you can't be cited for contempt for refusing to answer it."

Danny looked to Ralph.

"*Technically*, that's correct," said Ralph.

The short bespectacled attorney continued. "If I were you," he hurriedly explained, keeping his voice down to a conspiratorial hush, "I'd get out of here right now — before they can call you back to correct their oversight by putting you up on the witness stand again."

Danny again looked to Ralph while he wondered if it would be acting like a coward if he tried to duck a citation for contempt after all the preparation for a constitutional test. Ralph calmly puffed his pipe, thinking it over before replying.

"I don't think it'll make much difference. If they want to cite you for contempt, they can always call you back at some later date and direct you to answer the question, or much easier and done every day with these congressional committees even though it's not exactly legal, he'll simply tell the hearing stenographer to change the record so it shows that he *did* direct you to answer the question."

The bespectacled attorney still insisted that it would be best for Danny to disappear so he couldn't be summoned back to the witness chair. "Out of sight — out of mind," he stubbornly argued. "Why stick around to remind them?"

Danny hesitated. "I don't know," he said, not wanting to appear disloyal to his own lawyers.

Ralph Kaufman solved the dilemma. "There'd be nothing lost if you disappeared, Danny. Anyway, you didn't get much sleep last night. Why don't you go up to Ed's room at the hotel and rest a while? We'll meet you for lunch."

"I *am* tired."

"Just take an easy stroll down the corridor," suggested the lawyer who had urged him to leave. "There's a stairway just beyond the elevator. If anybody asks where you're going — tell them you're going to the men's room on the third floor because it's crowded on this floor. When you get down to the third floor keep on going down the stairs to the main floor and out of the building. No one will notice."

Ed Murphy, without comment, slipped his room key to Danny who shoved it into his side pocket while he glanced around. No one in the smoky corridor was paying any attention to their little group.

"Will you call George Hernandez in Schenectady" — Ralph removed the pipe from his mouth — "and tell him what happened so far this morning? I'm sure he'd like to know."

Danny promised he would call from Ed Murphy's room, and he wondered if he should phone Helen after he spoke to George.

Nodding goodbye to the three lawyers, careful not to give any indication that he was not coming back, Danny leisurely strolled toward the far end of the long corridor, weaving his way between the small groups congregated outside the courtroom.

No one seemed to be paying any attention to him as he idly wandered past the elevator entrance and aimlessly started walking down the stone staircase to the floor below. When he reached the third floor landing he kept going on down to the second floor, then down to the first floor and through the main lobby out onto the stone steps in front of the courthouse and then down the steps to the sidewalk.

The traffic signal was green when he arrived at the corner, and he filtered himself into the middle of the small jam of pedestrians crossing the street.

He silently berated himself. *"Coward! You want the dignity that goes with standing by your principles, no matter what the cost. And the next minute you're running to hide from your own bravery."*

Safe inside Ed Murphy's hotel room, after hanging the Do Not Disturb sign on the outer doorknob and locking the door with the key on the inside, Danny leaned back against the door.

How different everything had become. He already had the feeling that he was a wanted man, marked, different from the ordinary free citizen; the sword of Damocles which hung over the head of Julius Emspak was hanging by a slim thread over his head now — the same powerful forces who had been trying to put Julius behind bars would be after him now. He had made himself a target and now they could draw a bead on him to try to shoot him down.

Haunting visions of a lonely prison cell and separation from Helen and the kids, maybe forever if their marriage broke up, engulfed him again. The sweat wet his shirt under his arms, and the palms of his hands felt sticky and damp. Even though the room seemed so warm that it was uncomfortable when he entered it, he now shivered from the cold. Trying to pull himself together, he walked across the room and sat down on the edge of the bed. The bright sunshine streaming in through the windows depressed him, its sharpness hurting his eyes.

Maybe sleep would make him feel better. He hadn't had much sleep. But even though he was shivering the room seemed too warm and stuffy. He opened both windows a few inches at the bottom and drew down the green shades. Both beds were still mussed up — Murphy had slept in one of them, and he himself had used the other, the bed nearest the wall, when he came back there to telephone Helen. *Was that only last night?*

His shoes felt too tight. He unlaced them and kicked them across the room. Then he remembered he had promised Ralph Kaufman he would call George Hernandez in Schenectady. The switchboard operator took the number. About a minute later Danny heard Lisa Michaels talking to the operator, and then she called George Hernandez to the phone.

"Hi, George."

"What's up?"

Danny quickly summarized what had happened that morning over in the courtroom.

"How you feeling?" George asked.

"Fine," he lied. "It wasn't too terrible."

"Yeah?"

"It could have been worse."

"You all right?"

"Oh, sure."

"You sound worried."

"I'm just tired."

A pause. "You're all through there, aren't you?"

"I think so — I hope so — "

"Good. You'll be able to cover the district executive board meeting tonight and the district meeting tomorrow — in Elmira."

"No, George!" His howl of protest seemed loud even to himself.

"Why not?"

Danny knew George was laughing to minimize the violent protest he had heard.

"I've got to get back to Buffalo right away — "

"What for?"

George was still laughing in that aggravating way he had of making something you thought very important seem to be so completely inconsequential that you were put into the position of appearing to be very unreasonable if you insisted on having your way. Too angry to talk sensibly, Danny loudly cursed his boss. But George Hernandez was smart enough to keep on laughing while he explained.

"Somebody has to be at that executive board meeting tonight, Danny — "

"Not me."

"And somebody has to cover the district council meeting tomorrow — "

"Not me."

"To report what happened at this hearing and what's happening here in Schenectady. You know yourself some of the delegates are bound to ask questions —"

"To hell with them."

"About what's happening at this eastern end of the state, especially a few bastards who'll be there trying to whip up a storm against the union from within." George Hernandez was no longer laughing. "I'd go myself, Danny, but I have to stay here in Schenectady to handle the reaction to the job the local newspapers will be doing on us tonight and tomorrow with the comparison between Dampier's testimony and the testimony of you guys."

He paused, and Danny was able to break in. "Who was supposed to go there if I didn't get through testifying today?"

"Well, Danny" — George's smoothness infuriated Danny — "Julius Emspak was going to fill in for us if we needed him."

"We *need* him!"

"But it ain't right to ask him to handle our problems in our district when one of us can make it now, is it?"

"You bastard!"

"After all it is *our* district — "

"Go to hell!"

"And we know the delegates better than anyone from outside our district could possible know them. We know who's all right, and we know who to watch out for. We can do a better job by handling the situation ourselves. Ain't that right?"

He stopped for an answer and Danny swore at him, telling him to go fuck himself. What would Helen think of him if he put a meeting of the union's district council ahead of coming right home to talk things over with her? Her major complaint was that he thought more of the union than he did of her.

"Fuck it, George! Fuck it! And fuck you too! The whole damn bunch. You can all go fuck yourself!"

"Okay. — Okay. — Okay. — If that's the way you feel about it. — Okay — "

George sounded as if he was very hurt, and although Danny knew George well enough to know this was only an act for his benefit — it still affected him, as George Hernandez must have known from past experience it would. George continued, very righteously.

"Okay — if you don't want to go, Danny, it's up to you. No one can make you go if you don't want to go. But after all, there is such a thing as a sense of responsibility — a sense of political responsibility — to the people you represent, to the working people of this union and to the working people generally, and to all progressive peoples — "

"I want to get home, George!" Danny burst out, almost shouting. "I've got tremendous problems waiting there for me! Which I've got to solve right away!"

"With Helen?"

"Who else?"

"They'll still be there if you get home tomorrow night instead of tonight, won't they?"

"Fuck you, you sonofabitch! Fuck you!"

George laughed it off, coming right back, "How about it?"

"You heard me. Go fuck yourself, you dirty bastard."

But George only laughed louder. "How about it?"

Danny knew George was right. Getting angry and swearing at him was primarily a reaction to what happened at the hearing in the courthouse. And George can't go away from the situation in Schenectady. And he — Danny — *does* have a firsthand knowledge of the background of most of the delegates who will be at the district council meeting.

"How about me covering *only* the executive board meeting tonight?" he suggested. "Then I can grab a train or plane back to Buffalo late tonight or first thing in the morning — "

"Danny," George interrupted — he had Danny pinned down now — "if you're going to be there for the executive board meeting tonight, you might as well stay on for the full council meeting tomorrow." He talked fast to keep Danny from breaking in. "That's when all the delegates will be involved and that's more important than the executive board meeting tonight."

"Why? If nothing happens at the executive board meeting tonight, why is there any more likelihood that something will happen at the full council meeting the next day?"

"Because if we're going to have any trouble at all — we'll have it at the full council meeting. No one is going to try anything at the executive board meeting where they know we have a clear majority — they don't want to tip us off on what they're planning to pull the next day at the council meeting, not if they're seriously planning to pull anything — "

"What about the *other* organizers?" Danny weakly objected, knowing there was some truth in George's explanation, even though he was probably exaggerating the situation. "Why can't one of *them* handle it? They're going to be there, aren't they?"

"But you can do a better job, Danny —"

"Cut the shit!"

"How about it, Danny?" George wheedled. "Remember, you and me, we're officially the International Representatives in our district. We're supposed to be in charge of the field organizers. It's our responsibility for at least one of us to be at these meetings, isn't it?"

"Well" — Danny wavered.

After all, there was no use hurrying back to Buffalo. No happy welcome waiting there. Helen might have already left with the kids, on a train or a plane to Florida.

"What's the best way to get from here to Elmira?"

The phone conversation with George Hernandez done, Danny swung his stockinged feet up and stretched out on top of the bed. The rumpled blankets and sheets under his back felt very uncomfortable. He forced himself to get up and straighten them out, and then laid down again and covered himself with one of the blankets.

He realized he was still wearing all his clothes, including his jacket and his tie and his trousers.

Should he get up?

His clothes were sure to get all wrinkled if he slept in them.

Morosely staring up at the ceiling, too tired and disgusted with himself and life in general to care about such an inconsequential thing as his clothes, he tried not to think about Helen and the possibility that their marriage was going to break up. The drawn shades were flapping, letting in sudden stabs of bright sunlight, each stab of light shooting across the shaded room, and then the room darkened again. Exhausted, too tired to get up and close the windows to stop the drawn shades from flapping, miserably depressed, half awake and half asleep, so worn out there was a slow buzzing in his ears while he kept shutting his eyes and opening them — sometimes dizzily slipping away completely into slumber, then coming back abruptly to wide-awake consciousness while desperately wishing he could fall asleep and stay asleep, but at the same time knowing he was too emotionally disturbed to let go completely of his waking problems — the shades flapping — the stabs of sunlight shooting across the room — time dragging and dragging — thinking about Helen and the kids again — about jail again — about the loneliness of living alone in a furnished room in New York City during his years of acting — the loneliness of living without a woman in a prison cell — the loneliness of living in the empty house in Buffalo if Helen had already left for Florida with the two kids. Where could he go to get away from that empty house? Should he move to North Tonawanda where the bulk of their union membership in the western end of the state lived? But when you get through with a union meeting at night — whether it be in North Tonawanda or Buffalo or New York City — an empty furnished room is still an empty furnished room, and as Helen often reminded him, "You can't make love to the union — "

A furious hammering on the door startled him into leaping to his feet, flinging the blanket across the room. He stood in the center of the room, still not completely awake, all muscles tense, feet spread apart, arms flung wide, frantically searching around for a way out, an avenue of escape.

Where could he go?

The hammering on the door continued, and his heart was beating rapidly.

Who could it be?

A voice out there shouted something.

Had they come to haul him back to the hearing to set up the situation more properly for a contempt citation?

Then he recognized that voice shouting out in the hall, and he relaxed and let his arms drop to his sides. He could feel the chilled sweat on his face and neck, and he was still breathing hard. His feeling of relief was replaced by anger as he heard Ed Murphy hammering on the door and shouting again, the voice muffled by the door.

"Open up in the name of the law! The joint is raided! Open up in there!"

"Go fuck yourself!" Danny, boiling angry now, yelled back as loud as he could. Ignoring the hammering and shouting, he deliberately took his time, picking up the blanket and tossing it back on top of the bed before he started for the door.

Ed Murphy and Ralph Kaufman walked in, with Danny holding the door open for them. The two lawyers grinned like high school freshmen enjoying a wild prank. To conceal his embarrassment, thinking the lawyers had been making fun of the way he had run from the courthouse, Danny cursed them with every vicious swearword he could muster, and then lamely explained why he was so angry.

"You woke me out of a sound sleep," he lied.

They apologized, and he laughed along with them about how funny they had been, pounding their fists on the door like officers of the law coming after him to drag him back to

the hearing in the courthouse.
  Ha-ha! How funny!

Chapter 27

Danny and Ralph Kaufman listened while Murphy, speaking on the phone to George Hernandez in Schenectady, told how Jean Dampier had categorically denied present and past membership in the Communist Party, calling Julius Pearl a liar when Denilworth asked about Pearl's sworn statement that he had recruited Jean into the Communist Party, and then how Congressman Holling declared that someone was guilty of perjury, either Julius Pearl or Jean Dampier, and the Committee would see that the guilty man was prosecuted. After that, Holling brought the entire proceedings to an abrupt close with the announcement that no more witnesses would be called to testify and that all those subpoenaed who had not yet been asked to testify were released from the summons to appear.

Listening while he sat on the bed, Danny felt a great sense of relief that he couldn't be called back to testify any more at this hearing and he wondered if that would make a difference.

"Ready for lunch?" asked Murphy, putting down the receiver after saying goodbye to George Hernandez.

"Starving," said Danny.

Ralph wanted to check out of the hotel first. "We can take our bags along and eat near the railroad station."

They walked several blocks to the tavern across the street from the railroad station, the same place where Danny had eaten lunch with Murphy the day they arrived. That seemed, to Danny, to have been a long time ago.

Bill Kosciusko and Ray Foster were holding a table for them in the rear. It was a festive occasion — the hearing was over.

"Let's not pass up this legitimate opportunity to have a drink," said Murphy, and he called for a waiter and ordered a round of drinks.

Danny did not feel part of the group. He was aware of their sense of pride in having acquitted themselves well in the contest with the Committee, and he went through all the outer movements along with the rest — but he felt outside of

it; his inner tempo had slowed down to a very somber pace,
and he was still worrying about whether or not he had acted
like a coward by not going back into the hearing that
morning; and he was also thinking about how his
appearance before the Committee was going to affect the rest
of his whole life; he knew his troubles, especially at home,
were just beginning. He felt the nudge from Bill Kosciusko.

"Aren't those guys reporters?"

Danny looked and saw John Mason with several other
men. The reporters sat down at a table next to the opposite
wall — and Danny thought they had found a table as far
away as they could get from the union guys. But then John
Mason looked over and gave a friendly nod. Danny nodded in
return, and he wondered what kind of a story young Mason
had sent over the wires to Buffalo. Had Mason given him a
break because of Helen? But then he reminded himself that
it wouldn't make any difference what Mason wrote because
the final story would be put together by some rewrite man
who would handle it in a way that was sure to cause a real
storm back there.

Ralph went over and spoke to one of the reporters, a man
he knew, who worked on a New York City paper. When he
came back to the table he bent over Danny and whispered
into his ear.

"I've got a message for you."

Danny looked up.

"What?"

Ralph Kaufman whispered into his ear again.

"That reporter I know said to tell you he admires your
courage."

"Oh — "

Danny looked across at the other table, but the reporters
were busy ordering their lunch. He turned his face to the
lawyer.

"When you get a chance, Ralph, thank him for me."

Ralph nodded and went back to his seat on the other side
of the table and sat down. Danny ate his lunch along with
the rest, a roast beef sandwich and a bottle of beer. The few
words of encouragement Ralph Kaufman had passed on to
him had done wonders for his morale, but he could not
understand his own reaction — he was having a very hard

time controlling the flood of pent-up emotions released by those encouraging words; it was hard to eat with that choked feeling of almost crying.

When the reporters finished eating lunch John Mason came over and shook hands with Danny who rose as the young reporter approached.

"Danny, be sure to say hello to Helen for me."

"Thanks, I will."

"And good luck."

"Thanks — thanks — "

Mason hurried to catch up with the other reporters who were already at the front door of the tavern.

Ray Foster offered to drive Danny to Schenectady so he could get the plane there. They said goodbye to the others who were waiting for their trains. There was no place to park the car in front of The Regent, and Ray double-parked and waited while Danny rushed into the hotel to get his suitcase and pay his bill.

Alone in his room, Danny picked up the telephone and asked the switchboard operator to put through a long distance call to Buffalo, but he lost his nerve after giving the operator the number of his Buffalo phone. He jiggled the hook up and down frantically, luckily catching the operator before she completed the call.

"Yes, sir?"

"Will you cancel this call, please? I don't have time now to talk to Buffalo — I'll phone later — I'm late, operator — I have to catch a train — I've got less time than I thought — "

The telephone operator must be thinking he has suddenly lost his mind. She said she would cancel the call.

He put down the phone receiver and picked up his suitcase and started for the door. As he passed the door of the room next to him, out in the hallway, he wondered if his mysterious neighbor had already checked out. He would never know whether or not the man had been planted there to watch him.

Ray Foster started the motor when Danny approached.

They headed for Schenectady.

Chapter 28

When they arrived at the union office in Schenectady — Danny was given a big welcome by the organizers and secretaries and workers from the shop who gathered around him. Julius Emspak rested his hand heavily on Danny's shoulder. *We're in the same boat now*, that hand on the shoulder said.

"I see," said Julius, "you're asking them to toss you into the can and throw away the key."

Trying to maintain a lighthearted attitude for the benefit of the others, Danny said, "Looks that way, doesn't it?"

Before Julius could say anything else, Lisa Michaels pushed her way into the group and threw her arms around Danny's neck and kissed him. Then, embarrassed by her own enthusiasm, she pulled her arms away and backed off a few steps and blushed while she explained.

"That kiss is because I heard you were so wonderful. My mother called me. She was thrilled — the way you told them what you did."

Julius Emspak bitterly mocked her. "He was so wonderful they've got a little cell staked out for him in the can — right next to the one they've been saving for me."

"Well," said Lisa, with a petulant pout, "if he goes to jail I'll send him cigarettes."

"He doesn't smoke," said Julius, as if this was the final touch of irony.

George Hernandez came into the room with an armful of Schenectady newspapers. He shouted when he saw Danny.

"Hey, this says you took the Fifth."

Danny took a copy of the newspaper and scanned through the front page story. There it was. "All the union organizers used the Fifth Amendment to avoid answering questions concerning communist affiliations while Jean Dampier flatly denied any connection with the Communist Party, past or present."

"What do you say to that?" asked George Hernandez, coming back to Danny after passing around the rest of the

240

newspapers.

Danny protested, "I specifically told the Committee chairman I was *not* using the Fifth Amendment. Ask Ray. He was there — "

Ray Foster said, "That's right."

George Hernandez was enjoying himself. "The newspaper says you used the Fifth Amendment." He lit a cigar and held it up in the air like a comic in a vaudeville act, fixing his eyes on Danny with a very reproachful look. "Are you trying to insinuate," he asked, very seriously, "that this newspaper is lying? Be careful what you say, brother. If this newspaper says you used the Fifth Amendment, then so far as the people who work in this GE shop in Schenectady are concerned — *brother, you used the Fifth Amendment!*" He ostentatiously puffed his cigar and took it out of his mouth and flicked the ashes in Danny's direction. With a smirk on his face, he asked Julius Emspak to confirm what he had said. "Ain't that right, Julius?"

And Julius quietly said, "Fuck the newspapers," and then quickly apologized to the women in the room.

George Hernandez was through with that foolishness.

"Have you called Helen yet?" he asked Danny.

"Not yet."

"That," said George, sticking the wet end of his cigar butt into the right corner of his mouth while he swallowed a nasty chortle, "is a conversation I would like to hear."

"Go jump in the lake, you sadistic bastard."

George Hernandez ducked behind Julius Emspak to avoid the light punch Danny aimed at his shoulder, but Lisa Michaels playfully slapped him on Danny's behalf. Emspak, with an incredulous look, questioned Danny.

"Haven't you told your wife yet?"

"Not yet."

"How do you think she'll feel about it?"

"Well — how did *your* wife feel about it when you tangled with the Committee?"

"My wife? She would have traded me in — if I wasn't so old already I had no trade-in value." But he was laughing, and Danny guessed that he was only joking, and the rest of the organizers were hooting derisively at him. "You don't believe me?" Julius asked, looking around, trying to be serious. "You see what happens when Danny's wife hears he's going to be cited for contempt. You think it's a big joke, huh? Wait and see."

A pall came over the group, and they became silent.

"There's a possibility," Danny ventured, "they can't cite me for contempt, Julius — because the chairman of the Committee forgot to *direct* me to answer the question."

Julius Emspak laughed in his dry, quiet, bitter way.

"They can't cite you, but they *will!* I said they couldn't put me in the can for refusing to be a stoolpigeon" — he laughed at how green he had been — "but they gave me six months, even though I used the First Amendment and the Fifth Amendment, and the Supreme Court is still screwing around, afraid to uphold me because of the lousy political climate in the country."

He shook his head and warned, "Danny, don't bank on any technicalities to keep you out of the hoosegow. Only a substantial change in the political climate can do that. Not technicalities. Not even laws. When they want to get you because they think you're a real threat to their lushy private profit kingdom — they'll stretch the law so it fits to get you; they'll murder you if they have to do it to stop you, like they murdered Sacco and Vanzetti and like they murdered the Rosenbergs — as long as the people of this country let them do it. And right now the people of this country are still drugged with all the redbaiting which has been poured down their throats by the newspapers and the radio and the television. There's only one thing you can be sure of right now — "

He stopped to give Danny a chance to ask the obvious question.

"What's that?" Danny stared at that drained face which had become so bitter during the years Emspak had been carrying that six months jail sentence on his back. "What can I be sure of?"

The reply came, steeped with a suppressed anger.

"You can be sure the Committee will hang you if the people will let them do it. And right now the people are in a mood to let them do it!"

There was an embarrassed silence.

"Well" — Danny tried to grin about it — "then I guess I

better count on a contempt citation."

"There's no use kidding yourself. You might as well realize now what you're going to face in the months and years ahead." Emspak was speaking very earnestly, straight-from-the-shoulder. "Realize that now. Adjust to that now. It'll save you a world of heartache later."

"Hey-y-y — " George Hernandez grabbed Danny's arm and pulled him away, at the same time making a disparaging gesture at Emspak. "Let's get away from this crepehanger. He'll have you jumping out of a ten-story window if he keeps this up."

"Those are the facts," Emspak righteously shouted after them. "Those are the actual facts, and you might as well deal with the facts. There's nothing gained by kidding yourself."

George Hernandez got Ray Foster and Danny off in a corner by themselves.

Would Ray Foster drive Danny out to the airport?

He would.

George dug down into his pocket and handed Ray several dollar bills. "This will pay for your gas and oil."

On the way out to the airport Danny questioned Ray Foster, trying to learn from the other man's experience — so he would be prepared for what he might have to do now that he had challenged the Committee.

"Ray, have you been looking for a job since you've been fired?"

The man at the wheel kept his eyes on the road. They were out in the country now, outside the city limits. He answered the question without hesitation.

"Oh, sure. But nobody in this town would hire me."

The simplicity and the lack of self-pity or self-torture in his reply shamed Danny.

"What are you planning to do, Ray? You got a family, haven't you?"

"A wife and three kids."

"What do you plan to do?"

"I don't exactly know, but I'll do something."

"I'm sure you will — you have to. All of us have to."

Ray stopped the car for a red signal at a crossroad. The signal changed to green, and he drove on, resuming the conversation as he put the car into high speed again.

"I've been thinking of trying to borrow some money to open up some kind of business — I don't know what kind — any kind that doesn't take too much money to get started — some business where someone of my color will be accepted. You know how it is — "

"I know. Last hired, first fired."

"That's right."

"And it must be the same in business. They let you operate around the edges."

"That's right. But even if I could borrow the money and start a business — one hot blast in the newspapers could fold me up. People are afraid to talk to me now. How are they going to come into a store to buy from me, especially if the local Negro-haters and redbaiters start a boycott?" He laughed as though it was funny. "I think about opening up a business, but not too seriously."

"Can you keep going with just odd jobs the way you're doing?"

"For a while. We still got some money in the bank, and my wife's picking up a few odd jobs. But when our money's gone I may have to apply for relief."

"Will they give it to you?"

"There's only one way to find out —"

Danny was amazed at how calm and objective Ray appeared to be.

"I been thinking," Ray continued, while he watched the road ahead. "Maybe I'll take the wife and kids and go West. Maybe to California. I'll change my name and make up a phony background and see if I can't get a job somewhere out of reach of the FBI. They're on my tail all the time here, trying to pressure me into joining their stable of stoolpigeons. They think they can starve me into it."

"Rough," Danny muttered, shaking his head and clucking to show his sympathy. "Rough. I'm lucky I got a job with the union to go back home to." Then, feeling ashamed of the advantage he had, he added, "Of course, Ray, my job's liable to go down the drain if our union is wiped out by all this raiding and redbaiting. After they get through killing me with what happened in the hearing here — I won't have much chance to get a job or of making a go with any kind of business venture. I'll be in the same boat right along with you."

"You might have to follow my trail out West." Ray laughed along with Danny, as though they were telling one another jokes.

They discussed some of the problems involved in going to a strange city and changing identity.

"You'd have to start over with everything different," said Danny, really figuring it out loud for himself. "A different name. A different social security number. A new driver's license. New license plates on the car — you'd have to sell your old car somewhere, buy a different car under your new name. New life insurance — "

"Don't forget, " Ray reminded, "they got your fingerprints if you ever worked in a defense plant."

"Then you can't take a job where you'll be fingerprinted again."

"And you can't ever mix with the law on anything where they book you and take your prints."

Danny shook his head. "I never thought about it before. How hard it would be for guys like us to disappear and start all over new. Especially with a wife. And especially with kids."

"But if your back's against the wall what else can you do?"

They were silent while they watched an airliner descending above several automobiles, crossing the road ahead of them.

"Never a dull moment," said Danny.

"Life is very interesting," agreed Ray, "especially these days."

They slowed down to turn off the road into the driveway leading into the airport. Danny reached over the back of the front seat to get his suitcase.

Chapter 29

The airline hostess was leaning over Danny when he opened his eyes.

"We're coming into Binghamton now, sir. Snap on your belt, please."

The plane landed and taxied down the runway. The pilot braked it to a halt, then wheeled the plane around and taxied it over to the paved area in front of the small brick building which housed the ticket office and waiting room. Danny unsnapped his belt.

Leaving the plane, he saw Lou Cartman, a bald-pated old hand at the union organizing game who had come out of a farm equipment shop in the Midwest. Lou was to drive him to Elmira. But Lou had expected to meet Julius Emspak. Danny explained the switch. Lou insisted on carrying Danny's suitcase. Danny tagged along, keeping pace with the older man.

"I hear you told that Committee where they could put their questions, you redheaded sonofabitch."

"Has it hit the newspapers here already?"

"We heard it on the car radio. From Albany."

"It's hard to keep a secret these days," said Danny, thinking that Helen had also already heard the news, the same way Lou Cartman had heard it.

Out in front of the airport administration building Lou introduced Danny to Naomi Gatti and Carl Gawrys, two youngsters in their early twenties — they looked freshly scrubbed. As they walked through the parking lot to his car, Lou explained that Naomi and Carl worked at the GE plant in Schenectady — they were members of the rank-and-file volunteer organizing committee which was pitted against Jean Dampier's hardened political machine. Carl was a skinny young man with his hair cut so short that it looked like bristles on a toothbrush. Naomi was a wiry person, with a boyish bob. Both youngsters were peppy and bouncy, and Danny envied their youth.

"Want to stop off for a beer before we get out on the road?"

suggested Lou.

"No, thanks. We better get rolling if we're going to get to Elmira in time for me to attend that executive board meeting." Danny was in no mood to sit around and talk.

"Okay."

The two youngsters had already climbed into the back seat. Danny sat up front with Lou Cartman. As they started on their way he peered into the fiery sun, a red ball shining low in the west.

"How did the hearing go?" asked Lou, trying to start up a conversation.

But Danny refused to be drawn in.

"Okay."

He hoped the curtness of his reply would discourage any further talk about what had happened that morning.

"Weren't you scared?" the girl in the back seat wanted to know.

"Sure."

"Was it very exciting?"

"It was dull."

The young man asked, "Do they hound you?"

"Well" — (how could he answer that in a few words?) — "yes, and no."

They continued to probe for a little while longer, but his short replies were so unsatisfactory that they switched to talking among themselves about the situation back in the shop in Schenectady. Danny dozed off.

When he awakened he saw that the sun had set but the clear sky was still lit up with a twilight glow. They were on a road which ran alongside a winding river. He could see small islands in the middle of the river, islands overgrown with lush marshy vegetation, all turning green again now that spring had arrived. He tried to hang onto the picture of that green freshness, that fresh living color reminding him of the poem by Oscar Wilde, written while he was in prison, something about "a wistful look at that tent of blue called the sky"; and he thought he understood how Oscar Wilde must have felt, hungrily gazing from within prison walls up at that tiny patch of blue sky which looked down on all the richness of the tremendous world outside the man-made iron bars walling in his tortured spirit. Only half-awake, Danny hung on to the memory of those small green river islands, printing their picture firmly in his mind so he would not forget them — they would be *his* "tent of blue called the sky."

It was dark when they arrived, but Lou Cartman knew Elmira well. Lou's assignment to the Schenectady situation, Danny knew, was only temporary. His permanent assignment was to assist the local union at the Elmira branch of GE. They drove through the city streets.

"Good to be home, Lou?" asked Danny, engaging the driver in conversation to help wake himself up completely.

"I haven't seen my wife for almost a month," answered Lou, the dryness of his comment indirectly answering Danny's question.

The skinny young man in the back seat of the car howled, "There'll be a hot time in the old town tonight!"

"Oh, you!" The young woman punched him. "Stop talking dirty all the time."

"Ouch," he screamed in mock pain, "she broke my arm, she broke my arm — I want workmen's compensation — I'm going to file a grievance with the union — "

The horseplay continued in the back seat, but the two older men up in front ignored it.

"Danny, do you want to stop at the hotel first?"

"No, you better drop me off at the executive board meeting, over at the union hall." Peering at his watch as they drove by a street light, Danny saw that he was already more than half an hour late for that meeting. "I'm in no mood for any meeting, Lou," he wearily admitted, "but you better drop me off there first. I'll go over to the hotel when the meeting's done."

"Whatever you say."

They drove down the narrow main street of Elmira. The street was jammed with traffic, the sidewalks filled with pedestrians. Friday night was a busy night in this small industrial community which had once been primarily a farming center. Lou turned the wheel to the left and the car turned the corner and passed through the concrete archway of a railroad crossing viaduct. About half a block further Lou pulled the car over to the curb in front of a group of dimly lit stores. He pointed to the entrance sandwiched between two dilapidated stores, a restaurant and a secondhand furniture place.

"The union hall's upstairs."

Danny saw the union's name printed in scratched gold letters on the glass in the double doors. There was a weak bulb hanging by a wire inside, behind the doors, lighting up the steep stairway. As he got out of the car, Danny glanced up at the windows on the second floor. The lights were on up there. He assumed the executive board was already in session.

"See you later, kids," he said to the two youngsters in the back seat.

Lou Cartman brought him his suitcase. "Do you want me to reserve a room for you when I drop the kids off at the hotel?"

"I'd appreciate it. If it's no trouble."

"No trouble."

Lou said he would come back to the union hall after he picked up his wife, and Danny watched him drive away.

Putting off going upstairs to that meeting for a few more minutes, Danny stopped off in the restaurant for a quick cup of coffee. About five minutes later he slowly climbed the steep wooden stairs and stopped outside the door of the union hall, listening.

A woman's voice. Bill Becker's secretary, he guessed. Bill, as president of the district council, was undoubtedly chairing the meeting. The voice droned on. Everything sounded very peaceful in there.

His hand on the doorknob, he told himself, "They must already know what happened at the hearing." He turned the knob, thinking almost aloud, "Well, here goes nothing."

He quietly opened the door, suppressing a zany impulse to call out, *"Surprise!"*

Chapter 30

His exaggerated care in shutting the door noiselessly behind him let the executive board know that he did not want to interrupt their regular order of business — he hoped they would not stop everything to ask him to tell what had happened that morning.

Lanky Bill Becker, president of the district council, was chairing the meeting. Catching Danny's eye, Bill pointed to a heap of folding chairs piled up against the wall and slid his own chair over to make room for Danny at the head of the long conference table around which were gathered about a dozen members of the executive board. He repeated his invitation several times, vigorously beckoning to Danny to pick up a chair and bring it over.

But Danny just as vigorously shook his head, refusing the invitation. He put down his suitcase and pointed directly down at the floor at his feet, where he was standing up against the opposite wall, as far away as he could get from the long table around which the board members were seated.

"Okay," Bill Becker mouthed without a sound. Danny returned a slight bow, thanking him for the invitation. Bill Becker returned his attention to the long communication which Annie Anderson, his tall blonde secretary, was reading aloud.

"Hi, Danny —"

The whispered greeting came from Leonard Skop — Lennie, everyone called him — a young organizer with a face like a friendly puppy, in his middle twenties, assigned to the Elmira area to assist Lou Cartman.

"Here." Lennie held a folding chair.

"Thanks."

Lennie started to unfold the chair but Danny took it and carefully unfolded it himself, making sure there was no noise to draw the attention of the members of the executive board. Still wearing his topcoat, he sat down, hoping this would encourage Lennie to go away and leave him alone so the executive board members would stop glancing their way, but

Lennie didn't move. Danny, seeing that the young organizer was anxious to start a conversation, held up his hand in a gesture of thanks for the chair, which at the same time was an impatient warning that this was no time to talk. But this did not stop Lennie.

"Danny" — Lennie bent over to whisper into Danny's ear — "the local newspaper guy called and asked for a statement from us — about you and what happened at the hearing."

"Fuck him."

The vulgar retort came out louder than he had intended and some of the executive board members looked around, startled, wondering if they had heard right. Danny kept a perfectly straight face as though he had said nothing.

"We told him," Lennie went on, "to call back later and speak to you."

"How'd you know I'd be here tonight?" Though annoyed, Danny kept his voice down.

"I asked Bill Becker if *he* wanted to talk to the guy," Lennie explained, "and he said — tell him to call back later when you'd be here."

"The hell with it."

"What'll I say if he calls again."

"Tell him to go fuck himself" — a whispered response.

"Danny!" Lennie protested, twisting his gamin face into a gesture of utter helplessness at his inability to understand why the other man would not talk to the newspaper people. "I think you should give a statement to the newspaper. If you don't, they'll print a story all about how they called our union office and we refused to talk to them. — You don't understand. The newspaper is very influential in this town."

"Fuck 'em."

"Oh, for chrissakes," disgustedly exclaimed Bill Becker, angrily tossing his gavel down on the table and putting his hand on Annie Anderson's shoulder to stop her from reading any further, "let's have only one meeting here — okay?"

Danny contritely apologized, "Sorry, Bill," as Lennie scooted away from him like a water bug flicking over the surface of still water.

Duke LaDuca, a barrel-chested delegate from a shop in the central part of the state, jerked his thumb in Danny's direction. "This guy's been telling off that Committee all day

— he forgot how to shut off the spigot. The words keep spilling out like wine out of a barrel."

"Don't pick on my boy," warned Al Carmer, a husky executive board member from Buffalo, as he playfully aimed a clenched fist at Duke.

"He's my boy, too. He's my *In*-ternational *Rep*-resentative."

And the Duke turned to Danny, his jet black eyebrows forming two inverted U's as he made a very comical face. "Ain't that right, Mister *In*-ternational *Rep*-resentative?" And then his voice positively drooled with the delightful picture he conjured up in his mind as he asked, "Did you tell those bastards to go to hell?" He didn't wait for an answer. "Good," he hoarsely gurgled. "Good. That's the only way to handle those bastards." He turned back to the rest of the executive board members who were enjoying his performance, and he thumped his enormous chest and crowed, "That's my boy!"

"He's *my* boy!" argued Al Carmer, again cocking his fist to throw a punch at the Duke.

The Duke shielded his face from the impending blow he knew would never descend. "Our boy," he tactfully suggested as a compromise with a comical twist of his heavy face.

Al Cramer stuck out his hand. "You got yourself a contract!"

Bill Becker wearily tapped his gavel against the table while the two clowns cemented their bargain with a handshake. "If you two fat burlesque queens are through horsing around — may we go on with the meeting?"

"You," answered the Duke in a falsetto voice, "certainly can go on with the regular order of business now, darling," and he blew a ludicrous kiss to Bill Becker.

"Oh, honey," vamped Al Carmer, "I didn't know you really cared," and he stuck his tongue out between his fat lips and gave forth with a lusty rasping Bronx cheer which caused general laughter in which even Bill Becker joined. During the laughter, Danny stood up and took off his topcoat, draping it over a small table up against the wall, and then sat down. Bill Becker tapped his gavel again.

The Duke beat him to the punch. "Stop holding up the meeting, Bill. I pay my dues and I want action for my money. Let's get this meeting going. What's the big holdup?"

Bill Becker resignedly nodded to Annie Anderson who resumed her reading of the communications.

The telephone rang.

Lennie Skop, seated at the desk in the office area off to Danny's right, jumped up and grabbed the telephone receiver off the hook to silence the instrument. He motioned for Danny to come over and answer the phone.

Danny shook his head.

Thrusting his hands straight up into the air in a violent gesture of despair, Lennie Skop went through the motions of pulling his hair out by the roots, but Danny turned his face away and watched the executive board meeting across the room. Out of the corner of his eye he saw Lennie talk into the phone's mouthpiece for a while before he hung up the receiver. Lennie started toward him, and Danny made believe he was too completely engrossed in the meeting to notice the approach of the young organizer.

"Danny" — Lennie sounded very excited as he bent over and whispered, so close to Danny's ear that he could feel the young organizer's warm breath — "that was the publisher of the newspaper, a young guy who just took it over, and he says there's a story about you just come over the wires from Associated Press — "

Instantly alert for the worst, Danny froze.

Lennie rushed his words together: "The chairman of the subcommittee recommended to the full Committee in Washington — to ask the House of Representatives to cite you for contempt!"

Even though Danny had expected this might happen despite his cowardly flight from the courthouse, he had to concentrate to maintain his outward appearance of calm while the tempo inside him shot up to a screaming siren pitch. He looked up at Lennie.

"So?"

"He wants a statement from you." Danny tried to speak but no words came out, and Lennie rushed on. "You gotta give him some kind of statement tonight. They'll carry a big story about the contempt citation tomorrow morning in the paper. We *gotta* have some kind of statement from our side to counteract the damage that'll do to us with our people in the shop —"

"Let me" — Danny could see Bill Becker glaring their way, ready to blow up again — "let me think about it."

Lennie started to protest. Too agitated inside to be bothered with being polite about it, Danny gave the young organizer a gentle shove to make him get away. A hurt look on his face, Lennie reluctantly returned to the desk.

Danny tried to keep his mind on the executive board session. He was too upset to try to arrive at any decision now about the newspaper.

The executive board had already disposed of both old business and new business, all routine and without any unusual developments, when Lou Cartman came in with his wife and two youngsters from Schenectady. Under good and welfare, Bill Becker asked for a report on the situation at the GE plant up in Schenectady. While Lou Cartman delivered a longwinded report that dragged the meeting out almost beyond endurance, Danny debated with himself whether or not to phone the local newspaper publisher and give out a statement. He had not yet arrived at any decision when Lou finally ran out of words and sat down.

Bill Becker quickly closed the meeting before anyone else could get up and make another long speech. He rapped his gavel sharply. "A motion to adjourn is in order" — "It's been moved" — "And seconded" — "All in favor say, 'aye'" — "All opposed stay here and hold your own damn meeting!"

The meeting broke up immediately, the executive board members welcoming the opportunity to stand up and stretch their cramped muscles.

The telephone rang again.

Lennie Skop answered it and called out to Danny over the noisy hubbub of the board members, a pleading note in his voice.

"It's the newspaper again."

"Okay," he called back across the room — and he himself was surprised at how calm he felt about it.

The board members cleared a place for him so he could sit on the corner of the desk with the phone in his hand, and they quieted down so they would be able to hear. Lennie stood next to him while he put the receiver up to his ear.

"Hello."

The man at the other end of the line introduced himself.

His diction was good. He was Joel Haas, publisher of the Elmira newspaper, he explained, and his paper would go to bed at midnight — their deadline. Then, for Danny's benefit, he read the full Associated Press dispatch which said that Congressman Holling had issued a statement after the hearing ended, that the subcommittee was sending a recommendation to the full Committee on Un-American Activities, asking that body to recommend to the House of Representatives that Daniel Newman be cited for contempt because of his refusal to answer any questions of the Committee.

It's exactly what we wanted, Danny silently reminded himself. I should be happy.

The publisher asked, "Why didn't you tell the Committee where you were born, Mr. Newman."

"Here's why —" And Danny explained that he had nothing to hide, that he was born in the United States, but that he had not answered any questions at all in order to formally challenge the constitutionality of the enabling resolution by which the House of Representatives had established the Committee. The publisher interrupted to ask if he could come over with a photographer and shoot some pictures and get the full story.

"Just a second," said Danny. He put his hand over the mouthpiece and asked Lennie, "What kind of a guy is this joker? Will he give us a fair break? How's he treated you guys?"

"He's always been pretty fair with any statements we've given him."

Back to the publisher: "A straight story? No phony twist or dirty angles?"

"A straight story," the publisher assured him. "This is a hot news item, Mr. Newman, and we don't want to miss out on a statement from you while you're here. It'll make good copy and Associated Press will probably pick it up from here and send it out over their wires."

"Okay" — Danny thought that the Buffalo papers might pick up his statement if AP sent it out over the wires, and even if what the Buffalo papers printed was a distortion of what he actually said, that would be better than having only Holling's statement appear there.

"Mr. Newman," said the publisher, "I'll be there with my photographer in five minutes."

"Fine."

Lou Cartman and his wife invited Danny to go out and get something to eat with them after the interview would be finished — and then they would drive him to his hotel. Lou took his suitcase back out to the car so they wouldn't forget it later.

Danny sat on the edge of the desk, acting as though he was listening to the conversation buzzing all around him, but not really hearing any of it. He wondered if he should phone Helen and tell her about Holling recommending a contempt citation before she read about it in the Buffalo morning paper.

"Does it look that bad, Danny?"

He looked up and saw that Lennie had called the attention of Lou's wife and several of the board members to his silence and his sober appearance. He forced a silly grin.

"Oh, no, Lennie. This is just what we expected. We can't test the constitutionality of the Committee without a citation for contempt. As a matter of fact, this looks good for what we're trying to accomplish —"

"Then don't look so sad."

"Sad?" And Danny kept on grinning at the young puppy-faced organizer who was so ineptly trying to encourage him. "No, Lennie. This is how my face was shaped when I was born. My bone structure. You inherited the look of a pixy and I inherited the look of a sad sack. Neither of us had much to say about it."

"A pixy!"

Lennie snorted with disgust and walked away.

Danny was glad to be left alone a while to think of what he should say to the publisher of the Elmira paper.

Chapter 31

When Joel Haas, the young owner-publisher-editor arrived with his photographer, Lou Cartman suggested that they could get away from the noisy board members by going back to the meeting hall in the rear. In the bare hall the photographer placed Danny in a position where he was perched on the edge of a small table, with baldpated Lou Cartman seated, gazing expectantly up into his eyes, listening. Lennie Skop and Joel Haas watched from a vantage point close behind the photographer.

Danny estimated that Joel Haas was at least ten or fifteen years younger than himself. The young publisher was dressed in a well-cut dark suit with a fashionable double vent, seeming to have an air of ease and security that probably came from being born with enough money in the family to shield the spirit from getting too badly wounded by the outside world. He would get along well with Helen. Their conversation would contain many subtle nuances of meaning from which he, Danny, with his different background during his younger years, would be unconsciously excluded.

"Mr. Newman," suggested Haas, "why don't you talk to Lou — as though you're trying to justify your refusal to cooperate with the Committee this morning —"

Lou Cartman jumped to Danny's defense. "He doesn't have to justify anything. The Committee has to do some justifying to the American public — for what they're doing to our Bill of Rights!"

"I know, Lou." Haas hurriedly apologized — disarming Danny somewhat by his nice quiet manner — "but if Mr. Newman is talking to you it'll make a better shot."

The photographer waited for them to give him some action, and Danny leaned forward and said, "Well, Lou" — keeping his neck stiff, trying to look dignified and restrained, to give as good an impression as possible to the newspaper's readers the next morning — "you see, Lou, it was like this —"

An exploding white flash.

Danny relaxed, but there was a glaring round white spot still in front of his eyes. He squeezed his eyes shut and that felt good. How nice it would be to slump gently to the bare wooden floor and fall asleep. He opened his eyes and smiled at the photographer and recited a silly jingle to himself, "How now, brown cow?"

"Once more, please," said the photographer, very business-like, wiggling his thin black mustache as he worked fast, fumbling in his pocket for another flash bulb —" and lean forward a little more, please — and a little more relaxed, please — and a little more action, please." He aimed his camera again, with Lennie Skop and Joel Haas peering over his shoulder.

"Well, Lou" — Danny leaned forward slightly, his mouth frozen open in a half-smile, still very much aware that he was trying to create a pose which would create a favorable reaction when the picture appeared in the newspaper; he wanted people to say: *He looks like a nice, average, ordinary kind of guy.* Still hanging on to that smile, waiting for the flash bulb to explode, he remembered that picture of himself which had appeared on the front page of the newspaper in Albany, that wiseacre brazenly thumbing his nose at every reader. What if that one was printed now in the Buffalo newspapers? Goodbye, Helen.

The white flash again.

He shut his eyes to squeeze away the after-image.

"That's it," announced the photographer.

Haas told the photographer to hurry back to the office with the plates while he stayed behind to get the story to go with the picture.

The publisher began by asking some general questions about Danny's background. Where was he born? (Brooklyn) Where did he grow up? (Buffalo) Where did he go to school? (Buffalo) And when Danny told the young publisher he had a total of two years of college credits accumulated at three different colleges (University of Iowa, Canisius College and University of Buffalo) and through several army correspondence courses — he couldn't resist adding, "I played football in the Big Ten Conference," stretching the truth a little since he had played only freshman football, not varsity. It built up his ego to see that the publisher was puzzled. Haas asked how Danny had happened to become a union organizer, and Danny explained briefly that he had worked at an airplane plant and became active in the union, and that he had been fired and became a union organizer, and that he had been reinstated to the job at the airplane plant by order of the War Department — but had worked there only one day after his reinstatement, for the record, and then had continued as a union organizer with some time out for service in the army in World War II.

With this background out of the way, Joel Haas dug into the meat of the interview:

"Do you think, Mr. Newman," he asked, his pencil poised over the folded scratch paper, "that you'll be cited for contempt by the parent body — by the full House Committee on Un-American Activities? Do you think they'll go along with the recommendation of Congressman Holling?"

"No comment," said Danny, and he tried to appear very nonchalant and undisturbed, folding his arms and grinning — but not grinning so much that he might appear flippant or foolish. The skin on his face felt drawn tight again, dry and itchy like it had always felt when he was working in the chemical plant after he got out of high school, back there when it had been an everyday occurrence to get his face splattered and burnt with strong caustic — he knew that if the light hit the skin on his face at a certain angle anyone looking at him could see the streaks burnt in there by the strong chemical.

"Do you think, Mr. Newman, that if you *are* cited for contempt of Congress — and if it goes to trial in the courts — do you think the courts will find you guilty — under the present interpretation of the law?"

"No comment. I don't want to speculate."

"If you're found guilty and given a prison sentence — will you appeal?"

That required an answer, and Danny chose his words carefully.

"I think that in all probability I will be found guilty in the lower courts if this goes to trial, in which case I would probably be sentenced to a prison term. — But the issues raised are of such a nature, I think, that this matter will probably be finally decided only by action by the United

States Supreme Court."

"How long do you think that would take — to get a decision from the Supreme Court?"

"Your guess is as good as mine. Probably better."

"Two or three years?"

"Maybe. Maybe more. Maybe less. I'm going to play it safe and say, 'No comment.'"

Haas thought a moment while the three organizers watched him, waiting for the next question. The publisher tapped his chin with the eraser of his pencil — he stopped — he had his next question.

"You didn't use the Fifth Amendment — "

"That's right."

"Has anyone else ever offered this kind of a challenge to the Committee? Has it ever been tried before?"

"Well" — Danny ran his fingers through his hair and went through the motions of trying to recall something he didn't know for sure — "let's say this. Usually a witness may refuse to answer some *particular* question or some *particular* questions on the grounds that the Committee doesn't have the right to ask him — or make him answer — *that* question or *those* questions."

"But you," interrupted Haas, pointing his pencil, "say they don't have the right to ask *any* questions of *anybody*, is that it?"

"I say they don't have the right to exist! They're an illegal body! Unconstitutional! So they can't ask anybody anything!"

Haas scribbled down some more notes, and then looked up at Danny again. "Did you tell the Committee why you think they're an illegal body?"

"Yes —"

Danny became aware of the feeling of importance he felt being interviewed this way, but almost immediately the grisly thought flashed through his mind that this must be the same kind of sick importance felt by a man accused and convicted of murder and who faces the electric chair or the gas chamber or the hangman's noose. The attitude of the man asking the questions now is one of somber and restrained respect, the kind of muted attitude one assumes when talking about someone who is already dead and the deceased you are talking about is exposed in the same room in an open coffin.

"What reasons did you give the Committee for refusing to answer their questions?"

Danny reached his hand into his inside pocket where he still had his notes. "Would you like to hear all the reasons — or just those the Committee permitted me to give before they dismissed me from the witness chair? My attorney told the Committee we're going to mail in a statement embodying the reasons I was not permitted to give at the hearing."

Haas said he would like to hear all the reasons, and he'd decide later which he would use in his story. Danny glanced down at the yellow sheets of paper he had taken out of his pocket, to refresh his memory by looking at his notes.

"What's that?" Haas asked him.

"These are the same notes I took into the hearing with me. I had them on the table in front of me when I was sitting in the witness chair."

The publisher scribbled something down on his scratch paper. "Detailed human interest."

Haas continued to rapidly jot down the different thoughts as Danny explained — still referring to his notes — that he had refused to answer any questions on the grounds that the enabling resolution establishing the Committee was unconstitutional.

"Because the resolution declared certain ideas to be verboten;

"Because the words 'un-American' and subversive' embodied in the resolution were so vague as to lack any meaning except what the Committee itself wanted them to mean;

"Because the resolution had been used and could be used for illegal inquisitions by Congress into personal and private affairs;

"Because the resolution and the hearings conducted by the Committee served no legislative purpose;

"And because the resolution and the conduct of the Committee under this resolution represented an illegal assumption by the legislative branch of the powers of the judicial branch of our government."

Finished with the notes, Danny folded the yellow sheets and put them back into his inner pocket. Joel Haas thought a while before asking his next question.

"What about the members of your union, Mr. Newman?"

On guard, Danny said, "What about them?"

"Do you think they'll approve of this position you've taken before the Committee?"

"Well" — Danny shrugged and shoved his hand deep into his side pockets and tried to smile easily — "let's leave that to them. They'll decide that. Not me." And he added, "Let's make that 'No comment.'"

But both Lennie Skop and Lou Cartman interjected that they were sure the union membership would strongly agree with what Danny had done. Danny cautioned them to let the membership speak for themselves.

"I think I've got enough here for my story." Joel Haas glanced at his wrist watch before making a rapid check over his notes, running the point of his pencil down the edge of the folded scratch paper he held in his left hand. He stopped himself and looked up. One more question. "Are you married, Mr. Newman?"

"Yes" — *on guard!* — "I'm married."

"Any children?"

"Two daughters."

"How does your family feel about this?"

"What do you mean?"

"Well, how do they feel about your making this constitutional test?"

Danny hesitated. It would not help if Helen read a statement by him, saying what *she* was thinking. Like their union membership, Helen had a right to make up her own mind.

"I'd appreciate it, Mr. Haas" — trying to be pleasant and disarming — "if you'd leave my family out of it."

"Okay." The publisher surprised Danny by the readiness with which he complied with the request. He slipped his notes into his side pocket. "Thank you, Mr. Newman."

"Thank *you*."

They shook hands.

"You must lead an interesting life," said Haas, in a tone of voice which made it evident he was speaking only as one man to another — ("Stout fella!") — and not for publication.

"Too interesting sometimes."

Haas laughed warmly. "I see what you mean." He tightened his grip on Danny's hand which he still held. "Your wife must find it hard, doesn't she?"

The young publisher seemed to be very curious about Helen. Danny's first impulse was to answer coldly, 'No comment.' But, since this question was not part of the formal interview and he didn't want to unnecessarily offend Joel Haas, he changed his mind and answered — a curt reply intended to discourage any further questions on that subject:

"Yes."

He dropped the hand of the young publisher and led the way back to the small meeting room and the office area up front. Out there, among the local union's executive board members who were still hanging around and talking, there was no chance for the publisher to ask any further questions. They shook hands again and the publisher thanked Danny for being so cooperative.

Danny wondered what kind of story would appear in the Elmira newspaper as he watched Joel Haas descend the stairs.

Chapter 32

"Hey-y-y, Danny!"

Startled, he awoke, involuntarily jerking his body up straight and searching from one side to the other for the source of danger. Then he saw they were still seated in the booth in the crowded, noisy diner. The brightly colored jukebox across the aisle was giving out with a hot beat of raucous jazz. They were still waiting for the aging blonde waitress to bring their five orders of tomato juice and scrambled eggs and toast and coffee. Lou Cartman and his wife Rita and the two youngsters from Schenectady enjoyed Danny's startled reaction to the shout which had awakened him. The big grin on Lou's face hinted that he was the one who had yelled.

"Catching up on my sleep," Danny sheepishly apologized.

Lou Cartman attracted the attention of the customers in the nearest booths by insisting that he wanted to switch places so Danny could sit on the inside end of the bench and lean his head up against the wall and sleep more comfortably until the waitress would bring their order.

"Lou, I'll catch up on my sleep over at the hotel."

Danny's embarrassed protest did not stop the other organizer.

"You're not going to see the inside of that hotel until the wee hours of the morning," he warned, unceremoniously pushing Danny out into the aisle so they could trade places on the bench. "We're going over to the bar and meet the rest of the gang after we get through here."

Carl Gawrys, the young man from the GE shop in Schenectady, supported Lou. "We're all going to get soused tonight," he promised as an inducement.

"You young punk," Lou twitted him, while changing positions with Danny, "one boilermaker would put you under the table for the rest of the night —"

"Oh, yeah? I'll drink an old baldheaded coot like you under the table any time of the day or night —"

"Oh, look who's talking," said the girl who had come with

264

him from the GE shop in Schenectady. She put her hand on her hip and made a funny long face. "Did you bring your birth certificate along to show the bartender, sonny?"

The conversation continued briskly in this vein and faded from Danny's consciousness again. His eyes wouldn't stay open. They closed. Opened. Closed. Fluttered open and closed. And opened and closed, and stayed closed. He lost his balance as he fell asleep. His head cracked against the wall. He awoke, involuntarily grabbing hold of the sore spot where he had hit his left temple against the wall, pressing his hands there as hard as he could, to relieve the pain.

The others expressed their deep concern about him.

"Nothing serious." He rubbed the aching area. "I better get over to that hotel and into bed before I kill myself." He made an excuse to get them to leave him go. "I promised I'd call my wife and tell her what happened at the hearing."

"Haven't you called her yet?" Lou's wife, a gray-haired woman with a kind face, was amazed.

"I didn't have time," Danny lamely explained.

"She must be frantic by now, wondering what happened to you — she must have read about it in the newspapers —"

Danny was Mister Sincerity himself as he explained, "That's why I want to get right back to the hotel to call her."

The bustling waitress unloaded five orders of tomato juice and scrambled eggs and toast and coffee on their table. They pitched in, all except Danny, eating and talking about what they would do later. While beginning to get disgusted with his constant preoccupation with his hard lot, he thought that he was already living in an entirely different world from everyone else in that crowded diner. He was alone by himself now with a terrible weight bearing down on him. But he was sick of thinking about the threat of jail and the fear that Helen would take the kids and leave him.

"Danny, hey, wake up, wake up —"

The young man from the GE shop in Schenectady was snapping his fingers in a very annoying way.

"I'm awake."

"Oh, yeah!"

Lou Cartman's wife intervened. "Let him rest."

Danny tried to listen to the conversation but he almost immediately sank back into himself again. The warmth of the diner and the extreme fatigue which had piled up from getting so little sleep during the past few days combined to make him so drowsy that his head began to bob up and down again. He tried to stay awake by talking to himself. Too much inner searching and self-pity. About time that with all my experience in handling difficult situations I begin to plan what I'll do when I get back to Buffalo. The problem was how to combat the influence of other people on Helen. Especially her oldest brother, Robert — Bob. And Helen's mother. And that small slice of the Buffalo community into which Bob and Helen's mother fit. It gave him a spark of encouragement to know that the problem was at last beginning to take some objective form in his mind. What to do about it came next. But he decided that he would wait until he got to the hotel to think that through, so he would not be interrupted. He gave up the struggle and closed his eyes. His head again cracked up against the wall and the sting of pain brought tears to his eyes. Lou's wife took pity on him.

"For heaven's sake, let's take him back to the hotel before he kills himself."

They got the check.

Driving to the hotel, Lou Cartman and the two youngsters again tried to persuade Danny to come along to the bar and to make a night of it with them and the rest of the district council delegates. They would wait in the lobby until he finished his phone call to Helen. Lou's wife argued with them. Danny, too worn out to bother becoming actively involved in the noisy controversy, listened like a disinterested spectator.

"Let the poor guy get some sleep. He's out on his feet."

"You don't know this guy, Rita, like I know him," said Lou. "I've seen him in action before. The less sleep he gets — the more wide-awake he becomes and the quicker his mind clicks."

"But he wants to go to bed —"

Lou Cartman stopped the car in front of the hotel and helped Danny get his suitcase out of the baggage compartment.

"Say hello to Helen for me, Danny — and tell her not to worry."

"Thanks, Lou." Danny tried to suppress a yawn as he

called out to the others who had remained in the car, "See you in the morning."

A bellhop grabbed the suitcase from Danny as he entered the hotel lobby. The electric clock behind the desk across the lobby showed two minutes before midnight, and Danny was glad he was not starting off on a late drinking party at that hour — he had some planning to do. Walking beside the bellhop, he circled an area where two charwomen were scrubbing the tiled floor. As they passed by a line of pay phone booths, he wondered if any good could come from calling Helen. Probably not.

Before talking to Helen he had to work out a detailed plan of action which he could lay before her, showing her that it was still possible for them to remain married and continue to live in Buffalo — despite the bad publicity the newspapers would give him because he had challenged the Committee, despite the possibility that he might have a conviction for contempt of Congress hanging over his head for a few years and despite the possibility that he might — eventually, if not sooner — have to go to jail for a short while, or maybe longer than that.

They stopped at the desk.

"Do you have a reservation, sir?" the clerk asked, as he pushed the hotel register card forward and held out a pen.

Danny heard what the clerk said, but it required a conscious mobilization of physical effort to reach out his hand and take the proffered pen and focus his eyes on the clerk's face and get up the necessary energy to answer that very simple question.

"Yes." He was extremely conscious of the heavy weariness which had hit him on the head. "Yes, I have."

He very slowly wrote out his name on the registration card.

Chapter 33

12:07 AM . . . Saturday morning —

The elderly uniformed bellhop preceded Danny into the room, flipping the light switch as he entered. He made a big show of bustling around the room, setting Danny's suitcase down on the small luggage rest at the foot of the big double bed, turning on several lamps, checking to see if there were towels and soap in the bathroom, and matches and stationary on the desk.

"Should I open the window?"

He stood, with his right arm outstretched toward the windows, waiting for Danny's reply to trigger him into action. But Danny was anxious to be left alone.

"Never mind."

The bellhop headed toward the door, cupping his hand near his hip to receive the tip.

Danny switched off the ceiling light, leaving on only the table lamps. He tossed his topcoat down on top of the bed, crossed to the nearest of the two windows and looked down through the darkness. Elmira seemed to have died. The lines of street lights, seven stories below, seemed feeble and sick. Danny watched a lone automobile slow down at an intersection and then turn right to disappear around the corner; it seemed lost, trying to find its way through the maze of an empty city.

How easy it would be to pull up the window and take a long arching swan dive down to the concrete pavement. But oh what a mess when you hit bottom. Oh, you kid!

The memory of Uncle Harold came back to him. It had been a long time since he thought of Uncle Harold — it happened so long ago that try as he might he could never remember Uncle Harold's face.

"Seven floors down and plop!"

It struck him funny.

Wouldn't the reactionary bastards love it if he opened the window and dived through the darkness to the pavement below? *He must have been guilty of something or he wouldn't have jumped!*

He remembered how miserable Aunt Lena and his two cousins, Rachel and Yvette, were when they came to live with the family in Buffalo right after it happened with Uncle Harold in New York City. So many times since then he had thought about it — how easy it had been for Uncle Harold, walking out on his responsibilities because he couldn't swallow a business failure. Those whom Uncle Harold left behind suffered the pain for years and years and years, forever, their lives marred by that suicide which was always a suicide no matter how many years intervened between the event and the memory.

"No one," he told himself, "has the right to do that to those he would be leaving behind," and he was so emotionally wrought up he had to choke back tears — his throat clogged with an aching fullness.

He awoke in a state of terror, growling like a wild animal, whirling to shake off the hand which grasped his shoulder — striking out blindly with clenched fist at the new threat.

The heavy man bending over him hastily backed away and straightened up, avoiding the blow.

Danny's heart raced as he scrambled to his feet. The door was open. He tried to pull himself together to figure out what was happening. His brain found it hard to start functioning again. He kept his clenched fists raised in front of his chest.

"What the hell do *you* want?"

"House detective," the heavy stranger impersonally explained. "You left your door unlocked. Better lock it."

"Oh" — Danny relaxed and let his hands drop — "thanks." He explained that he had laid down to rest for a few minutes and had fallen asleep.

The detective went out, and Danny locked the door and made sure it was really locked good and tight this time. He stood there, leaning his head against the cool wood of the inside face of the door, his eyes closed. His mouth tasted foul and sticky, and his neck was sore from the way he had been lying in a twisted position on the bed. He wondered how long he had slept. He opened his eyes and looked down, without taking his head away from the door. His wrist watch had stopped running.

He phoned down to the switchboard and cursed out loud, with his hand over the mouthpiece of the phone, when the operator told him it was seventeen minutes past four. He asked her to call him at eight-thirty in the morning. That would give him about four more hours of sleep.

He sat down on the edge of the bed and pulled open his tie and slowly unbuttoned his shirt. The district council meeting was scheduled to start at ten in the morning. He wondered if he could get the council to pass a resolution supporting the position he had taken before the Committee. That would be a strong point from which to go back to the local unions in Buffalo and launch the whole plan of action to win tolerance of his right to a viewpoint which might sharply differ from that of the majority.

He thought about taking a shower or bath, and about shaving. He didn't have the energy for it. He decided he'd take a shower first thing when he woke up in the morning.

He remembered the interview with Joel Haas and wondered if the first edition of the Elmira newspapers had been delivered to the hotel. He could call down to the desk. But he decided to wait until morning. Too late to change the story after it's already printed.

"The hell with it," he said out loud, and fell asleep lying on top of the bed, awaking only a few moments later, laughing at himself, without any sound coming out of his mouth. Asleep again with all your clothes on. Becoming a habit. He laughed out loud, thinking he was being very funny as he upbraided himself, "Go to sleep, you drunken bum!"

Obeying the command, he stood up.

"Hang up your clothes, you drunken bum!"

He obediently staggered across the room to the closet — so tired he was acting silly. He removed his clothes and hung them up, hoping some of the wrinkles would be stretched out of his coat and trousers by morning. It was too late to send the suit down to be pressed.

He put on his pajamas. There was a toothbrush somewhere in his suitcase, but he didn't find it until after he had spilled all the rest of his things, mostly dirty clothes and books, in a heap on the floor. Then, after stuffing everything back into the suitcase, he remembered he had hidden the tube of toothpaste inside a clean sock when he packed at the hotel back in Albany.

"The hell with it, I'll brush my teeth with the hotel's soap."

He went into the bathroom.

"Oh, God," he said aloud, taunting the puffy-faced, tired, unshaven, red-eyed creature who peered between slitted eyelids back at him from the mirror above the wash basin. "Brother, you sure look like an awful miserable sonofabitch right now!"

The fresh pillow case felt nice after he climbed into bed and laid his head down. But he was still feeling very silly. There was a buzzing and whirring going round and round inside his head, as if he were drunk.

"Good-night, everybody," he announced to the empty darkness of the room.

He closed his eyes and took a deep breath and let out a loud sigh, as he wondered again what kind of a story the Elmira paper would carry. And then he was asleep, mouth wide open, noisily snoring, his face distorted in its collapse from total exhaustion.

Chapter 34

The fat black-lettered headline spread across the top of the front page of the Elmira newspapers was much more than Danny expected:

RED PROBE FIGURE AT MEET HERE

And underneath that banner headline, printed in only slightly smaller letters, the subhead:

UNION OFFICIAL DEFENDS PROBE QUERY REFUSAL

Underneath, surrounded by several columns of small print was the black and white photo, showing him talking to Lou Cartman, looking dark and funereal with his red hair a jet black.

"Why must you always look so heavy and serious?" Helen would ask. "Why can't you ever relax? And why didn't you take off your glasses?"

Standing in the lobby of the hotel, a few feet away from the cigar stand where he had bought the newspaper, Danny wondered if any of the local townspeople would recognize him.

He began to read. Halfway through reading the article, he became aware that the attendant at the cigar stand was staring at him. He tried to ignore the stare but out of the corner of his eye he could see that the attendant was checking the resemblance between him and the photo, noisily rustling the newspaper in his hand, the gaze from his faded blue eyes switching back and forth from the photo in the newspaper to the living object standing there in the lobby.

"You old fart, why don't you look somewhere else?" Danny said to himself as he folded the newspaper and thrust it under his arm. He briskly crossed the lobby, as if he had suddenly remembered he had to be somewhere in a very great hurry.

A hot and cold shower, followed by a shave, had started him off with some of the old zip — he felt human again. While he dressed, he reviewed the tentative plan of action he had blocked out for himself before he went to bed. His kickoff

would take place at the district council meeting when he
addressed delegates from all over the state. George
Hernandez was right to urge him to attend this meeting and
face the rank-and-file leaders as soon as possible after the
hearing. It was like getting up on a horse again immediately
after you've been thrown. This would be his chance to build
the broad background of support in the Buffalo-Tonawandas
area.

In the coffee shop a buxom blonde in a black dress very
brightly greeted him.

"Good morning, sir — "

"Morning."

"Just one, sir?"

"Just one."

He spread the newspaper out on top of the small table
and skimmed rapidly through the story, trying to finish
before the waitress came back.

As he read the reasons he had given for refusing to
answer the Committee's questions, he silently thanked Joel
Haas for giving him a break. Haas seemed to be trying to
create the impression that the union organizer was a serious
character — perhaps taking himself a little too seriously —
who decided as a matter of principle to challenge the
constitutionality of the enabling resolution by which the
House of Representatives had established the Committee on
Un-American Activities. Even his army service was
mentioned, with a quote to the effect that he had decided to
volunteer to fight fascism here at home in the same way he
had decided to volunteer to fight fascism when it threatened
the welfare of the nation in World War II. In cold black print
that seemed like he was waving the flag just a little too hard.
Yet he wished he could get a story like that into the Buffalo
newspaper. But then he decided against that — the big
headline would frighten Helen.

He saw the waitress approaching with a small glass of
orange juice and he carefully folded the newspaper with his
picture face down. When she left he unfolded the newspaper
and read the story again, slowly this time, studying it —
meanwhile wondering what kind of story appeared in the
Buffalo morning newspaper. Was Helen frantic? Had she
raced off to her sister in Florida, taking the two kids with

her? He saw the waitress returning with his scrambled eggs and toast and coffee — he folded the newspaper with his picture face down again.

Eating his scrambled eggs, he became aware that one of the other patrons in the coffee shop had guessed his identity. A fat man at a table across the room was directing the attention of his stout female companion to the picture on the front page of the newspaper he held in his hands. He pointed. Danny looked down at his scrambled eggs, trying not to appear disconcerted.

"More coffee, sir?"

"No, thanks. Check, please."

After he received the check and paid the waitress, telling her to keep the change he looked to the couple who had identified him.

They glared at him, the hate showing on their faces. He was glad when the door closed behind him.

"Bastards!"

Back in the hotel room, he sat down on the edge of the unmade bed and studied the front page of the newspaper again, reading it first as he thought Helen would read it, and then as he thought a total stranger might read it, and then as one of the friendly local union members back in Buffalo or North Tonawanda might read it — trying to figure out places in the article where different readers would have strongly favorable reactions and places where they might react unfavorably, and most important, *why* they would react that way.

The delegates to the district council meeting will have already read the front page of the newspaper by the time he arrives at the meeting hall. He would soon be able to check *their* reaction.

As for Helen — he decided not to show her the paper. The headline **RED PROBE FIGURE AT MEET HERE** would disturb her too much, killing any good which might come from the fairly decent story Joel Haas had written.

He wondered if he should phone Helen. That would be the quickest way to find out whether or not she was still in Buffalo. He decided it was too risky to phone her before he spoke at the district council meeting — he needed all the confidence he could gather together to put himself across properly at that meeting. If he phoned now and Helen wasn't there — if she and the kids were already on their way to Florida — he dreaded what that knowledge might do to his morale. And even if Helen did answer the phone she would probably be very depressed by what she read in the Buffalo newspaper about the threatened contempt citation. That wouldn't help his morale either. After the district council passed some kind of favorable resolution he would have something to use to counteract the damage done by the Buffalo newspapers.

When he paid his bill down in the lobby he sensed the clerk's cold hostility. He had to fight a growing feeling of panic as he left the hotel. Walking toward the meeting hall, he remembered how this had happened to him once before — back in 1948, in the early days of the Cold War, the Tonawanda newspaper had whipped up a wild hysteria against him in the community with scare stories labeling him as an outside red agitator (his home was in nearby Buffalo) who had invaded their community to foment strikes and class warfare; he remembered walking down the main street in North Tonawanda the same way he was walking down this main street in Elmira — and a car pulled up alongside him and the driver rolled down the window and showed his teeth when he screamed:

"You red bastard! Get out of town before we get a rope and hang you up by your nuts!"

Danny remembered how he plodded on, looking ahead, deliberately ignoring the threat, refusing to surrender his self-respect by increasing his pace — and nothing happened, the hysteria gradually subsiding over a period of several months.

He looked up at the blue sky and the bright sun and tried to lift his spirit by reminding himself that it was a nice spring day. He walked briskly down the main street, staring defiantly straight ahead, avoiding a clash of eyes with townspeople who passed by him on the sidewalk or who drove by in their automobiles. Nervous, he waited for some driver to roll down the window of his car and to scream, baring his teeth like that man had done in North Tonawanda in 1948:

"You red bastard! Get out of town before we get a rope and

hang you up by your nuts!"

And if anyone did scream at him that way he was determined to keep on plodding straight ahead, making himself ignore the threat as he had done in North Tonawanda back in 1948, and he hoped nothing more serious would happen to him now in 1954 than had happened to him then.

He walked steadily toward the union's meeting hall, keeping a stiff face, staring straight ahead.

The district council meeting had already started. Standing in the rear of the main hall where he had been interviewed by Joel Haas the night before, Danny quickly estimated that there were seventy-five or more seated delegates listening to secretary-treasurer Ed Hinton, his heavy spectacles perched on his nose, reading the minutes of the previous meeting.

Lanky Bill Becker, in the chairman's seat at the center of the long table in the front of the hall, beckoned and pointed to an empty seat in the first row. Several delegates turned their heads to see the object of the chairman's attention.

Danny hesitantly started down the aisle, unsure of the reception he was going to get from the delegates. He was very quickly reassured.

Hands waved.

Faces smiled.

Friendly voices, muted so as not to interrupt the reading of minutes, called out greetings.

"You're late, you agitating redheaded son-of-a-gun."

"Hey, Danny, why do you pick on those guys? All they want to do is cut your throat!"

"Hey, you redheaded bastard, where were you born?"

"He wasn't!"

"The milkman delivered him."

"The milkman, hell — the iceman — "

"You mean the mechanic who repaired the refrigerator."

"So you won't talk, you stubborn sonofabitch!"

"We taught 'em not to mix up with any guys from up around Buffalo and the Tonawandas, didn't we, Danny? From now on they'll know better — "

"Hey, Danny, go easy on those guys next time. After all, you gotta remember they're only a bunch of lousy no-good bastards!"

Overflowing with emotion, a choked feeling developing in his chest and throat, Danny walked slowly down the aisle, turning his head each time he heard a new voice, trying to locate and smile at each delegate who spoke to him.

He felt a hand lock itself around his left wrist. He looked down and saw chubby Walt Scheer and hawk-nosed Elmer Topolski. In 1948 it had been their local union leaders who had led the pack in whipping up the hysteria against him in North Tonawanda — because he had walked on a picket line in front of the Immigration Service office in Buffalo to protest against the deportation of Charlie Doyle, a union leader known to be a communist. Scheer, gripping his wrist, slid over to leave an empty seat between himself and Elmer Topolski.

"This seat is reserved for you."

He pulled Danny down into it. The three of them sat up against the wall, not saying another word, facing the rest of the delegates seated in the center of the hall.

Bill Becker rapped his gavel to bring the attention of the delegates back to the reading of the minutes. Danny saw that men and women in different parts of the hall were still winking and smiling recognition at him. Some raised their eyebrows and twisted their faces into comical expressions when their eyes met his. Some quietly waved at him. A few wiggled only their fingers to draw his attention and then formed a silent 'hello' with their lips.

Deeply stirred, Danny blinked and fought to hold back the wetness that filled his eyes. These were *his* people, from the shops: men and women he had helped to organize into unions; men and women who had sat with him at the bargaining table facing the company in negotiations; men and women with whom he had walked the picket line for weeks, and with some of them for many terrible months.

He smiled back at those who were signaling to him, as he fought not to cry.

Chapter 35

Danny stood in the front of the hall, facing the seated delegates. It took him a while to get out a word.

"Brothers — "

He stopped.

"Sisters — "

He stopped again, unable to go on.

He opened his mouth — no words came out. He tried again. And again. Each time he opened his mouth he had to close it again in order to control the flood of emotion trying to break out of his clogged throat and chest. He must look like a fool — opening and closing his mouth like a poor fish gulping for air. Why was he so emotionally disturbed? Thus far, everything had gone well at the meeting. And he had seen a copy of the Buffalo morning newspaper — a delegate from Buffalo brought it along — there had been a factual account of his refusal to answer the questions of the Committee, after a lead paragraph about Congressman Holling's recommendation that he be cited for contempt, and the story was buried deep inside the newspaper, not screaming from the top of the front page like the banner headline in the Elmira newspaper.

During the reports by local union delegates on important developments on grievances and arbitrations and wage talks and contract negotiations there had not been even a hint of redbaiting; the delegates had taken every opportunity to show him their friendliness. Bill Becker, chairing the meeting, had agreed that it looked like there would be no trouble and that it would be all right if Danny left after he made his report on what had happened at the hearing. Bill promised he would make Danny's report the first item on the agenda when the meeting reconvened at two o'clock after breaking for lunch. He also promised that he would arrange for one of the delegates to make a motion from the floor, putting the district council officially on record as supporting the position Danny had taken before the Committee.

There was no direct plane flight from Elmira to Buffalo

until the next morning. He could catch the early afternoon train to Buffalo but he would have to make his speech a very short one. Rather than phoning Helen to tell her when he would be arriving in Buffalo, he had sent a wire, phoning it in to the telegraph office, addressing it to "Helen, Ruth and Linda Newman" — saying when he would be arriving at the railroad station in Buffalo and asking them to meet him there; on impulse, he had added, *"Please stick with me."* And then: *"Love, Danny."* The operator asked the number of the phone he was using and he had to explain that he was calling from the union office, and she asked for his full name, and then read the message back to him, and he thanked her and told her it was all right, and then she dropped the official tone and said, "Good luck." He knew then that she had recognized his name and tied it to the story in the Elmira newspaper. Her sympathy caught him unawares and he had a hard time keeping his voice even as he replied, "Thanks — thanks."

The delegates were still waiting for him to pull himself together so he could make his report.

He started again.

"Sisters and brothers — "

He could see that some of the delegates were sweating out his embarrassment with him. He closed his mouth and awkwardly scratched the back of his head and tried to get control of the situation by laughing at himself.

"I don't know exactly where to start — "

He could see their sympathetic smiles.

He ridiculed himself. "That's something when Danny Newman is speechless."

Some of the delegates grinned encouragement, and Bill Becker behind him quipped, "This is something I never thought I'd see."

There was some nervous laughter in which Danny joined.

Then a dramatic silence settled over the delegates. Danny's eyes traveled from one face to another and he could see that they were waiting for him to go on, and he could feel their desire to help him, their friendliness — it was this very thing which made it so hard for him to speak; if there had been antagonism out there — if this were a no-holds-barred floor fight requiring an angry counterattack or a furious defense it would be easy — he could lose himself in the heat of the combat. But it wasn't like that.

He started once more.

"I — would — like — to — try — "

He stopped.

He could see they were straining to help him get the words out. He fumbled nervously with his tie.

"I — would — like — to — try — " he repeated. And then he went on, groping for the right words, nervously moving as he spoke — shoving his hands into his pockets and taking them out again, removing his glasses and putting them on again, fumbling with his tie, running his hand through his hair, shifting his weight from one foot to another, hunching up his trousers, rubbing the palm of his right hand back and forth along the underside of his jaw —

"I've asked the chairman — if it's all right — if I cut my report short — so I can catch a train to get home. — I haven't spoken to my wife since I appeared before the Committee yesterday morning — so I want to be sure to catch the train. — I've sent a wire asking my wife to meet me at the railroad station in Buffalo with the kids; and I don't want them to come down to the station and not find me there, and I hope I don't get to the station and not find *them* there — "

He stopped, wishing he hadn't said that. It sounded like a cheap bid for sympathy. His hands were still in mid-air, caught in the middle of that last sentence, and his mouth was still open. He closed his mouth and grabbed hold of his belt with his hands and hunched up his trousers.

He began again.

"Sometimes — "

His chest was heaving. Deep breaths. Inhale. Exhale. He could hear his deep breathing as he fought to control the turbulence which threatened to burst out of the confinement in his chest.

"Sometimes — . Sometimes — . Sometimes — I almost wish I didn't see things the way I do. — Sometimes — I almost wish I could be happy standing on the sidelines. Or even in the rear of the most reactionary section of people in our country. Because then — maybe I could just go along saying what it's good and safe to say — what it's good and safe to advocate in the way of ideas — and be very happy and

satisfied and smug with my little kingdom of happiness
— quiet and at peace with myself."

Breathe in. Breathe out. In. Out.

"But — "

Breathe in. Breathe out.

"But — . But — . But — you got to be what you are! — You
got to do what you can live with! — No matter what happens
— you always have to live with yourself — you can't get away
from yourself — and you got to do what you have to do — so
you *can* live with yourself — . Sometimes — I wish I were a
different kind of person. Life might be so much easier — for
me — and certainly for my family. At least in the short run.
Maybe not in the long run. Maybe not in the long pull of
things — if you can look at life with the long view — "

He stopped to collect his thoughts, to get back on the
beam. He realized he was wandering. Maybe he ought to
start back and make a fresh beginning.

"I would like to tell you — as quickly as I can — why I
refused to answer the questions of the Committee. — Please
don't think I wanted to be a hero. I don't, I don't. — Of
course, I wanted to do the right thing, the best thing, and I'm
honest enough to admit that I like to be praised and admired
— my heart still beats faster when I hear a brass band — "

He stopped. My God, he was beginning to sound
incoherent!

He took another deep breath, to pull himself together.

He began again, speaking slowly, steadily, hanging on
tight, making sure the words fitted together with solid logic.

"Believe me, I'm not trying to be a hero. I'm too scared to
be a hero. — But I *had* to do what I did. Don't get me wrong
— no one made me do it; no one except myself — *I* — *me* —
once I was convinced that the situation was right for
someone to make this kind of test; once I was convinced that
it was only a question of getting up sufficient courage to do
something which should, in all logic, have been done at the
moment; once I was convinced that, as part of the developing
resistance to the Committee's attack against the civil
liberties of the people, I should — if I could only get up the
courage — challenge the constitutionality of the Committee,
challenge the very existence of this Committee on
Un-American Activities which is the central spearhead of the

assault against our Bill of Rights and the freedoms which
flow from the Bill of Rights; once I was convinced of that,
rightly or wrongly, with correct or incorrect logic — *how*, I
ask you; *how* could I face myself if I turned and ran from my
responsibility to the people of our country, to the working
people of our country, to you, to my family, even to myself?"
He gritted his teeth, as if in pain, and he slammed his right
fist against the palm of his left hand. — "We all know what
happened in Germany under Hitler! Under the Nazis! . . .
Some of you know this, and some of you don't — *I'm a Jew!*
And all of you know what happened to the Jews under Hitler,
under the Nazis. — I can't help but think that if, in similar
circumstances, I had been a German, living in Germany
before Hitler and the Nazis succeeded in wiping out all open
opposition, and if I had been called before a similar
committee in Germany at that time — who knows, maybe
such an act would have helped to rally the forces who, in
their hearts, opposed Hitler and the Nazis but were afraid to
say it out loud — maybe it would have helped, at least in a
small way, to prevent some of the terrible things which
happened later in Nazi Germany. Thinking that way I *had* to
do what I did here — "

He paused, disturbed by his inability to say exactly what
he meant. It still sounded like he was trying to be a hero. He
burst out, trying to get across the idea to the delegates:

"Believe me, I didn't want to be a goddamn hero. But
knowing and seeing things as I did, *I couldn't be a lousy
coward!*"

He stopped. It still sounded all wrong. He reminded
himself that he was talking in circles. Get to the reasons why
you refused to answer the Committee's questions! Explain it
to them! Hurry up — you'll miss the train. Get to the point —

"I'd like to take a few more minutes to give you the
reasons, the legal reasons why I refused to answer the
Committee's questions. But first let me say — that while I
didn't use the Fifth Amendment, those who are using it are
acting very honorably to defend the Bill of Rights for
themselves and for all of us. Each person does what fits in
with the needs of his personal situation as he sees it; what's
correct for one person is not necessarily correct for another.
Some people decide to answer some questions and refuse to

answer others. Some people use the Fifth Amendment, some people don't. Each person does what he feels he's got to do."

He tried to explain to them how difficult it had been for him to arrive at his decision to refuse to answer *any* question of the Committee. He told the delegates briefly, concealing the worst of it, how he had argued with himself until early morning in his hotel room before he phoned his lawyer and told him he had decided he would challenge the constitutionality of the enabling resolution establishing the Committee.

He took his notes out of his pocket and unfolded the yellow sheets and slowly went through the reasons why the resolution establishing the Committee was unconstitutional. The delegates listened intently — he could see the interest on their faces, and there was absolute silence in the meeting hall.

When he finished he folded the notes and put them back in his pocket.

" So — "

He stopped and tried to think of what else he should say, but then decided he had said enough.

"Thanks."

There was no applause. He started toward the rear of the hall — on his way to catch the train, on his way back to Buffalo and all the problems waiting there. There was absolute silence in the hall. Several delegates stretched out their hands to grab his and give a quick squeeze as he went by.

Chubby Walt Scheer stopped him in the rear of the hall and solemnly shook his hand and congratulated him, giving him the greatest compliment he could give to any speaker. "You sonofabitch," Walt hissed into his ear, "I always said you should have been a lawyer!"

Except for the man behind the grating of the ticket window and the woman attendant behind the newsstand, Danny saw that he was the only person in the small waiting room at the railroad station. When he bought his ticket the man behind the grating told him the train was on time — it was due in four minutes. He hurried into the phone booth and put in a call to the union office he had just left. He recognized the voice on the other end of the line.

"Lennie, this is Danny — "

"Oh, hi!"

" Hi — I'm at the railroad station, Lennie, waiting for my train — "

"Oh, you made it!"

"Yeah, Lennie! Listen — I only got a minute before I have to run, so don't waste time."

"Okay."

"Lennie, did anyone introduce a resolution after I finished speaking?"

"What resolution?"

"A resolution about me!"

"About you?"

"Yes, about me and about the position I took before the Committee — a resolution of support. Didn't anyone make a motion from the floor?"

"I didn't hear anything, Danny. I came out here to the office after you finished speaking — I didn't stay back there in the meeting hall."

"Lennie, ask someone else around there. See if you can find out! Hurry up, Lennie, I've got to run in a second, I can hear the train coming in — ask if they passed a resolution about me. Hurry up. Please, Lennie!"

He heard Lennie call out to someone in the union office, asking if he or she had heard anything about a resolution supporting Danny Newman. He couldn't make out the reply of the other person — he could hear the roar of the train racing into the station on the upper level, directly above him. The building was vibrating from the pounding of the wheels of the train. And then he heard Lennie's voice again.

"One of the guys put a motion on the floor — full support, Danny — it passed unanimously!"

"Good! Thanks, Lennie, I gotta run, the train's here already, g'bye!"

He slammed the receiver down on the hook, yanked open the door of the booth, grabbed his suitcase, raced up the steps of the long stairway, jumping three at a time. There was the porter reaching down to pick up the wooden step. Danny yelled. The porter waited for him — and told him he was the only passenger who boarded the train there.

He found a seat where he would be able to spread out for a while and grab some sleep. The train was picking up speed again — he sat down next to the picture window where he could look out and watch the passing countryside — and think about how he could use the resolution passed by the district council as a stepping stone for further activity to create a favorable atmosphere around Helen and the kids back in Buffalo.

He both dreaded and looked forward to meeting Helen face-to-face, coming to grips with the problem of what to do about their marriage. He wondered if she would be there to meet him at the railroad station.

Chapter 36

A steady drizzle splattered the train window next to Danny's elbow. Dusk tried to hide the line of dirty factories and steel mills whose tall smokestacks, some belching fire, were silhouetted against the darkening sky. The train passed through a rundown section of Buffalo with crowded ramshackle houses. As a child he had lived in one of those houses a few blocks over to the right of the railroad tracks. He wondered if it had been this way back then.

"Buffalo — Buffalo — all out at Buffalo!"

Danny's eyes followed the train conductor passing through the car. When the conductor was gone he looked through the window again, identifying familiar landmarks — it would be another minute or two before the train would actually pull into the station.

The train moved slowly now, up on the elevated tracks over the warehouses, and Danny could look down on the harbor with docks lined up along the muddy channel that led into the lake. Out beyond the channel he could see the dark water of the lake and the stone breakwall — he remembered how, when he was a young boy, he dived off that same breakwall and almost drowned out there. A stranger saved his life, pulling him back to the safety of the breakwall. He saw the ore boats, enormous lake freighters which were also ocean-going vessels, lined up along the breakwall, a familiar sight reminding him of the time when he decided to be a sailor and went so far as to apply for his papers. Out beyond the breakwall, beyond the freighters, off into the misty gray of the rapidly descending darkness, he saw — recalled almost more than actually saw — the vast spreading expanse of dark, choppy, white-capped waters of Lake Erie extending as far as the eye could see, way out there to the light gray horizon in the west. The rain had settled down to a steady drizzle. He watched the beady drops of water form into thin rivulets running down the outside of the window pane next to his elbow.

There was a lot of activity developing inside the car.

Passengers were pulling down suitcases, putting on hats and coats and generally arranging personal effects to be ready to get off the train which was barely crawling along now as it approached the station. Passengers began to line up in the aisle. Danny sat motionless in his seat and watched them. He was in no hurry to be the first to get off the train.

The train creaked and complained its way into the station, and Danny's view through the window on his left was blocked by another train on the next track which had already unloaded its passengers. He looked across the center aisle and out through the windows over on the other side of the car, seeing the slanted roof sheds which protected the long narrow platforms between the tracks from the worst of the rain.

The train stopped moving.

Danny heard the familiar sound of metal striking against metal, as the conductor out in the vestibule at the end of the car slammed open the door which faced the station platform.

Other passengers started to file out of the car. Danny watched, waiting until the end of the line had passed him. He stood up and put on his topcoat and reached up and hauled his suitcase down from the rack, and then he stepped out into the center aisle and took his place at the end of the shuffling line of baggage-laden passengers leaving the train. Through the car windows facing the platform he could see some of the passengers who had already left the train being greeted by those who had come to meet them, and he envied them as he saw the embraces and kisses and hearty handshakes.

He stepped down to the concrete platform and looked around — there was no one there to meet him. He started walking, slowly, toward the brick building at the end of the long narrow platform.

The setting around him seemed totally unreal, like a mechanically contrived scene for a moving picture. Rain was falling, wetting the tops of the trains and the unprotected track areas between the platforms — and in the background he could hear all kinds of railroad station noises: train whistles, chugging of engines, steam escaping, squealing of metal wheels against metal tracks — and he felt like an actor, moving along, taking his cue from the director behind the camera, with no real personal connection with what was happening. Numb — mechanically weaving his way, blindly, through the different activities usually included as background in a railroad station scene: a group of men, working as a team, unloading heavy sacks from the mail car; a gray-haired woman bending over to kiss a small child; a uniformed sailor shaking hands with an older man who looked like he was his father; two bouncy teen-aged girls ecstatically throwing their arms around one another; — Danny saw all this activity developing in front of him, as he dragged along, trying to hold back, staring through it, searching for the familiar sight of a tall, slim, dark haired woman in her mid-thirties with two redheaded girls, a gawky long-legged adolescent and a fat-legged little child who would probably be so tired that her sister or her mother would be carrying her. Redcaps pushed their loaded baggage carts across his path and impatiently threaded their way in and out between the slower moving passengers.

He had seen this scene often in the movies, but this was the first time he ever had a feeling that he was living something exactly as if he was an actor being followed by a camera on a set. It gave him a peculiar sensation, as if it was all unreal. A man arrives on a train, hoping someone he loves will be there to meet him; he gets off the train and starts walking along the platform; a shot of some passengers jostling against him; a shot of some people greeting one another, making his loneliness sharper by contrast; back to him, moving stolidly ahead, alone, with passengers shoving past him; a shot of his suitcase in his left hand, heavy — his heart heavy, his suitcase heavy, he's all choked up, but he keeps his face a stiff mask, showing absolutely no emotion — that's what makes the scene so poignant to the movie audience, that's why the women reach into their purses for their handkerchiefs — and he keeps plodding ahead, each step calculated, each step measured, consciously keeping himself moving steadily ahead — step — step — step —

He stopped and stood still.

In an effort to break the unreal movie quality of what was happening — he put down his suitcase and flexed his fingers which ached from gripping the handle so tight.

He started off again, with the suitcase in his other hand,

continuing down that last mile to impending doom, with the imaginary cameras grinding away again, following behind, shooting over his shoulder, seeing what he saw; and at any moment the director would yell, "Cut!" — and then they would move on to the next scene inside the railroad station.

The waiting room was a dingy place, too deserted to make a good setting for a movie — not enough mechanical movement to hold the interest of a movie audience very long — and he lost the feeling of being followed by cameras and a movie director.

He sat down on a bench, to think things over and decide what to do. He was surprised to find that he was not as disturbed as he thought he would be. What happened — had happened and there was no use crying about it.

He looked up at the electric clock above the line of ticket windows. The train had come in on time. Even if Helen were a few minutes late she would have come by now. Maybe she had not been able to find a parking place. She might be outside in the car, waiting for him to come out of the station. That was not likely but he might as well take a look.

Stone steps in front of the old railroad station led down to the street level. On the sidewalk a line of taxicab drivers reached out their hands, offering to take his suitcase.

"Taxi! Taxicab! — Cab! Taxi!"

He walked along the sidewalk out in front of the station with the cries of the drivers following him.

"Taxicab! — Taxi! — Taxicab!"

He went back up the steps into the waiting room and sat down again.

There was a newsstand in the corner of the waiting room. He heard the lonely sound of the soles of his shoes scraping on the stone floor as he walked across the room.

What a going over the evening paper must have given me if it's thrown Helen into such a tailspin that she won't even come down to the railroad station to be seen there with me. Of course, she may have already gone with the kids to Florida.

He bought a copy of the evening newspaper. A quick glance at the front page. Nothing there!

He returned to the bench where he had left his suitcase and sat down and rapidly thumbed through the rest of the

Buffalo newspaper, scanning each page for the story about Congressman Holling's recommendation that he be cited for contempt.

Finally, he found it — a short, comparatively innocuous item, a few dirty digs, but really not too bad, nothing nearly as bad as he expected — he had been given much worse treatment by the same newspaper many times before. Even Helen must have expected much worse. But maybe it was the last straw for her, the extra ounce that toppled the pile of grievances. Had she been feeling so badly about the whole situation that anything in the newspaper at this time was too much to take?

He carefully folded the newspaper, crossed to a waste barrel and threw it in.

Back to his place on the bench. Maybe Helen decided it was too late to take little Linda out of the house. It was past the child's bedtime. Maybe she couldn't get a sitter to stay with the child. Maybe the whole family — Helen and Ruth and Linda — were home, waiting for him to phone from the railroad station.

The man at the newsstand changed a dollar bill for him. In the phone booth he dialed his home number. The buzzing sounded in his ear. The phone was ringing at the other end. It rang — and rang — and rang — and rang — and rang —

He hung up the receiver and went back to his place on the bench.

What happened to Esther, their college student helper? If Helen and the kids were gone, where was Esther? Back home with her parents in North Tonawanda? Or had she already found some other place in Buffalo near the college where she could work for her room and board for the rest of the school term?

Maybe Helen never received his telegram. She might have already taken the children and left for Florida. Where would she get the money to go? From her brother Bob or her mother. Maybe she took the kids and moved in with her mother over at The Park Lane. There would be room there for all of them.

Should he telephone there?

What good would that do? If she took the kids over to her mother's place it would be only to give her time she needed to get ready to go on to her sister's place in Florida. Or maybe she wanted to wait until Ruth was through with school. And if that's the way she wants it, to hell with it. He was too sick and tired of the prolonged emotional turmoil to do anything about it.

Ever since he had realized there was a possibility that he might be left alone his mind had been made up that he would not live in their big house which would only remind him continually of Helen and the two kids. A hotel room? But right now he had only two dollars and some change in his pocket. He could stay with some of his union people, or with one of his brothers, or at his sister's place, or even with his father and mother. But he was in no mood to be with anyone he knew, with anyone to whom he would have to explain why he was not going home. To hell with it. For the time being he'd go home and get a good night's sleep in his own familiar bed, *their* bed. And in the morning he'd figure out what to do next.

Down on the street level in front of the railroad station. Rain still falling. Darkness. The street lamps lit.

"Taxi! — Taxicab! — Cab! Taxi!"

A cab driver grabbed Danny's suitcase. Following the driver to his car, Danny thought that this would just about clean him out financially until he could get a check cashed somewhere, but he was in no mood for a long bus ride. The cab driver put the suitcase up on the front seat near the meter and opened the rear door for Danny.

Just as Danny ducked his head to enter the taxi he saw a light green car pull up to the curb in front of them. He recognized the car; he recognized Helen at the wheel; he recognized the two redheaded girls sitting in the front seat with Helen, Ruth holding Linda on her lap — and he saw the two kids waving frantically at him.

His brain was slow to react.

He stood there, stooped over, looking at the green car and Helen and the two kids; and then he realized he still had a family and he was able to make his arms and legs move again.

He casually waved back at the kids.

"Our wedding picture, taken in lobby of The Park Lane, March 21, 1941. The tuxedo had been loaned to me by a friend who later killed himself, which only in retrospect seems to be a harbinger of dark days to come."

"Rhoda and *THE CAKE ICER*, the first in a planned series of paintings of employees at Lippes Bakeries in Buffalo, N.Y. Photo, circa 1972."

Christmas at the Park Lane

"The Park Lane porch, part of luxurious restaurant and cocktail lounge which, after it was sold by Lurie family in 1968, was destroyed by fire and replaced by English style tavern. This Christmas card was sent out by their maitre d' Peter Gust Economou — in their employ so many years that he was considered part of Lurie family."

"Rhoda, center, in The Park Lane dining room, at height of her glamorous stage during our early married years, flanked by childhood friend Ros and husband Dr. Hal Millstone, close friends who pulled away from us during the McCarthy Period — advertising executive Ros pressed by her employer to break the friendship. Photo, 1946."

"Arguing with policeman who threatened to arrest Eddie Lewandowski and me for giving out leaflets without a permit, leaflets asking public support for some of our union members who were on strike. Plainclothes detective told cop we had right to give out leaflets. Circa 1954."

"Charles Warren Brown (later first Black to become licensed electrician in the city), myself and Eddie Lewandowski, giving out leaflets in downtown Buffalo, asking public support for striking American Safety Razor workers. Circa 1954."

"Volunteer organizing Committee of workers at Buflovak Division of Blaw Knox Corporation celebrating National Labor Relations Board election victory over raid by Steelworkers Union — raid illegally promoted and assisted by J. Edgar Hoover's FBI. August 1954."

"Lorrie and Mindy in living room of our home, 125 Chatham Avenue, Buffalo. Photo, circa 1954."

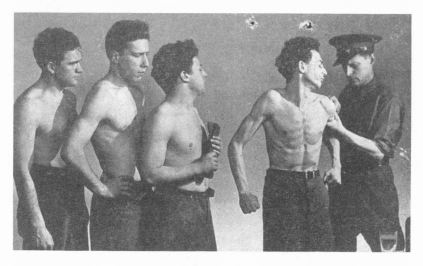

"Second from left, I was 22 when in 1935 I played the lead in Theatre of Action's *THE YOUNG GO FIRST* directed by Elia Kazan. In front of me is longtime friend Perry Bruskin, now a well-established New York theatre and film producer. — Back then I thought I was a weak-willed vacillating person compared to Kazan with his unbending commitment to idealistic goals of socialism. But almost 20 years later it was Kazan who cooperated and named names before the House Committee on Un-American Activities while I refused to answer any of their questions and challenged them to indict me so we could go to court to act on my charge that under our U.S. Constitution the Committee had no legal right to exist. Yet I still have a very warm feeling for Kazan, still think of him as nice guy 'Gadge' who was truly kind in 1935 to a very confused and unhappy young actor, and again in 1946, offering to launch me on a film career when I returned from army service in World War II, not sure what I wished to do with my life."

"*THE SWITCHBOARD OPERATOR* — one of a series of paintings Rhoda did of cross section of tenants and employees of The Park Lane. This is Irene, on whose lap Lorrie, when she was about 5, sat and (taught by Irene) operated the switchboard."

Confidential Informant advised on April 6, 1944 that had told him that she had contacted MANNIE FRIED to see if he would say a few words at the meeting, but MANNIE had not committed himself at that time.

- 5 -

"Typical blanked-out page in FBI dossier supplied me when I requested it under Freedom of Information Act."

"Mindy and Lorrie. Photo, circa 1953."

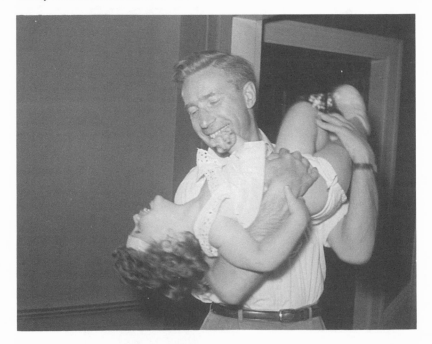

"Playing with Mindy. Photo, circa 1952."

United States Department of Justice
Federal Bureau of Investigation
400 U. S. Court House
Buffalo, New York

IN REPLY, PLEASE REFER TO
FILE No.

ALL INFORMATION CONTAINED
HEREIN IS UNCLASSIFIED
EXCEPT WHERE SHOWN
OTHERWISE

CONFIDENTIAL

September 6, 1950

"JUNE"

CONFIDENTIAL

9/18/80
CLASS. & EXT. SPS eschm
REASON-FCIM II 1-2.4.2
DATE OF REVIEW 9/18/90

Director, FBI

RE: EMANUEL JOSEPH FRIED
INTERNAL SECURITY - C

Dear Sir:

DECLASSIFIED BY 8042 PLJ/as
ON 4/13/86

        Reference request for microphone surveillance dated August
14, 1950 and Bureau teletype to Buffalo dated August 25, 1950.

        Referenced teletype authorized the installation of a
microphone surveillance in the subject's wife's apartment as per
referenced request.

        A careful survey of the location resulted in the decision
that a useable microphone could not be installed with the necessary
security factor being born in mind.

b7D/1

b7D/1
&
b7E/1

        If permission is granted to install a combination telephone
and microphone installation in this apartment the installation can be
made with full security.

                                          Very truly yours,

                                          H. G. MAYNOR
                                          Special Agent in Charge

                                          100-24586-44
                                          OCT 17 1950

                                          5

CONFIDENTIAL

memo. Buffalo
9/29/50

"Page from FBI dossier, which explains itself."

"Rhoda and I and Gentleman Charlie in living room of our Chatham Avenue home. This is room where, about 9 years earlier, shortly after Mindy was born in 1950, I came home one night and found Rhoda protectively huddled over the baby, all lights out, having just received warning phone call that gang of teenagers, steamed up by redbaiting stuff about me in the newspapers, were on their way to throw rocks through our windows."

"That's Rhoda on the left, me on the right, at Boca Raton, Florida, trip won because I sold million dollars worth of life insurance for United States Division of Toronto-based Canada Life Assurance Company, whose vice president had the guts to refuse to fire me after FBI tried to get his company to do what a series of U.S. companies had already done with me when — following my 1954 appearance before HUAC — I was blacklisted. Photo, circa 1958."

"Cast of MARK OF SUCCESS, winner of Catawba College (Salisbury, N.C.) 1962 New American Playwrights contest. That's Rhoda seated on sofa, my hand on her shoulder. Although I was still on FBI's blacklist, Theatre Department Director Donald N. Walters, standing behind me, had the courage to select and produce my play. Some years later, revised and renamed DAVID AND SON, the play was produced by Buffalo Ensemble Theatre."

THE UN-AMERICAN

by adolph dupree

Who's Afraid Of Manny Fried?

Producers and theatrical groups alike almost unanimously avoid original plays of unknown playwrights preferring instead the "BOX OFFICE" certainty of established works.

But if a playwright is to ever become established and if his works are to be recognized, then there must be a beginning somewhere.

Theatre Five in cooperation with the Buffalo Junior Chamber of Commerce established that beginning last week with the opening of an original drama by Emanuel Fried entitled "The Dead Hand" Staged at Hotel Richford's Off Broadway Theatre "The Dead Hand" will be followed by "Let's Not And Say We Did" an original comedy by Gerad Marchette.

Ironically enough Emanuel "Manny" Fried should be considered an "established" playwright. His one act plays have enjoyed sucessful productions in various coffee houses in Buffalo and a three act play, "The Mark of Sucess" won a national playwriting contest. In addition, "The Mark.." was placed on the supplemental list of Catalogue of New Plays for 1963 by American Educational Theatre Asso-

ciation (AETA). His once act play "The Dodo Bird" was one of eight plays listed by the Catalog in the main edition. "The Dodo Bird" is scheduled to open this fall in New York with Bob Costly starring in one of the roles

"The Dead Hand" could easily be considered autobiographical in explaining the "anonymous" Emanual Fried. Based upon individual concepts as opposed to group social standards "The Dead Hand" represents archaic ideas and non involvement. The frustration of chosing between leftist rights and social rights befalls heroine Barbara Wilson (Rose Elmstead) and is complicated by a subsequent marraige when her husband Gerald Hoke (Bert) deviates from earlier principles to fit the easier pattern of guilt free association.

Miss Wilson as the wife is confronted with a demanding role that allows little if any freedom from dialogue action and emotion. The fine young actress performs her assignment with professional style and is responsible for maintaining a reliable hub from which the spokes of support are able to revolve efficiently.

Equally effective was Gerry Hoke, naturally suited for his role in easy going manner. Gerald Fried, brother of the playwright was adequate as the "tainted" brother-in-law Mike and Maureen Donnelly appeared as the sister, Ellen Assistant Director Stuart Maguire appeared briefly as the father.

"The Dead Hand" was an interesting mixture of realism and avant garde with Brecht overtones employing the use of sound film and recorded voices. At times Director Gary Tunmore and Author Fried took different directions but basically the play overcame the minor defects. Mr. Tunmore and the Junior Chamber of Commerce with Theatre Five, Inc. should be praised for presenting a play with something important to say on stage and something definate being done in theatre. Buffalo and surrounding area certainly has the facilities and personnel to project beginning playwrights as well as potential theatrical stars. We can not plant a garden of roses without thorns or a field of grass without weeds. Together we must carefully avoid the thorns and patiently pull out the weeds if the final product is to succeed

WUFO Super Stars 1080

SUNDAY WUFO Literature From The Bible

Challenger Speaks WUFO (1080) At 4 PM

"Actors Marvin Goldhar, seated, Albert Waxman behind him, and Mel Scott, in Toronto production of my play *THE DODO BIRD* which opened March 2, 1966, one day after my 53rd birthday. Al Waxman, discouraged and planning to quit theatre business before this play, was catapulted into prominence by his performance, becoming Canada's leading TV actor, starring in serial *KING OF KENSINGTON*, followed by featured role in America's TV serial *CAGNEY AND LACEY.* — My plays blacklisted in my own country, I had turned to Canada where I was treated very well, for which I am ever grateful."

"Actor Salem Ludwig and actress Jean Alexander with me at New York's Astor Theatre where they appeared in my play *BROTHER GORSKI* in 1973. McCarthyism, contrary to those who thought it was all in the past, was still flourishing. Apparently because the play revealed how a corporation, with assistance of a Catholic 'labor priest', used redbaiting to oust honest union leaders they thought were too militant, a drama critic for one of the New York newspapers wrote that I — finally off the blacklist, teaching Creative Writing at Buffalo State College — should not be allowed to teach there."

"Actors Leo Cimino, down front, and behind him, left to right, John Randolph, Thomas Anderson and Walter Flanagan, in my play *THE DODO BIRD* which opened at New York's Martinique Theatre on December 8, 1967, to excellent reviews. Cimino subsequently had a prominent film role in *THE GODFATHER*; Randolph won a Tony for his performance in Neil Simon's *BROADWAY BOUND* and had a featured film role in *PRIZZI'S HONOR*."

From left to right, actors Thomas Anderson, John Randolph and Phil Sterling in my one-act play *THE PEDDLER*, presented with my one-act play *THE DODO BIRD* at New York's Martinique Theatre in 1967."

"My older daughter Lorrie talking to noted feminist writer Meridel LeSueur at Moushy's Pub in Pittsburg after Meridel and I read there from our work as part of a fund raiser for Mill Hunk Herald newspaper put out by rank-and-file steel workers. Photo 1983."

Chapter 37

Helen rolled down the window on her side, as Danny came around from behind the car to greet her before kissing the children — remembering an offhand remark she once made after he returned from some short trip out-of-town, about him hugging and kissing the kids before taking a peck at her cheek; she would be sensitive to that kind of thing now, and he tried to be extra careful.

As his lips brushed against her cheek he saw that she was deliberately staring straight ahead, breathing deeply, lips pressed together, holding in her anger which seemed ready to burst all over him if she let go of it. Instinctively, he decided to keep his mouth shut and not take any chances on making the situation worse. He hoped that what he would tell her about his plans for talking to her family, about the whole general counterattack he had in mind to create elbow room so she could breathe more easily in the community, including the beginning which had been made with the resolution of support passed at the district council meeting in Elmira — he hoped that that would ease the situation. But this was not yet the time to talk to her about that.

The two flaming carrot tops, Ruth and Linda, wedged themselves between Helen and the driving wheel, holding their faces up to him at the open window, shoving out puckered soft lips to be kissed. Helen flattened herself against the back of the seat, to make room for the girls to wriggle through on top of her lap, but she kept staring straight ahead over their squirming backs.

Little Linda gave him a snappy wet kiss and was ready to climb back to her place on the other end of the front seat. But her older sister, Ruth, wouldn't let go. She hung on tight, clamping one hand around the back of his neck, pulling him toward her, mashing her lips against the side of his mouth. He made several starts to end the kiss but Ruth wouldn't let him pull loose.

Danny sensed that she knew something was wrong. Did Helen tell her about going to Florida? Or maybe she guessed on her own.

Ruth pulled her face back to only a few inches away from his, still clamping her warm hand tightly around the back of his neck to keep him from getting away. He patted her round soft cheek — he wanted to do something or *say* something, somehow to reassure her —

"Honey, everything's okay — everything's okay, honey — "

He patted her cheek, feeling rotten because he wasn't able to express more freely how much she and little Linda meant to him, how cold and empty his life had been without their colorful warmth, these two lovely redheaded girls with their brown eyes — and how much worse it would be now if he were to be without them after he had already known what it was to have them.

"It's way past Linda's bedtime," Helen impatiently reminded, speaking apparently to no one in particular. "Ruth, you climb over into the back seat. You too, Linda. Let's get started."

"Daddy," said Ruth, not moving and still clinging to him, "we got mixed up. We went to the wrong railroad station first. That's why we're late."

"Oh — "

"Did you think — " She stopped and he was afraid she was going to cry. "Daddy, did you think — we weren't going to meet you?"

Her worried eyes searched his and he tried to grin reassuringly, "Honey, I thought you might have had a flat tire — or something." It sounded very flimsy.

Helen deliberately changed the subject. "You're getting wet out there in the rain. Where's your bag?"

"There — " He nodded toward the cab driver who was standing on the curb next to his taxi, suitcase in hand, patiently waiting. "I was getting a cab."

"You two kids," snapped Helen, "climb over to the back seat."

Ruth obediently climbed into the rear of the car but little Linda cried that she wanted to sit up front with Daddy. Not wanting to give any more rights to Linda than to Ruth, Danny quietly insisted that if her older sister had to move to the back seat then Linda also had to move to the back seat. The little redhead wailed her protest against his firm decision. Ruth interceded to tell him it was all right with her if Linda stayed in the front seat since she was such a young child. Danny noted how Helen kept herself aloof from the controversy, waiting until it straightened itself out without her help.

She gave him the keys to the luggage compartment. The taxi driver helped stow away the suitcase, receiving a half-dollar tip to compensate him for his assistance and for his loss of fare.

"Do you want to drive?" Helen asked when he handed the keys back to her through the open window on her side.

"Not particularly." He knew how sensitive she was about such things. (*Why must the woman always slide over to let the husband take the wheel and drive — the minute he steps into the car?*)

He walked around in front of the car and slid into the front seat from the other side.

Linda scrunched up onto his lap so she could see where they were driving. She was wearing her dark green snowsuit, the color sharply contrasting with the golden red curls prying their way out under the edge of her hat. Danny slipped his arms around her soft stomach and held her cozily tight against him, his chin resting lightly on top of her head.

But at the very same moment that he hugged Linda to him he felt two arms coming from behind to enfold him, and a soft face pressed against the side of his neck, and Ruth began to sob brokenly — she had held it in until she just couldn't hold it in any longer.

"I love you, Daddy — I love you, Daddy — " she repeated over and over through gulping sobs while he twisted his right arm around back of the seat and around her shoulders and hugged her to him.

"I love you too, honey" he repeated over and over, trying to soothe the sobbing child.

He felt completely ineffectual.

All he seemed able to do beyond repeating over and over that he loved her was to keep patting her back with the fingers of his right hand while he held on tightly to her.

But the deep sobs did not diminish.

She pressed her face into the crook of his neck and he

could feel the warmth of her tears on his cold skin. This must have been piling up inside her all day, maybe for several days, or even longer. If only she were old enough to understand. And if only he were smart enough to explain it properly to a child her age.

And then Linda joined in.

At first the little one on his lap hadn't known what to make of her older sister's crying. Completely bewildered, she asked what was the matter with Ruth and he told her that Ruth was just tired. But as Ruth's sobs continued, Linda began to whimper, and then Linda squirmed around and reached up her fat arms to hug her face next to his, and then her whimpers became louder and louder until she was crying even louder than Ruth.

Squeezing the two girls, the three faces pressed together, Danny glanced over at Helen. She stared straight ahead, deliberately ignoring the racket and he assumed that she was hating him thoroughly for the hurt he was causing the girls.

Ruth and Linda finally stopped crying but they refused to relax their tight hold around his shoulders and neck, their wet faces still pressed against his as though they feared he might go away — or be taken away — or that they might be taken away from him. He wondered if Ruth thought he was going to be put in jail now that Congressman Holling had recommended that he be cited for contempt of Congress. She must have read about it in the newspaper.

He steadily patted the backs of both children with his fingers, trying to reassure them that everything was going to be all right.

Ruth asked if she could use his handkerchief. He dug it out of his pocket and gave it to her. She wiped her face and gave the handkerchief back to him. Then she put her arms back around his neck and shoulders, fitting her face into the crook of his neck again.

"I love you, Daddy," she whispered, quietly, simply, and she kissed his cheek with her soft lips.

He rubbed his cheek against hers and whispered in return:

"I love you, honey — very much — very much."

"I know you do, Daddy."

She kissed him on the cheek again — a cool dry kiss, the purest.

And then Linda — not to be left out of all this — said, "I love Daddy too," and she smeared a wet kiss on his cheek.

"We all love each other," he told Linda, and he kissed her and wiped her face dry with his handkerchief. "All of us," he said, trying to let Helen know she was included. "We all love each other."

But he did not see any indication from Helen, either in her face or eyes that could be called a reaction to what he said.

They rode in silence, turning off Main Street, going west, and then turning north again, passing the high school where Danny attended school for five years, four years to graduate and an added year to waste away time during the big depression which followed the 1929 stock market crash — his name was on a bronze plaque hanging on the wall in the auditorium, awarded to the outstanding all-around scholar and athlete in the graduating class. One student the faculty doesn't dare to boast about now. He wondered if someone might suggest that his name be taken off the plaque.

Without warning, without any movement to prepare him, Helen spoke, the first time since he had gotten into the car in front of the railroad station — glaring straight ahead, and with a repressed fierceness that showed deep anger underneath the even tone.

"Why do you always have to dramatize everything?" He knew she was hanging on tight to keep from blowing up in front of the children. "Why did you send that highly emotional telegram?" Each word was deliberately measured and controlled. "Why did you have to do that? — Ruth was the only one home when it came. You scared the life out of her."

He mumbled how sorry he was.

They drove on in silence while he waited for Helen to go on. But she did not say anything further.

It was up to him. Since she had broken the ice it was up to him to keep the talk going. Silence was no good. They had to talk this out or their marriage would go down the drain for sure.

"I want to explain things to you later, after we get the kids to bed." And then, so Ruth wouldn't worry, he added, "Ruth,

I want to explain to your mother exactly what happened. I'll tell you about it later, maybe tomorrow, so you'll understand. — It's a legal rigmarole that involves a lot of explaining but you should know what it's about — if the kids in school or on the block mention it. — I'm going to tell Esther, explain it to her too, in case any of the students over at the college ask her about it." He improvised additions to his plan of action as the ideas came to him.

He remembered to ask Helen where Esther was, since no one answered the phone when he called from the railroad station. "Did Esther go home over the weekend?"

It was Ruth, not Helen, who explained.

"She went to some sorority affair on campus but she'll be back later to sit with me and Linda. Mommy asked her to stay over tonight."

Why did Helen ask Esther to stay over to sit with the kids instead of going home for the weekend to be with her parents in North Tonawanda? He didn't think it wise to ask Helen right now. In good time he would find out what she had in mind, and he feared what it might be.

When they entered the house Helen brusquely told Danny to put Linda to bed. From the tone of her voice he could not tell whether she meant that assignment as a form of punishment or if she was giving him a chance to be with the kids because he hadn't been with them for so long and she knew he always did get a real kick out of putting Linda to bed.

While he carried Linda upstairs he wondered if Helen was still planning to take the kids to her sister's place in Florida. The uncertainty was no good.

It was too late to give Linda a bath, but they had a good time while he changed her into pajamas and washed her face and hands with a washcloth and carried her piggyback to bed and brought her the milk and cookie snack and tucked her in under the covers and sat next to her on the bed and read a book story to her and then told her two made-up stories, one about their old friend Mr. Bluebird who visited Linda every night to talk over the good times, the other about another old friend, Minnie Honeybear, a small redheaded girl bear, exactly Linda's age, who always had exactly the same problems with her mother and father and older sister that Linda had with her parents and older sister and always found a satisfactory way for all concerned to resolve those problems and then went to sleep, happy and contented, and always snored while she slept — and the louder she snored, the happier that meant she was —

They were giggling in silly fashion in the half-darkened bedroom — the light shining in from the hallway — and they talked about Minnie Honeybear's latest adventure, meeting her Daddy at the railroad station just when her Daddy almost stepped into the taxi, and Danny was telling Linda how the car drove up with Minnie Honeybear in it with her older sister — he became aware of Helen standing still in the doorway, her shadow stretching across the floor of the child's bedroom.

He interrupted the story.

"What is it?" he warily asked.

"Are you tired?"

"Not particularly." Any other answer would have caused additional problems, since she had already arranged for Esther to stay overnight on a Saturday when Esther would have ordinarily gone home to her parents in North Tonawanda for the whole weekend instead of just Sunday. He would have to drive Esther out to North Tonawanda early in the morning. He hoped Helen did not have an all-night talk planned.

"We've been invited out tonight. Are you too tired to go?"

"No." He wondered who among Helen's friends had the courage to invite him over right on top of his appearance before the Committee on Un-American Activities.

"You sure?"

He realized she was giving him every possible chance to say he was too tired to go out and he wondered what her reaction would be if he would surprise her by saying that he was so exhausted that his bones ached and he could hardly keep his eyes open whenever he sat down. But that would be the wrong thing to say right now. The truth was — and he was to learn it from Helen later — at that moment she was ashamed to be seen anywhere with him and was hoping he *would* say he was too tired to go out.

"I feel fine," he said.

"I thought you might be too exhausted to go out."

"No." He welcomed this opportunity for what was almost a friendly conversation. "Where we going?" he asked in an offhand way as though it really didn't matter. He scratched Linda's back to quiet the little child's restless wriggle in his lap.

"Susan Lewis called," explained Helen. "She and Abe are having some people over at their house tonight. Your brother Joe and Hilda will be there."

"Anyone else we know?" he asked, thinking what a solid citizen Susan was turning out to be, though she looked like a flighty dizzy blonde.

"Some other people, including a couple from out of town. Susan said she doesn't think we know them."

"Okay."

Helen disappeared from the doorway. Danny went back to telling Linda about Minnie Honeybear and her adventures at the railroad station when she met her Daddy.

He wondered if his younger brother Joe and wife Hilda had worked it out with Susan and Abe to invite him and Helen over to a party at their house this Saturday night so they would not feel abandoned by everyone after he returned from the hearing. Each of the couples invited to the party had probably been told in advance that he was coming, so there would be no "incident" of someone refusing to stay at the party because of his presence. His brother's business and manufacturing friends would be conspicuous by their absence. — For a few fleeting seconds, while he tried to get Linda to go to sleep, he thought about how all of them had been kids on the East Side, he and his brothers and Abe Lewis and the rest of the gang playing stickball in the streets and occasionally getting mixed up in fights with other gangs. It was heartwarming to know that there were still people like Abe Lewis in Buffalo, now a successful physician, living in a nice home in a fashionable suburban development, who still had the principle and the courage to stick with one of the boys from the old gang — even though he disagreed with his radical politics and his union activity. As for his younger brother Joe — the big, warm, good-natured, good-hearted redhead, they had always been close to one another, and he was not surprised that this relationship still continued even after Joe became a wealthy manufacturer and businessman; it had always been that way with his brothers and sisters. They had grown up believing each one had the right to believe whatever he or she wanted to believe.

He finally got Linda to bed after the third drink of water, after she brushed her teeth twice because she wanted to be sure they were clean, and after she was carried in several times to Mommy and to Ruthie to say good-night, and again to say good-night to their college student helper when she came home from the sorority affair just as Linda had finally settled down to go to sleep. And then finally —

"Good-night, Linda."

"Good-night, Daddy."

He closed the door except for a crack of about one inch and stood there, listening a second to make sure all was quiet for the night in the child's bedroom. He then directed his attention to the other members of the household.

Ruth and Esther were provisioning themselves for the long Saturday evening camp-out in the den with the television set. Danny enjoyed watching them bring in potato chips, several bottles of coke and ginger ale, crackers and peanut butter and jelly, several sandwiches made with meat leftovers, and a bag of oranges; and when he kidded them about all the food they said they would get more from the refrigerator later if they became hungry again.

He went into the bedroom where Helen was already preparing for her bath. She was taking off her slip when he walked in and she hastily covered herself with a robe and silently slipped by him into the bathroom where he could hear the water running into the tub. Welcoming the opportunity to grab a few minutes of sleep, he stretched himself out flat on his back on the bed.

"Are you too tired to go out?"

He had fallen asleep. Helen stood there, all dressed. That had been a sound sleep, he thought, short as it was.

"Are you too tired to go out?" she repeated.

He sat up. "No, I'm all right."

"You better get started — if you're going to change your clothes."

"Do I have time to take a quick shower?"

"I suppose so."

He watched her go over to the dressing table corner she had made in their bedroom with the round mirror she screwed up on the wall and the small dressing table and chair she covered over with pink material.

"Helen — "

"What?"

"I'll tell you later about what happened at the hearing."

She sat down on the seat in front of the dressing table. "I'd like to hear about it," she said, surprising him. She picked up one of her dangling earrings from the mirror top of the dressing table and fooled with it. "What about this citation for contempt?"

"Don't put me in jail yet. — If they *do* prosecute — and there's always a chance they might not — it's a Supreme Court issue before it's really decided. It'll take at least three to five years before the final decision comes down."

"That's nice," said Helen, with a fine touch of sarcasm that made him wince inside.

"A lot can happen. This whole Cold War atmosphere can be dissipated long before then."

"Maybe — "

He watched her as she attached the shiny bit of golden jewelry to her ear lobe.

"Did you speak to your mother?"

Helen turned and looked at him, surprised.

"Why?" she asked.

"I just wondered what she said."

"About what?"

She turned back to the mirror, as she tightened the tiny screw on the earring.

"About me," he said.

"Mother hasn't said much. Yet. But wait until she talks to Bob. He'll give her an earful."

This was his chance to explain his plan. At least part of it.

"Why don't we all get together? Your mother. And Bob. And you and me. All four of us." He went on to explain his idea about getting together a council of her family so he could explain why he refused to answer the Committee's questions. "We can talk it over. All together at one time."

Helen seemed to like the idea. She suggested that Bob's wife also be included.

"I meant to include Millie," he said, and then tried to sound Helen out further by asking, "So you think it's a good idea?"

"Oh sure." She combed her hair, looking into the mirror, as she quietly added with a deft touch of just the right emphasis, "Not that it'll make much difference."

He had to ask the question, although he thought he already knew the answer —

"Why?"

Helen stiffly rose and walked across the room, not looking at him, and tried the door to make certain it was closed tight. — She stood with her back to the door, staring at him, defiant, resentful, cold.

"Do you think we're going right back to living the kind of life we were living before?"

The deliberately icy tone sent shivers down his spine. He was unable to reply.

Helen accepted his silence as a response. She went on, cold as ice. "I'm not going to stand by and see my children take a beating because of you and your activities — "

"They're my children too."

"And I know you love them. I know that. But I can't understand how you can set yourself up as a judge to decide that this will be better for them in the long run. — Look at how much you hurt them. Do you think they'll ever forget what happened today? I know *I* never will.

He could not look at her. "I'll never forget it either," he said.

She crossed to the dresser and got a cigarette and lit it.

"It's too bad you didn't marry someone else. I'm sure there are other families you know about in this city — among your union people — or among some of your middle-class left-wing friends — where you would be coming home the great hero today after the way you told off that Committee — and your kids would be full of tremendous pride for what you did." She took a deep suck of smoke and blew it out between her lips. "Did you ever think of that?" she asked, a bit of challenge in the question.

He waited for a moment before he decided to just nod his admission that he had thought of that.

Helen faced him. "If I was proud of you, then the children

would be proud of you, wouldn't they?"

"Maybe. Probably."

She went back to the dressing table and sat down. He watched her, studying her face in the mirror. She turned to him.

"I *am* a little proud of you. I really am."

"Thank you," he said, very soberly.

"But not enough to outweigh all the rest. All the crap I've had to take because of you. From my family and friends I grew up with."

"You've got the wrong kind of family and friends," he said, sadly trying to be funny.

"I didn't pick my family. And most of them are pretty nice. It's only those living here in Buffalo that I'm having any difficulty with. Bob and Mother." She brushed her hair away from her forehead and continued, "I could ignore my family if I had a lot of other friends who were completely loyal to us — to *both* of us — not only to *me*. There are lots of people in this town who want to continue being friends with me, but not with you. But that's no good. — We've got to get out of this city. And you got to change your work. Otherwise, there's no salvation for us."

"That's running. It doesn't solve anything."

"It's our only solution."

"I don't think so."

"We've got to get out of here. Away from this constant feeling of heaviness."

"Running away won't cure it. My ideas will be the same. Moving won't change them."

"At least we won't be living under the constantly critical eye of The Park Lane and that crowd."

"I don't think it's good for us to let *them* decide what we do with our life."

"I don't like running away either, but I can't take it anymore. Maybe I'm weak, but I got my mind made up." And then, as though she had finally decided this was the time to answer the question she knew was in his mind, she stood up and solemnly delivered her ultimatum. "I'm going to wait until the school term is over, so Ruth won't have her school attendance broken up, and then I'm going to take her and Linda with me to Florida — "

He could tell that she still had more to say. He waited.

"If you love us you'll come after us. And if you don't come after us, then you don't. And I'll know that's your decision."

He was silent, not knowing how to react.

"You think it over," she concluded. "You've got plenty of time to make up your mind."

He remained stiff and silent, resenting the ultimatum but not wanting to precipitate any showdown until he had a chance to figure out what to say and what to do.

Helen went back to the dressing table. "You better get going. You don't have much time for a shower. We're late as it is."

He went into the bathroom and undressed and pulled the shower curtain and turned on the water — welcoming these few minutes of privacy and peace and quiet before going to the party where he would have to be on guard every second he was there. He turned his face up to the spray and let the water fill his mouth and pour out, enjoying the relaxing feeling he got from closing his eyes and letting his face fall apart.

"Like a beat up prize fighter between rounds," he thought, surprised that he was amused by the complexity of his situation. It was a good thing that he could still laugh at himself.

Chapter 38

"Do you really want to go to the Lewises'?"

"Why?" Helen's question took him completely by surprise. — "Don't *you?*"

At that moment they drove past a street lamp and he saw that Helen was staring straight ahead. The light revealed a mask of white face and red lips and carefully penciled eyebrows and mascaraed eyelids, framed by dark hair above. The car sloshed through a big puddle and the water washed against the underbelly of the car with a loud slapping sound.

"Is the street slippery?"

"Not too bad," he said. "It's stopped raining."

"I'm glad I let you drive."

Wondering what she had in mind about the Lewises, he glanced at her several times, trying to read the riddle. But her face mask hid her thoughts and emotions.

He knew she had consciously dressed as glamorously as she could tonight — she wore a very expensive dress her sister Frances had given her and also the sable neckpiece Frances had bequeathed to her before moving to Florida.

Tonight, he thought, Helen Stack Newman has decided to show the world she is once again the glamorous Miss Park Lane. She has rejected any thought of herself as Helen Newman, wife of union organizer Danny Newman who was questioned by the House Committee on Un-American Activities concerning his radical beliefs and activities.

When she dressed so smartly — (her closest friend Lillian Fox, a high fashion advertising copy writer, told him that Helen could make a fortune modeling these clothes) — she seemed to step back into her Park Lane world in a way intended to shut him out completely.

"The Lewises are expecting us, aren't they?"

"Yes," Helen replied.

They drove several blocks further before she spoke again. "Let's stop somewhere and get a drink."

"We're late," he reminded her in a way that let her know he was willing to stop if she wanted to.

She was silent.

He swung the car wide to the left and they passed a dawdling truck.

"We can stop somewhere," he said.

She remained silent.

"Do you want to stop?"

"No, never mind."

There was only the sound of the water from the street puddles slapping against the underside of the car as they drove on without speaking. He wondered what she was thinking behind that haughty mask. Then he became acutely conscious that she was staring at him, and he tried to ignore the look he saw on her face each time they passed a street light.

Finally she spoke, quietly and deliberately.

"I wish I always hated you like I do right now."

His skin crawled and he clenched his teeth while he stared straight ahead, tightly gripping the driving wheel. She was waiting for him to swallow the bait and to start an argument but he was not going to gulp down the hook. An argument now would only make the situation worse and solve nothing.

"Life would be so easy," she went on, coldly, deliberately, "if I always hated you like this."

She stopped and waited. He refused to respond.

He heard the slap-slap of the water from the big puddles hitting underneath the car as he pointedly ignored the stare from Helen while she examined his face, challenging him to retaliate. He thought of asking her if she was enjoying herself but decided not to allow himself to be provoked even that much.

"How," Helen finally asked him, not shifting her stare away from his face, "did you ever become so smart?"

He refused to bite.

"Who taught you when to keep quiet? — You're so damn smart. You say nothing — and you let me shoot off my big mouth as much as I please — you let me get it out of my system — and I end up by arguing myself out of what I just finished saying to you only a minute earlier. And you never even get involved. It's marvelous. Who taught you to be so wise?"

He couldn't tell if she meant it or if she was being sarcastic. He gripped the wheel tighter, relishing the broad swerves the car made as he rotated the wheel with big rolling movements of his arms and shoulders. They were passing every car they approached on their side of the road.

"You're expecting too much." Her voice changed, becoming softer, and in response he stepped on the brake and slowed the car down so he could listen more carefully to what she said.

"You're pushing me too fast — you can't expect me to come all the way over to your side — you've got to give too — you've got to meet me at least half-way — on the things that really count."

He tried to figure out where she was heading but he did not attempt to reply.

"I know you've given in on many things," she continued. "You let me have my way on everything except the important thing, the one thing that really means anything — your union work and the politics which goes with it!" — His face stiffened. — She went on. "You let me run our social life. What there is left of it. You're always ready to go wherever I want to go. You let me pick the place where we live, a typical middle-class neighborhood among business people and professional people — even though you still have some fantastic idea about getting me to move with you some day into more of a working class kind of neighborhood — "

"Not so fantastic!" he muttered, unable to hold it in.

"Oh, yes! Fantastic, Danny! Yes, fantastic!" She welcomed his response. Call to battle. "You don't know me. After all these years we've lived together you still don't know me. If we ever move out of the house we live in now — it'll be into an apartment in The Park Lane, an apartment like the one in which I lived most of my life before we were married. — It's amazing! After thirteen years of marriage you still don't realize the kind of woman you married!"

He had a hard time keeping his voice under control but he held it in as he answered, "You still don't seem to realize the kind of man you've married!"

She took that in and thought it over for a long while — a long silence as they drove on. Then he saw her shake her head.

"You're wrong." She said it with a quiet sincerity which disarmed him. "You're all wrong. I realize the kind of man I married. I knew it when I married him. He's a great contradiction — a combination of strength and driving energy on one hand, and gentleness and sensitivity and kindness on the other hand —a person who is easily hurt —"

He was deeply moved. He had not realized she had given that much thought to the kind of person he might be under the tough exterior he tried to maintain.

" — He's the only man I ever fully respected, the only man I can't push around, which is probably why I fell in love with him, why I married him. — I was afraid of him but he's the only man I ever wanted to marry. — And I still love you even though right now I hate you and can't stand the thought of you touching any part of my body right now." — She was not looking at him. — "That's why I want you to go away from this town with me, so we can be happy away from all this heaviness and misery. — We could have such a happy marriage together if you would only do the one thing that would really count — if you would get out of the union and away from all your politics — "

"And become respectable — "

"What's so wrong with being respectable?"

"You know what I mean. You'd like me to become a *respectable businessman.*"

She turned to him, her anger breaking out again. "What's wrong with going into business and earning more money for your wife and children?"

"Nothing. Except that isn't all you want. You know that."

"What else do I want?"

"Would it be all right with you if I became a businessman and still remained a left-winger in my politics?"

"Yes! As long as you are smart enough to keep your mouth shut out in public — you have a right to think what you please!"

"You mean as long as I'm willing to be a hypocrite!"

"*Can't you just live your own life?* And not have to be thinking all the time about other people? Working people? The poor? *This* minority group? *That* minority group? — Everybody except your own wife and children? How about *us*? Don't you want us to have a nicer home? Nicer clothes?

A nicer car? Don't we count more than strangers?"

"You want me to cleanse myself!"

"No — "

"You want me to turn stoolpigeon!"

"No — "

"You want me to start running away from everything I've ever believed in!"

"No, I don't!"

"You do! That's exactly what you're saying! What it means. You know that!"

"I want you to start thinking of your own family!"

"Helen! You said you fell in love with a certain kind of guy because you respected him. Would you respect him if he turned and ran — when he's completely convinced it's the wrong thing to do? — Be honest! Be objective! Would you respect me if I folded up now? If I made believe that I don't think the way I do? *If I lived a life which is a complete lie?* "

Helen's voice rose with exasperation. "Why must you always be so damn dramatic?"

"Helen! I have certain beliefs! You knew that when you married me! Okay, do you disagree with my beliefs? Then argue with me. Argue for what you believe in, and I'll argue for what I believe in. — What the hell, I don't insist that you agree with me or that's the end of our marriage. Why should you insist that I have to agree with you or else?"

She didn't have an answer. He kept his eyes on the wet road — driving very slowly so they would have time to finish this important talk before they arrived at the Lewises'.

"The trouble," she finally said, "is that I don't have any definite beliefs of my own. If I knew exactly what I believed in — then everything would be easy. The truth is that sometimes I think that if I wasn't married to you I might hold beliefs very similar to yours. But being married to you and seeing how much trouble you invite for yourself and your family, I'm afraid to allow myself to agree with anything you say on politics. Unconsciously, I take the opposite viewpoint. I know whenever you're in a fight in negotiations or a strike I automatically defend the company's side because I know you'll take the union's side. Maybe to balance off for the radical side I know you'll take — "

"That's a helluva note."

"Isn't it? — That's another reason why I think we should go to Florida. Away from all the people I grew up with, I think I could become a much broader person. I could think more freely without worrying about what Mother or Bob or the people around them will say. I can never be free that way up here."

"You mean it's all right with you, Helen, if I remain exactly the way I am, so far as my political beliefs are concerned, believing exactly as I do now — but you want us to go to Florida so you can change your thinking without being condemned by the group you're concerned with here, the people around The Park Lane?"

"I'm not sure — "

"That wouldn't work, Helen — it's still running away — voluntary exile. Why should we? This is our home. We both have lived here most of our lives. Certainly where we can be most effective as people. Best fulfill our potentialities insofar as contributing towards making this a more decent world to live in. — Why must we run away because some people may disagree with my ideas or with your ideas?"

"Danny, we can't live here anymore. How many friends do we have left here who are willing to be seen out in public with *both* of us?"

"I've got lots of friends in the union."

"I'm not ready for that. Not yet. Right now I need friends among the people I grew up with — "

"Conservative middle-class — "

"I'm not ready to break away from them. Sometimes I wish I could. I know it's a shortcoming of my own that I feel strange and disliked when I'm with your union people and their wives or husbands — but I'm apparently still not ready for them. I have a long way to go yet."

She stopped there and was silent a long while.

He paid close attention to his driving while trying hard to figure out how to handle the last point she had raised: her relationship to the upper middle-class and to the working class.

"Helen — "

"Yes?"

"There's no reason why you have to break away from the people you grew up with. It would be false if you tried to force something like that. You can't wipe out your background. It's a fact of life. And you have to accept it. But you can be a person who is broad enough in her perspective to be able to associate with people who are conservative politically and also with people who are radical politically, no matter what your own thinking. Must everybody who associates together think exactly the same? That would make life awfully dull and stupid, wouldn't it?"

"Maybe."

"You know that I disagree with your mother and with Bob on almost everything political. But I don't find it very difficult to be with them. I think they're entitled to their own beliefs. Why can't they — and *you* — grant me the same right? — You're probably not aware of it, or maybe you are, that I used to be very ill-at-ease when you first took me into the world of The Park Lane — just as much ill-at-ease as you must feel when you're with me and meet union people — but The Park Lane was your world and I went along with you into it, and I finally began to feel more at ease with it, still disagreeing with many of its standards and certainly with its generally conservative outlook on life. — Why can't you do the same with me? And with the people in the union? Why can't you be big enough as a person to associate with union people just the same way you asked me to associate with your family and the people you grew up with — without necessarily agreeing with them? Why not? There are a lot of nice people in both groups."

"Right now," Helen reminded him, "the people I grew up with, The Park Lane crowd, don't want to associate with *you* any longer. Don't forget that!"

"Then the hell with them!" He was angry because what she said was true. "The hell with them! Let's move out to North Tonawanda where we'll be surrounded by friends."

"*You* might be surrounded by union friends," Helen acidly corrected him. "But I'm not ready for that. — The trouble is that I don't feel that I fully belong to *any* group. I'm caught in between — and it's very painful."

"I know," he said, trying to be sympathetic.

"*You don't know,*" Helen said, quietly. "*You don't know!*"

He kept his mouth shut. Those last words had come from way down deep inside her and they represented a great deal of very complicated thinking on her part which could not be fliply tossed aside. Sometimes she was too deep inside her own thinking for him to be able to follow her line of reasoning —

The host and hostess met them at the door and took their coats. Abe, prematurely gray and developing a big stomach, put a friendly arm around Danny's shoulders. Susan, shimmering in a fancy dress, her hair platinum blonde, with long glittering earrings hanging from her ears, jabbered about nothing, welcoming them to the party. Abe brought drinks and led them into the living room. Then they were left alone as host and hostess went off to see to the needs of other guests. Helen told Danny she'd be right back. He wondered if she was deserting him on purpose — an idea confirmed as the evening went on and she stayed away. He sat alone on the couch in the living room, a sickly smile on his face, trying to appear self-contained and completely at ease while he sipped his drink. There were a dozen or more guests, most of them strangers. Probably friends of the Lewises. Then he recognized a couple he knew very well, a successful factory owner and his wife. Arthur Steiner was another one of the gang who had grown up with him and his brothers and sisters on the East Side — and the success he had made with his factory, manufacturing modern furniture, was reflected in his self-assured air of being right in his opinions on any subject because he had been so right with his decision to make a new style of furniture. Danny was careful to avoid saying hello to Steiner or to his wife — he didn't want to be snubbed. They passed by him several times and ignored him, very pointedly. It was a wonder Steiner had even come. He saw the sour expression on Steiner's face when he looked toward the couch.

Danny's good-natured brother Joe, a redheaded two hundred pound husky with broad shoulders and narrow waist, came over to the couch with a stranger, a thick-eyebrowed man who appeared to be in his early forties. Joe introduced the stranger to Danny, describing him as the older brother of Sam Nathanson, a prominent local criminal lawyer. While Danny shook hands with the man, his brother Joe winked — reminding Danny of the incident that Joe had told him about Sam Nathanson: how Sam Nathanson had made a loud remark at a fashionable dinner party that Danny should be stood up against a wall and shot because of his political beliefs, at which point husky Joe had threatened to punch Sam's teeth down into his throat, a serious threat which had brought an immediate apology from the self-important criminal lawyer. With another wink back over his shoulder, Joe walked off with the man he had just introduced, leaving Danny alone — he sat down on the couch again.

It was a deadly evening. It was so obvious that the other guests were avoiding him. Anyone who accidentally became involved in conversation with him scooted away as soon as some polite excuse could be found to move on. Feeling awkward and self-conscious, he kept refilling his drink but it seemed to have very little effect.

Even the Lewises and his brother Joe seemed to find it very difficult to hit upon a subject of conversation to keep them standing and talking with him. He tried to figure out why this was so and he decided it was because they were trying too hard to find some other subject of conversation besides the one uppermost in their mind, the one subject they never mentioned — his appearance before the Committee in the State Capital — and it was very difficult to ignore that subject since he had appeared before the Committee only the day before, on Friday morning, and both Buffalo newspapers had carried a story on it in this morning's editions.

Several times he had a strong urge to slip out of the house and run for it — to sneak over to one of the taverns along the river where he would be sure to meet some of his union friends who worked in the factories over in that area.

Helen sidled up close to him.

"You better take me home soon," she whispered, "before I make a fool of myself," and when she spoke to him he could smell her breath — he wondered how many double shots of whiskey on the rocks had gone down into her stomach.

"We can go right now," he said, "if you want to — "

"You're always so agreeable," she taunted him, but keeping her voice down so none of the other guests would overhear what she was saying. "You're always so agreeable about things that don't matter too much."

He refused to comment on that.

"You stink," she said, breathing her alcohol breath into his face, and then she smiled at him as though she had said something very complimentary.

He bent toward her with a false smile of his own and whispered, "Thank you, dear — the same to you, in spades — and many more of them. . . . And please go fuck yourself, thank you."

"You always say the nicest things," she smirked back at him.

She waved goodbye and wandered away, leaving him standing alone, a silly grin plastered on his face, trying to hide the panicky feeling churning his stomach.

She returned a few minutes later, her coat hanging over her arm and her fur neckpiece dangling over her shoulder. Without a word she gave him her coat and he held it for her while she slipped her arms into the sleeves. The Lewises and Joe rushed over. Why are you leaving? The food hasn't been served yet. We're making coffee in the kitchen. Danny explained that he was exhausted and needed to get some sleep.

His younger brother pulled him aside in the hallway while Abe and Susan were talking to Helen, trying to persuade her to stay.

"Was it rough?" It was a quick whisper, and Danny nodded in reply. Joe looked worried. "Why didn't you use the Fifth Amendment? Isn't there a danger you'll go to jail this way?"

"I thought it would be better if I attacked the Committee instead of using the Fifth — "

"But you're risking jail!"

"There's a good chance I can win out — "

"How good?"

"A possibility."

"It'll have to go to the Supreme Court, won't it?"

"Probably — "

"In the meantime?"

Danny tried to laugh. "In the meantime I sweat."

"When will you know?"

"It's up to the full Committee to decide now whether or not

to act on Holling's recommendation — to ask Congress to cite me for contempt."

"And if they cite you for contempt — what happens?"

"A trial — to decide whether or not the Committee is or is not unconstitutional — that'll be the issue, the real issue. — I don't think the Committee's going to rush into that kind of a trial in a hurry — they've got more to lose than I have."

Joe made a face. "But they don't go to jail if they lose. You do."

"True."

His brother nodded in Helen's direction. "She's taking it hard, ain't she?" It was more fact than question. Danny silently agreed with a shrug. "I thought she was," Joe went on, "the way she's been drinking tonight."

And then Helen called to them, "You two big redheads stop whispering over there like a couple of conspirators."

"We're plotting a revolution," Joe called back, with a big grin. "We're going to make all workers capitalists, and all capitalists workers — and see if that makes any difference."

"No politics tonight!" screamed Joe's wife Hilda.

Joe put his hands over his head and ran into the clothes closet, pretending to be frightened, and there was a lot of laughter connected with the flurry of horseplay.

"Please don't turn me into the Un-American Committee," Joe begged when he was fished out of the clothes closet, his wife pulling him out by the ear. As Helen and Danny left the house Susan Lewis called after them from the front doorway that she would telephone Helen during the week to find out what they planned to do next weekend.

Danny held the door open for Helen to get into their car. She was careful to avoid touching him as she climbed in. He slammed the door shut and went around and got in on the other side of the car, behind the wheel. Helen slid over to the right-hand corner of the front seat and he thought of asking her if he had leprosy, but this was no time to try to be sarcastic or funny. The safest approach was to remain silent.

It was about five minutes of silence later that Helen spoke. "And you think we can still live in this town."

He couldn't think of anything to say.

It was not until they were in bed with lights out, after

Helen had smoked a cigarette in the darkness and had snuffed out the glowing end of the butt in the glass ashtray on the night table, that she finally spoke to him again. And it was evident she had made her decision.

"We've got to get out of town, Danny. There's nothing but misery for us here."

Disheartened though he was, Danny refused to surrender. He had come out all right in many a wage negotiation and in many a union election, even though at some early point the situation had appeared hopeless.

"Getting out of town doesn't solve anything. It doesn't change what's within us, the basic cause of our problem."

"What do we solve by staying here?"

"We try to do something about the situation — try to win people over — people you know — people I know. I don't see why Buffalo should be any different from any other big city in the country. Why shouldn't we be able to develop a fair-sized group of liberal and progressive business and professional people who'll be willing to work with some union people, to fight for what's decent and right, for greater political freedom for all, for a better standard of living for all, for an end to segregation in all walks of life, for decent low-cost housing to replace slums, better schools, for better hospitals — "

Helen interrupted him with a low cry of disgust.

"Oh, what's the use? I'm trying to figure out a way we can save *us*, how we can make *us* happy — and you're thinking about how you can set up a group to fight for public housing and civil rights for communists and socialists and equal rights for colored people. We don't talk the same language! Miles apart! Miles! Miles! — How did we ever get married?"

He was silent.

"Oh-h-h, what's the use?" The bed moved as she slid down under the covers. "Let's go to sleep."

She stopped moving around, and in the darkness — he was still sitting up — he could see that she was lying on her back, her head on her pillow, looking up at the ceiling. He knew he couldn't let their conversation end at this point. He had to project some hope, some possibility that they could work out their problem in Buffalo.

"Helen" — he wanted her to understand what he was

trying to do, why he was trying to do it — "I'm trying to figure out how we can establish some kind of group in this city into which we can both fit comfortably, a meeting ground which can include both working people with whom I associate and business and professional people with whom you associate. So you don't feel we're two alone against the world. You don't feel at home yet with my union people, you say. And your Park Lane crowd — for whatever reason — won't associate with me. — What else can we do except start digging in to create a new group — a combination of working people *and* middle-class people in this community — with whom we can have a comfortable social relationship? Otherwise, we surrender and admit we're two people alone in the world who are giving up and retiring into their shell to try subjectively to beat their brains out, berating one another, getting psychoanalyzed, psychoanalyzing one another, getting absolutely nowhere because we don't get at the basic causes and try to adjust them — "

Helen interrupted, raising herself up off the bed, propping her weight on her left elbow. "I'm not going to be *two* against the world — or even one against the world — not in Buffalo. At the end of Ruth's school term I'm not going to be in Buffalo any more! Did you forget that?"

She silently lowered herself flat on her back again, her head on the pillow. He made no effort to answer her.

Chapter 39

Sunday morning . . .

"Daddy! Move over — "

He opened his eyes. Little Linda, in pajamas, her hair tousled, crawled into bed beside him. He shifted his body to make room for the pink-cheeked redhead. She cuddled next to him and he enfolded her in his arms and kissed her. She practically purred as she gave him a gamin grin and pressed her lips together to keep from laughing out loud.

He looked over at Helen and saw her face, relaxed, eyes closed. She always looked her best to him this way, without make-up, when he could see the real woman without the reserved front she donned when she dressed and made up her face to go out in public.

The alarm clock on the corner of the dresser showed ten minutes past nine. Too early to get up on Sunday morning, he thought, wondering if there was any chance of getting Ruth to take care of Linda so he could get a few more hours of sleep.

Then he heard Esther's footsteps as she moved around upstairs in her room on the third floor and he remembered that he had to drive her out to the roadside restaurant run by her father and mother on the northern edge of North Tonawanda — now that the spring tourist traffic was starting up again she had to help her parents on Sundays.

He scooped the little redhead into his arms and rolled out of bed with her. "Shhh, Linda, don't wake up Mommy. It's time for us to get dressed — "

He carried her back into her room to dress her before getting into his own clothes, but the sound of Esther's heels clicking down the steps from the third floor forced him to flee wildly back to his own bedroom with Linda still in his arms — his pajama bottom was half torn off. Linda went out into the hallway to say hello and Esther took over the job of dressing her while Danny quickly threw on his clothes.

On their way out to North Tonawanda he told Esther what

had happened at the hearing in the State Capital, explaining to her that he wanted her to know about it so she would understand and would be able to talk about it if other students at the college brought it up. She listened with intense interest, pressing her lips together and emphatically nodding as she registered the ideas.

He told her why he had refused to answer any questions of the Committee as she, sitting in the front seat next to him, listened while she played with Linda who sat on her lap hugging a doll with long blonde braids. It was Esther's background, he believed, which made her such a sympathetic listener — her father still worked in the factory all year round, even though the family operated the small roadside restaurant during the tourist season; all her immediate family and close relatives were working class people; the same with her friends; and her favorite uncle — her father's twin brother — was a member of the union at one of the plants whose workers Danny had helped organize, in North Tonawanda.

"They ought to do away with those awful committees," Esther said. There was no question where she stood on the issue.

He drove along the river past the GM auto assembly plant, past the DuPont chemical plant where he had worked, past the Dunlop tire manufacturing plant, past the steel plants, past the metal fabricating plants, more chemical plants, machine shops, factory after factory lined up along the road which ran parallel to the river where there was a cheap supply of water, cheap supply of electric power, and access to cheap means of transportation. When he had been younger he had been frightened by the vast stretch of dirty smoke-blackened factories and the freight yards and the littered docks, and he had felt like a stranger in enemy territory, wanting to hurry through it to get into cleaner sections of the surrounding area; but later when he came to know the people in those factories, the people who stood around in dirty clothes in front of the dingy taverns, the people who crowded the ginmills on pay night, the people who swarmed in and out of the factories on change of shift — when he came to know these people he lost his fear of the factories and he began to revel in his knowledge of their strength and power to produce — these factories were what labor had built with its sweat, out of its muscle and bone, and he believed that some day labor would receive the full return of the value of the labor they produced and there would be no more depressions and no more hunger and no more unemployment.

He knew it was impossible to expect Helen to react like Esther; their environments had been so different. Yet Helen must have learned a great deal, having a girl like Esther in their house for almost a full school year. Helen continually praised Esther: what a mature girl she is, how capable she is, how down-to-earth she is, how she can handle herself in almost any kind of situation like an intelligent adult who has been out in the world all her life, while Esther had only recently celebrated her eighteenth birthday.

He parked the car off the highway in front of the clapboard one-story restaurant and Esther urged him to come in and have a cup of coffee with her Mom and Dad.

"And a chocolate milk shake for Linda!" she added, hugging the little redhead who squealed with delight.

Esther's mother and father, Peg and Art Bachman, came out to say hello. Danny knew they were his age, and it tickled him to think that if his own marriage had occurred about six years earlier than it had, his daughter Ruth would already be in her freshman year in college, studying like Esther to be a teacher, since this was also what Ruth wanted to be when she grew up.

"Hi," he greeted them as he got out of the car.

He shook hands with Art, a stocky sandy-haired man with a pleasant round face, wearing gray shirt and trousers.

"I see," said Peg, a brunette with a boyish body which made her look younger than her daughter except when you got close enough to see the lines in her face, "you brought my cute little girl with you," and she grabbed little Linda and kissed her. "I'll bet this girl would like a drink of milk," she said, starting toward the restaurant.

"A chocolate milk shake," Linda corrected her, hanging onto Peg's neck. Esther followed, carrying the doll with the long blonde braids.

The restaurant was empty, and Art explained that it was a quiet time of the day, between breakfast and lunch customers. They sat down on stools at the counter, all except Esther who put on a white apron and went to work to serve the others. She gave Linda her chocolate milk shake and served Danny and her father two big portions of delicious homemade apple pie — too fattening. After serving coffee to Danny and her parents Esther sat down to help Linda whose drinking straw had become pinched so that she could not draw her chocolate milk shake into her mouth.

So relaxed, Danny thought, looking at the Bachmans. So unpretentious, with no phony position to maintain in the community. He knew Art operated a screw machine, a skilled job, in one of the machine shops in North Tonawanda. The little restaurant had been started by Esther several years earlier, during her summer vacation, to earn money to pay for her college education. Now it had grown to where it required the attention of the three adults in their family over the weekends. There was a young son in the family who, Danny assumed, was off playing somewhere.

They talked.

Danny was very much aware that no mention was made of his appearance before the Committee though he felt certain that Esther had kept her parents posted.

They discussed the employment outlook, the different political figures in the country and in the area, the conditions in the South, the future of organized labor, the unsettled international situation, the atom bomb and the hydrogen bomb, the people of India, and the rotten contract which had been negotiated the week before by a company union at a shop in town.

At one point in their conversation Art said, "I wish Franklin D. Roosevelt was still alive. Things would be a lot different in this country now."

This was as close as the conversation got to anything connected with Danny's appearance before the Committee. Sipping his coffee, trying to forget about Helen and his splitting headache, Danny thought about how much easier life might be if he and Helen lived out here in North Tonawanda.

Reluctant to go home, Danny made a detour to drive by the zoo in Buffalo. Linda said she wanted to stop to see the monkeys. He held Linda's hand while they walked through the zoo grounds to the monkey house. It was more pleasant to be with the animals at the zoo than to be at home with Helen.

Somehow before the day is over he has to figure out an excuse to get over to see his brother-in-law Bob without Helen knowing where he's going. The showdown with Bob was long overdue.

"Daddy, I'm tired of the monkeys."

He looked down at the little redheaded girl and laughed, "So am I, honey. Let's go home where the animals are bigger."

She punched him.

"You're a silly Daddy."

He picked her up and carried her out to the car, hugging her face against his as he walked.

Chapter 40

Danny hurried up the short flight of concrete steps in front of his brother-in-law's house, after mentally noting that Bob must be home since his car was parked at the curb. Too absorbed with his thoughts to be careful, he tripped on the top step and fell, catching himself with the palms of his hands flat on the pebbly surface of the stoop in front of the door.

His heart beat rapidly as he picked himself up and brushed his scraped hands clean. Clumsy bastard. His hands really hurt. They were scratched but not bleeding. Dumb bastard! Can't walk without falling all over yourself.

He squeezed his eyes shut for a second trying to relieve the pain of the headache which still bothered him. Then he lifted the shiny brass knocker and gently tapped it against the panel of the massive wooden door. The hollow knocking sound was much louder than he expected, and he imagined he startled everyone in the house. Also, he was sure that all the neighbors in the genteel homes across the tree-lined street were coming to their windows to see who was making all the racket on the doorstep of the Robert Stacks on a quiet Sunday afternoon. He nervously glanced around, across the street, up and down the street, trying to appear self-contained and assured.

Should he knock again? Or give them a chance to answer the door if someone had to come down from the second floor.

How freely could he talk with Bob if his whole family were around? He should have telephoned and arranged to meet Bob alone. It was too late to retreat. Someone was unlocking the door on the inside.

It had taken some ingenuity to figure out how to sneak away from Helen to see Bob alone. When he returned from the zoo with Linda he found Helen already up and dressed, drinking coffee in the kitchen. She deliberately refused to answer when he spoke to her. A silence strike, he mentally noted and accepted that maybe it was better that way as long as they didn't seem to be able to speak to one another civilly. But it was a sad silent house.

Late in the afternoon he was given the opening to get away to see Bob alone. A phone call from one of his local union presidents, Stan Helowicz. After he put down the phone he told silent Helen that Stan wanted to know if he could borrow a ream of mimeograph paper to use for his local union's shop paper which he wanted to run off and distribute early Monday morning at the gates of the foundry where he worked. If she didn't mind he would drive down to his office and transfer a ream of paper from there to Stan's local union office which was right next door to his. Helen silently nodded that she heard him.

In his conversation with Stan Helowicz, Danny availed himself of the opportunity to ask about the reaction in his shop. Stan said he hadn't been able to tell anything yet because the newspaper items about Danny's appearance before the Committee hadn't been seen by the people in his shop until after they had already finished work and gone home for the weekend. He would be able to get their reaction when he went to work in the morning. But he gave Danny's morale a lift by telling him that he had already written an article for his shop paper in which he told why Danny had challenged the constitutionality of the Committee.

"I think we're going to come through all right. We can expect the same small group who tried to wreck the union before will try again. But it'll be only those few."

"You don't think they'll get anywhere?"

"This article should give the people the answers they want."

"Okay, Stash. I'll drop over to see you at noon tomorrow to find out what's happened."

"Meet me in the guard's shanty."

"Okay, Stash."

He had been worrying about Stan. There had been a time, not more than a year back, when Stan Helowicz had been the leader of the group trying to kick him out of the area because he had not properly cleansed himself of the charge of communism leveled against him, but lately Stan appeared to be willing to allow him to believe whatever he wanted to believe, even if it was over to the Left; and now it was good to learn that Stan was not turning on him.

He told Helen he would be back in forty-five minutes, knowing he could drive down to his office and back in about fifteen minutes with very little traffic to slow him down on a Sunday. That would allow him thirty minutes to stop off and talk to Bob.

Bob would not like what he was going to say, but there was no need to argue about their political differences. He was simply going to ask Bob as nicely as possible to stop putting the pressure on Helen.

What if Bob refuses to cooperate? What if Bob resents my coming to him this way to ask him not to talk to Helen? What if he gets angry and increases the pressure on Helen? What if he tells Helen all about this visit? What if he goes right to the telephone and calls her? — That could make the situation even worse than it is. But it's too late to retreat.

His heart was thumping and his face felt hot. He became aware that he was clenching his hands into tight fists. He made himself open up his hands and keep his fingers straight, with his hands at his sides.

One last quick reminder. It might be nice to get everything he felt about Bob out of his system but he couldn't afford himself that luxury. Handle yourself in such a way that when you leave this house you're still friendly with him.

Bob opened the door wide.

"Oh — "

Bob involuntarily exclaimed with surprise. His face revealed the question: what do you want that you come here without any warning? Then Bob remembered to be the gracious host.

"Come in." He opened the door wider and apologized for his pajamas, bathrobe and slippers. "Millie and I are spending a lazy Sunday at home for a change."

He went ahead of Danny, leading the way from the outer hall into the living room where Danny saw Millie, also in pajamas, bathrobe and slippers, stretched out on the sofa with her feet up on several fat cushions, the pages of the Sunday newspaper strewn all around her.

Danny wondered if he had disturbed them in the middle of having sex. He hoped not. That would not put them in a receptive mood.

Millie sat up when he came in. She was a woman of

medium height, beginning to put on weight, taking after a heavy mother. She had not put on any make-up yet, and her face looked very pale. She was his age, Danny knew, two years younger than her husband whose graying hair at the sides of his head and at his temples made him look much older than either Millie or himself.

"Where's Helen?" asked Millie.

"Home."

"Oh." Millie was not smiling. Her tone of voice expressed curiosity mixed with disapproval, as if she knew his coming alone could not be for a good purpose.

Still standing, not adjusted yet to the unexpected visit, Bob awkwardly tried to act friendly and polite, stepping aside and motioning for Danny to enter the living room through the wide entrance from the outer foyer. "This," he said, as he gestured for Danny to go into the other room, "is indeed a distinct, if unexpected pleasure," and then he bobbed his head around while he grinned like a bashful schoolboy, which Danny recognized as a very characteristic gesture of his brother-in-law.

Feeling ill at ease himself after he stepped into the living room, Danny shoved his hands into his side pockets to get them out of the way.

"Can I get you a drink of some kind?" Bob asked.

Danny remembered what Helen had said about Bob. He was always such a sweet guy and he had such a whimsical sense of humor until Dad died and he took over the job of running The Park Lane — and then he changed, becoming a very worried person and a serious man of importance with a little pot belly. Running a million dollar property made him a very harassed person. The responsibility killed his wonderful sense of humor.

"Scotch and soda?" Bob suggested.

"No, thanks. I'll take a rain check. Helen's expecting me back in a few minutes." He looked around. "The kids out playing?"

"Sandra's visiting one of her friends across the street," said Millie. "And the baby's asleep upstairs."

There was a long minute of silence, no one knowing what to say next.

"Why don't you sit down?" Bob urged, with what Danny

thought was a forced smile. He wondered if Bob assumed he had come to surrender — to abandon his union work and go into business as Bob had been urging through Helen.

Does he think that my experience with the Committee has so shaken me that I'm ready to hand my life over for him to tell me what to do with it? He's acting like a victorious general who's trying to be graciously generous to the surrendering military commander.

Bob pulled a big easy chair over to the edge of the grand piano for Danny, making a cozy grouping of furniture in the big living room, two easy chairs facing the big sofa where Millie was sitting, with a marble-topped coffee table in the center.

"Have a seat."

"No, thanks."

Danny remained standing, facing his brother-in-law. He was not there for a friendly visit and he did not want to mislead Bob by accepting too much hospitality.

"Helen will be expecting me back soon. I can stay only a few minutes."

Bob still gave him that forced smile of welcome, showing his white teeth.

"Helen doesn't know I'm here" added Danny.

Bob's smile vanished as he registered the inference that this was no friendly social visit.

"And I would appreciate it," continued Danny, "if you wouldn't tell her that I've been here. I'll tell her myself when I think it's right to tell her. — I think I know what I'm doing, and I'd appreciate it if you'd go along with me that much — "

Bob sat down, his face now sober, as he tightened the muscles in his jaw, waiting for his visitor to explain what he wanted.

"Bob, I know you and Millie differ with me on many things, especially politics."

"That would be putting it mildly," commented Bob with a dry laugh.

Danny gave his brother-in-law a quick impatient grin intended to keep the conversation on a friendly plane. But there was no time to waste if Helen was not to be made suspicious by his long absence.

"You certainly have the full right to differ with me all you want, Bob. You can think I'm a stupid jerk — "

A *well-meaning* jerk," Bob corrected him, with a nervous laugh.

Danny accepted the correction, with a slight bow and a quick tight grin.

"Right. A *well-meaning* jerk. You're entitled to your opinion. That's your own business."

"But Danny," Bob interrupted, still keeping his lips apart to show his white teeth in a stiff smile, "what good is it going to get you? You know you're not going to get anywhere. You're intelligent enough to know you're fighting a losing battle and you can't possibly win. You're trying to swim upstream against a strong sweeping current going the other way — "

"Bob!" The sharpness of it halted his brother-in-law's speech. Danny coldly continued. "I'm not here to discuss my political differences."

"No?"

"At least not now."

"But you're such a nice guy," insisted Bob. "You could go so far in the business world if you'd get all these nonsensical ideas out of your system and grow up — "

"Thank you," snapped Danny, sarcastically. Then he stopped himself to get his temper under control. He forced a grin, hiding his nervousness. It was wrong to get into a fight with his brother-in-law.

"Bob" — he nervously shuffled his feet on the thick nap of the rug — "Bob, you live your life, I'll live mine. Okay?"

"Okay."

Danny saw that Millie didn't like the way he was speaking to her husband. She turned her face to Bob in a way that prompted him to go on.

"Do you think you helped yourself by what you did?" Bob asked, leaning back in his chair, crossing his legs and clasping his hands behind his head with his elbows forced way back as far as he could move them. "Do you think you did the right thing refusing to answer any questions in front of a committee of the Congress of the United States?"

"Obviously, or I wouldn't have refused."

Danny saw his brother-in-law return his hands to his lap and shrug his shoulders in a disdainful manner, sniffing at his visitor's inability to see what was right and what was wrong in such matters. Fearing that the rising irritation was getting the better of himself, Danny sat down, gingerly resting his bottom on the forward edge of the easy chair.

"Bob, I did exactly what Albert Einstein advised everybody called before this Committee to do." He pulled his voice down. "Einstein advised those who are called before these Congressional committees investigating political beliefs to refuse to answer any questions, no matter what the consequences. He learned that from his experience with the same thing in Nazi Germany under Hitler!"

"That's easy for Einstein to say," said Millie. "A famous man, he can get away with it. He doesn't have a wife and two young children to worry about, I'm sure."

"What does Einstein know about politics?" Bob gave a disgusted flip of his right hand up into the air. "Einstein's a scientist, a physicist, a mathematician — an impractical dreamer who lives in an unreal world of figures and theoretical experiments. He ought to stay in his laboratory and keep his mouth shut!"

"The atom bomb wasn't such an impractical dream, was it? And it was Einstein who presented the idea to President Roosevelt!"

"That was back when everyone was fighting the Nazis," retorted Bob, his face flushed, resenting the way Danny snapped at him. "You must remember that the attitude of the general public today towards people like you — is exactly the same as it was back then toward the Nazis!"

That hurt. Danny rose to his feet to cut the conversation short by coming directly to the point of his visit.

"Bob! Let's not waste time discussing politics! I didn't come here for that!" He wondered if his own face was as red as Bob's. Millie was staring up at the ceiling with an expression of scornful distaste. "Bob!" Danny rushed on. "Helen told me not long ago that our problems, hers and mine, are greatly aggravated by the fact that *you* come into her studio while she's working on her book illustrations and *you* sit down and start to needle her about why doesn't Danny change his job — and why doesn't Danny give up his union work — and why doesn't Danny go into a business — "

He stopped to get control of the shakiness in his voice. His brother-in-law's face was white, no longer red. Millie glared with resentment: how dare you talk to my husband that way?

"Bob" — Danny forced a smile to take the sharp edge off what he was going to say — "if you've got anything to say about anything like that, say it directly to me! Not to Helen!" He kept his voice under tight control and spoke softly. *"You come and talk to me! Don't you go to Helen !"*

A tense silence followed as he waited for the reaction of his brother-in-law.

Then, catching Danny by surprise because he had been expecting a fight, Bob grinned sheepishly. "What's the good of talking to you? I can't get anywhere with you, can I?"

"But" — Danny still forced himself to speak softly, still held a smile on his face — *"don't talk to her!"*

"I don't see why I shouldn't talk to her." Bob was half-laughing and half-serious, trying to brush aside Danny's objections as though they were silly. "I'm trying to help you, and it's for your own good. You insist on sticking with your unions. Even though you're not getting anywhere. Even though you're getting smeared all over town. You're throwing your life away! Nothing I say to you seems to make any difference. Logic doesn't work with you. So I talk to Helen." He grinned, "I mean well, anyway — "

"I know" — Danny stopped, to quiet the agitation he felt — "I'm sure you mean well. — *But — cut — it — out!* "

Millie surprised Danny by taking his side, though it was apparent that she severely resented the way he was ignoring her husband's importance as a successful businessman and also his role as the central figure of the Stack family in Buffalo.

"I agree with you. I've told him not to stick his two cents in." Then she coldly looked at Danny and added, "It's up to you and Helen to work out your own problems."

She swung her feet back up on the couch and deliberately turned her head away from him, looking out through the window.

"Well" — Bob laughed with embarrassment. "I can't keep myself quiet when I see how Danny is messing up his own life and the lives of my youngest sister and her two children." He apologetically corrected himself, to Danny: "Your children too."

"*Bob!* " — Danny still had to fight to hold on to himself. "Bob! — *Try!* — *Try!* — *Try to keep out of our marriage!* I'm forty-one years old! No child! And your sister is only a few years younger! We're not children! We're old enough to make up our own minds and solve our own problems and take our own medicine if we make a wrong decision!"

"I suppose you are — "

"And your mother," added Danny, remembering something else Helen had told him, "she's also over twenty-one!"

"What about Mother?" Bob showed complete bewilderment. "Are you saying that I influence *her* too?"

"Don't you?"

"How? When? I don't know what you're talking about."

"Helen told me that at times your mother has agreed with something I've done or said — until you talk to her, saying exactly the opposite, and get her to reverse her own judgment."

"When did that happen?"

"Oh, never mind. I apologize for bringing her into this. It's none of my business what goes on between you and your mother. I'm not married to her. — All I'm saying is that for the sake of your sister's happiness, leave Helen alone and leave me alone. Allow us to work out our own problems one way or the other. Without any interference from you. Stop trying to put the heat on me through Helen. — Okay?"

"But don't you think you'd have a happier marriage if you'd get out of the union and go into some more respectable work?"

"Bob" — Danny, too agitated to sit down any longer, stood up — "leave that to Helen and me to decide!"

"She wants you out of the union, doesn't she?"

"Leave that to us!"

But Bob wouldn't let go. "She wants you out, doesn't she?"

"That's *our* problem! Not yours! Let *us* work it out by ourselves!"

"Well, at least don't you think you would make Helen much happier if you'd make some kind of public statement clearing your name of all the stigma of communism?" Bob, embarrassed at his own persistence, again showed his teeth in his characteristic bashful smile. "Then you can start working to make some money in a business — "

"Look!" Danny wiped the sweat off his hands with a swipe against his thighs. "You don't seem to understand what I'm saying! Leave Helen and me to work out our own problems without your help. *I'm not married to YOU!*"

"Thank God for that!"

They both had to laugh at Bob's vehement interjection.

Millie decided to comment on the situation.

"I agree with you, Danny," she said, coldly. — She alternated between staring up at the ceiling and out through the front windows of the house as she delivered her opinion. "I agree with you even though, *personally*, I could never marry anyone like you. — And I don't see how Helen can possibly stand it. I know I would find it completely impossible. An absolute nightmare! — I couldn't think of anything worse than to be married to someone who is always fighting for ideals. Even though I might agree with his ideals, in principle, in theory." She examined her fingernails coated with pink lacquer. "For instance, I believe someone should tell off that Un-American Activities Committee. I believe it is a detriment to our nation and to everything our country was originally founded on. And if someone else besides you had done it — *anyone else!* — I would respect them for their courage. But not you! It's none of my business" — she reached for a cigarette — "and I should keep my mouth shut, I suppose, but I don't think you had the right to sacrifice your wife and children by challenging the Committee — "

She stopped to light her cigarette with the flame of the silver-plated cigarette lighter.

"That's your opinion," said Danny, "and you're entitled to it."

"I think," Millie swept on, exhaling the first long drawn-in breath of cigarette smoke, "people have a right to their own beliefs whatever they may be. I even believe that anyone has the right to believe in communism, to be a communist. That can be their private belief. But you can't sacrifice others for that belief. That isn't right! — It's fine, and probably necessary, for some brave man to decide he's ready to go to jail for his beliefs — so he can test unjust laws and preserve the true meaning of the Bill of Rights. I agree with you. Someone should do that. But not someone married to my sister-in-law! That's too close to home for me. — I like to *read* about brave men like that. I don't want them in my family. They're too selfish. Their bravery comes before their family. — I know that if I were married to you — "

"Fortunately," Danny sharply interrupted her, "very fortunately, Millie, for both of us, we're *not* married to each other!"

Her face hardened and she took a quick puff on her cigarette while Bob rushed to her defense.

"Millie's right," he interjected, seeming more disturbed by the way Danny spoke to his wife than by anything said directly to himself. "I don't think Helen's so very happy with this kind of life, married to a martyr — "

Danny's anger got away from him.

"You let Helen decide that! Stop acting as though you're her father! You may be running The Park Lane! Inherited that! But you didn't inherit the position of being head of my family. In case you don't know it, feudalism — the system of the oldest taking over when the father dies, the system of primogeniture — is dead! At least where my marriage is concerned. You leave Helen alone! Then maybe our marriage might have a chance to survive! — You'd be surprised how often Helen has been very happy with our marriage until someone like you reminds her that it's wrong to be happy and well-adjusted with me! Until you deliberately make her feel she's supposed to be unhappy because of my union work and my politics! You'd be goddamn surprised if you knew how often it's happened exactly that way!"

Bob's face flushed a deep red. He was so agitated that he drew his robe tightly around him and stood up and walked in a circle around his chair, standing behind it for a second, unable to think of what he should say, and then coming around, completing the circle, sitting down again. Danny watched and waited to see how much more trouble he had created for himself.

"I — don't — think," began Bob, picking his words very carefully, a businessman making an extremely important statement to the board of directors, " I — don't — think — that — I'm — trying — to become — the head of the family."

He had his hands pressed together in front of his chest, like a churchgoer at prayer. "Certainly, not the head of *your* family — "

"Helen's part of my family — "

"She's still my sister and I consider her still part of my family too!"

"Well, for your own good as well as hers, stop trying to be her father! For chrissakes, Bob, let her break free! — Let her grow up! — Let her become an adult, mentally and emotionally as well as physically! — I tell you, Bob, it's hell being married to a child, to have three children where there's supposed to be a wife and two children. — Give her a chance to argue these things out with me on her own. So she can face some difficult situations and decide them by herself. No matter which way she decides! But let *her* decide! *Her! Her!* "

Danny stopped himself.

He became aware that he was breathing so hard that he could hear his own breathing. He thought he had gone too far, saying things which for years had been eating away down deep inside him where he had consciously buried them, thinking what good could come from speaking about them — they always seemed to entail problems too involved and too complex for him to be able to work out a solution. Both Bob and Millie seemed to be shocked into silence by his vehemence. They avoided his searching stare.

Bob stood up and adjusted his robe, tightening the belt which was knotted at his waist. The two men faced each other, two opponents measuring one another.

"You're asking me not to talk to Helen about this Un-American Committee thing — "

Danny interrupted, abruptly, coldly, in guttural tones. "I'm not *asking* you, Bob; I'm *telling* you!" The sound of his own words frightened him, but he had made up his mind that he was going to make a hard fight for his marriage, and this was one of the most important obstacles he had to overcome.

Bob quietly sat down again.

There was a long embarrassed silence.

Danny realized he would do best to try to ease the tension now that he had made his point. It wouldn't be good to leave Bob's house on this extremely sour note. After all, he had no way of compelling Bob to leave Helen alone. If they parted angrily now Bob could go to Helen and give her the worst possible interpretation of this visit.

"Bob" — Danny forced himself to smile — "let's try not to get too hot about this. I'm not here to argue with you. I don't want to interfere in any way with your life or in any way with your relationship with Millie. All I'm asking from you is exactly the same thing regarding my marriage with Helen."

He restlessly paced up and back between the piano and the opposite wall, twice, gathering his thoughts. Then facing Bob again, he went on. "All I'm hoping is that you think enough of your own sister to let her try to work out her marriage with me in our own way — let her deal with her problems like an adult — let her finally try to grow up to be an independent woman making up her own mind. And I can also tell you this, Bob. Some recent decisions I've had to make, decisions I'm in the process of making right now, are helping *me* finally to grow up into an adult myself, into an emotionally mature person who is capable of consciously trying to solve his problems and to accept the full responsibility for shaping the course of his own life within the context of the objective realities. And it's my opinion, Bob — I think a similar development would take place with Helen if you'd give her half a chance. That doesn't necessarily mean she'll decide to stay married to me. I realize that. And if she decides by herself that our marriage won't work, then okay, fine, that's the way it'll be, and I've got no squawk to make. But don't you be the one to persuade her it won't work. If you do, I think you'll be sorry. Because it's very possible that a few years from now, or maybe sooner, or maybe even sometime later, Helen may look back with different eyes and she'll really hate you for what you did. And the kids will despise you if you're responsible for taking them away from their father. And don't be surprised — it's very possible that in years to come, after this hysteria is cleared away, you — you yourself! — might look back with different eyes and you might thoroughly hate yourself — " The anger and heat had cooled off.

Silence.

Danny saw that Bob and Millie were engrossed in weighing what he had just said. He followed up, carefully pressing his advantage.

"Bob, I don't want to fight with you. I've never wanted to fight with you. As a matter-of-fact, strange though it may seem to you, except for our different viewpoint on politics and such, I've always respected you and liked you as a person. But this is *my* marriage, *my* life, you're monkeying with. And I'm not going to stand idly by and see my marriage broken up by interference from you or anyone else. Not without making a helluva fight, and no matter *who* I have to fight. There are too many lives in our family at stake in this thing for me just to walk away and let you or anyone else have your way without a battle. — And don't be too sure you know your sister. You may be surprised some day to learn that she doesn't disagree with my ideas as much as you think she does."

"Well" — Bob ventured a winning shy grin — "you're an extremely persuasive guy. I'm sure that if anyone lived with you as long as Helen has — you might persuade him to agree with you. But that doesn't necessarily mean you're right. It's only that you're a very sincere person and you make a good clean-cut appearance and everyone knows you're honest, no matter what else they may think about you."

"Thank you. — Then you agree that we may work out our problems if you leave us alone — "

"She may be persuaded to go along with you. But I don't think that's necessarily the best thing for her, or for you, or for the children."

The look on Danny's face needed no explanation.

Bob chuckled nervously to cover his embarrassment.

Millie interceded. "I keep telling him it's none of his business. It's up to Helen to make up her own mind. — I know that if I were in her shoes I wouldn't remain married for one minute to someone as intense as you who's always fighting out the problems of the world. But that may be just what Helen wants, just what she may need — to be happy."

Danny decided there was no use going over the same ground he had just covered with Bob, and he guessed that Bob must feel the same way. They had talked themselves out. He buttoned his jacket.

"Helen will probably invite you people to come over to the house with your mother. Probably sometime the early part of this week — so we can talk over why I refused to answer the questions of the Committee. Sort of a family council meeting."

"Exactly why did you refuse?" Bob asked. "I thought you might use the Fifth Amendment on some of the questions concerning your politics, but I can't understand why you wouldn't answer where you were born."

"I can explain if you'd like to hear."

"I'd like to hear how you explain it."

"Do you want the explanation that takes one minute or the one that takes five hours?"

"The one minute version will do. You can give us the long version when we come over to your house for your meeting."

Danny raced through the monologue, quickly summarizing why he had refused to answer the questions of the Committee — "the enabling resolution establishing the Committee unconstitutional — certain ideas *verboten* — the words '*un-American*' and '*subversive*' so vague as to lack meaning — illegal inquisition by Congress into personal and private affairs; — no legislative purpose — illegal assumption by legislative branch of powers of judicial branch — "

His audience was cold. Danny could not miss the expression of tolerant disgust on the lips of his brother-in-law whose face otherwise remained impassive. There was a broad sneer on Millie's face — deliberately exaggerated, he thought, so he would be sure to see it. He was sorry about Millie because he had always been fond of her and had hoped to keep her as an ally, especially since he knew she theoretically agreed with his right to his own opinions and his own choice of what kind of work he wanted to do. There had been a time not too far back when Millie and he had talked confidentially about the problems of in-laws married into a family whose members put their mother and brothers and sisters and the prestige they had by their connection with the luxurious Park Lane before the wife and husband they acquired by marriage. He wondered if, now that she felt that she had been accepted into full status in their family, she wanted him put clearly outside the pale of the family for all the community to know and see — so whatever he did would not reflect upon the family —

"Of course," smirked Bob, after Danny finished his

reasons for refusing to answer the Committee's questions, "you know I disagree with you."

"That," said Danny, "is probably one of the outstanding understatements of the year."

Even Bob smiled.

Danny started toward the outer hallway. "I better get going."

Bob stepped in front of him and led him out of the room. Danny looked back into the living room and saw that Millie had not stirred from her reclining position on the long sofa.

"So long, Millie."

"Goodbye," she said, up to the ceiling.

Out in the hall, Bob stopped with his hand on the doorknob.

"I won't say a word to either Helen or mother," he promised. But Danny could see how much his brother-in-law still resented some of the things he had been told.

"Thanks, Bob. That's all I'm asking."

Millie called to him from the living room. "What about this family council meeting you're planning?"

"What about it?" Danny stepped back to the entrance from the hallway into the living room. Millie twisted her head to face him.

"You haven't given us our instructions. Are we supposed to agree or to disagree with everything you say?"

Her sarcasm bothered him but his voice was cold and contained as he very deliberately replied, "It doesn't make much difference to me, Millie, as long as both you and your husband do it to my face and not behind my back."

Millie flushed as she squirmed around to sit up. "I agree with that," she said, somewhat apologetically. This time she stood up and followed Danny as he started toward the front door again.

Bob held the door open.

"If Helen calls," Danny reminded him, "it's best if you don't mention that I've been here. I'll tell her myself when I feel the time is right."

Bob somberly nodded agreement.

Danny heard the knocker clatter as the door closed behind him. He started down the front steps, glad that the session was over. As he climbed into his car out in front of the house he realized that his headache had disappeared. He laughed at himself, he was so obvious.

Chapter 41

So angry that she forgot she was not speaking to him, Helen looked up from the cup of black coffee when Danny walked into the kitchen.

"Where have you been?" she frigidly demanded.

"I got stuck," he lamely replied and started out of the kitchen to avoid further questions.

"One can always count on you!"

That stopped him.

"What the hell difference does it make whether I was here or down at the office?"

"Your daughter refuses to take a nap — she cried for an hour after you left — she wants her dear Daddy."

"Where is she now?" he asked quietly, knowing she meant little Linda.

"Up in her room, probably still awake. She's been waiting all this time for you. I phoned the office but no one answered."

"The phone at the office rang but I decided not to answer it," he lied. "I didn't know it was you."

"As usual, whenever I need you that's when you're not around." She said it to the wall, refusing to speak directly to him.

He refused to be drawn into a useless argument.

"I'll go talk to Linda."

"Well, you might as well get her up already. It's too late to take a nap now."

He spun around and left the kitchen and ran up the stairs, bounding up four steps at a time, relieved to escape. He stopped in front of Linda's door and slowly turned the knob and opened the door about an inch. The little redhead in her pajamas was sitting on the floor, playing with her dolls.

Linda looked up, saw him, stretched out her hands to him and began to cry. They hugged and kissed. And then he wiped her face dry with his handkerchief.

"Where were you?" Linda tearfully demanded.

"I just went down to the office for a while, honey — "

"I thought you went away for a long time again," said Linda, and he realized that she had tied in his disappearance that afternoon with his long absence when he had gone to Albany to appear before the Committee. And then he remembered how long he might be away from her if he was formally cited for contempt of Congress and if he was found guilty and sentenced to prison. He quickly shoved that thought aside, refusing to let himself dwell upon it.

He sat down on the floor with Linda and they played with her dolls. Helen silently came into the room and rummaged through one of the dresser drawers, picking out underclothes for Linda. She brought a little dress out of the clothes closet. She spread the clothing out on the small bed.

"You can take care of her this time."

"Fine," he said, trying to act happy in order to dispel some of the gloom in the house.

"I'd like to rest for a while," explained Helen.

"Okay" — he was most agreeable — "I'll go over and see my mother and dad, and I'll take Linda along. What about Ruth?"

"Leave Ruth where she is. She's having fun at her friend's house, playing phonograph records. Don't bother her."

"Okay."

Lifting Linda up into his arms, Danny watched Helen silently leave the room. A moment later he heard her close the door to their bedroom. He kissed Linda on the soft underside of her chin and laughed at the way the little redhead giggled.

Linda pushed his face away. "Is Mommy going to sleep?"

"She wants to rest."

"Why?"

"She's tired."

"Why?"

"She didn't sleep much last night."

"Why not?"

"We got to bed late."

"Why did you get to bed late?"

"Because we didn't get to bed early."

"Oh — "

He hated to leave Helen alone in the house to stew in her

melancholy juice about how rotten her life was with him because of his union work and his politics.

"Let's go ask Mommy if she wants to come with us." He carried the child across the hall to the other door and knocked. He heard the muffled question.

"What do you want?"

She sounded annoyed, but he went in.

"Wouldn't you like to come along with us?"

"No!"

Her abrupt reply angered him. But it wouldn't help either of them to allow Helen to isolate herself like this and keep brooding about their situation.

"It's a real nice day outside. It'll do you good to get out of the house."

A long pause before she replied.

"I want to rest — "

Still holding Linda with his left arm, Danny quietly opened the door and stepped into the room. Helen was sitting on the edge of the bed. She stared up at him, annoyed by this intrusion into her privacy.

"Helen" — he tried to be lighthearted and conciliatory without giving up any of his own dignity — "you may feel like you do about me and maybe you're going off to do what you plan to do" — he had to speak so vaguely because of little Linda — "but we're two grown human beings living in the same house. So let's try to act at least as civilly toward each other as we would toward a total stranger."

She thought that over, staring directly up into his eyes — he stared back, waiting.

"Okay," she said, so calmly she surprised him, "but I really am tired and I'd like to sleep for a while."

"It's the nervous strain."

"I know. I'm exhausted."

"Get some sleep."

Linda wriggled out of his arms to stand on her own two feet. He took her by the hand. "Come on, honey, let's get you dressed and go see Grandma and Grandpa."

Helen spoke to him again before he closed the door. "Danny, my mother's coming over to eat with us tonight. Do you mind?"

"No."

But he wondered why Helen hadn't mentioned it before and if her mother's presence would add to the tension which already existed in the house.

"Mother called up and asked how you were." Helen got up from the bed to retrieve her pack of cigarettes from the top of the dresser. He waited. He could tell that she had more to say about her mother's call. "Mother wants to find out from you what happened."

He had been afraid of that. A fine family council meeting they would have later. He had already spoken to Bob and Millie, and now Helen's mother!

"She's more on your side than you think."

"Oh?"

"She surprised me."

He didn't comment, lest he say the wrong thing. He wondered if her mother had anything to do with Helen's apparent willingness to be more ready to relax their private cold war.

Linda grabbed him by the loose seat of his pants and pulled. "Daddy, hurry up and get me dressed! I want to go outside!"

"Okay, honey."

He reached around behind him and swept the little redhead up into his arms, high into the air, and then hugged her and kissed her warm soft neck while she shrieked with delight. He started to close the door, but Helen stopped him.

"Do you mind stopping off at The Park Lane to pick up Mother on your way back?"

"No, I don't mind."

"When she's ready to leave I'll phone you. She'll be waiting in front of the main entrance."

"Okay."

He quietly closed the door behind him. Out in the hall he squeezed the little redhead and tried to kiss the soft warm spot on the side of her neck again.

"Let's go out!" Linda ordered, impatiently pushing his face away from her neck.

"Okay."

And he raced into the other room with Linda under his arms while she shrieked with delight. He closed the door to keep the noise away from Helen.

While dressing the child, he evaluated the latest development. It appeared that there was a good chance to win over Helen's mother. And Bob and Millie might be willing to maintain a position of hostile neutrality. Now, if he could spread beyond that and ease up the pressures on Helen in some of the surrounding areas of the community, maybe their marriage would still be saved. He felt better. Even if we do break up and separate, there's a good possibility we'll eventually get together again. But he hated to think of the pain and heartache the two kids would go through. They might be permanently scarred, emotionally.

He kneeled to tie Linda's shoelaces. She threw her arms around his neck and her damp soft lips pressed hard against the side of his mouth. She had a habit of kissing hard like that without any warning, and it was a shocking surprise which always melted Danny inside.

They briefly hugged and kissed and squeezed.

Then, ready to leave, Linda went into the other room to kiss Mommy goodbye, while Danny noted how careful the child was to match kisses evenly between parents.

And then they started out for Grandma and Grandpa's house.

His mother made the usual big fuss over Linda, taking the little child up on her lap and kissing her. Linda — still insisting on impartiality — immediately broke away from Grandma to run across the living room to hug and kiss Grandpa.

Then Grandma took Linda into the kitchen and gave her a big piece of cake and a glass of milk — the Sunday afternoon ritual for visiting grandchildren in that house. Grandpa pulled out the whiskey bottle from under the table in the kitchen where he hid it from the grandchildren. He set the bottle down on the dining room table and brought Danny a small glass from the fancy cupboard where the guest glasses and china were stored.

"Help yourself to a *schnappsel.*"

His usual good humor quite evident, Grandpa waved to Danny to help himself to whatever he wanted out of the bottle and then the vigorous old man returned to his favorite easy chair in the living room. He was wearing the same kind of knitted wool stocking hat that Albert Einstein often wore in his pictures in the newspapers. Danny and his brothers often poked fun at him about that hat but his father always took the ribbing good-naturedly. He wore the hat to keep his head warm, he always explained, and then he would show the heavy woolen socks which he wore all year round. He also wore sheepskin bedroom slippers. The old man was very wary about catching colds, explaining that at his age he had to be very careful of his health. His whiskey drinking, he insisted, was strictly medicinal. It was true that the doctor told him to take a drink at every meal. He was in his eighties, the exact age still a secret the old man refused to reveal to his children. He insisted that he was young enough to keep on working in his little notions store, refusing to retire despite the urging of his sons and daughters. The old man frequently referred to himself jokingly as "the young man."

He was also a scholar in his own way. The rickety end table beside his easy chair was piled high with a collection of Talmudic books which he pored through in all his spare moments with the aid of a very powerful magnifying glass.

"Help yourself," urged his father. "What are you waiting for?"

"How about you?"

"No, thank you, sir," his father answered with the exaggerated politeness which was part of his peppy sense of humor, "I already had my quota for the day."

Danny poured himself a shot from the whiskey bottle and held up the glass, a toast.

"Good health," he said to his father, in *Yiddish* — he knew the old man liked to hear his son speak a few words in *Yiddish* now and then; and Danny had heard it spoken so much in their house when he was a young boy that he was still able to understand much of it when it was spoken to him and he could still say some words in *Yiddish* that made sense.

His father gave him a very hearty "Good health to you!" also in *Yiddish*.

"Down the hatch," said Danny, smiling as he ribbed his father by using slang in contrast to the *Yiddish*. He held his glass high up in the air, waiting for the old man to reply to that toast.

"Down the hatch!" came the vigorous reply from his father.

Danny emptied the glass with one gulp. The hot liquid burned its way down into his stomach and immediately sent a warm glow out to the rest of his body.

"Have some cake," urged his mother, bringing in a plate piled high with chunks of sponge cake. His father also urged him to have some cake. The old man always used cake as a chaser after a glass of burning whiskey.

Danny helped himself to a small piece of cake and bit into it, while he kept his eye on Linda who was climbing onto her Grandma's lap again. The child got comfortable and sat there with a piece of cake in one hand and a glass of milk in the other hand, smugly relaxed against the warmth of her Grandma.

"Have another *schnappsel*!" his father insisted.

"I just finished one."

"Another won't hurt you. Good for whatever ails you."

"If you insist, sir —"

"I insist, sir."

"Thank you, sir."

"You're welcome, sir."

He raised his glass and bowed. His father returned the bow.

"Lachayim!" — Good health, in *Yiddish.*

"Lachayim to you, Pop!"

And down the hatch —

The preliminaries were over.

Danny knew that his father and mother were aching to talk about what had happened in Albany.

His father started it off.

"I see you told them not to waste your time," he said.

"What do you mean?" Danny was not sure whether his father was praising or criticizing what he had done. But the old man cleared that up right away.

"Let them go to the devil with their questions. *Momsers*!"

"Shhh!" Danny's mother held a finger to her lips, cautioning her husband to watch his language, even in *Yiddish*, with a little child there.

"The devil with them!"

"All right, all right, the devil with them. But there's no

need to get so excited — "

"Who's excited? I'm merely expressing an opinion, if you please, madam. Isn't a man permitted to express an opinion in his own house? What's the matter, do we have an Un-American Committee in this house already?"

Danny grinned openly at the familiar exchange which had been going on between his parents on one subject or another for as long as he could remember. This time it was the Un-American Activities Committee. But the friendly bickering back and forth, tongue in cheek, had been going on since he was a child. It was a familiar routine, with his father vehemently sounding off and his mother telling his father not to get so excited and his father insisting in return that he is not excited.

His mother silenced his father, with the same peremptory gesture she always used to put an end to his quibbling, and then turned to her son. Danny waited for the inevitable questions. He felt like a little boy who feared he was about to be scolded.

"What about this citation for contempt?"

Danny's eyes met the stern gaze from her deep-set blue eyes. He stared back while she brushed a wisp of her snow white hair away from her forehead. What a strong face she had, the same high cheekbones he had inherited. With the stern character lines in her face, she looked like a pioneer woman out of some painting about the settling of the wild West. She had always been the anchor in their family. Now, in her late seventies, she still tried to keep a tight check on everything going on. But she had trained her children too well, and they insisted on standing on their own two feet.

"What about it?" he asked, on guard and unbending, politely letting his mother know he wanted no criticism from her because of what he had done.

"Isn't there some danger?"

"Sure, there is."

"Then why did you do it?"

"Because I decided it was the right thing to do. I'm old enough to make up my own mind —"

"Of course, you are. I know you're over twenty-one."

"Mom, if they *do* decide to cite me for contempt and they prosecute me, then the whole question of the constitutionality of the Un-American Activities Committee itself will be thrown into question. That's what the courts will really decide — whether or not the Committee itself was unconstitutionally established. With the possibility that the Committee itself may be ruled out of existence. They'll think hard before they take that risk."

"But what if they decide to take that risk? Then aren't *you* taking a risk?"

"That's right."

His mother peered at him over the top of Linda's mop of red hair, fixedly staring with those deep-set blue eyes, examining his face to get every nuance of his reaction.

"You're sure you know what you're doing?" she asked with a critical note in her voice.

"I think so, Mom. I thought about it for a long time before I made up my mind to do what I did."

His father became impatient.

"He knows what he's doing. He's no child."

"You!" Her commanding blue eyes shocked the old man into silence for only a second or two before he bounced back, vigorously defending his viewpoint.

"This," he importantly announced, trying to make this mere woman understand the tremendousness of it, "is something which will have to be decided by the top Supreme Court of the United States. It's a big thing, Ma."

"I don't care how big it is," she said very simply. "I hope nothing will happen to my boy which will make him go to — well, which will not be very nice for him and his family."

"I hope nothing will happen either, Mom," said Danny. "I'm hoping that the people of this country are so fed up with all this witch-hunting that the courts will start to reflect this with rulings that such hearings into a man's political and economic opinions and thoughts and associations are unconstitutional. That's what I'm counting on."

"'The Supreme Court follows the elections!'" proclaimed his father. "That's what Peter Finley Dunne wrote. — *MIS*-ter Dooley! — Do you remember *MIS*-ter Dooley?"

And for the umpteenth time Danny's father told him about his favorite humorist, Peter Finley Dunne, who had died in the mid-Thirties, the creator of *MIS*-ter Dooley, a character who commented very sharply on the political, economic and social scene.

"*MIS*-ter Dooley said the Supreme Court always drags along behind the thinking of the majority of people."

The telephone rang and Danny answered it, expecting it to be Helen. It was her. She asked if he would go over to The Park Lane right away and pick up her mother at the front entrance.

His father insisted that he have one more *schnappel* before he left, but Danny refused it. Two *schnappels* had been enough on his empty stomach. He could feel them.

"Well, good luck!" cried out his father flamboyantly as Danny started out with Linda in his arms after the child kissed and hugged both Grandma and Grandpa to say goodbye.

"Thank you, sir," he replied to his father, with a mock bow from where he stopped in the doorway.

"Be careful," warned his mother. "Do what's right, but don't be too brave. Remember, you have a family. Don't take unnecessary chances."

"I'm thinking of my family, Mom," he assured her. "I just happened to be the guy who was there at a certain time in a certain place when it was ripe to do what I did. I couldn't duck away from it and still respect myself."

"I understand," said his mother, "but try to be as careful as possible — "

"Okay, Mom."

"Leave him alone," interjected his father, exasperated. "He's a good boy. He did a wonderful thing and I'm proud of him!"

"Don't you think I'm proud too?" his mother indignantly demanded. "Does that mean I still can't worry about what might happen to my son?"

"Nothing will happen," said his father, the perennial optimist. "Everything will come out all right." And the old man turned his attention back to Danny and dismissed him. "Are you going? Then goodbye! Go!"

They all laughed at this abrupt dismissal.

Danny carried Linda down the stairs in his arms while his parents called down goodbye to her and the child called back goodbye to them. If only enough people in Buffalo began to think and talk like his parents, Helen would find life much easier here.

And now there comes the scene with his mother-in-law. If only he had time to rest between these sessions.

Chapter 42

"I like to sit on Grammy's lap," said Linda, "the fur coat feels so nice," and she scrunched her little bottlom around on her maternal grandmother's luxurious mink garment. Helen's mother warned Linda to sit still or she would have to get off her lap and sit on the seat, and the child stopped squirming.

Danny reached across Linda and his mother-in-law to make sure the car door was locked on their side before he drove away from the front entrance of The Park Lane.

No one spoke for awhile.

"And how are *you*, Danny?" his mother-in-law finally said, laughing self-consciously at the fact that she had not spoken to him before, all her attention being concentrated on her grandchild.

Danny glanced at his mother-in-law and laughed. She was a gray-haired woman, in her sixties, meticulously dressed — anyone could see that she spent much time taking good care of her face. Danny knew she exercised her neck muscles and rubbed the skin around her eyes — to keep the circulation going and prevent sagging wrinkles— every morning and night, and she had her hair done at the hair dressers at least once or twice a week. Every wave was in its exactly right place underneath the modish hat she wore, a hat with a little feather.

He answered her question, drawling it out.

"I'm fine, Irene" — he refused to call her by any more intimate term than her given name — "thank you." He grinned at her girlish laughter and deliberately chuckled aloud to set her at ease.

She twisted her head back so she could examine him. "Well, you don't look like you had too terrible a time." He laughed again.

"Not too bad," he said flippantly and grinned. "I lived through it."

She became serious.

"I'd like to hear about it. After we eat. I'm very interested

351

in knowing exactly what happened."

"Okay." He was both surprised and pleased at her show of interest and he cordially nodded to express his willingness to fulfill her wish.

Little Linda, to get their attention, chose this moment to stand up in her grandmother's lap. Danny stopped the car until she agreed to sit down again. They continued on, with Irene clasping Linda on her lap.

"Danny," she ventured, "there is so much a person doesn't know about what's going on in the world, isn't there?"

"Yep." Not knowing what his mother-in-law was driving at, Danny didn't want to say anything which might turn out to be the wrong thing to say.

"I'm beginning to learn that," Irene continued, very earnestly. "Have you ever heard of the League of Women Voters?"

"Oh, sure."

"It's an organization," she intensely went on, "which is trying to make people understand why it's so important that they should be sure to vote at election time — it's a *very* important organization doing *so much good.*" She spoke with great conviction, as though she feared he might not give sufficient weight to what she had to say. "It's a wonderful organization. It has absolutely no axe of its own to grind. I joined it last week. "Well," she argued, as though he had questioned why she had done it, "I decided it's about time I learned what's going on in politics in my own country. In order to be a good citizen you have to spend some time to learn what the different bills are all about and who the candidates are and their backgrounds. That's the only way you can be able to vote intelligently."

She stopped to shift Linda higher on her lap. "Danny" — she turned her attention back to him — "what's the Bill of Rights?" And then she giggled with embarrassment. "Isn't that a stupid question? I've always wondered if it's got something to do with our Constitution but I thought I would appear to be such a fool if I asked anyone. I thought they would laugh at me for being so stupid."

"There's no reason to feel that way."

"I know, but I do. *Is* the Bill of Rights part of our Constitution of our country?"

"That's right," he answered her, being very matter-of-fact about it so she wouldn't feel self-conscious.

He saw a red signal up ahead and he stepped on the brake to slow the car down as they approached an intersection. "The first ten amendments to our Constitution," he explained, "are known as the Bill of Rights. As I recall it — very much offhand — after we had our revolution in 1776 delegates from all the states met in a constitutional convention and drew up a constitution to be submitted back to the individual states for ratification — and the convention delegates, many of whom came from the propertied classes with notions that they were going to be the homegrown rulers to replace the British profiteers, deliberately omitted from the first draft of the Constitution the guarantees of the very freedoms for which the average soldier had fought and for which the rank-and-file, the common people of the country, had endured great sacrifices."

The red signal changed to green, he pressed down on the gas pedal and the car picked up speed.

"A bitter political struggle followed — and out of that struggle came the first ten amendments to our Constitution of the United States, and they were known — they're still known as the Bill of Rights. It didn't come easy, Irene. Freedom never comes easy."

"The Fifth Amendment," she said, "the amendment there's so much talk about — that's one of the ten?"

"That's right."

He saw the perplexed look on her face and he waited for her to ask him the question.

"Danny, exactly what is the Fifth Amendment?" Despite her gray hair and sixty odd years, she reminded him of a young, inquisitive, extremely naïve and unsophisticated girl in her late teens or early twenties, trying very hard to learn about the great big world she had become aware of for the first time in her life. "Why," she asked, furrowing her forehead with the intensity of her desire to know, "is there *so* much argument about the Fifth Amendment? Can you tell why?"

"Well" — they were driving slowly through the park now — "the Fifth Amendment, among other things, protects the right of a person to refuse to testify to anything which might tend to incriminate himself or herself. — There's a long history behind the Fifth Amendment. As I recall what I've read about it — back in the old days, especially during the period of the Inquisition, people were forced to testify against themselves. And with enough torture almost any person could be forced to confess his guilt even though he had actually done nothing wrong. — It was a device used to convict people when there would be absolutely no other way to prove them guilty of some wrongdoing — you compelled them to confess, and that was the proof that they were guilty of whatever they had been forced to confess they had done and you needed no other witnesses or no other proof. — Well, as nearly as I can recall it, some stubborn character in England decided this was all wrong and he refused to testify against himself and he was sentenced to prison; his refusal to testify was proof that he was guilty! Otherwise, why wouldn't he be willing to testify? — Well, his imprisonment caused such a reaction among the people of England at that time that Parliament had to free him and also pay him damages for the time he spent in jail. I forget this character's name but he apparently was a really obstreperous stubborn man of principle — a noncomformist who refused to knuckle under! He absolutely refused to back off and to submit to what he believed was wrong, even though he had to go to prison to prove his point. — I admire the guy."

"Well," said Irene, with a shake of her head, "he must have been somewhat like you —"

Danny laughed and looked at her to see if she meant that. Her face was very serious. She was holding Linda around the stomach, and her attention was directed at the road ahead. He decided she meant it.

"Well, it was a lot harder then," he said, trying to be modest. "But we've still got our battles about the Fifth Amendment— they're trying to wipe out its effectiveness with phony pledges of immunity which will force a man to testify against himself and to convict himself publicly or be subject to charges of perjury if his testimony clashes with that of some stoolpigeon. They say he'll be immune from being prosecuted for whatever guilt he admits. But if a man is compelled to say he's a communist or associated with communists, who gets his job back for him when he's fired and who protects him and his family from being isolated in the community? What kind of guarantee of immunity is that?"

"Terrible — "

"But back then in England they didn't even have the Fifth Amendment or its equivalent. And this stubborn character still had to establish that principle by his own sacrifice. And then it became an established part of English Law. And later it was embodied in our United States Constitution as part of the Bill of Rights — because the mass of the common people of our country demanded that it be included or they were ready to fight another revolution right here!"

Irene shook her head slowly from side to side, and he thought she was entranced with the great wonder of such tremendous historic developments.

"That's so wonderful, isn't it," she said, so naively that he had to smile along with her. "Isn't it so wonderful how some people have had so much courage in the past to be willing to sacrifice themselves in order to advance the cause of freedom for all the people? They had such heroes in those days. People must have been much less self-centered then, much less selfish. They must have thought a lot more about helping one another. They must have thought of other things besides making more and more money — they must have been so much better people than we have around here today in the world."

"There are plenty of those kind of people around today, Irene."

"I don't meet them — "

"Sure you do, they're all around you. The unimportant people you never notice. There are millions of great heroes around us in our own country, ordinary people who meet and surmount problems which would have floored kings, queens, presidents and generals — in their struggle to support their families and themselves against, at times, impossible odds."

"I never thought of it that way," said Irene.

There was a long silence. Irene, still holding Linda snug on her lap, was deeply engrossed in her thoughts. She turned to Danny.

"There's so much to learn, isn't there?" she said.

"There sure is."

"I never thought much about our Constitution until your situation made me especially interested. Then I *had* to think about it — to make up my mind about you. After all, you *are* my son-in-law, married to my daughter, and I do know you as a person and as the father of my wonderful grandchildren."

She brushed several golden curls back off Linda's forehead, and the little redhead pushed her hand away — Linda was busy watching where they were going as they came out of the park.

Irene shook her head up and down slowly and spoke to Danny again, with a strong emphasis which revealed how hard she was trying to think it through. "I should know more about the history of our country! — Isn't history a *fascinating* subject? — Oh, how I wish I were younger! Wouldn't it be *so* wonderful to be going to school to study history — after you've been out in the world long enough to be able to really get so much out of it? When it would really mean something to you?— But people think they're too old to go to school when they're my age. They're too embarrassed."

Danny stepped on the brake and slowed the car down for the turn into their street. "You're not too old to go to school now, Irene. No one's ever too old to go to school and to learn — "

"No, no, I'd feel silly. I'm too self-conscious about how little I know. I'd be scared to death to ever open my mouth. But I do wish I knew so much more about what's going on in the world. I think my whole life has been too sheltered. — Isn't it awful when you stop to think of it? I've lived most of my life already — I'll soon be an old woman — and I don't know anything about the world outside of my tiny little shell around The Park Lane. Isn't that really terrible?" And then she exclaimed with an intensity which doubled up her fists, "*People waste their lives! — they never realize how empty their lives are until it's too late to change! I wish I had spent my life out in the world where I could get to know all kinds of people! Dad protected me too much!*" He knew she meant her husband who had died.

"It's never too late, Irene. You're learning right now. Otherwise, you wouldn't be questioning so many things about your present mode of existence — "

"That's so," she agreed, nodding to emphasize the point. "That is so. And I want you to tell me more about what happened. I don't understand parts of what I read in the newspaper. That article in the newspaper said you didn't use the Fifth Amendment. Is that true?"

"That's true."

"But you didn't answer any of their questions, did you?"

"No."

"Then I'm completely confused. I don't understand." They were approaching the house, and Danny gave his full attention to his driving. He steered the car into the driveway and after he switched off the ignition he turned to Irene.

"I challenged the constitutionality of the enabling resolution passed by the House of Representatives," he hurriedly explained.

Linda slid out of the car and ran up the driveway to the side door of the house to ring the bell. Irene had started to follow her but she stopped with only one foot out of the car.

"What resolution is that?"

"The resolution establishing a committee to investigate so-called 'un-American' and 'subversive' activity, without defining what was meant by that. If the resolution is unconstitutional, then the Committee is unconstitutional — it has no right to exist, no right to question anybody about anything; it's null and void."

"Oh-h-h. Is that why you wouldn't answer any of their questions?"

"That's the only way to get the constitutionality of the resolution tested in the courts."

"I see."

While she was nodding her head up and down there was still a puzzled expression on her face which made him wonder if she really did understand.

They walked up the driveway, with Danny following Irene, and he heard her begin to tell Helen at the door about their interesting conversation.

Helen had already prepared a batch of martinis and she brought the glass pitcher from the refrigerator. They adjourned to the living room to relax for a few minutes before sitting down in the dining room to eat. Ruth made ginger ale cocktails for herself and Linda, and they joined the adults in the living room.

"Don't fill my glass too high, Helen," her mother protested. "You know me, I become giddy after one drink." But Danny noted that she did not protest too strongly when Helen refilled her glass later.

Danny sipped his own drink slowly while noticing that Helen had adopted her mother's mood and that for the first time since he had come home from the hearing in Albany there was a relaxed friendly atmosphere in their house again.

"Danny," suggested Irene, between sips, "why don't you start telling us exactly what happened there. I'd like to hear all about it."

"Let's wait until after we eat," Helen quickly suggested, and Danny knew she meant wait until after the children were out of the way.

She still thought he had done something to be ashamed of, to be kept from the children.

When they finished eating, Helen took Linda upstairs and gave her a bath while Danny worked with Irene and Ruth, clearing the table, washing the dishes, straightening up the dining room and kitchen.

"Danny!" Helen yelled down from upstairs. "Bring Linda her snack."

"What does she want?"

"Milk and cookies."

"One order of milk and cookies — coming right up!" Danny yelled out, happily, feeling that the house was returning to normal.

Finally, Linda was tucked away for the night and Ruth was doing her housework — at the last minute, as usual — up in the den, watching television while she drew a map for geography class. The adults adjourned to the living room with their coffee. Sitting in a big easy chair, Danny faced his wife and mother-in-law seated on the sofa. Irene settled back comfortably for a long interesting conversation.

"I want to know everything that happened. Tell the whole thing from beginning to end. I want to know all about it.

Smiling to himself at her fresh enthusiasm, Danny started

off by telling about his decision to refuse to answer any questions whatsoever and how hard it had been for him to arrive at that decision. And then he went over the list of reasons he had prepared with Ralph Kaufman to give to the Committee to explain his refusal to answer their questions, and then he told them the reasons he had been permitted to give in the courtroom before Congressman Holling dismissed him from the witness chair.

His mother-in-law asked about the other witnesses and how did he feel sitting in the courtroom and waiting his turn? — how did he feel when he was up there in the witness chair, being questioned? — was he afraid when he told them he was not going to answer their questions? — did they yell at him? — did he get stagestruck? — did he lose his temper? — did he speak loud enough to be heard by everyone in the courtroom when he told why he wouldn't answer their questions? — did the photographers take his picture? — did the reporters talk to him? — did the people in the courtroom ever applaud? — did they hiss or boo?

She was like a curious child who has been taken backstage to speak to the star of a Broadway play.

"It's fascinating to be able to talk to someone who has actually been called before one of these committees, someone I know so well — who I know will tell me the truth about how it was. I've often wondered what it's *really* like, to be questioned that way. Isn't it wonderful in a way that I can find out from my own son-in-law?"

Time passed quickly, and Helen kept making fresh coffee as they drank cup after cup along with their conversation. Ruth came downstairs and said good-night and went up to sleep. And they still talked.

Danny had never before felt so free to speak his mind with his mother-in-law. She had never before been so receptive, so tolerant. But he wondered how much of a change there would be in this attitude after Bob spoke to her. He'd know — when they held the family council session. Irene thought it an excellent idea to hold such a session. "So Robert and Millicent can hear exactly what happened and why." He couldn't help wondering what her reaction would be if he told her he had already spoken to Bob and Millie and how they felt about it.

"Danny" — Irene primly folded her hands in her lap — "I agree with everything you've done so far, but I think you must do one more thing — to really make your position clear to everyone — to show that you're really not guilty of anything."

"What's that?" But he already had a premonition as to what she was going to suggest.

"Now you should draw up some kind of statement" — she took a deep breath — "that *you are not a communist!* — Sign it and give it to the newspapers to print. Then everyone will know you didn't refuse to answer those questions because you had anything at all to hide about your own politics."

Danny could feel Helen's eyes boring through him. She was waiting to hear how he handled that one. He decided not to duck it. In the long run, if he was to establish any kind of comfortable relationship with his in-laws, he had to face this question and win at least a minimum of agreement on his right to his own ideas. Avoiding the issue now would make it harder to face later.

"Irene" — he slowly shook his head, as he fumbled for the right words. "First thing, for all you know — maybe I *am* a communist "

"I don't think you are!" Irene indignantly interjected, with a toss of her head. "No matter what the newspapers have ever said about you!"

"But, Irene, maybe I *am*," he quietly corrected. "At least, let's assume for the sake of argument that maybe I *am* a communist. Okay?"

Irene hesitated, extremely reluctant to make that assumption. "All right," she finally agreed, with stiff lips and a wary expression.

"The next question: Do I have a right to be a communist? Do I, Irene? Do I?" He waited, forcing her to reply.

"Well — "

She stopped herself after that first huff involuntarily escaped her.

"Do I have the right, Irene," he insisted, quietly, demanding a direct reply, "the right to think whatever I please?"

"Yes," she said, with a strong nod of her head, conceding that much.

"Then I do have the right to be a communist?"

"You don't have the right to overthrow the government!"

"What does that mean?"

"*Revolution!*"

"Our country came into existence through revolution — "

"That was a long time ago. Now we have elections. If you want a change, vote for a change. You can get a change in the government peacefully by electing people who will do what the majority want."

"You mean — if the majority of people want communism, they can vote for candidates who favor communism? Or that even a minority who want communism could vote for candidates who favor communism? That anyone who wants communism should have the right to vote for it?"

He stopped and waited for his mother-in-law's reply.

Irene hesitated.

Danny saw that Helen was also waiting to see what her mother would say.

Irene was thinking it over, a puzzled expression on her face. Then she nodded.

"Ye-e-s." She dragged it out. "Ye-e-s. Why not?"

"Then you're saying that a person can believe in communism and peacefully advocate that people should vote for communism, for candidates who are openly permitted to be known as members of the Communist Party?"

"You have the right to believe in anything," she firmly responded. "You have a right to your own beliefs. That's what our country is founded on. Freedom of belief!"

"Then why, Irene — just assuming that maybe I *am* a communist — should I have to give out a public signed statement that I'm *not* a communist?"

"Well," Irene tentatively ventured, after a moment's hesitation, "if you were a communist, it would be wrong to give out a statement that you are *not* one "

"Even though it would mean I might lose my job and not be able to get another job, and my family and myself would be subjected to all kinds of terrible difficulties — if I told the truth?"

"Well" — Irene was not sure of herself now — "you shouldn't have to lie. It shouldn't be that way."

"But right now, with rare exceptions, it *is* that way."

"People shouldn't have to lie."

"Okay. Now let's assume the other side of the coin. Assume I'm *not* a communist. Should I give out a statement to that effect?"

"You'd be telling the truth, wouldn't you?"

"But wouldn't giving out that kind of a statement imply that those who *are* communists and who can't or won't give out such a statement should be hounded, blacklisted, subjected to all kinds of indignities in the community. Otherwise, why must anyone give out a statement to protect himself?"

"Well — " She was stuck.

"If I give out a statement, protesting that I'm clean of any taint of communism or socialism, wouldn't I be helping to create the very hysteria which is then used to destroy not only the basic rights and freedoms of people who *are* communists, but also the basic rights and freedoms of all people, including the great majority who are *not* communists. Look around you. Isn't that what's happening in our country? Isn't it?"

"Well," Irene reluctantly conceded, "you have a strong argument there." He could see that she was trying to think it through and be fair, despite her deep antagonism against communists and communism. He pressed on, primarily for Helen's benefit. She was listening, not saying a word.

"What's *communism*, Irene? What's *communist*? It goes back to the same thing as: What's *subversive*? — What's *un-American*? No two people give exactly the same definition. Now I personally happen to believe that people should get the full value of their labor in return for the work they do, the labor power they sell — that none of the value of the full labor power expended, of the energy they take out of themselves and put into their work, should be taken away by others who don't perform that labor. Is it a crime to believe that? Should I be put into jail for having such thoughts? Or for expressing such thoughts — like I'm doing right now to you?"

Irene shrugged her shoulders. The answer seemed almost too obvious to bother putting into words.

"Why should you be put in jail for something like that? But I'll tell you right away that I disagree with you! What about the man who puts up the capital? You have to consider him! He provides the money to work with! He risks his capital! He's important!"

"Okay, Irene" — he grinned at her ardent defense of her class position — "your opinion is sharply different from mine. But let's not argue about that. The point is that you have a right to your opinion and I have a right to my opinion and we argue about it. But neither of us should be persecuted for our opinions, should we?"

"Of course not!"

"Then, Irene, it's not a crime, is it — to believe in communism and to argue for your belief?"

Irene hesitated a long while, shaking her head, trying to get away from the necessity to answer the question. But she finally nodded.

"No-o-o, it's no crime. That's why we have a democracy. People can think what they please. That's what makes our country so great."

"Then — is it right to put people into prison because they *are* members of the Communist Party? Because they advocate communism?"

"No, that's wrong! We shouldn't permit that! Not in *our* country!"

"They should be allowed to work, earn a living, even if they are communists, shouldn't they?"

"Yes."

He looked over at Helen to see what she thought of her mother's answers, but she wouldn't give him the satisfaction of letting him see her facial expression. She bent her head way down over her cup and stirred the cold remains of her coffee with a spoon.

He was in bed when he heard Helen come up the stairs. She walked into the bedroom, without switching on the light, and she quietly undressed. In the semi-darkness he watched her slip out of her clothes and into a nightgown.

She went into the bathroom.

He heard her coming back into the bedroom and he watched her open the window. Then she slipped under the covers on her side of the bed, nearest the window, keeping far away from him.

He stirred his body around to let her know he was awake.

"Are you up?" she asked, though the question was superfluous.

"Yes," he replied, and he hunched his head up off the pillow as if to see what she wanted.

"Mother was a real surprise, wasn't she?"

"Yes," and he stopped right there; it was better to say too little than too much.

"But wait until Bob goes to work on her — she'll change her viewpoint to whatever his is."

"Maybe," he said, "and maybe not."

Helen didn't say anything else. She slid down under the covers, way over on the farthest possible edge of her side of the bed.

There was a moment of complete silence.

"Good-night."

He thought her voice sounded friendly but still there was enough coolness in it to let him knew she was keeping a gap between them.

"Good-night, kid."

Poor Helen, he thought. It was tough for anyone to live with a union organizer, and it was especially tough for someone with her background. She was caught in the middle. He lay there for a long time, thinking about some of the difficult problems of adjustment she was having. Then he heard her smooth breathing. Thinking she was asleep, he carefully reached over under the covers and gently patted her behind. Without a word she took his hand and pushed it away.

Chapter 43

Monday morning —

Danny found Fred Woeppel in his local union office up on the second floor of the two-story unpainted clapboard Labor Hall in North Tonawanda. Through the wide window Danny saw the double set of railroad tracks on top of the built-up grade which raised the tracks over the paved street passing in front of the hall. Through the front window he could see one of the plants of Remington Rand Corporation, a four-story concrete and glass structure, over across the street — he could hear the constant pounding of the presses which, he knew, were located on the third floor over there.

Fred Woeppel was hunched forward over a typewriter, pecking at the keys with one finger.

"Hi, Fred."

Fred looked up.

Danny knew he was at least eight or ten years older than Fred Woeppel, but Fred's bulging stomach made him look like he was the older one. "A sign of prosperity," Fred termed his big belly whenever Danny kidded him about his weight. "We've got a good union — and we get good wages for our members. This stomach is an advertisement for the union — it pays to belong to our union." Fred Woeppel was a good union man, an idealist who did not get paid for his position as chairman of the strategy committee of all their local unions in that end of the state or for his post as president of his own local union; he worked in the shop like any other worker in their union, getting paid by the union only for his time lost from work when union business necessitated that he be out of the shop.

"How's the jailbird?" asked Fred, with a big grin, swiveling his chair to face the union organizer.

"Don't rush things," said Danny.

"I'm starting on our weekly shop paper," explained Fred, with a gesture toward the typewriter.

"Working second shift this week?" asked Danny, referring

to the clean street clothes Fred was wearing — white shirt, tie, pressed trousers and shined brown shoes.

"Third shift. I go in tonight."

Danny straddled a folding chair, sitting on the seat with the back part of the chair pressed against his stomach and chest — "Fred, what's the talk around town?"

"About what?"

"Me."

"What do you mean?"

"What's the reaction? Favorable or unfavorable?"

"Oh. I'd say it's good, at least from what I've heard in my shop and wherever I been around town."

"Fred, don't make it sound any better than it really is."

"I'm not. I didn't hear any bad talk anywhere about you."

"Don't spare my feelings. I want to know the worst so we can plan intelligently how to handle it."

"I told you — "

"There must be some unfavorable reaction. Everybody around this town doesn't love Danny Newman. Didn't *anyone* ask why I refused to answer the Committee's questions? Wasn't there *any* sniping?"

"If there was, Danny" — Fred held his right hand on his heart to vouch for his sincerity — "*I* didn't hear it. Maybe, knowing how I feel, they wouldn't talk in front of me, but I went all around the shop on Saturday — there were a lot of us working overtime — and I talked to all the stewards — I thought there might be some trouble and I was looking to see if there were any fires I had to put out." He picked up his pencil from the desk and pointed it at Danny. "What you don't understand, Danny" — and Fred smugly smirked — "is that the people never expected you to answer the Committee's questions. They expected something different. Something spectacular. That's the kind of reputation you got around here. The people actually expected you to tell the Committee off." He laughed in a friendly way. "They would have been disappointed if you'd done anything different. More than disappointed. *Disillusioned* ."

"That's horseshit, Fred."

"No, it ain't. You don't realize the kind of reputation you got. I'm telling you — when the word first came back to the shop late Friday afternoon that you refused to even tell the

Committee when you were born, some of the good guys in the shop went wild — they ran all over the shop, laughing like hell, yelling that Danny wouldn't even tell those unamerican bastards whether or not he was born!"

Danny heard the door downstairs at the foot of the steps on the first floor slam shut, and Fred called out, "Who's there?"

"Me!" a voice called back.

"What stupid bastard is *me*?" Fred shouted back, laughing, since both he and Danny recognized that the voice belonged to Art Manchester, the North Tonawanda field organizer who, together with Danny, covered that end of the state.

"Three guesses," said Art quietly as he approached the open door of the local union office, and then a bespectacled graying head peered around the edge of the doorway into the room. "Is this where the conspiracy against the government is going on?"

"This is the place," said Fred. "Have you brought your bomb along?"

"It's right here in my back pocket," said Art.

"Good," said Danny, "then you can come in. The admission fee is either a bomb or two straight pins or one safety pin and five shirt buttons."

"It's a good thing I got my bomb," said Art. "My wife sneaked all my pins and buttons out of my pocket this morning. She's always keeping me broke." He walked in, taking a pack of cigarettes out of his pocket and offering it around. Fred and Danny refused. Art lit his own. "What are us reds conspiring about today?"

Getting serious, Fred explained what Danny was concerned about. "I told him there's nothing to worry about here. You agree, don't you?"

Art pulled a folding chair over to the desk and straddled it the same way Danny straddled his chair. "You did just what the people out here expected you to do — "

"That's what I told him," said Fred.

"You took the offensive," Art continued. "You told the Committee to go to hell. That's what the people out here expected from you."

Danny stopped biting the fingernail on the thumb of his

left hand. "Do you think they'll still support me — if the House of Representatives votes to cite me for contempt — if I'm still indicted and it goes to trial?"

"Why not?"

Danny shrugged. "Just wondering."

"I'd put it this way, Danny." Art cocked his graying head to one side, thinking it out as he went along. "Back in 1948 — when you took a similar position, refusing to answer questions about your political opinions and it was blown up in the local newspapers — there were a lot of fights in the bars around this town. But those fights were a defensive thing — they started *after* other people tried to run you down."

He hunched his chair closer to Danny. "Now, in 1954, it's different. Our people are taking the offensive. I heard them, Danny, Friday night — our guys boasting in the bars — they're proud how their union representative took on the Committee and told them to go to hell. Nobody's disagreeing! At least not out loud! — That's the great difference between now and back in 1948 — "

Fred said, "You don't have to worry this time, Danny. You got plenty of support. The people were waiting for someone to do what you did."

"Thanks." Danny grinned his appreciation but at the same time felt embarrassed — it sounded like he was asking them to praise him for what he had done. But what they said did give him a good feeling inside. He wished it could mean as much to Helen. She needed that kind of boost to her morale more than he did.

He mentioned his problem, in an offhand self-conscious way, so they would be aware of it and be ready for any future developments in his marriage relationship — *if* they occurred.

"Helen's worried as hell."

"It's rough on the wife," said Fred.

"She's afraid I'll be smeared again and the heat will go on, like it did before."

"I don't think," said Art, "it's going to be that way this time."

"Neither do I, but something has to happen to prove it to Helen."

"Like what?"

"Well, if we can get some kind of demonstration of support—"

"What do you want?" asked Art. "A resolution pledging support? We can get it. Easy."

"Well, it would help if you fellas could get our local unions out here in North Tonawanda to go on record, voting to support the position I took before the Committee — maybe pass motions condemning the Committee and asking that it be abolished."

Fred said he would write up an article immediately for his shop paper and Art said he would talk to the other local union presidents in North Tonawanda about carrying similar items in their shop papers.

"You can show the shop papers to your wife," Fred suggested. 'That might help. She'd see that you got support in the union anyway. And we'll bring it up at the next membership meetings and get formal resolutions passed."

Danny felt the need to apologize for injecting his personal problem into the union situation. But Fred cut him off in the middle of his apology.

"It's not a personal problem, Danny. What you did was for the good of the membership, not yourself."

"Oh, it was for my own good too — "

Fred went right on. "It was for the good of our union and all organized labor and the whole country. So the least we can do is back you up. Especially when you're the one who's risking jail, not us."

"He's not going to jail," said Art, shaking his graying head, and he pointed his finger at Fred. "I'll bet you they won't even indict him! There's too much rank-and-file support in the shops. I wouldn't be surprised if we had a few walkouts in our shops if they indict him."

"Oh, I doubt that." Danny shook his head, skeptically.

"Oh, yes!"

"You're underestimating the fear when that kind of story is spread across the front page of a newspaper."

"No, I'm not. I know what it was like the last time. But you don't know the feeling out here now."

"Oh, I think I do."

"No, you don't! I know a lot of people who would

spontaneously take a walk out of the shop if they tried anything on you, and others would walk with them."

"They didn't walk when I was subpoenaed!"

"But now it's different. After you challenged the Committee head-on."

"Well, I wouldn't count on it," said Danny, still skeptical.

"You're a hot potato," insisted Art. "They're not going to take any chances on arousing the people in the shops in this area to take any kind of strong action. That kind of demonstration would hurt their program more than putting you in jail would help it."

"Well, maybe," said Danny. "Maybe." But he was still not convinced.

"The more publicity we can give to the case," said Fred, "the less chance there is that they'll prosecute you."

During the next hour the three of them mapped out a program of resolutions, leaflets, shop papers and news releases. They drew up a tentative schedule of speaking dates for him during the next two weeks — when he would talk to executive boards, steward councils and local union membership meetings.

It was after eleven o'clock when they broke up their planning session so Danny could start back to Buffalo.

"Stan Helowicz has an article in his shop paper this morning," he explained to the others, "and I want to see him at noon and find out how it went over."

They went with him to the stairway.

"Don't worry, Danny." Fred patted him on the shoulder.

"You've picked up strength," said Art. "Your position out here is stronger than it's ever been."

As he walked down the short flight of steps outside the Labor Hall, Danny remembered how there had been a lynch spirit whipped up against him out here — so bad he had moved all his things from the North Tonawanda office to the Buffalo office. That had not been very long ago. He got out of the army in 1946 after the end of World War II, and two years after that it happened — in 1948 when he publicly refused to answer whether or not he was a communist and the Buffalo and Tonawanda newspapers blasted him on the front pages. He wondered if it could happen again.

Chapter 44

"Going to be long, Red?" the uniformed plant guard at the Bufalo Foundry and Machine Division of Blaw Knox asked Danny when the union organizer parked his car in one of the spaces reserved for front office personnel. "Only a few minutes, I'll be right out of there."

The guard had come out of the one-room brick building, the guardhouse, which stood between the street and the group of old brick buildings which covered an area equal to several good-sized city blocks. He held the guardhouse door open for Danny who looked inside and saw husky Al Carmer and Stan Helowicz sitting in there, eating their lunches out of their black sheet metal buckets.

"I want to talk to those jerks for a while," said Danny, loud enough so Al and Stan could hear.

"Okay, Red."

Danny saw that the guard stayed outside when he shut the door, and he assumed that the guard did not want to overhear the conversation between himself and Stan and Al who were the chairman and vice-chairman of the shop grievance committee. Through the windowed upper half of the door he saw that the uniformed guard was also unofficially keeping watch so they would not be interrupted without warning.

"How's it going?" Danny asked, and he pulled up a chair and sat down near the two other men.

"How's *what* going?" growled Al, pretending to be tough, while he chewed on a bite of sandwich.

Danny looked at Al's grease stained face and he knew that Al was playing a game with him. "Why," he asked Al, keeping a straight face himself, "don't you ever wash your face?"

Al stared back, not blinking, completely deadpan. "Why should I — it'll only get dirty again." He bit off another big chunk of his sandwich and washed it down with a gulp of coffee from his thermos bottle.

"What are you waiting for — Saturday night?"

"What's Saturday night?"

"Bath night — "

"Who said so?"

"That's what it was — when I was a kid."

"You're not a kid anymore."

Danny looked over at Stan Helowicz, slim, hollow cheeked, all color drained out of his face, a few streaks of dirt on his forehead, dressed in faded blue shirt and old work trousers — he knew Stan worked in the same department as Al Carmer, the machine shop, the union's strongest spot in the plant.

"A comedian," he said, jerking his thumb in Al Carmer's direction. Stan Helowicz changed the subject.

"You don't have prison pallor yet," he said, making believe he was examining Danny's face closely for signs of effects of prison — at the same time shoving the last bite of sandwich into his mouth, swelling out his sunken cheeks."

"Wait until they put me in prison," said Danny — "for the present you're slightly premature."

"Nobody's going to put you in prison," growled Al Carmer.

"Don't say that too loud," said Danny. "They might hear you and decide to prove you're all wet."

"Don't worry about it — "

"I'm not worrying — "

"Oh no?" Al laughed, a friendly chuckle.

"Go screw."

Danny turned to Stan.

"What's it like in there?"

He motioned his head towards the group of sprawling brick buildings which housed the foundry, machine shop, fabricating division, power house and all the rest of the operations of the Buffalo Foundry and Machine Division.

"A few of the Shouters tried to whip it up this morning, but they couldn't get much started."

"Who was it?"

"The same handful." — Stan pawed through the crumpled wax paper in his lunch pail and found an orange and began to peel it, tossing the peeling back into his pail. — "They didn't get anywhere."

"Stop worrying," said Al — "they can't attack you in this shop. By now, after ten years or more of working with these guys, everybody in this shop knows where you stand on politics. If they don't, they're too dumb for you to have to worry about them. — Some of the guys may disagree with you, but most of the people in the shop don't care — your politics is your own damn business — all they're interested in is that extra dime you're going to get them in the next negotiations. They know you're a good negotiator and they got the best wages and best contract of any plant like it in the area. They don't care about what you do outside on your own. As long as you keep on doing a good job in this shop you don't have to worry about these people. And when you stop doing a good job I'll be the first one to boot you in the ass."

"Thanks."

"You're welcome."

"Who's going to boot *your* ass?"

"That's for you to do."

Danny knew that much of what Al Carmer was saying was intended to bolster Stan. He knew that Al thought Stan was still very susceptible on the redbaiting issue — and while Danny went along with Al, both seeming to be doing a lot of kidding back and forth with one another, he knew that Al was just as serious as he was, underneath the light banter they were tossing back and forth. He sounded out Stan. "Does it look solid to you, Stan?"

"I don't know. Some of the guys are worried about this red issue — they're getting cards signed for another union."

"They're *trying*," said Al, "they're *trying* to get cards signed and they're using this red issue for propaganda. They don't give a damn about it one way or the other themselves. They're being pressured, at least some of them are — and the others are just company sucks who think they'll get ahead with the company this way — they got their eye on a foreman's job."

"But they're getting some cards signed," insisted Stan, "to make a switch in unions."

"Not enough to take the shop."

"No, but they're getting some."

Danny listened to the two men bickering back and forth, with Al Carmer decrying the efforts of those who were attacking the union from within, and with Stan Helowicz insisting that the Shouters were making some inroads and something had to be done to counteract their propaganda.

"Danny" — Stan poured some hot coffee from his thermos bottle into the metal cap he had unscrewed from the top of the container — "Danny, I think you ought to write a letter to the newspapers, explaining why you refused to answer the Committee's questions. I think it would help a lot more than anything we print in our shop paper or in leaflets we give out from the union."

Danny looked at Al for his opinion.

"Why send a letter to the newspaper?" Al wanted to know. "They'll never print it — so why give them the satisfaction of thinking you're panicky? You only encourage them to step up their attack on you. They'll only stir it up more if they think you're being hurt by what's happening from what they printed already."

"That's possible," said Danny, trying to sound neutral, to encourage the two local union officers to argue it out between themselves. Personally, he favored writing a letter, hoping at least some of it would be printed and get through to the people of the community; but he preferred to have Stan and Al arrive at that decision without his interference.

"And even if they do print it," Al continued, "they'll twist it up and leave out the important parts the way they always do when they're trying to hang you," and he closed his lunch bucket; he was through eating.

"Why don't you send a letter," suggested Stan, "and then mimeograph copies of it. We can distribute them to all our union members in the area — and then we know our own people have the full letter without any distortions. — You can print a note on the bottom of the leaflet, telling the people to watch the newspapers to see if they print the letter exactly as it is."

"That's an idea." Danny looked over at Al. "You go for that?"

"Well" — Al didn't want to commit himself too definitely — "it can't hurt too much doing it that way," he grudgingly admitted.

"Okay, then I'll send a letter to the newspapers." Danny took paper and pencil out of his pocket and made a note to remind himself to write the letter. "I don't think we'll get anything printed in the News but we might get somewhere with the Courier."

"Try them both," suggested Stan.

"Why not?" Danny readily agreed.

"Send them both the same letter and then let's see what each prints. In that note on the leaflet say that you sent the letter to both newspapers."

"I will." Danny put away the paper and pencil. "You know, my father-in-law knew one of the editorial writers on the Courier. Could we lose anything if I went up to see him?"

All three of them thought it over for a moment.

"I don't see how," said Stan.

"The worst he can do," growled Al, "is have you tossed out on your ass and that wouldn't bother you, would it?"

Danny kept a straight face. "No, I get tossed out on my ass every day — out of the best places — it's part of the job description for a union organizer."

Al Carmer broke out into a hearty laugh. "You shit too," he growled between chuckles which shook his shoulders.

"Oh, yes, that too," said Danny, with mock seriousness. "*Anything* for the union."

Al stood up and playfully swung his lunch bucket at Danny's head. "Let a poor hard-working stiff get back to work."

Danny ducked. "You lazy bastard, you don't know what the hell the word *work* means."

"Listen to this guy," laughed Al, calling upon Stan to join with him against the organizer.

Stan closed his lunch bucket. "Organizers don't work," he said, getting up and following Al Carmer who was walking out through the door of the guardhouse into the plant yard. "All organizers do is talk. Anybody can learn to throw that clever line of bullshit."

Laughing along with them, Danny stopped in the driveway, allowing the guard to slip past him back into the guardhouse. "I'll go see this editorial writer as soon as I can," he called after the two local union officers who were continuing on their way to the machine shop in one of the brick buildings which extended the length of a short city block. "Let me know what happens," Stan Helowicz called back over his shoulder. "Call me up."

"If I were you," Al Carmer yelled back, "I wouldn't lose any sleep over this shop. You don't have to worry about us — go somewhere else where you got real troubles."

"Okay, fellas," he called after them, and he started toward his car. The guard waved goodbye to him through the window.

As he prepared to drive away, he wondered about Helen. What would she say if he told her he was going to see editorial writer Ted Allen who had been a friend of her father? Would she resent him using her father's name? "Probably," he told himself, "probably, because her father also disagreed with me." If her father were still alive would he line up with Bob against him? That would be a difficult combination to buck. He drove slowly down the driveway toward the street. Several workmen in dirty coveralls, their faces black with grease, waved to him as he passed. He waved back. Maybe it would be better to forget the editorial writer. He could send a letter to the editor for the People's Forum on the editorial page. Even though they might express a viewpoint contrary to the editorial policy of the newspaper, such letters were often printed. A workman running to get back into the shop before the whistle blew at the end of the lunch period yelled at Danny as he turned left into the street. He looked around and recognized the workman as one of the union stewards. Danny rolled down the car window and yelled. "Run, you sonofabitch, you're late!"

"Don't you think I know it?" the steward screamed back, waving his hand wildly over his head as he continued to run on into the plant yard.

Chapter 45

His next stop was to see Ben Russell who worked at the big Westinghouse plant. Although the local union there had been the biggest one in the area to secede from his union because of the red issue back in 1950, Danny had been working for several years with some of the leaders of the seceded local union, trying to cement the split. He issued a shop paper weekly at the plant gates, explaining why the two unions should unite their forces on day-to-day issues and eventually join into one union again.

The local newspapers reported that there had been a battle inside Ben Russell's local union over the weekend on the issue of whether or not a grievance should be filed to ask for reinstatement of workers fired by the company for using the Fifth Amendment to refuse to answer questions of Congressional committees. The forces upholding the right to use the Fifth Amendment had won out for the second time at a stormy special meeting of the local union.

Danny knocked on the side door to Ben Russell's house. The door was at the end of a long narrow alley between two frame houses. From where he stood on top of the stoop Danny could see the rear brick wall of a machine shop which butted almost smack up against the back of Ben's house.

He heard Ben's voice yelling that he would be right out — it came from underneath the house. And a moment later he saw Ben slide out from under the house, flat on his back, his well-muscled body covered with dirty overalls, a grimy locomotive engineer's peaked cap on his head and a heavy wrench in his right hand.

"Hi, Danny." Ben smiled a welcome.

Danny grinned back. "Still at it?" He gave Ben his hand and helped him to his feet. Ben brushed the dirt off the hind end of his blue overalls. "There's always something to fix in these brokendown old houses." He shoved the wrench into a back pocket. It fell out and he picked it up and leaned it against the bottom step. "Let's go inside."

"I'll only take a few minutes, Ben," Danny apologized for

interrupting the man in the middle of his work.

The door which led into the kitchen was painted a bright fire engine red, the rest of the house a drab gray. Danny knew Ben had done the painting himself, as he did all other maintenance and repair work around the house.

Following Ben into the kitchen, Danny explained the reason for his visit. "I'd like to get a little more dope, Ben, on what happened at that special meeting your local held Saturday."

Ben grinned. "I thought you'd be around after you read the story in the newspapers."

Ben's youngest boy, not yet old enough to attend kindergarten, ran to Ben and hugged his thigh while Ben hobbled over to the kitchen sink ignoring that extra lump of live weight hanging on to him. He washed his hands, wiped them across the front of his overalls, and then fondly patted the shy youngster on the top of his closely cropped little head to let the boy know he had nothing to fear from the visitor.

"Want to go inside? Or stay here in the kitchen?"

"Whatever you want."

The breakfast dishes were still on the table. Ben explained that it was his job to wash the dishes since his wife had to rush off in the morning to teach school while he didn't go to work until the second shift in the afternoon. "Let's go into the living room."

The youngster followed them, stepping on Danny's heels in his anxiety to stay close to his father. Ben sat down on a worn bench in front of an old upright piano. Danny sat on the edge of the overstuffed red mohair sofa, across from Ben. The young boy climbed up beside his father, sitting on the piano bench, leaning his head against his father's chest, keeping his bright curious eyes fixed intently on Danny. Ben fondled the boy's neck with his right hand while he talked.

Danny reached into his pocket for paper and pencil and as Ben talked he took notes. Ben told him what had happened before the membership meeting finally voted to back up any of their members who used the Fifth Amendment to refuse to answer questions before the Committee on Un-American Activities or any similar committee.

"To my way of thinking," said Ben, "the most important development there was the split in the heretofore solid ranks of the ACTU bloc."

Danny knew that the Association of Catholic Trade Unions — ACTU — in Buffalo consisted of Catholic cells established in some of the shops and trade unions, coordinated on a city-wide basis within the St. Joseph's Guild under the direction of the "labor priest" associated with the Buffalo Diocesan Labor College. The priest had come to see Stan Helowicz and asked Stan to establish a Catholic cell within his shop to guide the policy of his local union, but Stan refused and told the priest that he opposed organizing blocks within the union along religious lines because it would split the union and make it easy prey for the company to put across its speedup and wage cutting program; Stan told Danny the whole story, and Danny told him he believed it was up to the Catholic workers in the union to see to it that no Catholic organization tried to take over and dominate any labor union — just like it was up to workers of other religious faiths to see to it that their church hierarchies did not try to take over and dominate and use the labor movement to further their particular program. Stan said he agreed with him one hundred per cent.

"Danny, no one else took the floor on this issue except the ACTU guys themselves — they fought it out between themselves. I thought it was best if I kept my mouth shut as long as these fellows were carrying the ball themselves."

"I agree."

"The president of the local was pushing the resolution," Ben continued, as Danny scribbled away, taking notes, knowing this development was important if he was to evaluate correctly the community situation and the possibilities for developing a more liberal atmosphere in the area.

"Some of the president's strongest supporters in the past — some of his personal buddies, Danny — all part of the same group — some of the worst redbaiters in the local, Danny, hit the floor again and again, insisting that the basic freedoms guaranteed by the Bill of Rights of our Constitution must be preserved for everyone or they would be lost for everyone! — They all knew in advance that the purpose of this special meeting was to decide whether or not to support anyone who the company fired for using the Fifth Amendment to refuse to cooperate with a Congressional committee; from the speeches on the floor it was obvious that the poeple had been doing a lot of deep thinking and a lot of reading on the subject before they came to this meeting. These guys brought in all kinds of clippings to back up their arguments. One of them had a complete copy of the Constitution with him and he read off the whole first ten amendments, speaking from the floor. — "I tell you, Danny, it was a real education to be at that meeting and to hear that hot debate raging back and forth — a real education for me and for everybody there — "

"I wish I could have been there."

"You, Danny, you especially would have loved it — it would have made you proud of working people. I don't have the words in my limited vocabulary to describe how dramatic it was — more exciting than any movie or television show I ever seen. Maybe because I was right in the middle of it and I was part of it."

"Probably."

"You should have heard our local president, Danny! He wrapped himself in the flag. He appealed to patriotism and love of country. Religion and love of God. He asked them to vote to bar union support to anybody who did not answer all questions the Committee asked — that this was the only way they can back up George Washington and Jesus Christ! — I'm telling you, Danny, I never heard anything like it before in my whole life! Never!   He must have been coached in advance! Well, he definitely was coached; he said so himself — that several clergymen of his faith had come to him and urged him to bring up this resolution; that some government agents — everybody figured he meant FBI — had told him this resolution must be passed by the local union to preserve our country against the *boring-from-within-subversive-efforts-of-communist-rats!* He screamed at us. And then he begged and pleaded with us. And then he prayed that the membership would support their God by voting for the resolution. He shouted and he even cried, actually broke out in tears and mopped his face with his handerchief. — Then he finished by threatening to resign from office if the membership wouldn't pass the resolution. He said he could no longer continue to serve as president of any organization which would refuse to support our God and our Country — "

Ben stopped for breath.

Danny shook his head. "Sounds like an overpowering appeal."

"It was! It was, Danny! I thought this is the end. But these other ACTU guys got up on the floor and took the president on. They shouted back at him. Some were veterans of World War II. One was a World War I veteran. I was so surprised I couldn't believe it was happening. Really thrilling to watch and to listen. I'll never forget it as long as I live. What a meeting!"

Danny couldn't help smiling at Ben's enthusiasm.

"The people who hit the floor, Danny, to argue with the president — they were the same poeple who usually back him up — that's what was so amazing! I tell you, Danny, there's a new kind of spirit there — a realization is taking place among working people — they see what all this redbaiting is leading to — and they're not going along with it. It's so damn heartening, Danny — heartening as all hell to us guys who've been fighting a defensive battle for so long. — I tell you, Danny, I got renewed respect for the working people in our country — they weren't fooled, they knew what was behind all the propaganda, and when it really counted most, *the people in our shop and in our local union stood up!* "

"Good," said Danny, "good, good." But he couldn't help wondering about the German working class. "Why didn't they stand up when the chips were down — when Hitler moved into power? Could it happen here? Or do we have a more fundamental democratic tradition? Or did we learn from what happened in Germany?

Ben went on with what happened at the meeting. "One of our organizers brought in your name, Danny. I thought he'd attack you, you being UE and he being IUE, against UE. Believe it or not, he defended you. He said if you wanted to use the Fifth Amendment or to refuse to answer any of the questions to the Committee — you had a right to do that — "

"He defended me?"

"Yes."

"I can't believe it, Ben."

"He did. I was surprised myself, even though I was right there."

Danny lifted his eyes to the ceiling. "Ducky-wucky, the sky is falling."

Ben's boy got a real kick out of that. "Ducky-wucky, the sky is falling." He couldn't stop giggling, and he buried his face against his father's chest. The two men laughed warmly at the little boy's reaction, and Ben hugged the youngster to him.

While Ben went on, reporting in further detail the specific arguments presented at the union meeting, Danny found himself thinking about Helen and how good it would be for her morale if she could know someone like Ben Russell — she would lose that feeling of being alone against the world. He mentally charged himself with the responsibility to help Helen lose her fear of working people.

He became aware that Ben was silent, waiting for him to come out of his reverie.

"My mind was wandering," he apologized. "I started to think about something else."

Ben laughed good-naturedly.

Danny wondered if he could talk to Ben about his problem with Helen. But he felt too embarrassed to raise the subject just nakedly like that, and he put it off to some time when the opportunity would present itself for him to speak about it more naturally. He got up from the kitchen table.

"I better run along, Ben. You got to get ready for your second shift." Ben followed him to the door, and the boy still clung to his father's leg, all the way across the kitchen floor.

"I didn't tell you," said Ben, holding onto Danny's hand when they said goodbye, "what I thought of the way you handled youself before that committee. It was an inspiration to the rest of us who were waiting to see what you would do."

Danny shrugged it off. "I was scared stiff, Ben."

"I don't believe that."

"I *was*," Danny insisted. But he could see that Ben still didn't believe him. Ben thought he was trying to act modest.

As he walked out through the narrow alley back to the street in front of the house, Danny wondered if Ben still would respect him if Ben knew how much he wavered and how he actually wept before he finally made up his mind to refuse to answer any of the Committee's questions.

What would he think of his shining golden hero?

Chapter 46

Tuesday—

The next morning Danny drove down to the smaller Westinghouse plant in Attica, a foundry which supplied parts to the big plant where Ben Russell worked. He timed the trip to arrive just when employees were starting their lunch hour. As he parked the car across the railroad tracks from the plant he saw Milt Reynolds, the chief steward of the local union, come out of the red brick building and start toward him. The bareheaded man in soiled gray coveralls moved with a peculiar slow gait, and Danny wondered if Milt had acquired that way of walking as a result of the years of farming he had done before he had gone to work in the foundry. As Milt came nearer, Danny could see his weatherbeaten face — Milt still farmed a few acres — and he was crinkling the skin around his eyes behind the gold-rimmed glasses he wore, smiling a welcome.

Milt stretched out his hand.

"Welcome to Attica."

"Thanks."

The two men liked each other. Each respected the other's dedication to a cause. With Danny, it was the cause of the working people. With Milt Reynolds, it was Jesus Christ, the Saviour of Men. — Milt lived his religion, choosing to be chief steward in the local union to help his fellow men in a practical way to improve their wages and working conditions, merely another way of practicing what Jesus Christ preached.

Danny had telephoned the night before to ask Milt if a noon hour meeting could be arranged so he could personally tell the people there why he had refused to answer the Committee's questions.

Milt expressed surprise that Danny had not used the Fifth Amendment. "But I knew," he drawled over the phone in his slow way of speaking, "there was some good reason for what you did. You're not the kind who loses his head in a tight

384

spot."

"Oh, I got plenty scared up there, Milt."

"Of course, you did. That's why they do what they're doing, isn't it? To scare people?"

"Sure — "

"Isn't that their only purpose? To scare everyone into silence? Into conformity? — Dictatorship! Isn't that what they want? And they'll try to crucify anyone who dares to stand up against them — like Jesus Christ was crucified! You and me know, Danny, that if Jesus Christ came down to preach out in the streets today — they'd arrest Him! Wouldn't they?"

"I guess so, Milt."

"They'd call Him a subversive and a traitor! Wouldn't they?"

"I suppose so — "

"They'd denounce Him before some Congressional committee as a spy and an agitator and a rabble-rouser! Wouldn't they? — Wouldn't they?"

Milt insisted on an answer, and Danny said, "I guess they would, Milt."

"Sure they would," Milt echoed. Then he abruptly switched the subject back to the reason for Danny's phone call. "I'll pass the word on to the department stewards in the morning. They'll get the people out to the usual meeting place across the tracks. We can start some time about half-way through the noon lunch hour period."

"Thanks, Milt, I'll be there a little early — "

"How's the family?"

"The family?" Danny was glad Helen had gone over to see her mother, so that she didn't hear him discussing her. "Oh, the family's fine, Milt, fine, thanks."

"How Mrs. Newman?" Milt asked, and Danny smiled at the way Milt always spoke so formally whenever he referred to Helen.

"Oh, she's fine, Milt, fine."

"Is she all right?" Milt insisted.

"Well — yes, she's all right, Milt. It's hard on her but — " He stopped, not knowing how to complete the sentence.

"It's usually harder on a woman," Milt said, "because she isn't as directly involved as the man. Danny, you're too busy fighting these things to have much chance to dwell on them in your own mind like your wife does. She probably has too much time to think about her predicament — without much opportunity to do anything about it except to try to influence you. Of course, that makes it hard on you too, doesn't it?"

"Kind of — "

"If it'll help you any, you can tell Mrs. Newman that my wife and me and our whole family prayed for her. Well," he added hastily, sounding embarrassed, "actually, we prayed for *all* of you, for your whole family — but especially for your wife and most especially for the children. It's the children who are most affected by these things and who can do the least about it, and they're still too young to understand why these things are happening — that's why we prayed most for the children."

"Thanks, Milt, thanks — "

"I don't know how much you believe in prayer, Danny. But we hope you don't mind because we prayed with a Christian prayer — I know you and your family are of a different religious faith — and we hoped we weren't doing anything contrary to your faith — and that you wouldn't be offended — "

"Oh, no, Milt! Just the opposite — I'm just embarrassed because 1 don't know how to properly thank you — "

"Oh, there's no need to thank us."

"1 really appreciate it. And I'm sure Helen will appreciate it too when I tell her about it."

And then Milt apologized — "I suppose, as good Christians we should have prayed for everyone who is called before the Committee, for all the rest of the organizers and the others who were questioned there, but we know only you personally and we were concerned about you — about you and your family."

Danny didn't know what else to say — except to repeat that he appreciated what Milt Reynolds and his family had done. His inadequacy seemed to give the wrong impression to Milt Reynolds who apparently mistook Danny's hesitancy and inability to find words to express his thanks properly — mistook that for disapproval by Danny of the use of prayer.

"You don't believe too much in prayer, I guess," Milt ventured.

"Oh, Milt, I'm not opposed to prayer — "

"Well" — and Milt laughed in a friendly way — "not exactly opposed, but I know you don't think prayer accomplishes too much."

"That isn't exactly it either, Milt." Danny laughed along with the chief steward. "But my father always says: 'God helps those who help themselves!'"

And Milt chuckled loud enough for Danny to hear him and to imagine how that red face of the farmer was all crinkled up, enjoying what the religious Jewish father had said.

"Well," Milt drawled, "I suppose there's a lot of truth in what your father says. Yes, I would say there is a lot of truth in what he says."

When he told Helen about Milt and his family praying, Helen was very moved by the thought that someone had been thinking that much about her and her problems. She said that Milt Reynolds was a very exceptional person, that most people were selfish and thought only of themselves. Danny disagreed, saying that most people were well-meaning and wanted to do right by others, that the selfish person was the exception. Helen told him that this was what was wrong with him — he was an impractical idealist who thought people were good when they were, with few exceptions, "selfish stinkers!"

Danny and Milt Reynolds sauntered over to the small clearing next to the enormous tree under whose branches the men from the foundry usually held quick meetings on shop problems during the noon lunch period. From that spot Danny could see the woods off to the left of the plant — the tops of the trees disappeared into a valley, and way beyond that there were more wooded hills; off to the right of the plant he could see the rolling farm and dairy country, with low hills and the valleys between those hills; and behind him, he knew, was the village of Attica, a farmers' village. The Attica prison was also there, a sharp contrast to the farming countryside in which it was nestled. Many of the Attica Westinghouse workers doubled as guards at the prison.

Danny had heard many stories from the men who worked

in the Attica Westinghouse plant — about exciting meetings
they had held in this clearing. Back in 1946, during the
nationwide strike against Westinghouse, the men built a
wooden shack in the clearing across the tracks — where he
and Milt Reynolds were standing — and used the shack for
strike headquarters. The shack had been torn down but
"*Let's go across the tracks!*" still remained a battle cry used in
the shop whenever any union members wanted drastic
action to compel the company to settle some grievance on
which the men felt they were getting a runaround — it was
like the coal miners, for whom emptying the water bucket
meant strike.

The "tracks" were a series of railroad tracks which passed
between the plant and the clearing under the big tree's
branches. Danny had never seen any passenger trains come
through on these tracks — he had been told they had been
eliminated many years ago because of lack of passengers on
the line; but long freight trains groaned and creaked and
squealed their way by the plant several times a day, and
Danny himself had often seen a freight train stop to drop off
a few boxcars or to pick up a short string of loaded boxcars
in the company's yard.

"The men in the shop are angry," said Milt as the two men
squatted down on their haunches in the small clearing to
wait for the rest of the people to come out to the meeting.

"About what?"

"The runaround they got from Congressman Yates."

"Oh — "

"They think he didn't try very hard to prevent that
Committee from calling you." Milt picked up a dry twig and
drew a line on the ground. "They think he deliberately lied to
us."

Danny laughed. "Milt, you didn't expect anything different
from him, did you?"

"Oh, no" — Milt laughed and threw away the twig he had
been holding — "he's a weakling, and he probably feared
they might call even him a red if he spoke up for you. But
there was no harm in contacting him, was there?"

"No — "

"At least our people got an education — they learned
something about Congressman Yates. I knew it already but

some of the other people learned it here for the first time."

Danny saw a group of workmen come out of the plant. "They're starting to come over."

Milt Reynolds looked and said, "They'll all be coming now. They've had time to finish their lunch."

The union organizer and the chief steward remained still, squatting on their haunches in the middle of the clearing under the branches of the tree, watching the men as they straggled out of the plant and came across the tracks — some of the men were eating an orange or banana or a piece of cake, their dessert, others were smoking cigarettes or pipes or cigars, and some were chewing tobacco or sucking on snuff; some were pushing and shoving one another, tickling one another, playfully punching one another; and some were reading newspapers or magazines or paperback books; and a few were walking with heads down, looking tired and worn and lonely and disgusted with their lot in life.

They came across the tracks singly and in small groups, strung out in a long uneven line; and as they came into the clearing under the overhanging branches of the big tree, they nodded in the direction of the two men squatting there — a few spoke to Danny and Milt by name, and the union organizer and chief steward spoke back to these few men — and then the workmen bunched up in a semi-circle around Danny and Milt and waited for them to begin the meeting. Some of the men squatted on their haunches, in the same position as the organizer and the chief steward; others sat down on the grass; others knelt on one knee; a group playfully pushed one another back and forth, wrestling for the restricted space on the running board of a car parked near the edge of the clearing; and the rest, the majority, stood and waited.

"Let's get this meeting started," someone yelled, and Danny recognized the man because of his bushy hair —— he was a steward and he was grinning with good humor when Danny looked at him.

Milt stood up and announced that they were waiting for the rest of the men to come out of the shop, and then he squatted down beside Danny again.

While Milt made his announcement, Danny looked around at faces, trying to find some sign of direct hostility toward himself; a few men nodded in return when his eyes met theirs —— but he did not see any sign of antagonism.

They all seem friendly," he whispered to Milt.

"Oh, there's a few who are strongly opposed to you, Danny" — Milt was still watching to see if there were more men coming out of the plant to attend the meeting — "but I don't think they have the nerve to come out here and face you. They know they'll be in the minority."

"What about the talk inside the shop?"

Milt Reynolds kept his voice down so the other men could not hear him. "I think the people in this shop are more disturbed with Congressman Yates than they are with you — the way he let them down after he promised to do something. Some of the men in the foundry this morning were talking about sending a delegation to tell him what they think of him — and to file a protest against this threat by the Committee to cite you for contempt. What do you think?"

"That might help."

Milt touched his arm and said quietly, "I'll tell one of the men from the foundry to introduce a motion about sending a delegation." He stood up and walked toward the tracks. Danny watched Milt stop and talk to a bulbous-nosed fat man whose red face was still smeared with thick black greasy soot from his work in the foundry —— that was "Smiley" Lajacano, the vice-president of the local union. Milt talked earnestly, his head bobbing up and down, and Smiley nodded agreement.

There was a shrill yell.

"Hoooo-ray, the president's finally arrived!"

And then the same shrill voice razzed the local union president.

"Booooooooo — "

And then shrill laughter.

Danny saw that young Joe Storey, the local union president, had returned from eating lunch at home. Joe got out of his beat-up muddy sedan. And Danny grinned at the chorus of friendly boos and catcalls which greeted the freckle-faced union president as he came toward the clearing.

"Hey, Joe, where you been" — someone yelled out in a bull voice — "kissing S.N. White's pure white behind?" And there was loud laughter because everyone knew S. N. White, the plant manager, was engaged in a running dog-fight with the union.

"Hell, no," Joe Storey yelled back at the heckler after the long laughter had subsided enough for him to be heard, "*he* was kissing *mine!*"

This snappy rejoinder brought a chorus of derisive hoots.

Milt Reynolds rejoined Danny. "The motion's all arranged."

The local union president joined them. Milt shook his hand. "You better start the meeting right away." Milt seemed annoyed with the local union president for being so late. "It's getting to be almost time for the first whistle to blow."

"You could have started the meeting without me," Joe Storey angrily replied. "*You* could have introduced Danny — he's going to do the talking, ain't he?"

Danny wondered about Joe's anger. He was aware of a significant look he received from Milt Reynolds. Joe Storey squatted down beside them.

"You," he said very innocently to Milt Reynolds, "can introduce Danny."

Danny made note of that. Joe wasn't going to put himself in a position where anyone could accuse him of taking the lead to rally the workers in his shop to defend someone accused of being a red. Milt deliberately turned his back on Joe Storey and spoke to Danny. I'll call the meeting to order," he said hurriedly, "and I think it'll be better if I say a few words of introduction before you speak — so the people know I'm fully in support of you."

And Danny silently nodded his thanks.

The men had gathered in closer, expecting the meeting to get under way now that their local union president had arrived. Milt stepped forward to take charge of the meeting — and Danny wondered how many of the more astute stewards and executive board members of the local union would notice that it was the chief steward, not the president, who was conducting the meeting and how many would understand the significance of this.

"Men" — Milt raised his voice to get the attention of the gathering of about a hundred workmen from the foundry — "we're going to start the meeting now."

"About time," remarked several men in different parts of the group, not maliciously, but loud enough for everyone to hear. And Milt Reynolds stood perfectly still, waiting for silence before he went on.

"I want to say a few words before I introduce our international representative, Mister Newman — "Milt caught himself and looked over at the union organizer and laughed. "Danny doesn't like me to call him *Mister Newman.*" Some people laughed good-naturedly. Milt went on, speaking seriously. "But I call our union representative *Mister Newman* because I respect him, both the man and his ability. — Brothers, I've met many different kinds of people in this world of tears, and I want you to know that of all the people I've ever met I can say this for certain about this man I've known for the last four years or more — *Mister Newman* is a *man!* — He's done something which I don't think I would have the courage to do, and I don't know if there's anyone in this group here today who would have the courage to do it. He's done something very few people would do with their eyes wide open. He's deliberately stuck his neck out, risking jail to defend our rights. Your rights! And my rights! Along with his own rights!"

Feeling very self-conscious, Danny slowly squatted down beside Joe Storey and picked up a dry twig from the ground and began to trace meaningless line patterns in the earth. Milt's voice rang out with conviction, the sound carrying across the railroad tracks and bouncing back from the brick walls of the plant. Danny saw that a group of men and women from the front office had gathered on the stone steps of the administration building. Milt was just beginning to warm up, and Danny realized there wouldn't be much time left after the chief steward finished. A glance at his wrist watch revealed there were only a few minutes left before the first whistle would blow.

He wasn't worried about not having time to talk. Milt was doing a much better job than he could do. Milt Reynolds was one of the people from the community, a man from the farms who still kept up his dirt farming each day and milked his cows every day; he had lived in Attica all his life with these people who had gone into the shop from the farms — they knew him and they trusted him as one of their own. As for himself, Danny knew he was still an outsider, an outlander, a man from the big city, even though that big city was only forty miles away, even though he had been working with some of the same Attica people in the union for almost fifteen years. The less *he* said now, and the more *Milt* said on his behalf, the better off *he* was.

Milt spoke very rapidly, excitedly, telling the story Danny had already heard several times — how Milt had been persecuted in his Baptist Church because he differed on a point of gospel with the local minister; how the minister had excommunicated him along with all his family who were pronounced guilty by association with him after they refused to condemn Milt before the rest of the congregation.

Milt dramatized the story, making it live again as if it had happened only the day before. Danny kept his face impassive, stiff, solemn, while he directed his attention along with the rest of the audience to the emotional speaker, but inwardly he grinned with full appreciation of the marvelous job Milt was doing.

Then Milt suddenly switched away from his own story to speak with a fervent passion about Jesus Christ and how He had been persecuted because He fought against the money-changers. The deep religious conviction of the man was evident, and Danny's spine tingled as the unschooled chief steward anxiously groped for the right words to fully express what he wanted to say.

Danny knew that Milt had practically no formal education. Most of his reading had been confined to the Bible. But the necessity to find words to express what he felt was strong enough to enable him to find words, hesitatingly and with painful slowness at times, and in fluid tumbling rushes of words and phrases and sentences at other times. Often, he didn't use exactly the right word but his deep conviction gave a greater and more right meaning to that word than most men would have given with use of the more correct word. You felt deeply with the man as he struggled to say it in a way that you would know exactly what he was trying so hard to say. The audience of workmen were motionless, concentrating and straining to help him find the right words — they were *with* him.

Suddenly, complete silence.

The audience waited, caught.

Milt Reynolds glared at the semi-circle of men crowded into the clearing. Danny could see the right side of the chief steward's ruddy face — Milt was working his lips around as though he was trying to shape together the next word in his mouth before spitting it out. The small muscles at the corner of his mouth were moving in a steady circular motion. Nervous spasms, Danny thought. And he realized that the chief steward was very worked up inside.

Then Milt spoke out again —

"And now they're trying to crucify Danny Newman!" — The shock of hearing his name linked this way to Jesus Christ brought Danny's head up sharply and he could feel his face flush hot. He wished Milt wouldn't talk that way about him. It was painfully embarrassing to be spoken of that way in your own presence. — Milt's voice reached a high-pitched intensity. "They're trying to crucify Danny Newman because he's leading our fight against the money-changers of today! They don't want to nail him to a cross — that's old-fashioned! That's" — he tried to say the word "medieval" and stumbled over the pronunciation so badly that he jumbled it up into a non-existent word, but everyone seemed to know what Milt meant, and Milt went right on. — "They're trying to crucify him the modern way! They're threatening to try him for contempt of Congress and put him in jail — to take him away from his wife and children and lock him up away from the open fields and the blue sky and the sun overhead and the grass under our feet. As old farmers — as men who have spent much of our lives out in the open, alone in the fields, under the sky, close in communication with our dear Lord — most of us who have farmed the fields know what it means to be taken and hidden away from all this — "

Milt swept his arms over his head, taking in the whole sky and the spread of the fields and woods running off into the surrounding hills and valleys. He looked like one of those old pictures of the prophet in the Bible speaking to his people about the Day of Judgment — even though Milt lacked the long flowing gray beard of the prophet.

"Men!" — a long pause, while Milt stood absolutely motionless, and the men strained for that next word — "Men! I don't blame Danny Newman if he has contempt for this

Congress we got now!"

Another long pause.

Danny saw that Milt was glaring around at his audience, looking for disagreement. But every face silently agreed with the speaker.

And then Milt's voice unexpectedly soared to an even higher peak, with a rich fullness and with such hypnotic power that Danny almost answered the question the speaker asked —

"Can *you* respect them?"

And a lone voice answered, quietly, but clearly enough to be heard by everyone, "Hell, no — "

Milt rushed on. "Can you respect a man like our own Congressman Yates who is nothing but a messenger boy for you-know-what-corporation-I- mean?"

The same lone voice repeated, a little louder, "Hell, no — "

And Milt raced on. "Can you respect a man like that who is in the service of the devil?"

"Hell, no!" several voices chorused, and Danny thought that the meeting was beginning to take on the character of a religious revival — he realized that he himself felt a strong impulse to say, 'Hell, no!' along with the others; he actually was saying it to himself, not out loud, but along with the rest.

"Can *you*" — Milt's voice soared out into the hills — "put your faith in an agent of the devil like that man is?"

"Hell, no!"

"Can you trust him?"

"Hell, no!"

"Did he keep his word with us?"

"Hell, no!"

And a voice in the back of a crowd shouted out, "Let's send a committee to tell him what we think of him!" Danny wondered if it was Smiley Lajacano, the vice-president of the local union, the bulbous-nosed man to whom Milt had spoken earlier about sending a committee from the union to see Yates.

"Why waste time going to see that faker?" another voice yelled from over on the left side of the clearing.

"Bring the green stuff when you go to see him," a short man on Danny's right called out — "you gotta buy him to get anything out of him, and you gotta pay more than the others are paying — he represents the highest bidder."

The comments of the men interrupted the rising flow of Milt Reynolds' sermon. Danny could see that the chief steward seemed flustered. Bumped off the theme of his talk, Milt floundered around trying to get back on the main track again but he didn't seem to be sure where he wanted to go with his talk — what point he was trying to make. And then the factory's first whistle blew.

Milt stopped speaking.

He looked around, realizing how late it was, not knowing what to do about it.

Then he apologized to the men for having lost track of time and he introduced the union organizer.

"Danny wants to say a few words — "

The men were already edging away, and Danny knew that he could not speak for more than one minute, the final whistle was about to blow. He stood up and stepped forward and started to speak.

"I'm not going to make a speech, brothers," he called out, to stop the men who were already moving away, and he hurriedly went on, speaking quietly but with great energy, with great intensity — to grab his audience immediately and hold them. "It's too late for a speech, and there's nothing I could say that would be one inch as good as the wonderful talk Milt just gave on the subject. — On my way driving down here I wrote a long speech in my mind, to tell you the reasons why I didn't answer any questions for that Committee; but that whole speech can be summed up in a few words: — *I don't think anyone has the right to take away the dignity of a human being; and when you tell a man he doesn't have the right to think what he darn well pleases then you take away his dignity — then you destroy something in him — the most important part of him — you cripple him inside — and he'll never again be completely whole inside — never again! Once you take that away from him and he consciously permits you to take it away — no one can put it back there again like it was before!"*

He saw that the men had stopped moving away. "I'm no different from you or anybody else; I don't want to go to jail. — But isn't it better to risk jail for the body than to be a groveling coward and volunteer to put your own mind in jail while your body is permitted to appear to be free — "

He moved his hands around, and he saw that all their eyes were staring fixedly into his.

"*You* — *you* have a right to *your* own beliefs and come what may, no matter what the cost, I insist on keeping *my* beliefs —— whatever they are; and that means it's nobody's damn business but my own what they are!"

He saw that they were ready to stay and hear more even though it was late. But he decided to end his speech right there with only a few words to finish it off. And he spoke very quietly.

"Basically, gentlemen, brothers — that's the reason why I refused to answer their questions. — I say that you — and I — can believe in anything we damn well please — including communism — yes, I said it, including communism — if we want to believe in that — and it's our own business. To me — that's freedom! And anything less — is jail!"

He stepped backward, and with a nod and a wave of his right hand let them know that his speech was done. There were a few friendly yells and a smattering of applause, and the men started back across the tracks. Two stewards from the machine shop came over and briefly shook hands with Danny before starting after the others. The recording secretary and financial secretary of the union wished him good luck. Joe Storey hung back until all had left except himself and Milt Reynolds; and then he shook hands with Danny and told him the men in the shop were supporting him. Danny thanked him. Joe Storey left, following after the others.

Milt Reynolds and Danny, side by side, walking very slowly, brought up the rear of the long straggling procession of men in working clothes who were slowly crossing the series of railroad tracks, going back into the red brick building, returning to work. Milt apologized.

"I shouldn't have talked so long."

Danny affectionately placed his right hand on the older man's left shoulder. "You did much better for me, Milt, than 1 could have ever done myself."

"1 meant every word of it — "

"Thanks — "

The men were bunching up at the entrance to the plant, waiting to get into the building. The union organizer and the chief steward stopped a few yards away from the men grouped around the doorway. Milt told Danny he felt bad because the man who was supposed to make the motion to send a delegation to see Congressman Yates had not done it.

Danny laughed. "We didn't give him much of a chance, Milt."

"No, I guess not," Milt agreed. "That's probably the reason he didn't do it. But we'll get the executive board together either tonight after work or during lunch hour tomorrow and we'll get authorization to send a committee to see Yates."

They shook hands preparatory to saying goodbye. "Danny, I don't think you have anything to worry about. They're smart; they've got their fingers on the pulse of the working people in this area and they must know the people in the shop are backing you up; they must know that if they do anything to you — there will be a sharp reaction. — And the last thing they'd want to do, it seems to me, is to make a martyr out of you."

With his left ear cocked toward the older man, Danny kept nodding, registering the fatherly encouragement Milt was giving him. "My hunch," said Milt, still gripping the union organizer's hand, "is you'll never hear another word from them. They'll let it drop."

The other men had disappeared into the plant.

Danny thanked Milt for getting the people out to the meeting across the tracks and for making the wonderful speech on his behalf.

Milt stepped into the doorway — he looked back — he and Danny waved to one another — Milt walked into the red brick building — and Danny saw the door close.

The forty mile drive back to Buffalo went fast.

"Tonight," Danny reminded himself while he kept his eyes fixed on the narrow country road winding ahead, "is the family meeting, the tribal council, when I'm supposed to explain to them exactly what I've already explained to them, and I'm supposed to make believe — at least with Bob and Millie — that we haven't discussed the subject before.

The car window was open.

The singing sound of the tires was so loud he had to shout when he swore at all his in-laws and consigned them to the hot place below.

And then he laughed at his own childishness.

"Tonight's the night!" he shouted as loud as he could, hearing the sound of his own voice above the rushing noise of the wind going past the open window of the car. "And they can all go to hell!"

Chapter 47

"It's a question of ethics, what's right and what's wrong—integrity."

They were talking about ethics.

"How much money can you get for *that*" — Bob interrupted — "when you try to sell it on the market?" And his wife, his mother and his sister Helen smiled politely. But there was too much underlying tension to permit any real laughter.

Danny could see that no one was enjoying the family council session, at the same time as he tightened his grip on his glass of scotch and water and made himself add his own grin to the polite smiles of the others. Sitting in the living room, he could hear the sound from the television set upstairs in the den where Ruth was supposed to be studying her homework — he hoped the noise would not wake Linda who had been put to bed some time earlier.

"Some people still have ideals, Bob. More people than someone like you who doesn't have them any longer would ever believe." He kept his eyes on his brother-in-law while he bent his head and sipped his drink.

Bob flashed his bashful boy smile. "I've learned that it's either the very poor man without a dime who is always full of ideals — by which he means he wants some of the rich man's money without having to work for it — or else it's the very rich man who's already made his big bundle of money by ignoring ethics and ideals who then can afford to get ideals and ethics after he's got his big bundle safely salted away where it won't be affected by his ethics and ideals."

Bob's mother nodded agreement with that and Danny wondered if he was going to end up with Irene lining up with Bob and Millie against him. Helen might feel she would be isolating herself from her family if she leaned his way.

"And the man in-between" — Bob spoke tolerantly from his mountain-top position of self-righteousness — "the man who's neither very poor nor very rich, he can't afford to have ideals or he'll quickly become very poor."

400

"Could be," said Danny quietly, keeping the mask of affability fixed on his face. "But what kind of a country would we have if everyone felt that way?"

"Fortunately" — Bob smiled back with that nervous bashful bobbing of his head — "very fortunately for the majority of us, every age has its fanatics and martyrs who are anxious to sacrifice themselves to preserve the freedom of their fellowmen. — This age is no exception."

The obvious inference hurt, but Danny sipped his drink and tried to appear very self-contained.

The others were waiting for him to reply. He reminded himself to smile, broadening the mask of affability.

"Oh, I don't think that's very true, Bob." He tried to be very offhand about it. "It's the cynic who doesn't think people are any good and that life isn't worth living. He's the man who's anxious to throw it away in some sort of grand suicidal gesture. He hates people and doesn't think much of them because he hates himself. He'd just as soon throw away his life in some grand grab for fame. But the idealist is a man who's full of the desire to live, who wants to be out there in the midstream of life, to deal with the realities of life. He believes that man doesn't live alone, that man can't take care of only himself and be happy."

"That sounds good," said Bob, "but it would sound much better if you were standing on a soapbox," and he quickly added his bashful grin.

"Oh, I imagine it's been said on soapboxes quite often," Danny conceded, trying to keep the mask of affability plastered on his face. "I imagine even Tom Paine used a soapbox."

Bob shrugged. Danny sipped his drink, and Millie crossed her legs and pulled down the hem of her dress to cover her knees to let them know she was going to say something.

"If you know your history," she reminded Danny, "then you know that Tom Paine had sense enough not to get married again after his first wife died. People who are such fanatic idealists" — making it very clear she included Danny in that category — "have no right to marry and certainly no right to bring children into the world."

Danny shifted to face his latest opponent while desperately warning himself to keep smiling and speak quietly. Helen hated arguments between himself and her family. They unsettled her for days.

"Such people," Millie repeated for his special benefit, "have no right to marry or to have children; and after his first marriage Tom Paine had sense enough to know that."

"Millie" — Danny sipped his drink, using the moment to figure out a reply. — "Millie, isn't it possible that Tom Paine might have been even a more effective fighter for freedom if he had married again and had had some children of his own? After all, a parent usually fights more desperately for his children than for himself. A man alone can run away, but a man with a wife and children stays to fight to protect them. — Don't you think it's possible that Tom Paine might have understood — even better than he did — what freedom means in terms of human beings if he had had a family of his own? Isn't it possible that such an experience would have given him a broader understanding and helped him to express himself in terms which would have brought an even stronger reaction than he was able to create without that kind of a personal experience?"

Millie sneered. "I disagree with that. Tom Paine knew it wasn't fair to any woman to ask her to marry him once he decided he wanted to be the great martyr for freedom." She tossed a sharp look at Danny. "People like that have no right to marry."

Danny could see that this was disturbing Helen. "I'm no Tom Paine, Millie," he said lamely, unable to think of anything better to say.

Millie boldly sailed on, strengthened by the weakness of his protest. "It's very fine for you to stand up before the world for your ideals," she declared, her voice cold and loaded with accusation, "and I'm sure it must give a person a wonderful feeling to think that he's maintained his personal integrity despite all kinds of pressure — "

He could see that the others were straining to get every word as Millie continued.

"But how does that help when your children are not invited to parties because of you? When after they grow up they are kept out of sororities because of you?"

Her haughty look of contempt wiped away his mask of affability. "There are worse things than not being invited to parties," he harshly countered. "Worse things than being kept out of sororities!"

But now Helen entered the argument.

"Not for children," she interjected. "There's nothing worse than that for children."

Danny swung around to face her. The way it was going, this family council was making things worse instead of better.

"You were blackballed out of a sorority, Helen," he reminded her, "weren't you?"

"Yes, I was."

"It didn't kill you!"

"But I've never forgotten it! I've never been hurt so much in my whole life!"

He swallowed the retort which he wanted to make and instead forced himself to speak quietly.

"Let's not lose our tempers."

"I'm not losing my temper."

"I'm sorry if I lost mine. But don't you see the difference between getting blackballed out of the sorority and whatever effect there'd be if the kids are blackballed account of me?"

"I see no difference' — "

"You weren't blackballed on account of your father, were you?"

"No. Someone was jealous of me for some silly reason. At least that's what I was told by my friends. But I don't see the difference."

"This is the difference." He tried to sound very reasonable. "If our kids are blackballed out of a sorority because of their father, they won't blame themselves like you blamed yourself. Our kids will know it's because of me."

"Do you think," asked Helen, "that will help any?" Her eyes were narrowed with what seemed to him like real hate.

"I do, I do, Helen. I really do. — The kids may be too young to understand now, or even later when they're only in high school and they're blackballed from some high school sorority. But sometime in the future they'll finally get to understand. And even though they may not agree with me and my reasoning, they'll still get to understand why I acted as I did. I think, I hope, they'll admire their father for what he did. More important than that, I hope they'll develop a better sense of honesty and personal integrity for themselves as a result of what is happening now — "

He stopped.

There was absolute silence in the living room. Helen refused to look at him.

And then Bob decided to try to be funny.

"You mean" — Bob held his hand to his forehead in a mock gesture of despair — "that if Ruth or Linda are called before a Congressional committee, God forbid, they'll do the same thing you did?"

Danny laughed along with the others at Bob's clowning. Then he said seriously, "I hope they do, Bob. I'll be very proud of them."

Millie snorted.

"*You* might be proud," she said. "But what about Helen? She's their mother. Would she be proud?"

And they all turned to Helen and waited for her answer. Danny saw that Helen was hesitating, unable to make up her mind. "Well," Millie prompted her, "you wouldn't want your children to do what Danny did, would you?"

Helen bit her lip — she wrinkled her forehead — she stared down at the rye highball she held with both hands in her lap — and Danny could tell that she was having a hard time.

"It wouldn't be the same thing," her mother suggested, trying to save Helen from having to answer the question. "After all, the children will be *women*, not men, when they grow up."

Helen's head snapped up.

"Mother!" Her face reflected her indignation. "Why should *that* make a difference?"

Danny silently thanked Helen's mother for the tactless remark which aroused Helen's sense of loyalty to womanhood. Helen would defend the right of her children, women, to do exactly what their father, a man, had done.

Irene tried to back out. "I thought it would make a difference. After all, Ruth and Linda are girls. And we know that girls — "

Helen wouldn't let her go any further.

"Women have as much courage as men. — The trouble with you, Mother, and with too many women is that you willingly accept the inferior role that some men are stupid enough to try to hand us women. Then men wonder why they have such rotten marriage relationships — after they've deliberately prevented it from being an equal give-and-take relationship."

Irene didn't know what to say. She sat still with a stupefied look on her face.

"Don't tell me, Mother," Helen fired at her, "that men are more courageous than women. Because it just ain't so!"

Millie joined Helen, stridently expressing her agreement. "I believe women have just as much courage as men."

This prompted Bob to try to be funny again, hoping to extricate his mother from her embarrassing position. He shifted his head around with his face set in that smirking grin. "They probably have even *more* courage than men." He tried to include Danny with himself. "Who are we to argue? We're outnumbered by the women. We better agree with them."

Danny looked down into his drink, refusing to give Bob the satisfaction of even acknowledging what he had said.

Helen got up. Danny watched her cross the room to get a cigarette out of an opened pack lying on top of the upright piano. She came back to her chair, sat down, deliberately struck a match and held the flame to the end of her cigarette. Danny watched her inhale deeply and exhale a stream of grayish blue smoke. A bit of tobacco stuck to her lip. She wiped it off with the tip of her fingernail.

Then she spoke, very slowly, thinking out loud. "I would think that if the children were to grow up in an atmosphere such as exists in this situation" — she spoke as if she were making an observation about people with whom she had no emotional ties whatsoever — "were to grow up with a father whom they love very much — I think that in this situation they would tend to react the same way as the father did when he was called before the Congressional committee."

Danny kept his face blank as Helen went on. "When the children get older — there probably would be a great deal of talk in the family about what the father had done — why he had done it that way — and the children would be adult enough then to discuss it intelligently with their father and mother. So — "

She stopped.

The others silently waited for her conclusions.

"So, under those circumstances" — she looked from one face to another, from her mother to her brother to her sister-in-law, and then to Danny; then she kept her eyes on her cigarette as she tapped the burning end against the edge of the glass ash tray on the coffee table — "it would seem to me that if the children were thrown into a similar situation such as this, after they had grown up, after they had become adults, they would tend to repeat the pattern set by their father. They would put defense of ideals and ethics and personal integrity before their own immediate personal physical and financial well-being."

She turned and looked directly into her sister-in-law's face. "Don't you think so, Millie?" she added.

"Well — "

Millie fidgeted with her hands and crossed one foot over the other and pulled her dress down to cover the exposed knee. It was apparent that she was reluctant to give any reply.

The others waited.

"Well," Millie repeated, and then she reluctantly agreed. — "Yes, the children would tend to do what the father had done — unless they had been hurt so much by what their father had done that they hated him and turned against everything he stood for."

"I don't think the children will ever hate Danny," said Helen. "You can say whatever else you want to about Danny but he's a good father."

Danny looked at her. She looked down at her cigarette, refusing to let him catch her eye.

"Oh," agreed Bob, "I know he's a good father" — Danny hated the way he was being discussed as if he were not there — "which is why," continued Bob, "I can't understand how he could jeopardize the welfare of his children by getting involved in a fight with a Congressional committee."

Danny couldn't hold himself in any longer.

"Bob! — "

He stopped and tried to regain control of his temper.

"I wish," Bob went on, "you'd explain it to me. I'd like to know, Danny, how you rationalize your great love for your children, which I'll concede is there — how you rationalize that with the provocative way you conducted yourself in that hearing, just asking for trouble — "

"Bob! — "

Danny stopped himself again. Whatever he would say while he felt so angry would not help the situation. Who the hell did they think they were, stripping him naked this way, discussing him and his personal relationship with his children as if he were a two year old infant who had wet his pants in public? The resentment filled him up.

"Bob" — he kept tight control, speaking very quietly — "I don't think you'd ever understand. We look at everything through different kinds of glasses."

"Thank heaven for that!" exclaimed Millie, lifting her eyebrows and letting out a breathy laugh. "I'd hate to have my husband called before a Congressional committee and then have him gain notoriety in the community by refusing to cooperate with a committee of our government." She stuck a cigarette between her lips and held it in the corner of her mouth without lighting it, while she went on. "I can tell you — it would be the end of our happy marriage if Bob ever did anything like that — he could go off and live by himself and be a martyr and enjoy it to his heart's content, alone."

Danny watched Millie scratch a match along the rough strip on the bottom of a book of paper matches. She held the flame up to the end of her cigarette as she puffed several times. She drew in a deep draw of smoke and then let it slide out slowly between her moist lipsticked lips. And then she became aware of the tense silence which had followed her pronouncement about how she would treat *her* husband if he ever did what Danny had done. She looked around at the faces.

"Well," she said, defensively, "it would be *his* choice, not mine. If he decided he wanted to be a hero, he would have to do it alone."

The silence which followed was deadly.

Bob tried to laugh up the situation.

"Honey, you mean you'd leave me all alone to face the cold, cruel world just because I decided to lay down my dear life to defend our Constitution and the rights *of* the people, *by* the people and *for* the people?"

Millie refused to be a hypocrite.

"I would leave you," she said, with a defiant stare that made Bob's face become sober and slightly pink in hue, "and I'd take the children with me. And I think I would be doing the right thing for the children and also the right thing for your own good, to bring you to your senses."

"Well" — Bob made another effort to laugh it up — "at least I know where I stand, and I better watch my step." He lifted his drink in Danny's direction and gave a toast. "Here's hoping I never find myself in your position, Danny, or I'll be without my happy home and my happy family."

Danny could see the bewildered look of hurt in his brother-in-law's eyes, even though Bob was still laughing, and Danny felt sorry for him. He lifted his glass in reply to Bob's toast.

"Bob," said Millie, with a bitter look on her face, "can't you stop acting like an immature high school freshman?"

He shrugged, embarrassed, but made no attempt to reply. Irene came to the rescue. "Robert, I don't think Millicent would ever actually do anything so very drastic, even if you had done exactly what Danny did." She stretched her hand out toward her daughter-in-law and smiled ingratiatingly. "Millie, you'd be surprised what you might do if it actually came to something like that. Look at Helen — she's very hurt, I know — and I know she's extremely troubled — but I know she never even would think of anything like leaving Danny and breaking up the family."

Danny looked at Helen.

Their eyes met.

They kept their faces expressionless.

Bob rose to his feet. And Danny guessed that his brother in-law wanted to break up the embarrassing situation which had developed.

"We have to go home. Our sitter has to get up for school in the morning."

Helen immediately urged everyone to wait a few minute's before leaving. She had bought some special cinnamon rolls to serve. Bob sat down again. Helen went into the kitchen to heat up the rolls. Danny went into the kitchen to help her.

He was filling the coffee pot with water when Helen suddenly kissed him on the cheek.

He turned to her.

"Don't get any ideas," she said quickly, and she backed away.

"I don't have any ideas," he told her, wondering exactly what she meant.

"Just don't get any ideas," she repeated, and she walked away, refusing to explain further.

"I won't," he said, as he guessed that she meant for him not to get any idea that just because she kissed him that she had decided not to leave him. Whatever was going on in her mind now was too damn complicated for him to even try to figure out what it was.

A proper amount of time passed after the serving of the cinnamon rolls and coffee, and then Bob and Millie left, taking Irene along to drop her off at The Park Lane.

Danny thought Helen might want to talk to him — now that the others had gone. But she went upstairs to send Ruth to bed. When she came down again she went into the living room. He came from the kitchen to the entrance into the living room and saw that she was reading a book. She refused to look up or acknowledge his presence in any way.

He went upstairs and watched television in the den until midnight and then undressed and went to bed. Lying there in the darkness, alone, he thought about his plans for the next day. He was going to see the editorial writer at The Courier. He hoped something good would come out of that. He heard Helen moving around down in the kitchen, probably getting herself a cup of coffee, while he thought of what he might say to the editorial writer — he fell asleep before Helen came up to bed.

Chapter 48

Wednesday morning —

"Those who want to destroy the protections guaranteed in our Constitution are the radicals," said Ted Allen, chief editorial writer for the Courier, "and we" — Danny noted with pleasant surprise that he was being included — "who are trying to preserve the protections of the Fifth Amendment and the First Amendment, the right of the people to think as they please, are the conservatives."

The tall man with the brown mustache gave Danny the feeling that he was back in school again, a bug-eyed freshman listening to the learned professor expound an excitingly new viewpoint.

He was glad he had not found it necessary to use his father-in-law's name to get in to see Ted Allen. When he asked the shirtsleeved elevator operator where he could find the editorial writer, he was directed to the fourth floor. Through an open door he saw the wide office area, with several rows of desks lined up on the dark plastic-tiled floor; and for a few moments while he got his bearings he watched some men and women seated at desks, engrossed in typing or making notes; and he assumed that these people had something to do with the editorial staff, maybe *were* the editorial staff.

He stepped through the doorway. A man with a shiny bald head — he was seated behind a railing off to Danny's right — looked up and nodded for Danny to come over and state his business.

"I'd like to speak to Ted Allen."

"Ted's gone downstairs but he'll be back in a few minutes." The man with the bald head swung the gate inward to permit Danny to enter his small enclosed sanctum. "Come in and sit down." He pointed to an empty chair at one of the three desks behind the railing.

"Thanks."

Danny entered through the gate and sat down. "Would

410

you mind if I read this while I wait?" Danny pointed to a thick volume of Shakespeare's works lying on the nearest desk.

"Go right ahead, read it, read it." The man with the bald head seemed pleased. "Do you like Shakespeare?"

"Oh" — Danny hesitated, then answered, "Yes," the answer the other man obviously would be pleased to hear.

The man with the bald head beamed. "I'm always glad when I come across someone who is still interested in reading Shakespeare instead of comic books and detective stories."

Danny nodded, thanking the man for the compliment. He had asked to read the book because he had nothing else to do while he waited for Ted Allen, but apparently he had done the right thing to win this man's favor.

He read a few pages, then became aware of a lanky man with a bushy brown mustache approaching the railing gate.

"Someone to see you, Ted," the man with the bald head called out. "He likes to read Shakespeare."

The lanky man with a touch of gray in his mussed hair, turned to take a good look at Danny, as though he was one of an inside fraternity to which the three of them belonged. Danny felt like he was perpetrating a fraud, cheating; he grinned to hide his embarrassment. Ted Allen grinned back, a friendly spread of thick lips which stretched and narrowed his bushy brown mustache. Danny remembered to rise respectfully while he waited for the writer to speak to him.

Ted Allen beckoned.

"Sit down over here."

He pointed to a chair beside one of the other desks.

"Thanks."

"I'll be with you in a minute."

Danny returned the thick volume of Shakespeare's works to the place where he had found it and crossed to the chair where Ted Allen wanted him to sit. Meanwhile, the editorial writer went over to see someone on the other side of the room. A few moments later he returned and sat down at the desk, an old-fashioned rolltop piece of furniture — he pushed aside some other papers to make room for the papers he had brought with him — he bent his head down over his work — he rapidly scribbled notations as he scanned through the typed lines on the sheets of paper in front of him.

Danny kept his eyes fixed on the writer, waiting for him to finish. Meanwhile, he wondered how to begin his story. What would be the reaction when the editor learned that his visitor was *the* Danny Newman, the very same radical whom the Courier had often charged with following the communist line? There had been several editorials attacking him. Ted Allen might have written them. And now —

He saw Ted Allen put down his pencil.

The editorial writer swing around to face his visitor, giving Danny an encouraging smile which said, "Now you can tell me what you want, and don't be afraid to speak up."

"My name is Danny Newman — I'm a union organizer." Ted Allen took a moment to remember the name, and then he remembered.

"Oh!" There was a look of surprise on his face, and then he vigorously nodded recognition and pointed his index finger at Danny. "You're the man who took that novel position before the Un-American Activities Committee at that hearing in Albany." The editorial writer nodded his head up and down, with his lips pressed firmly together. Danny watched and waited, thinking of the flood of remembrances that must be going through the editorial writer's head about this radical seated here: the strikes in which he'd been involved; the furious inter-union and intra-union battles, with all the name-calling and smears hurled at him in the newspapers; the severe criticism leveled at him because he publicly objected to interference by several clergymen in the operations of the union; the frequent stories in the newspapers accusing him of being a communist-liner — "

But Ted Allen was still smiling as he nodded his head up and down, and Danny had the feeling that the writer was cross-checking his preconceptions about his visitor with the culprit sitting there in the chair in front of him. Danny knew that people often were surprised after reading all the unfavorable publicity about him, expecting to meet some evil-looking character, some standard movie villain, instead of the light complexioned, blue-eyed redhead who looked somewhat younger than his forty-one years.

"Have you heard anything further on the contempt

citation?" Ted Allen asked in an absent-minded way as if he was still thinking about other things.

"No. Congressman Holling asked the full Committee to cite me, but — so far as I know — they've done nothing about it, yet."

Danny was aware that Allen's dark brown eyes were studying him.

There was a long silence while Danny awaited the decision. He wondered if it would help if he were to mention the name of his late father-in-law. But he decided against saying anything about that —Allen might resent any attempt to use that kind of influence; he seemed to be that kind of person.

The writer narrowed his eyes and cocked his head to one side. "I never did get clear in my mind exactly what position you did take before that Committee. I know you refused to answer any of their questions, not even where you were born." And then he sharply questioned Danny as if he were trying to catch him off guard. "Where *were* you born?"

"In this country. In Brooklyn, New York. When I was only a kid, just starting grammar school, my parent's moved here to Buffalo with all nine of us children."

"Why didn't you tell that to the Committee?"

"Well — "

Danny launched into a long explanation of his reasons for refusing to answer any questions of the Committee, that in order to test the constitutionality of the very existence of the Committee it was necessary for him at the very outset to refuse to answer *any* of their questions — and the first question had been: Where were you born? Danny noticed that the man with the bald head and the green visor was also listening.

There was no change in Ted Allen's facial expression until Danny finished his explanation, and then the writer relaxed and leaned back in his swivel chair, with all five finger tips of his left hand pressed against their counterparts on his right hand; he twisted his lips around — his brown mustache stretched and shrank — and then the face became still. Danny guessed that the editorial writer had reached the decision.

"I think," Allen said slowly, his head inclined forward, his chin pressed down against his chest, with only his eyes looking up at Danny, "we ought to do something to get this information out to the general public. This explanation about your refusal to answer the questions of the Committee. To be fair to you — the public should know why you refused to answer."

Danny saw that the bald man was still listening.

Ted Allen pulled his head back and looked up into the air. "I don't think we could write an editorial on the subject. At least, not yet. If the full Committee cites you — and if the House of Representatives votes to cite you — and if the grand jury indicts you — that would change the situation; that would justify an editorial dealing with the reasons you gave for refusing to answer any of the questions of the Committee — "

The writer started swinging his swivel chair slowly from one side to the other; and Danny guessed it was an unconscious nervous movement, since Ted Allen seemed too absorbed in his thinking to be aware of his physical activity.

The chair stopped moving.

Allen looked up at Danny again but kept his head bent, his fingertips still pressed together in front of his chest.

"Do you know our labor reporter, Rockland Hayes?"

"We've spoken to one another on the phone." — Danny decided he better add an explanation about his relationship with Hayes, to let Ted Allen know he was not hiding any of the disagreeable facts. "Our conversations were none too friendly. He's phoned me several times for statements and I've always told him off, none too politely — because I believed he wanted a statement from me only so he could twist it around and use it as a platform from which to launch other statements against me personally and against my union."

The editorial writer did not appear to be disturbed by what he heard. "But you've never met Hayes in person, have you?" he asked, inferring that he thought that might make a difference.

"Well, yes and no. We've seen one another in action at various public meetings and conferences, but we've never spoken to one another except on the phone."

"I think" — Ted Allen lifted his eyes up to the ceiling while he thought out loud — "you two ought to have a talk with one another, a long talk," and then his eyes came back to Danny. "Hayes might be able to work up some kind of article for his Sunday feature on labor — to help put you into proper perspective in this community."

But Danny was still fearful about what Rockland Hayes might tell Ted Allen about their relationship. He decided that he better prepare the editorial writer for the worst.

"Of course" — Danny mustered a grin — "Hayes thinks I'm a wild-eyed radical."

"No-o-o-o," said Allen, and he leaned way back in his swivel chair and peered at Danny in a kind fatherly way — his thoughts seemed to be buried deep inside himself. "No-o-o-o, I don't think, in this instance anyway, I don't think you're a radical, Mr. Newman." He seemed to be smiling to himself. "I think, at least in this instance, you're definitely a conservative!"

"A conservative?"

Ted Allen went on to explain what he meant.

"My definition of a radical is a man who wants to tear established things up by the roots, who wants to destroy foundations, who wants to wipe out all sense of tradition, who wants to wreck what we have built up instead of building on top of that to make something better, using what we already have as the starting point from which to advance. Those who want to destroy the protections guaranteed by our Constitution are the radicals, and we who are trying to preserve the protections of the Fifth Amendment and the First Amendment, the right of the people to think as they please, are the conservatives."

Danny thought he detected a twinkle of amusement in the writer's eyes. He knew that his own bewilderment must be showing. Ted Allen seemed to be enjoying turning things upside down.

"Yes" — Ted Allen locked his hands together behind his head — "I would say, Mr. Newman, that you are a conservative in this instance. You *do* want to conserve our Constitution, don't you?"

"Yes, sir."

"Especially our Bill of Rights?"

"Yes, sir."

"You want to conserve the right of the people of our country to all the protection they can get from the Fifth Amendment?"

"Yes, sir."

"Without use of the Fifth Amendment being construed as a sign of guilt?"

"Yes, sir."

"And you most certainly want to conserve the First Amendment — the right to freedom of speech, freedom of thought, freedom of religion, freedom of association, and all the rest?"

"Yes, sir."

The soles of Ted Allen's shoes smacked loudly against the tiled floor as he rocked forward in his swivel chair and brought his hands down into his lap. "Mr. Newman! I don't know too much about how you proceed with your labor relationships with the managements you deal with — how radical or conservative you are in your union business — but here, regarding the Constitution of our country, it's my opinion, after talking to you — you're a conservative! Perhaps we might best term it, 'A progressive conservative!' Someone who wants to improve on what we have, but who wants to make sure we keep the tried and tested good things we already have. Wouldn't you say that's about it?"

Ted Allen waited for a reply. Danny thought that the last word he himself would have used to describe himself in any respect would have been the word 'conservative'. Yet, as Ted Allen had explained it, the word did seem to fit. The best Danny had expected out of this interview was that Ted Allen would characterize him as a radical who should be tolerated lest the freedoms taken from the radical be destroyed at the same time for everyone else. And now Ted Allen was calling him a conservative!

The editorial writer swiveled away from Danny and picked up the telephone. "I'll try to get hold of Rockland Hayes — "

But Hayes was out on an assignment.

"I'll speak to him later and ask him to get in touch with you."

Allen rose to his feet and Danny knew the interview was over.

They shook hands.

Danny remembered the suggestion Stan Helowicz had made, back in the guard's shack at the foundry, about writing a letter to the editor.

"Mr. Allen, some of our local union officers have suggested that I ought to write a letter to the editor, explaining why I refused to answer the questions of the Committee, just as I've explained it to you — "

The other man thought a moment before replying.

"I don't see why we couldn't print something like that. Write it up and send it in. Try to keep it as short as you can — we're restricted on space for those letters. And clip a little note to your letter, saying you spoke to me about it."

They shook hands again while Danny thanked him.

"Mr. Allen" — they were still shaking hands — "I think you knew my father-in-law. He died a few years ago. Milton Stack. The Park Lane.

Ted Allen held onto Danny's hand while he tried to fit his visitor into the scheme of personal relationships which could link together Milton Stack and a left-wing union organizer.

"Milton Stack was your father-in-law?" He seemed to find that hard to believe.

"I married his daughter Helen."

"Helen?" Ted Allen puzzled over the name a moment, and then he recalled. "Oh, yes, Helen, the youngest. A very attractive girl. — So you're married to Helen."

Danny nodded confirmation.

"Do you have any children?"

"Two daughters."

"Wonderful, that's wonderful."

"Thanks."

"I'll make a note to remind myself to be sure to speak to Rockland Hayes, and he'll get in touch with you. I think there should be some kind of interesting story here, and it's about time we created a better perspective in the community regarding a person like you." The writer nodded his head thoughtfully. "I think it's about time we did that."

Danny thanked him again.

They shook hands again.

The bald man also called out good-bye, and Danny called out his thanks and waved good-bye to him.

At home on Friday morning he read his letter on the editorial page of the Courier with not one word changed — even though the letter took up almost three-fourths of a full column.

Danny made breakfast for the kids. While they ate, he read the letter again, trying to read it as if he were a stranger reading it for the first time. It seemed to read all right, and he thought it would get a good reaction from most people who would read it that day.

Helen was still asleep, upstairs. He decided not to wake her — they were still feuding.

He showed the newspaper column to his older daughter.

"Read this, Ruth."

She read the letter while she chewed her toast.

"That's nice," she said, smiling up at him, and he took the paper from her and kissed her on the cheek.

Little Linda demanded, "Read it to me!"

She nagged him until he began to read it aloud to her, but she became bored after the first three paragraphs and ran upstairs to watch television.

Ruth left for school.

Danny went upstairs and stuck his head in through the doorway into their bedroom. "Helen, I'm leaving. You better get up and take care of Linda."

She stirred and murmured sleepily, "Okay."

"And if you feel like it, Helen, there's a letter on the editorial page you might want to read — "

She rolled over so she faced him, her eyes open and suspicious, despite her drowsy face.

"Who wrote the letter?"

"I did."

She stared a moment, and then her voice was cold: "You never know when to leave well enough alone, do you?"

"Good-bye." He suppressed the impulse to slam the door shut.

"Good-bye." Her reply was just as short and harsh. He went into the den where Linda was watching television and kissed her good-bye — she didn't take her eyes away from the screen — and then he left for the office.

Shortly after he arrived there, the phone rang. He recognized Helen's voice.

"That was a nice letter," she said.

"Thanks."

"Mother and Bob called right after you left. They both liked it."

"Thanks."

"Some of their friends called them about it."

"That's interesting."

"Was it your idea to write the letter?"

"No, some of the local union officers suggested it. They helped me write it."

"It was a good letter."

"Thank you."

"It sounded very honest."

"Thanks."

"Well, I better let you get back to work."

"Okay."

"Good-bye, Danny dear."

"Good-bye, Helen."

"I'll see you later."

"Okay."

He heard the click of the phone as Helen hung up. He put down the receiver at his end and cradled his head in his arms on top of the desk. Was it worth all this shit to save this marriage?

That afternoon Rockland Hayes telephoned.

"You're a highly controversial figure in the community, Danny. And there's never been a story in the newspapers about your whole background, has there?"

Danny laughed. "There's been a lot of stories about me, Rocky. But none that I would consider exactly unbiased. Of course, I'm probably a bit prejudiced — "

"This story I have in mind, Danny, would be completely unbiased."

"Oh, sure — "

And Hayes immediately protested against the sarcasm in Danny's voice. But Danny could not put aside his suspicion. Rocky Hayes had written some stories about him in the past, twisting his words and acts beyond recognition in order to fan the flames of redbaiting. He couldn't believe Hayes was ready to change his approach to write an unbiased story about Danny Newman. Better no Sunday feature article at all than one loaded to turn the community even further against him. A bad story now could wipe out whatever gains he had made with the printing of his letter to the editor.

"Rocky — "

"Yeah?"

"I'll tell you the truth. I don't trust you further than I can throw City Hall with one hand — "

"Danny, I promise you. This one will be completely objective, with no angles rung in — "

"No hooks, Rocky?"

"Absolutely! A completely objective story to let the people in this town know what and why Danny Newman really is what he is."

Danny laughed. "That could mean anything, Rocky."

"Danny, this will be a completely unbiased story — to put you into proper perspective in relation to this community."

Those were almost exactly the same words Ted Allen had used. It sounded good, a wonderful opportunity to get to the whole community with the true story — to change the picture the newspapers had created about him thus far.

"Okay, Rocky, I'll take your word — no hooks."

"No hooks, Danny."

But he still didn't trust the reporter. He feared he might find himself on the receiving end of a grand double-cross which could stink up his relations with Helen even more. He wondered if Ted Allen would kill the story if Hayes wrote something that would bitch up his position in the community worse than it was already. They made an appointment for next Wednesday, and Hayes said he would come up to Danny's office to interview him there.

"And no hooks, Rocky," Danny reminded the reporter again.

"No hooks — "

Danny still didn't believe the reporter, but he decided he had to gamble on Allen keeping Hayes in line.

Chapter 49

Tuesday morning —

A serious case of influenza forced Danny to hole up in bed.

Helen borrowed some kind of electric contraption from her mother — it threw steam out of a spout when you filled the aluminum container with water — and Danny sucked the steam into his lungs through the narrow opening at the small end of a cone he made with some newspapers. It was boring, but the doctor warned him to take good care of himself or his influenza could develop into pneumonia. His temperature had hit a high of 102.8 degrees the night before, and the doctor, an old friend of Helen's father, came to the house to shoot in some penicillin. Danny had his appointment the next day with Rocky Hayes and he wanted to be well enough to be there.

The house was quiet. Ruth had gone to school, Esther was over at the college, and Helen had taken Linda over to The Park Lane to stay with her mother, so Danny could have a peaceful house in which to rest.

"Psychosomatic," Helen called his illness. "Probably a reaction to all the pressure you've been under the past few weeks. You need plenty of rest to get well."

He didn't argue.

It was Helen who insisted on calling the doctor Sunday afternoon when Danny told her he felt utterly exhausted. He protested that he was just tired from not enough sleep, but Helen insisted it must be more serious than that — his face was so pale.

The telephone rang.

Danny tossed the newspaper cone aside and grabbed his bathrobe. The sweat was pouring out of all the pores of his body. Wrapping the robe around his shoulders, he dived across the room to pick up the phone from on top of the dresser. The voice at the other end of the line sounded vaguely familiar, "Is Danny there?"

"Speaking — "

The caller identified himself. Bill Sully. A reporter for the Evening News who had frequently smeared Danny in his by-lined articles.

"Yeah?" Danny was not friendly.

The reporter went on, with sugar in his voice. "Danny, I've got that release you called in here yesterday.

About that letter you received from Albert Einstein."

"Yeah?"

"I just wanted to check it with you to see if I got it straight." He slowly read the letter aloud. *"I am convinced"* — the reporter kept his voice flat and toneless — *"that you did the right thing and fulfilled your duty as a citizen under difficult circumstances."* There was a pause, and then Sully asked, "Was that all, Danny?"

"That's all." Danny, shivering, pulled his robe tighter around his shoulders. "Just that, and then his signature."

"Danny "

"Yes?"

"Danny. — Exactly how did it happen that a famous guy like Einstein sat down to write you a letter?" Bill Sully bubbled with a big laugh, "Do you have any interesting ideas on how it happened?"

Danny's reply was coldly impersonal, as he deliberately refused to respond to the reporter's attempt to make the conversation friendly. "I wrote him a letter." He carefully selected words which could not be given a twisted meaning. "I told him that the advice he gave to someone else who asked for it, not to cooperate with Congressional committees invading the freedom of one's mind, no matter what the consequences; I told him that his advice had a great influence in helping me reach my own decision not to answer the questions of the House Committee on Un-American Activities."

He stopped there, deciding not to tell Bill Sully that he had called George Hernandez to ask George what he thought about the idea of writing to Einstein, that George had said it was a good idea and that he was sure there would be a reply — George would talk to some people who knew Einstein — and there would be the kind of reply that Danny could release to the newspapers to strengthen his position.

"Danny" — Bill Sully bubbled up another laugh, as if they were both getting a great kick out of talking to one another — "did Einstein give you permission to release his letter?"

"Permission?" Danny stalled. "What permission?"

"Permission to release his letter, the letter you got from Einstein."

"It was *my* letter — "

"But, Danny" — Bill Sully kept on laughing — "the question is: did Einstein authorize you to release his letter to the newspapers?"

Danny held his robe together at his neck. "I assume," he began hesitantly, refusing to give Bill Sully a pointblank answer to his question "I assume Einstein knew I wrote to him with the idea of getting back a reply I could use." Danny wiped the sweat off his forehead. "Einstein's not that naive, Bill, to send me a letter, in reply to the kind of a letter I sent him, without expecting me to use it — publicly — " Danny guessed that the reporter had news of some development which he was concealing. Sully was too confident — he had something in his pocket. "Doesn't that sound logical to you?" Danny suggested, trying to get Sully to reveal the additional information he had.

The sweat rolled down his face and he blew several drops off his upper lip. His entire body was drenched with sweat.

"Danny," the reporter began, and he wasn't laughing any more; he was giving it to Danny, slowly, significantly — "Danny, Einstein says he never meant for you to use his letter for publicity purposes."

Danny felt a terrible urge rise up within his throat to get the whole lousy business out of his system; he tightened his throat and swallowed the sour mess.

It was a little while before he could talk.

"What do you mean?" he managed to croak, all cockiness gone, as he visualized how this could wipe out the gains he had made in trying to win over or at least neutralize the community.

"I've got a statement here, right in front of me, from Einstein," said Sully, seeming to be enjoying himself. "He admits he wrote you the letter, but he says it was private — without authorization for official use. This is a direct quote — '*It was not right for him to use it that way.*'" The reporter was silent for a while, letting the knife sink in a little deeper. "That's what he said."

Danny felt heartsick.

He knew how Sully would blow this up and how it would affect Helen. The sweat poured down his neck, his chest, his legs — streaming out of every pore of his body. Everything had suddenly turned very bitter. No one was to be trusted or depended upon. Not even Einstein. That god had turned into just another ordinary human being who didn't care what effect his statement would have on him.

"Did he say anything else?" he asked Bill Sully, stalling for time to think, keeping his voice calm.

"That's it, Danny, that's all."

And Danny mustered a sarcastic laugh. "I guess that's enough."

The reporter's laugh this time really sounded friendly. "I would think so." And then he invited a comment, what Danny recognized as baiting a trap for him. "He's given you a rough deal — "

Danny had sense enough to keep his mouth shut. He wasn't going to let himself be drawn into a public wrestling match with an internationally famous scientist like Albert Einstein.

The reporter nudged him, "Don't you want to comment on his statement?"

Danny thought quickly. Should he say that he thought Einstein meant for him to release the letter to the newspapers, that otherwise he would not have released it. He himself couldn't understand it. Einstein must have expected him to use the letter. Otherwise, why write it? — Was it so I would save the letter for my grandchildren and tell them I received it from the great scientist? — Einstein must have known that his repudiation of the use of the letter would cause problems.

"We're going to carry *his* statement, Danny," said Bill Sully, warning that it would be wise for Danny to say something in his own defense.

"I'll call you back in a few minutes, Bill." Danny swiped the sweat off his face again. "I'll draw up some statement or something." But he still wasn't sure he wanted to say anything publicly. Maybe it was best to let the whole matter drop, to flush it down the drain along with everything else including his marriage and go somewhere else alone and start a completely new life where nobody would know him. "I'll call you back, Bill, in a few minutes."

Sully pressed for an immediate statement, warning that he had a deadline to make and Danny might miss out if he didn't give a statement right away, but Danny stood his ground and Sully finally agreed to wait for the return call.

Danny put down the phone.

He went into the bathroom and used a Turkish towel to wipe off the sweat soaking his face. His pajamas felt cold and clammy underneath his bathrobe. He tightened the robe around his neck and shoulders and went back into the bedroom and sat down on the bed.

He slid under the covers. The shades were still drawn. He switched off the lamp beside the bed, and the room became almost completely dark. He lay with his head on the pillow, staring up at the ceiling. The odds against him seemed too great to keep trying. But then he thought about the kids — what kind of visiting rights would any judge award him after the opposition's lawyers had finished doing a job on him because of his political beliefs? The thought of being separated from the kids that way, maybe never seeing them again all the rest of their childhood lives, forced him to try to figure some way out of the latest setback.

He finally decided to send a wire directly to Einstein. It took him almost a half an hour to word that short message exactly so —

"*My deepest apologies. I mistakenly assumed you sent me your message to be used publicly. Surprised to hear otherwise from newspaper reporter. Sorry.*'"

He telephoned the telegraph office. Then he telephoned Bill Sully who took down the wire and then tried to get Danny to comment on whether or not he thought Einstein had been fair in giving out the kind of statement he had given to the press. Danny sensed that the reporter was trying to embroil him in a public pissing match with Einstein, a contest which would make him appear a stupid fool — he felt too much like that already.

"He wasn't fair to you, was he, Danny?"

"No comment."

"You thought he meant for you to use his letter. He gave you that impression, didn't he?"

"No comment."

"Isn't that what you're saying in your telegram, Danny? Aren't you saying you thought he meant for you to use his letter publicly?"

"The wire speaks for itself."

"Then that's what it means, that you were given the impression that it was all right to use his letter. Is that how you want to be quoted, Danny?"

"No comment."

"Well, then what *does* the wire mean, Danny?"

"No comment."

"You don't think he should have given out that kind of statement, criticizing you for using his letter, do you, Danny? You thought he meant for you to use his letter publicly, didn't you?"

"No comment."

"But he wasn't fair to you, was he?"

"No comment."

"Did you use the letter deliberately, knowing he didn't want you to use it?"

"No comment."

"Then you *did* use it deliberately, knowing he didn't want you to use it."

"No comment."

"Danny, what are you afraid of?"

"No comment."

And Bill Sully gave up and said, "Okay, Danny — "

"No comment."

The reporter laughed heartily.

"No comment," Danny repeated, flatly, dully, like a phonograph record.

"Okay," Sully conceded, "no comment."

"No comment," Danny repeated again, in the same monotone.

"Hey, Danny" — Sully seemed to be enjoying himself — "can't you say anything else?"

And Danny had a strong impulse to say, "Yes, go fuck yourself, you dirty sonofabitch, you rotten bastard!" But he restrained himself. "No comment."

Sully said good-bye and hung up.

Danny telephoned The Courier and spoke to the man on the city desk. Yes, they also had Einstein's statement. Danny read off the telegram he had sent to Einstein, and the man on the desk said he would call Danny later if the reporter assigned to the story needed any further information.

About an hour later Rockland Hayes telephoned. Danny assumed Hayes had called about the telegram.

"Danny, I've been trying to reach you at your office."

"I've been home all day, trying to get over a case of the flu."

Hayes expressed his sympathy and then told Danny he was calling to postpone their Wednesday appointment for the interview. "I've got another feature I've been assigned that has to go into the business and labor section of the paper this Sunday. Something special the front office wants me to handle right away, Danny. Maybe I can get to your story next week."

It sounded like a brush off, and Danny wondered if this was the result of what had happened with Einstein. He could think of nothing to say to Hayes.

"I'll call you some time next week," the reporter said. "We'll arrange some other time."

"Thanks," Danny mumbled.

"Take care of yourself."

"Thanks."

Feeling completely whipped, Danny slid back into bed.

His eyes opened.

Helen was standing in the doorway, her hand on the doorknob. A shaft of light shone into the dark room from the hall. The shades were still drawn, but he could tell that it was nighttime already. Helen strained forward, trying to see his face, to see if he was awake.

"Hi," he said, quietly, and he reached over and switched on the lamp on the night table on his side of the bed.

"How do you feel?" Helen asked, and he knew right away — from the sound of her voice and from the look on her face — that she knew about Einstein saying he had no right to give the letter to the newspapers. She had left home in the morning full of smiles and all kinds of optimism and friendliness. Now she was cold and distant again.

"I feel all right." He heard the sound of the television set in the den. The kids must be watching television. He wondered if everybody had eaten already.

"Are you hungry?" Helen asked. "Do you want to eat something?"

"No, thanks. Not right now." He was afraid that if he ate anything now he would throw up.

"Have you read the evening paper yet?" Helen asked.

"No." — She must know he had no way of seeing it. — "I haven't seen it."

"Einstein says" — her voice was filled with accusation — "you weren't supposed to give his letter to the newspapers."

"I know — "

She jumped him. "Did you know that he didn't want you to release his letter and yet you released it?"

"I didn't know."

"Then how did you know about him criticizing you for giving the letter to the newspapers — if you haven't read the paper tonight?"

He sat up in bed and pulled the bathrobe around his shoulders, covering his neck. The sweat was beginning to run again. He refused to look at Helen while he explained, "The newspaper reporter called and asked me to comment on what Einstein said." Then he realized how completely he had been trapped and used by Bill Sully. "Did they report the wire I sent to Einstein, apologizing, explaining it was a mistake?"

"There's nothing about any wire from you. Just a headline on top of a long story about Einstein saying you weren't authorized to reveal his letter."

"The hell with it." He closed the robe tighter around his neck to keep out the draft. "The hell with it."

Helen leaned her shoulder against the door frame. With a wan smile on her face, she shook her head slowly from side to side. He saw that she was feeling sorry for him. "How did it happen?" she asked.

"The hell with it." He didn't want to talk about it anymore.

"Mother had three phone calls already from her friends," said Helen. "They want to know the true story. They didn't think you would give out the letter without first getting permission."

"What did *you* think?" he challenged, trying to hide the anger and the hurt.

"Me?"

"*You.*"

"Well — "

She didn't seem to know what to say. He waited, relentlessly forcing her to reply.

"Danny, I — " She stopped.

He waited.

"Danny — I — I didn't know what to think — "

"Thanks," he said, coldly acknowledging her lack of loyalty. "I never thought about it. I took it for granted he sent me the letter so I could use it publicly in the community. I never dreamed there would be any kickback like this."

Helen stared at him for a long while before she slowly shook her head and let out a heavy sigh.

"You poor guy. You always do the wrong thing, don't you?"

"I thought he meant for me to give out his letter so it would help get a friendly reaction in the community. I thought he was going out of his way to help me — "

"Well, you can be sure of one thing now," said Helen. "This hasn't helped you, not the way it's worked out. You would have been better off if he had never written you a letter."

"I know."

She stood there in the doorway, not knowing what else to say, and he didn't want to say anything else to her. He wanted to be left alone in the darkness without interference from her or anyone else. He hated the world, he hated himself.

"Aren't you hungry?"

"No."

"You should eat something."

"Not now, thanks."

"Do you want something later?"

"No, thanks. I'm going to rest." He turned the switch and the room was in darkness again.

Helen stared into the room, trying to see his face in the darkness. "I think I'll sleep on the studio couch in the den tonight."

"Okay." His voice sounded very gruff when he heard it.

"You'll be more comfortable," said Helen, "with the whole bed to yourself in here."

He was too heartsick to answer.

Helen closed the door and he was alone in the dark.

A long while later Helen returned, bringing some hot chicken soup and a plate of crackers on a tray. Without a word she opened the door and switched on the light in the room. She put the tray down on the edge of the night table and went out.

He ate. And then he sat there, mulling over the situation.

The kids came and stood in the doorway — far away from him and his germs — to say good-night to him and throw kisses to him before they went to bed. Esther was with them and she asked Danny how he felt and then went up to her room on the third floor.

The telephone rang. He let Helen answer it downstairs. She came up the steps and called to him that Art Manchester was on the phone — she offered to tell Art that he was sleeping, but he said he would talk to Art, using the extension phone in the bedroom. He got out of bed.

"Hi, Art — "

"How you feeling?"

"Fair. What's up?"

Art Manchester told him some of their local union officers were puzzled about what Einstein had said. They couldn't understand why he had knifed Danny that way.

"Neither can I, Art."

Art Manchester told Danny not to worry about it. "The sentiment in the shops is good. Two local unions out here in North Tonawanda have already passed resolutions supporting your position. There wasn't a single dissenting vote at either meeting after I told the full story about why you refused to answer any questions."

Back in bed after talking to Art Manchester, Danny thought over the entire situation. The news about the action taken by the two local unions was encouraging, but he couldn't conquer the tremendous feeling of despair which filled him up to choking every time he thought of what was happening to the campaign he had mapped out to win over or at least neutralize that section of the community whose favor Helen felt she must have in order to be at peace with herself.

He switched off the light and stretched out on his back in bed. He couldn't understand it. Einstein's a brilliant man, smart enough to know he was pulling the rug out by giving out that kind of a statement. Such a big man. Why did he act so small?

His bitterness flowed over. Heroes, he told himself, even the greatest of the great minds — are human beings who go to the toilet like everyone else, and they have human failings like everyone else, and it's a great mistake to expect more from them than you would expect from people you live with and work with every day.

He thought he had learned an important lesson the hard way — that the best of people, those you trust and believe in the most, can fail you, especially when you need them the most, when the pressure is on.

He heard Helen moving around in the den and guessed that she was getting ready to go to bed. He listened to her go back and forth to the bathroom, and then there was silence — he knew she was lying on the studio couch. He lay awake for a long time after that, wondering if there was any sense in trying to save their marriage from falling apart. Wouldn't it be better to cut it cleanly in two, without all the ragged edges which come from trying to fight against the inevitable? Wouldn't it be better to try to start a new life, based on a firmer foundation than the one on which Helen and he tried to build their marriage? He covered his sweaty face with his cold hands. He knew other people who had started over again, even though they also were past forty, even though they had kids by their first marriage — kids they had to leave behind with the first marriage partner; they started over and built a new life for themselves — and got some happiness out of life. He dug his fingernails into his cheeks as he wondered if he also could do it.

Chapter 50

The following Monday —

"Danny" said Lillian Fox, her pretty face glowing with excited anticipation of his reply, "I've been wanting to ask you — "

The two of them were seated in the living room. Helen had just left them, going into the kitchen to look at the pot of stew she was cooking with a new recipe which Lillian, her best friend, had brought over that afternoon. Danny returned Lillian's gracious smile. She was always the lady, always dressed in the latest fashions offered to milady in Buffalo's highest priced specialty shops — and she had been a very good friend to Helen for as long as he had known anything about their relationship, which extended back to their early high school days.

"What do you want to know?" He kept the smile on his face, though he was apprehensive about what was to come.

Lillian flounced her loosely pleated skirt and pouted. "Now, Danny, why didn't you get permission from Einstein before — "

His face hardened and he stopped listening. He watched her face shifting animatedly as she worked hard to overcome his resistance. She knew he had withdrawn from her and she was trying hard to reach him. He didn't want to be reached. He didn't want any more discussion on that subject. She finished talking with a breathy giggle of anticipation, her head thrown back, her eyes bright and twinkling, her black hair framing her small features — the white face and black mascaraed eyelids and the black penciled eyebrows and the moist red lips.

"Tell me how it happened — "

"It happened," he said, flatly.

"You must have asked Einstein for permission. Didn't you?"

He shrugged.

"Why didn't you?"

"I never thought of it. I got the letter from him and I gave it out."

"Oh, Danny" — an expression of horrified disapproval — "you know better than that."

Feeling like a stupid jackass, he shrugged, too fed up to try to explain.

"It's too bad," said Lillian, "it's too bad."

Fortunately, at that moment Linda and Lillian's little girl Sandra came whooping down the stairs and provided Danny with an opportunity to change the subject. He met the two children at the bottom of the stairs and swept both of them up into his arms. The two children yelled to be put down and he told them they would be put down if they stood still for a few minutes and finished the ginger ale that had been brought in for them earlier. They agreed. He handed Sandra to Lillian and held Linda on his lap while the overheated little redhead drained her glass of ginger ale.

"That's the girl," he said to Linda, deliberately making conversation about nothing to keep the talk away from the disturbing subject. Linda squirmed off his lap, and he patted her small hind end playfully. "Take Sandra upstairs and watch television, quietly, and rest."

Linda took Sandra by the hand, and the two children raced up the steps, laughing and giggling.

"Crazy kids," Danny said to Lillian, and he made a great show about looking up the steps after them and listening to the noise they were making upstairs. "But they're good kids. I guess all the noise is normal."

He returned to a seat in the living room.

He wished Helen would come back from the kitchen.

"Do you have a light, Danny?"

Lillian Fox puffed several times to get her cigarette lit and then she leaned forward and looked past Danny toward the kitchen. He wondered what she had in mind now — and then he realized that she was checking to see if Helen was still busy in there. He heard the sound of the refrigerator door being opened in the kitchen, and then there was the sound of the door slamming, and then the sound of Helen's footsteps hurrying back and forth between the refrigerator and the stove and the sink.

"Danny" — Lillian Fox moved closer to him, so she could

speak lower, and he smelled the fragrance of her pungent perfume — "Danny, you know I'm your friend."

She stopped there, waiting for him to acknowledge that.

"Yes," he said, politely, but at the moment he wasn't sure he had friends anywhere except among the people in his union.

Lillian Fox tossed her head. "I probably should mind my own business — "

He didn't want to be rude, so instead of agreeing with her he remained silent. Lillian rushed on, moving her face close to his so she wouldn't have to talk too loud and risk being overheard by Helen in the kitchen.

"I can't be quiet when I see how miserable Helen is. We've been friends for so long — I've never had a sister — and I've always considered her more like a sister than only a friend. I think it's my duty to her to say something now. You're probably too close to her every day and you don't see what's happening to her as clearly as I do — "

He kept his eyes fixed on her earnest face as she pressed her moist lips firmly together and folded her hands in her lap.

"There's no happiness for you or Helen or your children in this town. You two have been our best friends — we'll hate to be without you here — but for your own good, for the good of Helen and the children, I think you've got to leave this town and go somewhere else where you're not known and you can start off without the stinking reputation you've acquired here in this town. You can start all over again, someplace where nobody knows you — and you can start with an absolutely clean slate."

She put her hand on his elbow to keep him from interrupting.

"Danny, you must face the fact that you'll never be able to overcome all that's been said against you in this town. You're through here. You don't have a chance if you stay here. You've become a symbol. And those forces who are opposed to you and what you stand for are determined to break you. And they'll stop at nothing until they do!"

"I'm not going to run away." He stubbornly shook his head.

"It isn't running away! If you're standing in the middle of

the highway and an automobile is racing at you, you've got to move out of its path, don't you?"

He stubbornly shook his head, resenting her insistence. But she pressed on.

"Danny, believe me — I'm in your corner. I've talked to a lot of people in this town about you, defending you. I'm your friend, Danny, your friend, believe me!"

He silently nodded.

"But you're done here, Danny! You're done! — It's too late, it's too late — you're convicted and condemned and sentenced, in their minds, and they're never going to give up until they hang you as an example to anyone else who might be thinking the same thoughts you have. I've argued for you, but instead of winning friends for *you* by arguing — we are losing all the other friends we have in this town, they're afraid to be seen with us" — she hesitated and added, "like we're afraid to be seen with you."

Feeling like he had been whipped over the head, he avoided her eyes. He could hear sounds from the kitchen — Helen taking dishes out of the cupboard.

Lillian started again. "Danny, you ought to know this — so you know the situation you're up against. A number of our friends have given us an ultimatum. They won't be seen with us any longer — if we continue our friendship with you and Helen."

"I'm sorry," he said.

Lillian gave him a quick smile and then became serious again. "Don't you think you'd be happier away from this town?"

He toyed with the cigarette lighter.

"Has Helen spoken to you about her plans?" he asked.

"About going to Florida?"

"Yes — "

"Well, she told me something about it."

"Did she tell you that I disagree with her?"

Lillian raised the cigarette to her lips but did not put the end of the cigarette into her mouth. "I knew you would, Danny." She gripped the end of the cigarette with her red moist lips and breathed in and then blew a stream of bluish-gray smoke up into the air over her head. She had her left hand on her hip — and he thought that she always posed, unconsciously, like a fashion model in a magazine illustration.

"Obviously, Danny, you think it's best to stay here and fight it out. But if you do that, will Helen be able to take it? You won't have many friends. Some of us who want to be your friends simply can't afford to be seen with you. Especially if you continue to remain in the public limelight by trying to fight this thing through. I'm being brutally honest with you, Danny, for your own good."

"Thanks, I prefer it that way — and I appreciate it. But I feel this way about it, Lillian. Once you start running, there's no end to it — you have to keep running the rest of your life."

They stared into one another's eyes for a moment, and then Lillian dropped her gaze.

"That's your point of view," she said quietly, "and I admire you for it — but I don't think you're going to be able to work things out with Helen if you continue to live in this town." She reached across the coffee table and tapped ashes off the end of her cigarette. "You probably are too close to this to be able to be objective, Danny, but I think you should know that Helen's at the end of her rope — she's on the verge of a nervous breakdown — "

"I think she'll come through."

"Don't be too sure."

"Running away won't help her. And it won't solve our marriage problems. I think I know Helen well enough to know that she would never respect me fully if I caved in and ran. We'd have a lousy marriage after that."

"This way," said Lillian, with a dramatic upward glance, "this way you will probably have *no* marriage."

"Or a darn good one if it works out — "

"*If* it works out — "

"I'd rather have it that way, Lil. The other way it would be so bad we'd be better off if we broke it up."

Lillian flashed her bright smile. "I'm sure you know what you're doing." She called out to Helen. "Do you need any help with the stew in there?"

Helen called back, "No, I'll be through in a minute — I'll be right there."

There was an awkward silence after that.

Danny wondered what Lillian was thinking. He tried to

smile at her.

"Danny" — Lillian impulsively reached over and put her smooth long-fingered hand on top of the clenched fists he was resting on the edge of the coffee table. "Danny," she repeated, staring deep into his eyes to let him know she was expressing the greatest depth of sincerity. She wet her lips with the tip of her pink tongue.

"Always remember one thing, Danny — "

He warily waited while she squeezed his fists with her cool long fingers.

"I'm always your friend, no matter what happens. Always remember that." She looked towards the kitchen and then spoke very fast, trying to finish what she had to say before Helen returned. "I know you're good for Helen. You've changed her so much — for the better, as a person. She's beginning to work steadily on her illustrations. And she's beginning to feel like she can accomplish something in her life — that she has a purpose — that she isn't just a sex box for some man to come home to so he can satisfy his needs without regard for her broad needs as a human being. That's what Helen always resented so much about being a woman. — And you've helped her so much, she's changed so tremendously in that respect. I give you full credit for that, Danny. You've probably saved Helen from an awful unsatisfying mixed up life. You deserve full credit for that. But you're going much too fast for her now. She hasn't been able to keep up with you. Slow down. Give her a chance to catch up."

Helen was coming in from the kitchen.

Lillian took her hand away from his clenched fists and sat back and took a long drag on her cigarette.

Helen's face was flushed from rushing around in the kitchen and working over the hot stove. She sat down in a chair beside the coffee table.

"What were you two talking about?" she asked.

Danny wondered how much of their conversation Helen had overheard — and he looked at Lillian, letting her answer Helen's question.

"Oh," said Lillian, very bright and brittle, "we were talking about you and Danny and life, — and I gave my opinion which I probably should have kept to myself — that I think the two of you will be much happier if you get out of this town for a while until all this unpleasantness blows over and is forgotten." She smiled at Danny, with dimples forming in her cheeks. "And your stubborn redheaded husband, the stubborn thing that he is, listened to me and was too polite to tell me to mind my own business — but that's what he was thinking, weren't you, Danny?"

Her combination of flippancy and directness drew from Danny a smile of appreciation — she had handled this embarrassing subject so gracefully. But Helen was even more of a surprise to Danny — she appeared to be completely undisturbed as she lit a cigarette and picked up one of Lillian's children's stories.

"Let's talk about something more pleasant," she said and went on to discuss one of the bits of action which she thought would be a good subject for an illustration to go with the children's story.

It was not until Lillian left with her little girl, taking Linda along for a ride, that Helen asked Danny what Lillian said. He told her all he could remember, withholding nothing. Helen listened without comment until he was through.

"It's Harry," she said, simply, still surprising Danny by not appearing too disturbed — Harry was Lillian's husband — "Harry refuses to be seen with you because he's afraid he might lose some of his patients." She started to collect the dirty cups and saucers form the coffee table. Danny picked up the two glasses the children had used.

"Well," he said — following Helen toward the kitchen —"what Harry or Lil thinks or says or does shouldn't bother you much longer. Ruth will be through school in a month or so and you'll be leaving for Florida."

Helen stopped in the passageway to the kitchen, blocking his path. Both of them knew he was sounding her out.

"Danny — "

"What?"

"Would you be willing to come to Florida with us to look around and see if there's anything down there you might want to do? You can always come back here if you find you don't want to stay down there."

She waited for his reply — and he knew she must have

figured this suggestion out as a means of solving the clash between them. But he also knew that such a course of action would solve nothing, merely put it off. She was still waiting. He felt very sad.

"Helen, we've got to lick this thing here." He saw her eyes fill up with tears, and he tried to explain. "There's no use going anywhere until we lick it here. If we lick it here I'm sure you won't want to go anywhere else, any more than I do right now. It's no good going somewhere else unless it comes naturally out of what we're doing, out of my work and out of your work. It's no good to run away."

She looked away from him. "You won't compromise, will you?"

"That's not compromise, Helen. That's surrender!" But he wondered if he was being unreasonable. "That's surrender to the worst possible thing we could do. Running away!"

She shook her head, disagreeing, but unable to speak.

"Yes, it is," he insisted, "it's surrender — but with some sugar on it to make it taste better. Let's not fool ourselves. We can't be happy in Florida if we go there without settling the problems we have up here now. Those problems will haunt us wherever we go, and they'll seem much worse down there in Florida because we'll be running away from them, while up here we're grappling with those problems, dealing with them, trying to do something about them, trying to find a solution."

She stared into space. "What problems are you talking about now?" she asked, and he thought she sounded completely disgusted with him.

He explained.

"The problem of you and me reconciling our different backgrounds and our different experiences in life — the different viewpoints we have as a result of these different backgrounds and experiences. How to maintain our integrity as human beings while we reconcile those differences. How to live together as honest people. How to have an honest marriage — one where we both give something to the other — and where both of us get something from the other — "

He was fumbling.

"Danny," Helen cut in, "I don't think you know what you really want —"

"I wouldn't say that."

"I would."

"I may not be able to put it into exactly the right words, but I think I generally know what I want — at least the general direction in which I want to travel with my life, our life. The direction in which I would like both of us and the children to travel. A way of life which will be happiest for all of us in the long run. A way of life which has solid foundations rooted in the realities of life — "

"You don't know what you're talking about — "

"I think I do."

"I don't think you do!"

"I think I do!"

"And I think you don't!"

They stood there, glaring at one another, Helen holding the cups and saucers, Danny holding two glasses.

"You want a happy family life," Helen accused him, "and yet you want to live as though you don't have a single responsibility to one other person in the whole world."

"That isn't true!"

"It *is* true!"

"It isn't true!"

"It is true!"

Suddenly the ludicrousness of the situation hit both of them — and they laughed guiltily.

"It's a draw," said Danny, trying to be funny.

But his attempt to make a joke out of it had the opposite effect.

"It's nothing to laugh about," said Helen, becoming grim and serious as she went on into the kitchen.

Danny followed.

Helen dumped the dirty cups and saucers into the sink and went over to the stove and lifted the cover off the pot of steaming stew. She stirred the stew.

"I'm sorry," said Danny, after he had put his two glasses into the sink.

She didn't bother to reply, and he became full of regret at the inept way he had disposed of her attempt at compromise. He belatedly thought of a number of more tactful ways he could have handled the situation but it was too late to try to go back and do it over.

"Go out and get the kids," said Helen coldly, "and get ready to eat."

"Okay."

He dutifully went out to perform the errand Helen had given him.

Chapter 51

Friday —

Danny and Helen did not talk to one another all week. They continued to sleep in separate rooms. Although the North Tonawanda newspaper did carry reports that several local unions voted full support to the position Danny had taken before the Committee and although Danny left a copy of the newspaper in the kitchen where Helen would be sure to see the encouraging news item, Helen gave no outward sign of having read it.

But something did happen on Friday. Danny received an anonymous letter, a Jewish greeting card for Passover contained in a square envelope.

Passover — the holiday celebrated by Jewish people to commemorate the deliverance of their forefathers from slavery in Egypt — carried many fond memories for Danny. As far back as he could remember, each year there had been a joyous noisy Passover celebration at the home of his parents, with more and more grandchildren piling into the upstairs flat as the family multiplied.

He examined the card and wondered who had written the short message on it — there was no signature. Then he heard Helen moving around in the kitchen and he put the greeting card back into the envelope. He walked into the kitchen and silently held out the letter. Helen eyed it suspiciously while she wiped her hands dry with a paper towel. "What is it?" Her voice was cold.

"Take it. Read it."

She took the letter. "Is it open?"

"I opened it."

Helen slid the greeting card out of its envelope. It was made of parchment-like crackly paper. She looked at Danny, puzzled. "What is it?"

"Read it."

He stood beside her while she read it. **"Passover Greetings"** was printed in English on the front page of the

442

folded card, and there were also two Jewish words on the same page. He recognized one Jewish word (he could joke with his father and tell him that all the years of study at Hebrew School when he had been a boy were not completely wasted)— the word meant **"Passover"** — and he assumed that the other word which he could not translate meant **"Greetings."**

Printed in bright colors on the same page were two bunches of beribboned purple and yellow pansies.

"What's it for?" Helen, her forehead wrinkled, turned her face to him.

"Read inside — "

Helen unfolded the greeting card. She pointed at the three lines of print. "Is this Jewish writing?"

"Printing — Jewish printing. There's a difference between the written and printed script in the Jewish language, just like there is with the English language."

"Oh." Helen nodded and turned back to read what was written in English, in purple ink, underneath the three lines of printed Jewish script.

Danny leaned over and silently read it again, with her: *"With admiration and respect from your many friends."*

"Who do you think sent it?" Helen asked, and he detected a soft, somewhat awed quality in her voice.

"I haven't the slightest idea."

"It's nice of them, whoever they are." She read aloud the phrase printed in English on the inside of the folded card:

"'May the Passover season be joyful and bring new inspiration to you.'"

She turned the card over and looked at the back of it, but there was nothing printed there except the manufacturer's name and trademark.

"Don't you have any idea at all who might have sent it?" She handed the envelope and the card back to him.

"No." He sat down on the top step of the small kitchen ladder and studied the short written message. "This writing is very stiff."

Helen looked at it. "What does that mean?"

"Well, it's also written under the holiday message printed in Jewish instead of under the holiday message printed in English." He pointed that out to her with his forefinger.

"What of it?" she wanted to know.

"In all probability the person who wrote this message is more at home with the Jewish language than with the English language. Probably an older person who doesn't speak or write English too well."

"Do you know anyone like that?"

"Oh, sure — it could be some friend of my father and mother — or one of some Jewish people who work in the shops we represent."

"Maybe it's somebody you don't know at all — "

"It could be."

"Maybe somebody who read about you in the newspaper and agrees with what you did."

"Could be." He pointed at the writing again. "See how cramped that is — whoever it was who wrote it had a hard time. Couldn't write English well. Look at that, how they made a mistake and wrote over the word to correct it."

Helen looked where he was pointing. "Very interesting," she said, and she went back to the stove.

Danny remained seated on the small step ladder, keeping himself occupied with the greeting card while he pondered on how deeply Helen had been affected by it.

"Will you set the table for me, please, Danny?" Her voice sounded very friendly.

"Sure —"

"Esther's not coming home until late. This is their Friday night supper over at her sorority."

"Where's Ruth and Linda?"

"Upstairs, watching television. Leave Ruth up there. She keeps Linda quiet as long as she's with her."

"Okay." He slipped the greeting card into his pocket as he got up to start setting the table.

"Thanks," said Helen, and she went to the refrigerator.

While he was in the dining room, setting up four place mats and laying out the silverware on the table, he heard Helen bustling around in the kitchen. When he came back into the kitchen he saw that she was making the salad, slicing up a head of lettuce into the big wooden bowl.

"You drinking milk tonight too?" he asked her, and she looked at him and nodded.

"If you don't mind," she said, quite pleasantly.

"I don't mind," he said, trying to keep alive this friendlier relationship. "Four glasses of milk coming up," he announced as he proceeded to pour the milk and carry the brimful glasses into the dining room. Helen was slicing a stalk of celery into the salad bowl when he returned to the kitchen a moment later. She looked up.

"There must be many people in this community who admire you for what you've done."

He shrugged his shoulders, trying to be modest about it, and he stood and watched her finish slicing the stalk of celery. She glanced up at him.

"That must make you feel good — doesn't it?"

"Sure." He kept his tone of voice apologetic and humble, not wanting to break her friendly mood by appearing boastful. "Sure it does."

Helen reached for a shiny green pepper. "I wish I knew some of those people, like the person who sent you this card."

"I often get the feeling," Danny said, "that I'm all alone." He wanted her to know he was also unsure of himself, so she wouldn't be so disturbed by her own unsure feelings. "But then I realize that can't be so — or forces on the right would be making more drastic moves against me."

"Where *are* all these people who are in agreement with you?"

"Around — "

"Where?"

"They're there, Helen — "

"Where?"

"Everywhere. In many walks of life." And then he thought that perhaps he was acting, talking, too optimistically, too definitely, and she might resent his seeming to be too sure of his position. He hurriedly corrected himself. "At least I think they're there, Helen. I hope they're there. That's what I'm counting on."

He was silent as he watched Helen slice open the shiny green pepper. She stopped, holding the two halves of the pepper in her left hand. She was motionless for a moment, thinking hard.

"I think they're there too," she finally said, very slowly. It seemed to be a very hard concession for her to make. She looked at Danny. "It's too bad they don't show it more. That would make everything so much easier."

"In these times people tend to be afraid — and you can't blame them for that."

Helen silently cut up one half of the green pepper and started to mix the salad with her bare hands. She stopped moving her hands and turned her face to him, her eyes examining his.

"What makes *you* so damn courageous?" It was a simple, straightforward question that prompted him to drop his defenses.

"I'm afraid too, I'm scared to death."

He went to the refrigerator and got the salad dressing for her. Helen took the bottle from him and doused the mixture of raw vegetables in the salad bowl with the oily dressing. She used the big wooden spoon and fork to stir and toss the salad.

"They're too afraid," she said — and he knew she was speaking of the people in the community who agreed with him but hadn't openly indicated their support — "and you're not afraid enough!"

"Maybe," he conceded, trying to avoid an argument.

"Somewhere in between is just right. People should have the courage to openly stand for what they believe in. But they shouldn't do it alone, too far out in front of the others, like you."

He answered slowly, carefully thinking it out. "Somebody always has to be out in front. Without much choice on his own part, somebody is always made into a symbol. You don't decide you'll be a symbol; the opposition attacks you and builds you into a symbol of what they oppose — and then you can't back down, because their attack has also made you the symbol for those on your side, for those who believe as you do in freedom of speech and freedom of thought. — Once they've made a symbol out of you, embodying in your person the conflict on important issues — you can't back down without doing great damage to the cause of the people, without hurting the morale of all those people who have taken courage from the fact that you have not folded under the attack; and if at that point — once you've been built into a symbol — you retreat, you destroy not only yourself — but you help to destroy the moral courage of all those for whom you have been built into the symbol of what they believe is right. — So, almost despite yourself — and sometimes in a manner which is frightening as all hell and you wonder what will be the final outcome — you're compelled to stand firm in defense of what you have been made to represent, as a symbol, by both those who are for you and by those who are against you; and you hope that since these are modern times and we're far from the days when crucifixion and burning at the stake were the usual practice — you hope a short prison term will be the worst that may happen to you if those who are determined to crush the symbol they created win out."

Helen silently handed him the bowl of salad.

He carried it into the dining room where he placed it in the center of the table he had set. He returned to the kitchen and saw that Helen was mashing the potatoes. He stood beside her.

"Need any help?"

"You can put the salt and pepper and the ketchup in on the table."

"Okay."

When he came back from the dining room Helen was dishing the mashed potatoes out of the pot into a big china bowl. "You can take this inside now."

"Anything else?" he asked when he returned. It felt good to work together, close and friendly this way.

She gave him the dish of cooked vegetables and he joked, "Look at the steam," as he took the dish into the dining room. When he came back to the kitchen, Helen was removing the meat from the hot oven, a small roast; she carefully set the hot pan down on top of the stove and then turned to him.

"It must be wonderful to feel so confident that there are many people in the community who respect and admire you — "

"Well — "

"I wonder how they would feel if they had to live with you and take all that I've had to take because of you?"

She hadn't sounded bitter but he decided it would be wisest not to make any comment. Was she warning him that this greeting card, this expression of admiration from some nameless person or persons in the community, did not settle their personal problems?

Helen busily transferred the small roast from the hot pan to a large meat platter. He reached for the platter to carry it into the dining room but she stopped him, touching his arm.

"You go upstairs and make sure the kids get washed. I'll take this inside."

After they had eaten, Helen telephoned her mother. Danny listened to her tell Irene about the greeting card; he thought she sounded proud. Later that night, without a word of explanation, Helen moved back to their bedroom. But she slept way over on the far side of the bed, making very sure that he understood that they still had some sharp differences despite the greeting card and its **"With admiration and respect from your many friends."**

Chapter 52

Tuesday —

Rockland Hayes surprised Danny with a telephone call to the union office in the morning. Could Danny spare about an hour for the interview — so the feature article could get into this Sunday's morning newspaper? And Hayes said he'd be right over — he was calling from the newspaper office only two blocks away.

Danny had been working out a rough draft of the union's shop paper to be given out at the Westinghouse plant. The paper was supposed to be a weekly but since he had appeared before the Un-American Activities Committee he hadn't been able to make himself face the sharp ridicule he expected to get from some of the more vicious redbaiters working at that shop.

He couldn't keep ducking his responsibility and he planned to resume distribution of the shop paper that week, dealing primarily with simple bread-and-butter issues so the opposition characters would find it hard to point to anything in the shop paper they could snipe at. He still felt plenty squeamish in his stomach about the hot reception he expected to get from the redbaiters at the plant gates but he had to face it and start changing the situation by dealing with it as best as he could.

After Rocky Hayes called, Danny put away his notes, cleared his desk and tried to clean up the dusty office. The landlord was adding another floor on top of the old roof just above Danny's head, and a construction crew had already broken through some of the walls down the hall so they could hook steel girders for the new floor to the old steel framework of the building; a thick film of brick and plaster dust coated the furniture and the tile floor in the office. Danny found a dust rag in the bottom drawer and started to clean up the top of his desk and to wipe off a few chairs.

The outer office door opened and a young man in his late twenties or early thirties, wearing a gray business suit, stepped into the office. "Danny Newman," he said, telling Danny he knew him even though they had never met before.

"Rocky Hayes," Danny replied. He tossed the dust rag down on his desk and crossed to meet the visitor. Gripping the reporter's hand, Danny took the opportunity to measure the other man for a few seconds. Hayes had a stocky build and a round face with a light complexion. Even though it was chilly outdoors he was not wearing a topcoat or hat; short hair, dark brown, neatly trimmed and combed.

"How about going out for a cup of coffee?" Danny suggested.

Rocky Hayes was very pliable. "Whatever you say."

They started for the door and Danny, leading the way, did not bother to pick up his own topcoat. Like the reporter, he wore no hat. Hayes followed after him, down the narrow stairway, down three flights of steps, talking about the weather all the way down to the main floor.

"A little snappy out," Hayes said, "but the sun's shining."

"I like it this way," Danny said.

They walked briskly down the block, Danny guiding the reporter to a nearby restaurant where they sat in a booth.

They ordered coffee and Rocky Hayes took out pencil and paper for the interview. Danny watched the reporter make a few preliminary notes at the top of the folded sheets of paper.

"Did you go to some journalism college?" he asked Hayes. "I'm just curious."

"Columbia," Hayes said, and he crinkled the skin at the outer corners of his eyes in a nice friendly way.

The waitress brought their coffee. And the official interview got under way. Rocky Hayes started at the beginning. "Where were you born?" And then he followed along, through Danny's childhood, through his youth, right on up through his adult life to the present.

Danny sensed that the reporter was searching for an angle — the key to what makes Danny run. Not trusting the reporter, he was very careful with his answers.

Rocky Hayes seemed surprised when Danny told him that Buffalo had been his home most of his life, that his family had moved here from Brooklyn when he was a very young child. "That's strange," he said, "I just never thought of you as a local product."

"I went to School 47 and Hutchinson High School here," Danny said, "and even to Canisius College here for a while, a few months."

Hayes wanted to know all about it and he wrote down the names of the schools. Did he take part in any athletics? Danny told him about his football and track letters, and the award he had won as the best all-around student in his high school graduation class — and about the athletic scholarship to cover his tuition in college.

"Why didn't you finish college?"

"Well — that was back in the depression days." He could see that this meant nothing to the reporter. "Back in those days — nothing seemed exactly worthwhile. — Finish college? What for? I spoke to a lawyer and he said don't study law, too many lawyers. I spoke to a doctor and he said stay away from medicine. I spoke to a business man and he said don't go into business, too many businesses failing. College graduates back then were a dime a dozen on relief — so why squeeze every penny out of your family just for the honor of being a college graduate? Why break your neck to work your way through college? Now it seems different, but back then it seemed like a wasted effort."

Hayes nodded and made some notes, but Danny could see that the reporter didn't understand — Hayes could never know what the real thing was like unless it happened again. And then he'll remember it with a great big paralyzing hole of fear opening up in his gut each time he thinks of it.

"How did you happen to become a union organizer?" Hayes wanted to know.

Danny raced through the surface facts, telling the reporter how he had quit working in an A&P grocery store to go to New York City to make himself a theatrical career and how, eight or nine years later when he was starving in the big city, he had come home to direct an amateur theatre group which was trying to produce shows with material about current social problems.

"That's where I met my wife," he told Hayes. "Her sister brought her down to see our first performance. A year later we got married. Meanwhile, I went to work at the Curtiss airplane plant to make a living — the theatre group had disintegrated because of lack of money and World War II.

Hayes scribbled away while Danny told how he had become active in the union at the airplane plant, how he had been fired as an "undesirable" by order of the local representative of the Army Air Corps. There was no use trying to hide that fact — Rocky Hayes probably knew all about it. He told Hayes how he had carried on a pressure campaign on his own after conservative union leaders retreated because he was too hot to handle, and how he developed enough support from the community to get the War Department to reverse itself and to remove the "undesirable" tag, how he had proved he had been fired for union activity — and he told Hayes about the triumphant day when he walked back into the airplane plant and worked only that one day "for the record" and then told the foreman he was quitting. He explained to Hayes that by then he was already working as a union organizer.

"Danny, do you have any brothers?"

"Yes, six. And two sisters."

"Nine children?"

"Yes."

"Your father and mother living?"

"Yes."

"In town?"

"Yes."

"Do your brothers and sisters live here?"

"Five of my brothers and one of my sisters live here, and one brother and one sister are living out of town."

"Wonderful, wonderful."

Danny couldn't figure out why Hayes sounded so pleased.

"None of your brothers and sisters are connected with union, are they?"

"No." Danny fiddled with his coffee cup while he watched the reporter write a note about that. "What difference does that make?"

"I don't know — yet," said Hayes.

But now the reporter seemed more sure of his questions. He seemed to have found his angle.

"Is it true, Danny, that your wife's family own The Park Lane?"

"What bearing does that have on this situation?"

"It's an interesting fact, if it's so."

Danny argued vehemently that he didn't see any need to mention The Park Lane or his wife's family in this kind of article. "Off the record, my wife's family disagree about the work I'm doing. They'd resent being hooked up with me in an article of this kind. I don't see why they should be brought into it."

The reporter cocked his head to one side, thinking about it, and then conceded, "I should be able to get across the idea without actually referring to them or to The Park Lane."

"What idea do you want to get across?"

"Oh — your background — human interest — "

That explanation did not satisfy Danny. He wondered if he had been too honest with the reporter.

Hayes switched back to direct questions about Danny and the different jobs he had held from the time he had started selling newspapers when he was a little boy, methodically listing the jobs as Danny reeled them off — candy butcher at the ball park, grocery delivery boy, theatre usher, bellhop, elevator operator, balloon vendor on the streets, control chemist in the chemical plant, grocery clerk, busboy, dishwasher, waiter, assistant manager of the chain grocery store, actor, artist's model, hospital guinea pig, would-be playwright, theatre director, template-maker in an airplane plant, union organizer — and, in between, other odd jobs and some plain old fashioned bumming and hitch-hiking to see the country.

And then Hayes asked Danny the question which, only later, he realized should have tipped him off on the angle the reporter intended to use.

"What would your family like you to do for a living?"

"What do you mean?"

"How does your wife feel about your work as a union organizer?"

"Well" — Danny tried to laugh it away — "with the beating I've been taking in the newspapers lately I imagine she wouldn't complain if there were no attacks for a little while."

"Has she ever suggested doing something else?"

"Like what?"

"Some other kind of work. Something she might consider more respectable."

Danny defended his work. "A union organizer's job is

respectable."

"Does your wife think so?"

"Sure, she does." But Danny knew the reporter thought he was lying.

"What are you driving at?"

"Your mother," continued the reporter, ignoring Danny's question, "she must have been surprised when you became a union organizer."

"Why?"

"When you were younger she had no reason to think you would ever become a union organizer, did she?"

"She probably never thought of it. Neither did I."

"All your brothers and sisters are professional or business people, aren't they?"

"So what?"

"Doesn't it seem strange that you ended up as a union organizer — when all your brothers and sisters ended up as professional people or business people?"

"Why *strange*?"

Hayes tried to smile away Danny's suspicious frown. "It's certainly different."

Danny worried that this was the angle Rocky Hayes intended to use as the central theme of his article.

"Rocky, how many people are doing the work they planned to do when they were youngsters?"

"Very few, I imagine."

"It just happened that I ended up as a union organizer."

"And you like it — so you stuck to it."

"Yes."

"Why?"

Danny repeated the reporter's question — "Why?"

"Yes, why did you stick to this job as a union organizer when you didn't stick very long to any of the others?"

"Well, maybe it's because I feel I'm doing something really worthwhile. With this kind of work I've got a good reason for living. And I needed that badly when I was younger." — Danny forced himself to laugh about it, as he tried to get the reporter to understand. — "Life was always too much with me when I was in my late teens and in my twenties. Looking back, I can see that I was an extremely unhappy guy — and that's why I went into the theatre even though I had absolutely no training or background for it. I had to get away from the kind of life I was living and going into the theatre was an escape mechanism for me. But even after I went into the theatre I was very dissatisfied with my life. Gradually, I worked my way from the carriage trade theatre toward the progressive theatre, the off-beat theatre groups off Broadway, the left-wing and trade union theatre groups — and there I found myself a philosophy of life which made it possible for me to live at peace with myself."

Hayes seemed very interested. "Do you still believe in that same philosophy?"

"Essentially the same — "

The reporter stared sternly at Danny for a short while, and then asked, harshly, "Is it the *Marxist* philosophy?"

Danny laughed out loud. Did Hayes think he was so stupid that he'd get involved with him in that kind of a discussion? He was still laughing when he answered the reporter's question.

"I don't know enough, Rocky, to be able to tell you its official title."

"Well, what *is* your philosophy?"

"My philosophy" — Danny pushed his cup and saucer away and leaned his elbows on the table and rested his chin on his hands — "is to deal with life as it is, to face the reality of it— and where there's something wrong — to head right into the heart of it, to deal with it, and try to change it *no matter how difficult the job seems to be.*" He summed it up: "To deal with reality as it is. And to try to change it for the better."

"And you think *right now* that you can do this best as a union organizer. Is that it?" Hayes studied Danny's face, waiting for the reply.

"*Right now?* Yes."

"And in the future?"

A shrug. "Who knows? This union organizing game is rough on a man over fifty. But that's nine or ten years from now."

"Do you have any idea what work you might want to go into then?"

"If I change jobs?"

"If you change jobs — "

"Something worthwhile — where I can continue to deal with reality and help try to change it."

"You haven't any idea what kind of work it will be?"

"Nope. I'm counting on developing into it, whatever it might be — if I change jobs — just as naturally as I happened to develop into this union organizing job."

Hayes nodded wisely as though he had the answer he wanted, and he made some notes.

Danny waited to see what tack the reporter would switch to.

"And now — what about your children?"

"What about them?" Danny asked.

And Rocky Hayes asked a lot of questions about Linda and Ruth — how old were the children, did they mind his work, did they associate with children of union people or children of professional and business people, did they have any problems with their friends — especially Ruth, the older child — because of the stories about their father which appeared in the newspapers?

Danny sweated through the answers.

By now he was fairly certain of the angle Hayes intended to develop in his article, but he didn't know what he could do to stop the reporter from going through with that theme: Why is Danny Newman a union organizer when he should be a professional or business man like others in his family and in his wife's family? — He was much more guarded in his answers as the reporter continued to probe away.

Danny saw that the restaurant had filled up with luncheon patrons. There were a number of men and women standing up front, waiting for seats. Danny broke the interview by suggesting that they give other people a chance to sit down and eat. Outside the restaurant Rocky Hayes told Danny he'd telephone the union office the next day and read the first rough draft of the article to him.

"I want to check all my facts with you."

"Call when you got it ready," said Danny. "I'm anxious to hear what it sounds like."

On his way back to the office Danny wondered how much added headache he had let himself in for now. If Rocky Hayes did a vicious knife job on him with this article on Sunday — !

He sat at the desk in his office the rest of the afternoon, thinking, trying to figure out some way to nudge Hayes into writing an article that would help him instead of digging his grave deeper. But he couldn't come up with a worthwhile idea. And that night he had a hard time falling asleep. Helen, still hugging the far edge of her side of the bed, snored a little as soon as she dropped off to sleep. She would be mortified, he thought, if he told her she snored. But with relations steadily improving, why needle her about her snoring?

Then he remembered that he had meant to tell her that Rocky Hayes said he had contacted the U.S. Attorney's office to find out if they were planning to prosecute him for contempt — and the Attorney's office said they knew nothing about any plan to prosecute Danny Newman for contempt. But maybe it was best if he didn't mention Rocky Hayes to Helen until he saw what happened with the article in the Sunday newspaper. He lay there, awake, racking his brain to think of some way to influence Hayes to write a favorable story. He might be able to get some local unions to write letters to Hayes, or he could send Hayes copies of the resolutions which had already been passed. But they would arrive too late. He fell asleep, still without an answer.

When he awoke the next morning he thought of phoning Hayes at the newspaper office and asking him pointblank what central theme he planned to use to thread the story together — force the issue out into the open so he would have a chance to argue about it. But if Hayes was trying to hang him, a telephone call would let Hayes know he was on the right track to do the most damage. And if Hayes wasn't trying to hang him — then there was no need to telephone. Helen was still asleep. He quietly dressed and went downstairs and made breakfast for himself and the children before leaving for work.

Late that afternoon Rocky Hayes telephoned. Danny acted cordial as all hell when he spoke to the reporter, but inside he was scared and shaky — his stomach had been upset all day. Hayes dug right in.

"I'll read you this first draft, Danny. But remember — we're checking only for facts now. Only for facts. The interpretation I give those facts is my own interpretation and I'm sure you won't completely agree with me. We won't get into any argument about that. But you be sure to correct me wherever I've made a mistake on some factual matter. Okay?"

"Okay."

"Ready?"

"Shoot."

Hayes read each sentence slowly. The article began by introducing Danny Newman as a very controversial figure in the community about whom there had been much speculation. What makes Danny Newman run? The reporter did exactly what Danny had feared he would do. The facts about Danny's background were accurate; the facts about his brothers and sisters were accurate; the facts about the Stack family and The Park Lane were accurate. Hayes added it all up and then asked: "Why does this man who has been called a communist — and refuses to deny the charge — continue to cast his lot with the working class when all the rest of the members of his family and his wife's family are respectable members of the professional and business group in our Buffalo community?" — Without saying it, he insinuated that Danny was a radical screwball.

Danny listened without comment until the reporter finished reading.

"What do you think?" Hayes asked.

Danny didn't know what to say. The phone receiver was slimy with sweat from his hand.

"The facts," the reporter prompted, "are all correct, aren't they?"

"Rocky — your facts are right," he began slowly, keeping his voice as light and unconcerned as he could despite the sickness in the pit of his stomach. "Your facts are all right— as far as they go." He tried to laugh about it. "But, of course, what you do with those facts — your interpretation of those facts — "

Hayes interrupted. "I'm sure you don't agree — "

"Not quite," Danny said louder than he intended, and he forced a laugh. "Not quite," he repeated, "But you're getting paid to write the article. Not me, Rocky. And if that's your interpretation of the facts, then that's your interpretation."

"What do you disagree with?"

Danny quickly decided there was no use asking the

reporter to change his main theme: that there was something twisted and insidious about a person of a middle-class background lining up closely with organized labor, making that his life work, instead of striving to become a doctor or lawyer or dentist or teacher or businessman; and there was no use letting Hayes know how much trouble the article would create for him with Helen by publicly reinforcing the view already held by some people in the group about which Helen was most concerned.

"Rocky — "

"Yes?"

"For your own good — I don't think it's exactly the wisest thing to actually mention The Park Lane."

"Why not?"

"After all, Rocky, they're a steady daily advertiser in your newspaper, plugging their dining room and cocktail lounge. I don't think the Stack family would like it if you link me with their place when I actually have nothing to do with it. They can't help it that one of their daughters married me. Of course, personally, Rocky, I don't give a damn" — he was trying to act very unconcerned — "whether or not you leave the article the way it is or if you change it, but for the record, Rocky, I'm calling it to your attention now so you can't say I approved mentioning The Park Lane. So far as I'm concerned, you can decide to print it the way you've got it written now and you can leave yourself open — but that's up to you to decide now, after I've warned against doing it —"

"You don't think I should mention The Park Lane —"

"What do you gain? You stick your own neck out and invite trouble. They'll file a complaint with the editor, sure as hell."

"I suppose you're right —"

"It won't hurt the main theme of your story to leave the name out —"

"I suppose not."

"You can still give me the needle without needling them."

The reporter laughed. "Okay, Danny, we won't mention them. Otherwise, how do you like it?"

"You got the facts there, Rocky." He tried to sound very indifferent and objective. "And you're getting paid to write the story the way you want to write it."

"What's wrong with it? What don't you like?"

"It's your story, Rocky."

"What don't you like?"

"I love every bit of it, Rocky," Danny said, with broad sarcasm.

"What part do you object to?"

"You write it, Rocky. That's your job."

After he said good-bye to the reporter, Danny sat at his desk for a long while, trying to figure out his next move. He had to act quickly to get his people ready for the newspaper blast. That would not be too difficult. All he had to do was to telephone all the other organizers for his union in the western end of the state and ask them to pass the word along to all the local union presidents, warning them what to expect in the Sunday feature article; the local union presidents would pass the information along to other local union officers and to the chief stewards; the chief stewards would pass the information along to the department stewards in the shops; and the department stewards would tell the union membership in their shop area about the article, preparing them for what would be printed in Sunday's paper.

He mentally checked over the situation in each of their shops in the area. Fortunately, it appeared, there was no immediate *time of decision* in any one of the shops: no contracts running out, no election, no strikes. There might be some unfavorable reaction to the kind of article Hayes wrote, but it would dissipate itself before any opposition could capitalize on it and use it against the union in a serious way.

But Helen!

The newspaper would be delivered to their door Sunday morning about nine o'clock. He would have until then to decide whether or not to tell Helen anything about the story before she read it herself.

Later that afternoon Helen telephoned. She sounded friendly.

"Danny, will you stop at the grocery store on the way home and buy a loaf of bread. I forgot to get it."

"Sure. How you feeling?"

"Good. How you feeling?"

"Good. And you?"

"Good."

"That's fine."

"See you later."

"Hurry home."

He hung up. Why the hell hadn't he left well enough alone? In his anxiety to change the atmosphere in the community around Helen he had stuck his feet deeper into the quicksand. If he had left it alone Helen might have come out of it completely by herself as she seemed to be doing already. He rapped his knuckles sharply against his forehead. "You're too damn smart for your own good." That hurt. He pressed the palm of his right hand against the spot where he had hit himself.

Chapter 53

Friday —

"Why must *you* stand out on the sidewalk handing out leaflets?"

No matter how often Danny explained it, Helen found it impossible to conceive that it was important for him to pass out the union's leaflets.

His mother felt the same way. "Why should a grown man do work like that? Can't you pay small boys a half dollar to do that? Is passing out printed sheets of paper on the street a job for a man who holds such an important position in your organization?"

Danny could understand their feeling that way because he had felt the same way when he had first started his union organizer job. He still had a touch of embarrassment each time one of Helen's friends happened to pass by and see him distributing leaflets.

But he had learned that outside of going to visit people in their homes and talking to them there is no better way to keep your fingers on the pulse of the thinking of the men and women in a shop than to stand frequently in front of the plant gates offering them leaflets to read as they go in to work. The philosophy embodied in the message printed or mimeographed on your leaflets becomes identified with you as an individual, the people going into the shop start reacting to *you* the way they react to the philosophy embodied in your leaflet's message.

Danny was nervous this morning when he drove out to the gates of the Westinghouse plant — the first time he had appeared out there to distribute the weekly shop paper since he had appeared before the Committee in Albany. But he realized how important it was for him to get out there again and face the people if he was to carry on the campaign to re-unite the membership of the two competing unions, his UE union and the IUE union which had been set up with the help of the government to wipe out what they termed "the

462

communist-dominated UE."

Shortly after he had started to distribute the weekly shop paper regularly at the plant gates a young worker took a leaflet from him and tore it up and threw it back into his face, saying, "You tell Danny Newman I won't read any of his lies." — In return Danny grinned the challenge, "Listen, pal, I'm Danny Newman — you tell me what's a lie in this leaflet and I'll eat the damn thing." The young worker, carrying a lunch pail, had already walked by, but he stopped after Danny answered him. "You're Danny Newman?" — "Sure." — "Oh." — And the young fellow walked on into the shop without another word. — The following week the same young fellow took a leaflet without making any comment to Danny. After that he took a leaflet sometimes and then some weeks he didn't. That in itself became another way to gauge the thinking of the people in the shop.

There were many other workers at these same plant gates whom he had come to know as distinctive individuals even though he didn't know their names, where they came from, what work they did inside the shop or anything else about them other than their individual reactions at the plant gates when he offered them leaflets. And it was the reaction of this group of specific individuals which revealed to him the trend of the thinking of the thousands of workers who streamed in to work through the main gate where he always stood when he distributed the UE union's weekly shop paper, a leaflet with a mimeographed message on both sides of the long sheet.

Danny and the men who were going to help him distribute the shop papers parked their cars up against the tall wire fence near the big gate. He felt very nervous. He would soon find out the reaction of the people in this shop to his appearance before the Committee and also to the letter and subsequent statement of Einstein. These thousands of workers came from all sections of the city and surrounding countryside and towns; they represented different nationality groups and different religious groups and different racial groups — they were a cross-section of the entire working class community in the western end of the state.

A gray morning —

The sun, Danny saw, was still low in the east, struggling to break through the heavy clouds which spread all across the sky, creating a narrow strip of bright yellowish glow bordering the horizon.

Stan Helowicz had brought a crew of four men from his shop to help distribute the leaflets. Danny sent three of the men around to cover the less important entrances on the other side of the plant, one man to an entrance; and he and Stan and the fourth man who had come with Stan — a steward from the shop — walked over to what they called "the main gate" which led from the tremendous parking lot into the winding tunnel that passed under the outer walls of the plant to the different stairways leading up to the many assembly lines and feeder departments.

Danny knew this plant well. He had worked here when it had been an airplane factory. He had been fired as an "undesirable" when he was co-chairman of the volunteer committee trying to organize the workers into a union. He and Stan Helowicz and the chubby steward spread out across the wide opening in the high fence which was still topped with the barbed wire that had been placed there during World War II. They faced out towards the parking lot, with Danny in the middle acting as the point to split the stream of workers in two as they poured through the main gate into the wide tunnel. He would give out most of the leaflets, passing the mimeographed sheets out to both his left and his right, and Stan and the steward would catch the overflow on both sides of him. In the next half hour or so, the three of them at this main gate would give out almost four thousand leaflets to day shift workers who would jam past them.

"We're early," Stan Helowicz called to him.

Danny saw that the vast graveled parking lot was quite empty except for cars belonging to night shift workers. Those cars were parked about a half a mile away from where he was standing in front of the main gate. A few early arrivals were slowly straggling across the big parking lot.

He looked at his wrist watch.

"Twenty after six."

He and the two other men knew that within ten minutes the automobiles would start speeding in a steady stream into the parking lot; and within twenty minutes the main gate where they were standing would be clogged with men and women in working clothes, carrying their lunch buckets or holding brown paper bags containing sandwiches and cake and fruit under their arms; and about ten minutes before seven o'clock, starting time, the crowd would be so thick that workers would be jostling against one another as they hurried through the main gate to get to their check board and hang up their time checks; and by two minutes to seven the rush would be over — so suddenly it was always a surprise to Danny — and there would be only a few latecomers running to try to reach their check board in the plant before the seven o'clock buzzer would ring.

An early arrival approached.

Danny recognized the man who was wearing a white shirt and a tie.

He had the man pegged as a foreman in some small section, a petty straw-boss of some kind.

The man with the white shirt and tie did not look at Danny as he walked by. "Aren't you in jail yet?" he sullenly snarled under his breath.

Danny made himself grin, but said nothing; he was not going to permit himself to be provoked into an argument as long as none of the other workers were around to be affected by what the man in the white shirt said.

"What's the matter with him?" Stan wanted to know.

"He never takes a leaflet. He doesn't like me and what I stand for."

"The hell with him," said the steward who was with them.

For the next ten minutes or so there was an uneven flow of individual workers and small groups of workers coming from the parking lot, walking past the three leaflet distributors; some people took the leaflets, others refused to take them, silently most of the time, occasionally making some quiet remark along with the refusal. And then the flow of workers from the parked cars into the shop became a steady ever increasing stream of men and women in working clothes.

Danny heard a loud yell.

"Hey-y-y, you redheaded sonofabitch, are you back again?"

It was a friendly yell, despite the language; and Danny knew by sight, not by name, the man who was yelling at him — and this was the man's way of showing his good will. As the man approached, Danny could see his wild hair and deeply lined face glowing with warmth; the man extended his hand to take a leaflet from Danny.

"How you doing, Red?"

"Okay, pal."

The big man stood aside and carefully folded the leaflet and put it into his pocket, while talking to Danny who continued to swiftly pass out leaflets to other working men and women who poured past him.

"I thought they'd have you in jail by now, Red — "

"Not yet."

"Good." The big man with the deeply lined face patted his pocket where he had put the leaflet. "You're doing a good job, you old redhead. Keep it up."

"Thanks," Danny called after him, and the big man with the deeply lined face disappeared into the crowd hurrying through the tunnel.

The stream of workers thickened.

Danny was too busy handing out leaflets to do more than just glance at each face as it went by. There was no time to stop and talk to anyone. The men and women in working clothes lined up for leaflets as they passed, single file on either side of him, holding out their hands to him; and he peeled off the leaflets as fast as he could, one after another, concentrating on whipping off the top leaflet, over and over and over, to shove it into the next outstretched hand — and the next — and the next —

With a tremendous feeling of gratification he became aware that the people were talking to him more than they usually did when he distributed leaflets at this gate. They weren't saying a lot. A few words. And an occasional hand touching his shoulder. Or a squeeze on his arms. Or maybe just a smile.

"Hello, Danny —"

"Hi, Red —"

"Thanks," after taking a leaflet from him.

"You're back, huh, Red?"

"Glad to see you, kid."

"Good morning!"

And he threw back a reply to each one of them, a quick answer — "Hi!" — "Thank you!" — "Here I am!" — "Morning!" — always throwing the reply back without looking at those who had spoken, because they had already passed by him.

But there was still some redbaiting.

Danny knew most of the redbaiters by sight — they had been baiting him consistently, week after week, for several years, every time he appeared at the plant gates with the shop paper. He usually tried to answer their baiting with some quick retort for the benefit of others who overheard what had been said. The people — and he himself — enjoyed the spontaneity of the exchange of words.

One of the redbaiters, wearing a red leather hunting cap, approached. Seeing him, Danny furiously worked, distributing the mimeographed handbills, waiting for the usual baiting remark, alerting himself to make a quick reply.

The redbaiter passed by.

"Why didn't you print it on red paper?" he flung back at Danny out of the corner of his mouth.

And Danny clicked right back at him — "You're so color blind you wouldn't know the difference!" — tossing the retort over his shoulder at the redbaiter while continuing to pass out leaflets.

Other workers commented on the exchange.

"Pay no attention to him, Red."

"Ignorance is bliss."

"Thanks, Red" — taking the leaflet from him.

Then he saw the young worker who had once told him to tell Danny Newman he wouldn't read any of his lies and who, after that, sometimes had taken a leaflet and other times refused to take one.

The young worker walked by, and Danny felt a pang of disappointment.

But the disappointment was short-lived because Danny saw the young worker stop and come back and take a place in the line of men and women who were sticking out their hands to receive a leaflet as they filed by.

"Good morning, Red," he said to Danny, quite stiffly, when he took the leaflet.

"Hi," Danny replied, hurriedly, continuing to hand leaflets

to the people in the line which flowed past him — but Danny noticed how the young worker stepped aside and stood there, about a yard away, carefully folding his leaflet and slipping it into his pocket; and then the young fellow caught Danny's eye and gave him a nod of good-bye before starting on into the plant again. That helped a lot.

By now it was apparent that he had picked up support among these people. He had no way to gauge whether that support would have been greater or less if he had not communicated with Einstein and if Einstein's subsequent complaint about the release of his letter had not appeared in the newspaper.

Several people did refer to Einstein and his letter.

"That was a nice letter, Red, from Einstein."

"How's your buddy, Einstein, this morning, kid?"

"Say hello to Einstein for me next time you see him — "

"Has Einstein explained his theory of relativity to you, Red?"

And then one of the most vicious redbaiters came along, and Danny prepared himself for the blast he expected to receive.

The baiter snarled, "Tell that sonofabitch commy friend of yours, Einstein, to go back to Germany!"

Danny snapped around and flung his right arm out at the baiter in an imitation of the Nazi salute and shouted, "Heil Hitler!"

The baiter stopped in his tracks, stunned by the suddenness of the counterattack, then he flushed bright red and swore a string of filthy oaths at Danny who repeated over and over, "Heil Hitler, Heil Hitler, Heil Hitler!"

The baiter gave up and retreated, going on into the plant.

And Danny saw how the other workers skirted away from the baiter as if he was something contaminated.

A gray haired stooped working man wearing rimless bifocals — Danny affectionately called him "Pop" although he knew the older man only from seeing him often at the plant gates — grabbed Danny's arm and gave it a friendly squeeze.

"Good boy," he said into Danny's ear.

And he took a leaflet while Danny grinned his thanks.

A few minutes later Danny saw another one of the men who served as a sharp indicator of the thinking of the people in the shop — a man with whom he regularly exchanged friendly enemy remarks. "Whitey," Danny called him because of his white hair.

Whitey was a man in his fifties, tanned, wiry, full of bouncing energy. Danny liked Whitey, especially his good sense of humor, even though there was a sharp disagreement between the two of them in regard to political and economic matters. They had worked out an improvisational vaudeville routine which was a source of amusement to themselves and to a group of riders that Whitey drove in to work in his car. Whitey never took a leaflet from Danny, but as he passed by he would toss off some heckling remark, making Danny the butt of a joke about the current political situation; and then it was up to Danny to try to top that remark with his comeback — and the group of men who rode to work with Whitey would decide who had won the heckling exchange of words that morning, by yelling out "Whitey took this round"; or "Red gets the decision this time"; or possibly "It's a draw." The routine had originated as a bitter exchange, several years back, with Whitey and Red playing to hurt one another, to win over those who were listening; but since then the two men had come to like one another and to respect one another's wit, though they were still trying to affect those who listened to their exchange.

Danny kept flashing the leaflets off the top of the pack, giving them out as rapidly as he could, while he waited for Whitey to make a wisecrack about his appearance before the Committee or about the threat of jail or about Einstein. Whitey had plenty to choose from this morning.

Whitey and his group of riders came near and started to pass Danny.

"How are you, you redhead?" Whitey called out. Danny looked over at Whitey, alert to hear the wisecrack, straining to be on edge to snap right back with a smart reply. Whitey smiled and waved as he walked on. "You got guts, Red," he called out, and he kept on going with his group of riders following behind him.

It took Danny a moment to realize that Whitey was not going to make any wisecrack that morning — and then he yelled out, "Thanks, pal!"

Whitey lifted his arm straight up into the air so it could be seen above the crowd of heads of people walking through the tunnel; he waved his arm back and forth several times, acknowledging that he had heard Danny, and then the arm disappeared.

Chapter 54

Sunday —

As usual, little Linda woke Danny up Sunday morning by crawling into bed next to him. He started to complain sleepily that it was too early in the morning and they couldn't sleep three in such a small bed — "It's too crowded, honey." — and then he remembered about the article by Rockland Hayes.

"Where you going?" Helen sleepily asked.

"I'll be right back."

"Don't let Linda make you get up this early. You only spoil her by giving in to her." She closed her eyes.

"I'm going to the bathroom," he lied. "Let Linda stay here until I come back."

Helen's eyes were still closed and he saw that she was asleep again. Little Linda was still under the covers. He tucked the edge of the sheet and blanket in around the child's soft neck and kissed that grinning redheaded imp on the warm pink cheek. Linda enjoyed the attention. Danny heard the gleeful giggle as he carefully closed the door behind him.

Barefooted, he ran down the stairs and opened the front door. The chilly blast of air made him shiver and clutch at the neck of his pajamas.

There it was! The Sunday morning paper, fat as usual, lying there on the front stoop where it had been tossed by the newsboy. His bare feet felt the shock of the cold stone as he quickly stepped outside, grabbed the newspaper and jumped back into the house, looking wildly around to see if anyone observed him dancing in and out so foolishly — fortunately, there was no one else out on the street.

He spread the newspaper out on the linoleum-covered floor in the kitchen and crouched down on his haunches while he rapidly leafed through the pages until he found the page devoted to business and labor feature articles. He could feel his heart pounding; his hands and armpits were hot-wet

471

with nervous excitement. He searched the page — quickly! — but no article with Rockland Hayes' by-line! No article about Danny Newman without a by-line on top of it!

Maybe it had been shifted to a more prominent spot in order to give it more weight with the public. On some occasions in the past Hayes' weekly feature on labor had been moved up to the front page to emphasize its importance that week.

He turned back to the front page. No article there. He carefully went through the entire newspaper, one page at a time, examining each page, column by column. The article was not in the newspaper.

He knew that Rockland Hayes had written the article for this Sunday edition of the newspaper — the reporter had read the rough draft to him over the phone earlier in the week.

Had Ted Allen or someone else on the editorial staff disagreed with the reporter's central theme which chided the subject of the article because he had lined himself up with organized labor while the rest of his family had chosen to become professionals or went into business? Or had Hayes or someone else on the staff of the newspaper realized that the approach used in the article would develop increased support from organized labor even though it might make their subject's name a little more dirtied with much of the upper middle-class group in the community, especially with that slice of the community that Helen worried about most.

Danny folded the newspaper.

In any case he had been granted a reprieve. Temporary? Or permanent? Would the article appear next week, possibly with some changes? Maybe they were making it worse, not better. He wondered if it would be wise to telephone Rocky Hayes during the week and ask what happened. Or would that be inviting trouble? It might be best, he decided, to just let nature take its course and let what would happen — just happen.

And then he heard Linda calling.

"Daddy? — Daddy? — Daddy?"

Linda's plaintive cry came from the top of the stairs, up on the second floor. He tried to keep his voice muted so as not to wake up everybody else in the house, "What do you want, honey?"

He heard the rapid patter of Linda's little bare feet rushing down the steps, and then the grinning redhaired ragamuffin burst into the kitchen and rushed into his arms, almost knocking him over backwards. They hugged one another, tight.

"Daddy?"

"What?"

"Why did you come down here?"

"To read the newspaper."

"But you said you were going to the bathroom — "

"I changed my mind."

"Why did you want to read the newspaper?"

"To find out what's happening in the world."

"Did you find out?"

"I certainly did."

"Then — make my breakfast now. I'm hungry."

Chapter 55

Sunday — a week later —

LABOR LEADER CONTROVERSIAL FIGURE
That was the heading on the feature article which appeared under the by-line of Rockland Hayes the following Sunday; and the subhead: **Newman Thrives on Disagreement.**

Linda had awakened bright and early, as usual, and Danny had come downstairs with her, hand in hand. He sneaked outside in his pajamas and grabbed up the Sunday paper. On his hands and knees in the kitchen, with the newspaper spread out on the floor and with Linda sitting on his back, riding horsey, he found the business and labor section page — and there in the upper left-hand corner, with a small photo of his face under the subhead, was the story. Helen wouldn't like the picture. She'd say he looks too heavy and depressing, and he thought that he did look like a gloomy caricature of a funeral director.

He didn't get the chance to read the article right away.

"I want breakfast, I want breakfast" — Linda started to jump up and down on his back — "I want breakfast, I want breakfast — "

He set aside the newspaper while he got up and peeled an orange for the little redhead so she would let him read the article in peace.

"Here, honey" — he picked her up and plunked her down on top of the small kitchen ladder — "sit here and fill your face with orange while I read this story in the newspaper."

The child gleefully chortled, "Fill your face! You're silly, Daddy! Fill your face!"

"Okay," he said, to calm her down, and he put a piece of orange into her open mouth and she began to chew on it while he knelt down on the floor again to quickly scan the article written by Rocky Hayes.

He could tell right away that the article had been changed a great deal since Rocky had read it to him over the

474

telephone. The broad theme was still *What makes Danny run?* And there were still some sharp barbs in it. But most of the dirtiest sharp hooks which had been in the first draft were gone now. The angle that Danny Newman had chosen to work with organized labor when he should have been a professional man or a business man like others in his family and that such choice on his part was an evil choice — that angle had been deleted completely. Instead Rocky Hayes wrote that Danny Newman was a man — *"aged 41, but looking boyish with his short red hair and his ready grin"* — who had been searching for a philosophy of life; who had left home at a comparatively young age and worked at many odd jobs, trying to find himself; and who had found the philosophy for which he had been searching — found it when he came in contact with the theatre of social significance in New York City. And all this, wrote Rocky Hayes, explained why Danny Newman clung so tenaciously to the principles in which he believed, despite the terrible pressures which had been exerted against him in an effort to break him down. A few short paragraphs about Helen and the children followed — Hayes wrote that Danny Newman had married Helen Stack — *"a member of a socially prominent Buffalo family"* — and that the couple had two daughters. Then there was a gentle thrust — so Danny thought — where Hayes said Mr. Newman's family will be glad to hear that some of his former friends are starting to say hello to him again on the street. He remembered he had mentioned this to the reporter with no idea in mind that Hayes would use it for the article.

Linda interrupted his thoughts.

"More, more, more orange," she cried out.

"Okay, honey."

He got up and peeled another orange for her.

Back on his hands and knees on the floor, he re-read the article, trying to get out of it everything the average reader would get and he concluded that the article as it stood would help him a great deal — it made him out to be a human being, not perfect, but also without the horns of the devil.

He thought it would help a lot with Helen.

He wondered if it was editorial writer Ted Allen who had brought about the change from the first draft Rocky Hayes had read to him over the telephone.

He re-read the article several times, each time trying to gauge the reaction of different groups in the community as each would read it.

Later he showed the article to Esther when she came downstairs. She seemed to be breathless, she thought it was so wonderful. "I'm going to buy a copy of the newspaper and clip this out and paste it in my scrapbook!"

"What's a scrapbook?" Linda wanted to know.

Esther playfully grabbed at the little redhead. "Come here, you little doll, you. I'll put *you* in my scrapbook. That's where I keep all the things I want to save for later."

Linda shrieked and ran, with Esther playfully chasing her.

Danny could hear them still playing while he went upstairs to dress so he could drive Esther out to her parents' roadside restaurant in North Tonawanda. He called down to them later, asking Esther if she would dress Linda so the child could come along, since both Helen and Ruth were still sleeping.

While they were driving they talked about the article. "It's about time," Esther said, hugging the child seated on her lap, "it's about time the newspapers said something nice about your daddy, Linda, isn't that right?"

"Yes," parroted Linda, "it's about time they said something nice."

"It sure is," said Esther, and she kissed Linda on her fat cheek — a loud smack.

When Danny returned home with Linda, Helen was sitting on the top step of the small ladder in the kitchen, sipping a cup of black coffee. He saw that she had slipped into a pretty pink housecoat.

"Where's Ruth?" he asked, for lack of anything else to say.

"Asleep," Helen answered without looking at him and he knew immediately that she had not recovered from a bitter argument they had had the day before.

He turned away from her and took off Linda's quilted jacket and leggings. "Go upstairs and wake up Ruth, honey. Tell her it's time for all sleepyheads to get up, even on Sunday."

Linda shouted, "Okay," and raced off on her errand.

With Linda gone, Danny turned his attention back to

Helen.

"Did you" — he shoved his hands into his pockets and leaned back against the sink — "read the morning paper?"

Helen gave him a cold uncomprehending stare.

"No — "

Danny found the newspaper where he had left it on the dining room table. He opened it to the page where the article by Hayes was printed and then — without a word — returned to the kitchen and handed the paper to Helen. He pointed at the article. Without relaxing her cold stare, Helen began to read. Danny watched her face, waiting for some reaction to set in. He hoped that the article would counteract the anger still in her as a result of the bitter day-long argument they had had the day before.

The whole past week had rushed by, eaten up quickly for Danny by a series of grievance meetings and wildcat work stoppages and special lunch hour meetings at the Buffalo Foundry and Machine Division of Blaw-Knox where the company had deliberately violated the seniority provisions of the contract, laying off several long service men while keeping on some recently hired men. The union had filed a grievance for each of the men who had been laid off out of line with seniority. There were several wildcat walkouts by whole departments. The men returned to work when the company agreed to sit down and negotiate immediately on the grievances. Danny and the local union committee met with the company. And they held plant gate meetings on all three shifts, round the clock, reporting on the progress they were making. This went on all week and Danny spent very little time at home.

Saturday the plant was not working and he planned to spend the day at home with Helen and the kids to try to make up for being away all week. He awoke with the ring of the alarm clock at nine o'clock. He sat up on the edge of the bed, still feeling exhausted from averaging only three or four hours of sleep for the past few nights. He was dressing when Helen came into the bedroom. She stiffly stood there, looking at him while she fiddled around with a sweater she was holding. He could see she wanted to talk to him but she wanted him to open up the conversation.

He finished buttoning up his shirt before he asked her, "What's up?"

"One of these days," she reminded him, ominously, "you and I have to sit down and talk things out. We have to decide what's going to happen with us."

He faced the mirror. "Helen, I'm completely pooped right now, through and through. Let's go into this some other time, sometime when I have a little more energy."

Helen flung her sweater across the room. "You've always got enough energy to go to another one of your damn union meetings!" She stormed out of the room and slammed the door.

He had intended to stay home all day but the atmosphere in the house was so strained he went down to the empty union office and stayed there until early evening, clearing off odds and ends of correspondence which had accumulated on his desk during the week.

The telephone rang.

"You coming home sometime today?" Helen sarcastically asked.

"Sometime, I imagine."

A pause, and then she sounded more relaxed as she asked, "Would you like to go to a movie tonight?"

"Anything you say — "

She taunted him, "*Anything* I say?"

"About a movie tonight."

There was a long pause before she asked, "When are you coming home?"

"Right now" — and he couldn't resist adding, "if it's safe to walk into the house."

"It's safe."

"Should I get a hat somewhere on the way home and toss it into the house before I walk in?"

"Joke," said Helen, her voice deliberately flat to deflate his attempt at humor. "Stop trying to be a smart aleck and come home so we can eat. Everything's on the table and we're waiting for you."

"Yes, dear."

"Hurry up."

"I'll be right there, dear."

"Oh, you — "

"Yes, dear."

Helen slammed down the receiver at her end.

After they ate and tucked Linda into bed for the night, they went to a neighborhood movie house to see some cheap gangster picture, leaving Esther and Ruth to watch television. After the movie they got into the car and Danny started to drive home. Helen was very silent. Danny guessed that she wanted to talk about their situation again but he was fed up with talking about it — he desperately wanted to rest from it for a while. Helen seemed to have read his mind.

"We're going to have to talk some time," she finally said, breaking the silence.

He warded her off, asking, with feigned ignorance, "About what?"

"About us."

"Has anything changed in your mind?"

"No."

"Nothing's changed in my mind either at the moment — so what's there to talk about?"

She was silent for a while and then asked, "Do you want to stop somewhere for coffee before we go home?"

"If you want to, but let's not have any heart-to-heart talks tonight. I'm sorry but I don't feel up to it, I couldn't take one of those tonight. I've had a rough week. My rear end is dragging and I can't take it right now to stay up until two or three in the morning over a cup of coffee or a drink, baring our souls without resolving anything. I'm sorry but I can't take that right now, now when I'm so thoroughly exhausted my bones ache."

"Let's go home," she said with teeth clenched. "If your bones ache that much I don't want to interfere with your health."

"Goddamit, Helen, can't I say *anything* to you without you getting angry at me?"

She did not answer.

He drove over to a coffee shop where they frequently stopped off for coffee and toasted French pastry on other Saturday nights. He parked the car and got out and walked around and opened the door for Helen.

She didn't budge.

"Don't you want coffee?"

"I told you," she said, staring straight ahead, "I don't want to interfere with your health."

"Okay." He thought she wanted him to plead with her but he was in no mood for that. He shut the door on her side and walked around behind the car and got into his seat and drove away.

Not a word between them all the way home.

In the house, Helen went upstairs and chased Esther and Ruth to bed. Danny sat down in the kitchen with the newspaper. When Helen came down he saw she had changed into her pink housecoat and had a book in her hand. She looked at him and turned around and went into the living room. He read for a short while and then went in and said good-night to her. She did not answer.

He went upstairs to bed.

He didn't know how late she stayed up. He fell asleep the moment his head touched the pillow and slept until Linda woke him up the next morning when he went downstairs to read Hayes' article in the Sunday paper.

Danny watched Helen's eyes moving back and forth while she slowly read the article by Rockland Hayes. Suddenly, her face snapped up. He could see the mixed expression of anger and disgust.

"Did you tell them that you married *'a member of a socially prominent Buffalo family?'*"

"No — "

"Why did you have to drag me into this thing with you?"

Instantly he realized what was bothering her. How stupid not to have realized it before.

She was ashamed of him!

She was ashamed to have the fact that she was married to Danny Newman given any publicity in the community, especially in the tiny community that meant anything to her, the ostentatious sliver of Buffalo upper middle-class society to which the Stack family belonged.

She was ashamed of him! A feeling of revulsion came over him, a feeling of self-loathing, of self-hate; he felt as if he were choking — he had to consciously inhale and exhale his breath.

Fortunately, at that moment Linda came dashing into the

kitchen and shouted that Ruth was getting up. And then the little redhead grabbed his legs. Danny lifted her up and hugged her, hiding his face from her and Helen by kissing the child on the back of her neck — he kept his face hidden there while he regained control of himself. When he looked up he saw that Helen was reading the article again.

He couldn't hold in his resentment. "I told the reporter to leave you and your whole goddamn Stack family and your goddam pretentious Park Lane out of this whole thing."

Linda began to whimper.

He kissed her on the cheek. "Everything's all right, honey." She clung to his neck.

He turned his attention back to Helen, staring directly into her hostile eyes. "The reporter apparently decided to still keep in a reference to you as a member of what he calls 'a socially prominent family.'" His bitterness began to get the better of him. "Those were *his* words, not mine. I've never thought of you or your family as 'socially prominent.'" He was too hurt to stop there, even though Linda started to whimper again. "In fact, in case you don't know it yet, what I think of your family and what I've thought of them for some time now — *is very unprintable!*"

Not a muscle in Helen's stony face moved. He whirled around and left the room with Linda still in his arms. He fought against the tears filling his eyes. He took his topcoat and Linda's quilted jacket and leggings out of the closet. Helen came and stood in the doorway, holding the newspaper in her hand. He was aware of her standing there and watching him while he put on his own topcoat and started to help Linda put on her leggings.

"Where you two going?" she quietly asked.

Rejecting her effort to make peace, he answered abruptly, "Out!"

"Don't you want a cup of coffee?"

"No! Don't strain yourself. A *socially prominent woman like you* might lower her social standing if it ever got out among her *socially prominent friends* that she drank coffee with someone as vulgar and low in the social scale as a union organizer. It's bad enough she's been sleeping with him. But drink coffee with him — my God, you'll be ostracized!"

"I'll risk it."

"No, thanks."

He was conscious of her silently watching while he zipped up Linda's quilted jacket. He stood aside while she stooped to hug Linda when the child went to her to kiss good-bye. Before he could get started with Linda he heard Ruth pounding down the steps. He saw her worried face and then saw her bare feet — she was still in her pajamas.

He pointed. "Where's your slippers?"

"Upstairs."

"Go up and put them on before you stub your toe and hurt yourself."

"In a minute, Daddy — I will."

She stood there on the bottom step, her face on an even height with his.

"Go upstairs and put on your slippers," he said again.

"Where you going, Daddy?" she asked, without moving, and he thought her voice sounded troubled.

"Out," he said, too sharply, and then tried to reassure her by adding in a softer tone of voice, "out for a little walk, honey. For some exercise. I'll be back soon."

He gently touched her neck with his right hand while he wondered how much she had overheard. She studied his face and he grinned to reassure her.

"Where are you walking?" she asked.

"Nowhere in particular. Just out for a walk. Maybe I'll stop somewhere and get a cup of coffee — in some restaurant."

"Why don't you have coffee here?"

"I want some fresh air first."

She turned her face and kissed his hand and then she threw her arms around him and hugged him tight. He stroked the back of her red hair gently. Eleven year old children, he thought, are too damn wise sometimes. She kissed him, and he knew she was trying to ease the hurt which was choking him. It embarrassed him to think that his inner feelings were so damn obvious even to a child when he was trying so hard to conceal them. He felt a tug at his coat and he looked down at the little redhead.

"Daddy," Linda wanted to know, "will you buy me some waffles when we get to the restaurant?"

"Sure I will, baby." He and Ruth disentangled themselves.

Linda took his hand again. He started out of the house with her. Helen still stood in the doorway leading from the kitchen into the hall. He walked by her without a word.

"Daddy," Ruth urged after him, "come back soon."

"Don't worry, honey. We'll be right back in a little while."

Helen called out, "Good-bye, Linda."

"'Bye, Mommy," Linda replied.

He closed the door behind them.

It was good to get away from Helen. He wondered if it might not be best if he were cited and tried for contempt and sentenced to six months or a year in jail. That would put an end to the marriage. He thought he was hanging on to this marriage only because he couldn't bear to be separated from his two redheaded daughters.

Linda held his hand while they walked down the block.

The sidewalks were deserted except for three small children across the street who were riding on their tricycles. He recognized two of the children, sisters, whose parents did not like them to play with Linda because she was the daughter of the notorious Danny Newman, Helen had told him.

An automobile horn sounded and a small car pulled over to the curb a few yards ahead of him. He heard his name being called.

"Hey, Danny — "

He had difficulty seeing the face of the man inside the car because of the reflections on the car's windows. Then he saw the face and recognized Jack Ross — they had gone to high school together, and Jack lived around the corner. Jack Ross had not dared to say hello to him for a long time, because Jack was a civil service employee working for the state in a minor administrative post. There was a hand sticking out through the open window.

"Hello, Danny — "

"Hi, Jack." Danny was surprised by the note of cordiality in the other man's voice.

They shook hands.

"Daddy," Linda screamed, "I want to say hello too." He lifted her up so she could shake hands with smiling Jack Ross — a man in his early forties, with a black mustache. Danny held her so she was sitting on his right hip.

Stretching across the front seat of his car so his head was next to the open window on Danny's side, Jack Ross said, "That certainly was a nice article in the newspaper about you this morning."

"Wasn't it?"

"I was glad to see something like that for a change — instead of what they usually write about you."

"I was glad to see it too."

Ross laughed in a friendly way. "I'll bet you were!"

"I sure was."

"So was I," said Ross. "You don't know how very glad I was to see something like that."

They talked for a little while longer, then shook hands again before Ross drove away. Danny took Linda's hand and they continued on their way to the restaurant.

Ahead of them Danny saw one of the neighbors on the block, a doctor, come out of his house. Every time he saw the doctor he recalled that it was the doctor's wife who had stopped her daughter from playing with Ruth because, she explained, that kind of boycott will force Danny Newman to change his politics. The doctor was walking toward his car parked out in front of his house but he seemed to be slowing down. He got into the car but he didn't close the door. He leaned out and waited for Danny and Linda to come closer, and then he smiled at them, showing a set of big white teeth.

"Hello, Danny — "

It was the first time the doctor had spoken to him in over a year — the doctor and his wife had been giving him the frozen treatment whenever they passed on the street. Danny was torn with conflicting emotions. Should he say hello to the doctor or should he get even now by giving the doctor the cold freeze, just as he had been given it several times after he had already said hello to the doctor and his wife? He decided he would be a much bigger person if he would accept the olive branch the doctor extended.

"Hello," he replied, and he politely nodded as he walked by, tightening his grip on Linda's hand.

"Spring is here," the doctor called after him, trying to keep the conversation very friendly.

"It sure is," Danny replied over his shoulder with a polite smile.

The doctor and Danny gave a last pleasant nod to each other. The doctor slammed his car door shut and drove away. Danny continued on, quickly evaluating what that little episode meant. The doctor must have seen the article in the morning paper.

Danny tightened his grip on Linda's hand as they crossed the street at the corner. The restaurant they were going to was four blocks from their house. Along the way, Danny waved several times in reply to the sound of a horn being honked at him. He thought that some of the people who lived in the neighborhood were trying to make up for the past year or so — trying to get him to melt the frozen face he had donned in public in self defense against the unexpected snubs which so often followed after he said hello to people he thought were still his friends and acquaintances. It bothered him to think that only one feature article would have such an effect on them. If that's all it took to thaw them out, couldn't another article — or maybe it would take two or three articles — freeze them up again? Or would it be much more difficult to freeze them up again now that they had found the opportunity to thaw themselves out? He was still thinking about that when they came to the restaurant.

He lifted Linda up so she could sit on a stool at the counter and he sat down next to her.

"Waffles and a glass of milk for the kid," he told the waitress. "And coffee for myself. Black."

He was amused at the number of fathers who were out with their children, getting them breakfast here. This is the morning when the wives sleep late. He saw a few couples with their children, all dressed in their Sunday finest; he guessed that they had stopped in either on the way *to* church or *from* church. It was nice, he thought, for a man and wife to stop in with their family to eat breakfast or brunch that way. He envied them. He saw a few familiar faces, people he had seen around the neighborhood, and he was aware of some nudging going on between several customers seated across the room — a fat man was nodding in his direction while whispering to a short shapeless woman with bleached blonde hair. Danny made believe he didn't notice anything unusual going on around him. He hid his embarrassment by becoming very engrossed with the job of brushing Linda's hair off her forehead. A man wearing rimless glasses, sitting in a booth across the room, caught Danny's eye and smiled at him. Danny smiled back but he didn't think he knew the man. In the past when there had been smear attacks against him in the newspaper Danny had been aware of a similar undertone running from person to person in a group or between groups of people in a restaurant like this, but then it had been a hostile undertone. This time he thought the undertone was a friendly one. Several times when he happened to raise his eyes he met someone else's glance — the other person nodded a little and Danny nodded back.

The waitress brought their order.

Danny concentrated on helping Linda, cutting her waffle up into tiny squares, dousing the squares with molasses. Linda was a slow eater and he had to keep pushing her, shoving the food into her mouth with a fork. He had an extra cup of coffee. Linda finally said she couldn't eat any more, leaving about half of the gooey mess of waffle and butter and molasses still on her plate. He washed her face with a paper napkin he dipped into her glass of water. And then he helped Linda put on her leggings and jacket. They walked over to the cashier. He let Linda pay the bill.

"Good-bye, Newman — "

Danny turned to see who had spoken to him. He saw an elderly man seated alongside a white-haired woman in a booth; the man was leaning out into the aisle, smiling at him. Danny couldn't place the face of the man or the woman but he nodded to thank them and said with a smile, "Good-bye."

He waved in an awkward way at them just before he took Linda's hand and led her out of the restaurant.

Linda clutched his hand tight as they started for home.

"Daddy — "

"Yes."

"Who was that man who said good-bye to us?"

"I don't know, honey."

"You said good-bye to him."

"He said good-bye to me first."

"Why did he say good-bye to you if you don't know him?"

"He wanted to show he was friendly."

"Do people say good-bye when they want to show they're friendly?"

"Sometimes."

That satisfied Linda.

They walked on in silence, holding hands.

When they reached the block where they lived Danny noticed that more people were walking around outdoors than there had been when they had left the house; and more people broke the deep freeze they had been giving him, calling out friendly greetings or waving to him.

And while still maintaining a polite reserve he replied to each greeting and to each wave.

Helen and Ruth met them inside the door.

Ruth kissed Danny's cheek and hung her arms around his neck while Helen took the leggings and jacket off Linda. Ruth let her weight rest against him.

"Okay, honey." He disengaged Ruth's arms from his neck. — "I'm not a lamp post and you're no featherweight."

"Don't insult me, sir," protested Ruth, drawing back in mock horror. "Are you insinuating, sir, that I'm overweight?"

He gently brushed past her and hung up his topcoat in the hall closet.

"Sir," Ruth began again —

"Honey, enough is enough! Please!" He was weary of his family; the moment he had entered the house he had become aware of the tensions again. He thought that one had to keep trying so hard to keep all the balls juggling up in the air in order to maintain an armistice. He wanted to be left alone for a while. "Ruth," he suggested, "will you take Linda upstairs to watch television for a while? Please, honey — "

Ruth took Linda by the hand and with mock indignation declared, "Well, if we're not wanted here we're not going to stay where we're not wanted. Come on, Linda, we'll go upstairs."

"Thanks, baby."

He brushed his hand lightly over the top of her hair and Ruth impulsively turned her head and kissed his arm. She took Linda by the hand and started up the steps with her. Danny stood with Helen, watching the two children scamper upstairs. He heard the door to the den slam shut. And then the house was perfectly quiet. Helen looked at him but he

didn't want to have anything to do with her at the moment —
he started up the steps.

"Where are you going?"

He stopped. Helen was offering the peace pipe. He knew
how hard it must be for her to back away like this. But at
that moment he didn't want any peace pipe; he wanted only
to be left alone.

"Helen" — he did not turn around — "I'm not going any
place. Do you mind if I lie down for a while? I'm pooped."

"Let's be friends."

"Okay."

"I'm sorry if I said anything that hurt you."

"That's okay."

And unexpectedly she was up the steps, her arms around
him, her wet face pressed into the crook of his neck.

"I don't want to hurt you."

"That's okay." He turned around and held her.

"I'm sorry."

"Okay."

They stood there a while, holding one another.

"Danny?"

"Yes — "

"Are you really tired?"

"Exhausted — mentally, emotionally, spiritually, every
other possible which way. You can't imagine how completely
dried out I feel. Completely dried out and dead inside."

Helen straightened up her head and they separated. She
wiped her hand under her eyes. "Then go to sleep for a while.
I'll take the kids and we'll go over to visit Mother. She phoned
a little while ago and she's alone. The house will be quiet
here so you can really rest."

He suddenly realized what had happened while he had
been out with Linda. "Your mother called you?"

"Yes, a little while ago."

"She read the article?"

"She thought it was really wonderful!"

He had guessed right.

Helen, apprehensive, asked him, "What's the matter?
What's wrong?"

"Nothing — "

"What is it?"

"Forget it."

He started up the steps again but Helen reached out and put her hand on his arm and stopped him. "What's bothering you? Mother was thrilled. She thought it's the most wonderful thing she's ever read!"

"That's good."

"What's wrong?"

It was hard to explain, to put into words, but Helen was waiting and he decided to try. "Helen, I can't help thinking—"

He stopped himself. What would be gained by telling her? The only result could be more unpleasantness.

"Thinking what?" Helen prompted.

"Helen — " He opened and closed his mouth several times before he could decide whether or not to go on. "Helen" — he swallowed and then let it come out — *"what if your mother had disliked the article like you originally did?"*

"What?" — She didn't understand what he meant, and he was sure she was not aware that she was digging her fingernails into his arm.

"What do you mean?"

He couldn't look at her.

"Helen, what if your mother hated it?"

"What?"

"Would you still be ashamed of me? Would you still be completely disgusted with me?"

"Oh, Danny." — It was a sad moan.

"Does my whole life and my entire relationship with you" — he kept his voice down so the children upstairs in the den would not hear him — "does my right to have a family and to be with my kids — does all that depend on whether or not your mother or your brother or somebody else happens to smile or frown each time I blow my nose? Does it?"

Her hands let go of him, and without turning around he heard her feet heavily descending the stairs. He continued on up to the bedroom without looking back. He carefully closed the door behind him and stretched out on the unmade bed, face down. He reached back and took hold of the rumpled covers and pulled them over his head.

Chapter 56

Monday —

"Daddy" — Danny looked up at Ruth; they were seated in the breakfast nook, eating lunch — "Daddy, do you have an extra copy of that article about you in yesterday's paper?"

He grinned at her. "Well, honey, it might be possible for me to find an extra copy if you really need it badly." — He had ten copies of the Sunday newspaper in his car out in front of the house.

He had stopped off for lunch with Ruth who came home from school at this hour to eat. He had just come from the union office in North Tonawanda where he had met with Art Manchester and several local union presidents to discuss where they would be heading in coming contract negotiations. After lunch he was due at a negotiating session between the local union committee and the representatives of Blaw-Knox with a federal conciliator assigned by the U.S. Department of Labor — the session was scheduled to take place in the front office of the shop in Buffalo where the failure of the company to satisfactorily resolve the seniority grievances threatened to cause a complete shutdown of the plant.

Helen was making Ruth's lunch when he unexpectedly walked into the kitchen. Without a word she doubled the order, making the same lunch for him. Not acknowledging his thank you, she told Ruth she was going upstairs to make the beds and Linda ran after her to help Mommy.

"Why do you need the article, honey?" he asked Ruth.

"Our teacher told us to cut it out and put it in our notebook on the history of Buffalo."

"No kidding?" This was just the opposite of what he had feared would happen with Ruth. For once she had a chance to be proud of him when she was with her school friends.

"It was in current events," Ruth excitedly explained while she tried to keep on eating her tuna fish sandwich. "The teacher asked how many of us had read Sunday's paper

490

carefully. The whole class put up their hands. Then he asked, 'How many read the article about Ruth Newman's father?' Most of the class put up their hands again. Then he asked, 'How many of you liked the article?' Most of the class put up their hands again. Then he gave us an assignment to cut out the article and paste it into our notebook we're keeping about the history of Buffalo."

"I'll give you a copy after we finish eating, honey."

She nodded and took another big bite of her sandwich, puffing out her right cheek as if she had a swollen jaw from a toothache. He cautioned her to take smaller bites so she could chew her food well and digest it properly.

They ate silently for a while.

"So the teacher really liked it, huh, baby?"

"He must have" — Ruth was sternly logical and detached, as befits a sophisticated seventh-grader who can't understand why grown-ups like her father sometimes ask stupid questions — "or he wouldn't have told us to cut it out and paste it into our notebooks."

"Did you tell your mother what your teacher said?"

"I told her soon as I came home."

"What did she say?"

"She didn't say anything."

"She didn't comment at all?"

"No, she just listened."

"Thanks."

They ate on in silence, finishing their sandwiches and drinking their milk, and then they started on the plate of cookies.

Ruth looked at the electric clock on the wall above the refrigerator. "Daddy, it's getting late — will you drive me to school?"

"Sure."

"Hurry up. We can pick up some of the kids along the way."

"Okay."

They both yelled good-bye up the stairs to Helen and Linda. There was no answer from Helen but Linda came screaming down the steps, asking them to wait so she could hug and kiss them good-bye. They hugged and kissed, and Linda scampered back upstairs to help Mommy finish making the beds.

On the way to school Ruth directed Danny to stop each time they passed a group of girls, loading ten young schoolgirls into the small vehicle, sitting three deep in the back seat.

"Oh, Mr. Newman — "

He looked up into the mirror and he saw the face of the young girl who had spoken to him. She was sitting on top of two other girls.

"Mr. Newman, that was a very nice story about you in the newspaper."

He remembered her face. She was the daughter of the doctor who had said hello to him the day before. He wondered if her parents had told her it was all right now for her to be friends with Ruth again.

"Thanks, Ethel," he said, and he gave her a quick smile over his shoulder. He drove on, pleased that he had remembered her first name.

Chapter 57

Tuesday —

The block looked deserted when Danny swerved the car into the street where he lived, deliberately making the left-hand turn so sharp and tight that the tires squealed. It was past midnight. Not another car moving on the street. Not a person out walking. All the houses — except the Newman house — already dark.

He wondered if Helen was waiting up for him. He pressed his foot down on the accelerator and raced the motor — jammed on the brakes — swerved the car in a tight U-turn to the left around the narrow island strip of grass which split the street pavement into two equal alleys — a loud squeal of the tires — raced the motor — brakes — a sharp swerve to the right into the driveway beside the house — a final squeal of the tires — brakes — quiet. He switched off the ignition, glad to be home again from the regular monthly membership meeting of the Westinghouse local union down in Attica.

Helen was in the kitchen, ironing, when he walked into the house.

"Hi," he said from the doorway.

She looked up and soberly nodded but did not reply. He went into the dining room and deposited his briefcase in the corner where he usually left it overnight. Helen spoke to him when he returned to the kitchen.

"Some night," she warned him, not looking up while she kept on vigorously ironing one of Linda's small dresses, "you're going to break your neck. I could hear the tires on your car squealing all the way up the block."

So she had heard him. That was the only reason why he had indulged in that kind of shenanigans, like a high school youngster showing off with a hot rod jalopy to draw attention to himself.

"I'll grow up one of these days," he said to Helen.

No reply.

"Did you" — he reached into his coat pocket and took out

493

a clipping — "see this in tonight's newspaper?"

Helen warily set aside the hot iron and hesitated before taking the piece of paper from him. "What is it?"

"Something I tore out of today's newspaper."

Helen took it from him. He watched her read it. She looked up and gave the clipping back to him. He carefully folded it and slipped it back into his pocket. Helen was coldly staring at him, uncomprehending.

"It's a list of people the full Un-American Activities Committee are asking the House of Representatives to cite for contempt."

"I read that."

"My name isn't there." She didn't get what he meant. "They're not going to cite me for contempt."

"How do you know?"

"The people named in that clipping appeared before the Committee *after* me — "

"That doesn't necessarily mean anything."

"I think it does. I've been following the Committee's hearings closely. All the people named here answered *some* questions before they balked on *particular* questions which they refused to answer. They challenged the right of the Committee to ask those *particular* questions. They didn't challenge the right of the Committee to ask *any* questions, the constitutionality of the very Committee itself. I think the Committee is afraid of a constitutional test of its right to exist. Too risky. They might lose. Otherwise, they'd include me on that list. No other reason for them to skip me."

Helen picked up the iron. "Aren't you smart?" she said, her dead tone of voice wiping away all his enthusiasm.

A deadly silence.

"This means, probably, that I won't be cited for contempt. There's no longer any threat that I might have to sit in the can for a while." She looked up. "In jail," he translated for her.

Helen put down the iron and slipped Linda's little dress onto a wire hanger and hooked the hanger over the door handle on one of the white wall cabinets. Then she gave him a chilling stare.

"What happens the next time they call you before another committee? Do we go through the same thing all over again?"

She turned away from him, not expecting an answer.

He watched her take a wrinkled blouse out of the big wicker basket on the floor and flatten it out on the ironing board. She sprinkled it with water and picked up the hot electric iron and swept it back and forth, ignoring his presence. He leaned back against the top ledge of the kitchen sink, watching. He was hungry after the prolonged tension which went with driving very fast after dark all the way from Attica after a long hard day of constant wrangling over shop problems.

"Would you like a sandwich?" he asked her, quietly.

"No, thank you."

"I'm going to make one for myself. No trouble to make one for you."

"No, thank you."

"Okay." He went to the refrigerator and opened the door. "How about a glass of milk?"

"No, thank you."

He made a cheese sandwich, poured a glass of milk and sat down on the small kitchen ladder, using the top of the stove for a table. The only sound in the kitchen was the squeaking of the ironing board joints as Helen pressed down and slid the shiny hot iron back and forth.

"Are you almost through," he ventured.

"Almost," she replied, without looking at him.

He chewed a little while longer. "Have you been ironing all evening?"

"No, I watched television with Ruth until she went to bed."

"The kids all right?"

"They're fine."

There was a long charged silence while he finished chewing a bite of his sandwich, swallowed, and then downed a large gulp of cold milk. Helen finished the little blouse and hung it up. She reached out to unplug the electric cord attached to the iron.

"Leave it," he suggested. "I'll straighten out the kitchen."

She stopped and looked at him, hesitated, then abruptly nodded.

"Thanks. Be careful with the hot iron. Don't burn yourself." She began to drape the ironed clothes over her left arm.

"Leave some for me," he suggested. "I'll bring them up later."

Without replying, Helen stopped piling the clothes on her arm and left with what she had already gathered together.

It was good to be alone.

Danny took his time finishing the sandwich and milk and then straightened up the kitchen. When he finally went upstairs with the rest of the ironed clothes Helen was already in bed. She had turned out the light in their bedroom. He stood in the doorway and spoke softly so as not to wake her if she was already asleep.

"Helen?"

"What?"

"Where do I put these clothes? I don't want to wake up the kids."

"Leave them in the den. I'll put them away in the morning."

"Okay."

He followed her directions and came back into the bedroom and undressed in the darkness before going into the bathroom. When he returned to the bedroom later he wondered if Helen was asleep. He silently slid under the covers, still way over on the edge of his side of the bed, the armed truce still in effect between them.

"Are you" — Helen's voice unexpectedly came out of the darkness — "going to be home tomorrow night or do you have another meeting?"

"I'll be home," he answered, although he had set up a session with the grievance committee at Blaw-Knox to talk over what to do about those unsettled seniority grievances. He would shift that meeting to some time during lunch hour or immediately after work, at the shop or at some ginmill near the shop. "I've got nothing on tomorrow night. Why?"

"My brother Nat is flying up here to see us.

"Good." His better judgment kept him from asking Helen why her other brother was coming back to Buffalo.

"I called him long distance tonight," Helen went on. "I asked him if he could get on a plane and come up to see us tomorrow."

"Swell."

"I thought he might be able to help us get some better

perspective on our situation."

Danny didn't think it wise to comment on that. Helen continued, somewhat hesitantly.

"Nat agrees with what you think about unions, and he has the same background I have. At least, being my brother, we're part of the same family and we were living in the same home until he left town. Maybe he can help us find a way to reconcile our differences."

Danny hesitated. He wanted to prepare Helen for a difference of opinion between him and Nat. But he had to be careful how he did it.

"I'm glad he's coming, Helen. It'll be good to see him again. But don't forget, his solution was to leave Buffalo. Move away."

Helen rushed to defend her brother. "I don't know if leaving town was supposed to be his solution to whatever problem he had. So far as I'm concerned, he left here and it's none of your business or mine why he left."

"He says he'll never come back here to live."

"He has his reasons."

"All I'm trying to point out to you is that Nat is certain to tell us we should leave here — the same thing he did."

"Maybe he's right."

"Maybe he's wrong. But he can't admit, probably not even to himself, that he might be doing the wrong thing moving out of town to live in Greenwich Village. He can't admit he solved nothing."

Helen was quiet for a long while. Then he heard her voice — intense, low, bitter — come out of the darkness again. "Do you want me to wire him not to come?"

"No. Let him come. Maybe coming at it with a fresh viewpoint he can shed some new light on our situation. At least we know he's sympathetic to both of us. Same background as you, but essentially in agreement with me about the importance of organized labor in our modern society — "

"If you want me to," Helen interrupted, "I can still wire him not to come."

"No. Maybe he can help." He tried to joke. "At least we'll be able to talk freely to one another through an interpreter who speaks both our languages. Someone we both trust even though neither one of us wholly agrees with all his viewpoints on all current topics and problems."

Helen didn't laugh.

"Good-night," she said, in a way that let him know she agreed they should not stop Nat from flying up the next day.

He answered, "Good-night," and then lay awake a long while, wondering about the role Nat would play in their situation.

Chapter 58

Wednesday —

In the morning Helen telephoned Danny at his office and told him that Nat had phoned from New York City to ask them not to tell anyone else in the family that he was coming. He wanted to be met at the airport and he wanted Danny to bring along the letter from Einstein.

It was already dark when they watched Nat descend from the plane. They waved at him until they caught his attention. He waved back and he hurried toward them. Danny couldn't help thinking that Nat always looked at though he had just stepped out of a New Yorker magazine advertisement for college men's clothes — even though Nat had been out of college for almost twenty years. Nat leaned over the top of the shoulder-high wire fence and kissed Helen, and then he reached his hand over to grip Danny's hand tight. Danny admired his brother-in-law's sun-tanned face. Nat came around through the gate in the wire fence to join them. Danny shook hands with him again.

"Nat, you look as if you just got off a plane from Miami instead of New York City."

"My sun tan?"

"You look too damn healthy."

Helen said, "What a gorgeous tan."

"Purely synthetic," Nat laughed, enjoying their flattery. "A sun lamp."

"You look like you're in terrific physical shape," Danny said. They were still shaking hands.

"Thank you, thank you. You look pretty terrific yourself."

Helen hugged her brother. "You look wonderful, Nat."

There was a big overjoyed smile on Nat's face. "Thanks!" And he explained, enjoying the telling of it, "I go down to the club every day and bake myself to a crisp under a sun lamp and keep my body in good shape by swatting a ball around a few hours each day. Handball or squash."

"You look terrific," said Danny, as they started toward the

499

administration building.

Nat beamed. "Thanks — "

Danny took hold of his brother-in-law's elbow. "What about your baggage? Your bags?"

Nat laughed at Danny in a very bouncy way, his teeth showing in a big grin. "I didn't bring anything! I'm only going to stay up here a couple of hours! Then I'm going right back! That's why — "

Danny saw the disappointment on Helen's face. At the same time he became aware that Nat was gushing out words like a swollen stream pouring over its banks, out of control.

"I asked Helen not to tell Bob or mother I was coming up. As a matter-of-fact, I'm going to grab a plane back as soon as we get through with our bull session." Nat kept laughing and beaming in a forced over-excited way while the words poured out of his mouth. "I wouldn't have come up at all — but Helen told me how much trouble you two are having — I didn't want to say no to her — I don't know exactly how much help I can be to you — I'm not in the best shape myself right now — I'm not exactly myself — not my *best* self anyway — and it makes me nervous to get too excited — I find that I get too emotional when I get into an argument or into a heated discussion with people — and you know mother and Bob — "

He abruptly stopped walking and turned to face Danny. They had just entered the lobby of the administration building.

"You know how mother and Bob are," he said, and he put his hand on Danny's shoulder, holding it there while he made believe that he was both his mother and his older brother. "'What are your plans, Nat?'" And Nat shook his head disconsolately while he gazed with a sour face at Danny. "'After all, Nat, you've got to do *some* kind of work, don't you? You're past forty, Nat — you can't be a playboy all your life! You've got to get hold of yourself by your bootstraps! You've got to pull yourself up! And make a man out of yourself!'" He slapped Danny on the shoulder. "'You know you can do it, Nat, if you'll only try. Stout fella! Old boy! Old kid! After all, my dear son and brother, you can't keep on living off the fat of The Park Lane all your life without doing any work — that's sinful! That's atheistic!

That's — that's — that's — '"

HIs hand dropped away from Danny's shoulder. He suddenly seemed to lose all zest for the game he had seemed to be enjoying so much. The tanned finely featured face became clouded and serious and sad.

"Maybe Mother and Bob are right after all." He added apologetically, "I'm working on a few projects — I've got several irons in the fire and I have to wait until they heat up — it takes time to work these business ventures out if you don't want to go off half-cocked — there's no use going into any old thing merely to be able to say that I'm working" — he smiled in a haunting winsome way into his sister's face —"is there, baby doll?"

Danny saw Helen try to return the smile, but she didn't say anything. Nat put his arm around her waist and pressed his cheek against hers.

"How are you, cutie pie?"

"I'm fine, Nat," she said very quietly.

"You're looking terrific," he told her, beaming in an excited way again as he stepped back so he could take a good look at her full-length body. "Wonderful! And you've lost weight in your face. On you those hollow cheeks look good, baby doll. You should keep on worrying. Problems agree with you — I wish they agreed with me as well as they seem to agree with you."

He made an abrupt gesture of disgust, a shrugging movement of revulsion that involved his whole body. "The hell with me and my problems for a few minutes! I didn't fly up here to talk about that. After all" — he gave a great big shrug — "when the time is ripe I'll find something in keeping with the fine bourgeois tradition of the Stack family. Something very respectable! Something where I can make a lot of money! Something where mother and Bob can boast about what I'm doing — so they can stop hiding the skinny skeleton they've got tucked back there in the family closet!" He put his arm around Helen's waist again and he laughed hilariously while he squeezed her. "They'll finally be able to tell all the friends of the family in Buffalo the truth about me! They can stop stuttering! They can stop stammering! They can stop changing the subject every time someone asks them what young brother Nat is doing! They can send out gilt-edged formal announcements letting all their friends and business associates know that Nathan Stack Esquire has finally bought a seat entitling him to membership in the ranks of the money-grubbing bourgeoisie — "

Helen interrupted him. "What's that mean — booshwahzee?"

"What does it mean?" Nat laughed and patted his younger sister affectionately on the cheek.

"That, baby doll, is a fancy word to describe that section of the upper-middle and upper-upper class which strives continually to keep ahead of the Joneses — they've got to get ahead — they've got to get somewhere, to make themselves into somebody who stands out from the mob. And the way you prove you're getting up there is to buy a shiny new Cadillac or whatever happens to be the equivalent badge of conspicuous consumption the bourgeoisie happen to be wearing in your particular community at the moment. And if you're really big, really important, you wait until everybody else gets a Cadillac — and then you buy a tiny Ford to prove you're so important that you can drive a beat-up old Ford and still be counted as a very important guy among people who are driving Cadillacs." He laughed in a high-pitched voice. "Like the debutramp who wears a dirty sweatshirt and blue jeans to the big formal dance — that really makes her *something!*"

They were standing still now in the lobby of the administration building.

"Nat," Danny interrupted, "let's get situated here. Where do we want to go?"

"Let's find a bar close by," Nat suggested; "you name it."

Danny turned to Helen with an inquiring look. She nodded — a bar was all right with her. But then Nat asked them to wait a minute while he checked his return flight reservation. They watched him walk over to the ticket counter. He glanced at Helen and saw that this was not what she had expected to happen with Nat. He tried to make conversation to break the awkward silence.

"I thought Nat was working again."

"So did I" — her voice was flat — "but I guess he isn't if he's spending his day playing squash and handball and getting a tan."

"Doesn't sound like it."

They watched while Nat stood in line waiting his turn at the ticket counter. From across the lobby he looked like a young college freshman. It was only when you stood close to Nat that you could see the mesh of finely penciled lines on his face. Danny glanced at Helen. She looked sad. He patted her back gently. She pulled away from his touch and fumbled hurriedly in her purse. She found her dark shell-rimmed reading glasses and slipped them on. That meant she was crying or about to cry. He gently gripped her elbow and this time she didn't pull away.

"Maybe," Helen whispered, surprising Danny by the calmness of her voice, "we shouldn't ask him anything about us. It might only upset him and make him worse."

"He seems to be really sailing," Danny agreed, wondering how they could avoid asking Nat to go over their problem with them after he had taken a plane here to meet them expressly for that purpose.

"When he's like this," said Helen, "I feel like taking him in my arms and holding him there, protecting him from all the things that hurt him. I wish I knew what's troubling him — so I could help him."

"Life is very difficult for some people," said Danny. "To get up in the morning and function all day as a human being can be a real burden."

"Poor Nat — I keep forgetting until I see him again."

Danny tightened his grip on Helen's elbow.

They drove over to a fancy motel about five minutes away from the airport to find a quiet cocktail lounge where they ordered something to drink. Danny glanced at his watch. Two and one-half hours to fill up with conversation before Nat's return flight was scheduled to leave the airport.

Nat lifted his glass, straight whiskey on the rocks. "A toast to a long and happy marriage for the two of you. A marriage lasting as long as mine was short. A marriage as happy as mine was lousy." He saw that they were embarrassed and he quickly added, "Let's drink to my brother-in-law who had the nerve to tell the Un-American Activities Committee to go to hell." He laughed, showing all his white teeth, a handsome contrast with the dark of his tanned skin. "Sir — it's an honor to be related to you." He emptied his glass.

Helen and Danny self-consciously sipped their drinks.

Nat put down his glass. "Did you bring that letter you got from Einstein?"

Danny slipped the letter out of his inside coat pocket and passed it to his brother-in-law. Nat examined the scientist's name and address in the upper left hand corner of the envelope.

"Great," he muttered. "Great. Great."

He took the letter out of the envelope and read it, muttering as he read, "Great. Great. Great." Still muttering the same word over and over, he re-read the letter several times before passing it back to Danny. "You can show that to your grandchildren. Be sure to put it some place where you won't lose it. In a safe deposit box or something. One hundred years from now it'll be quite a collector's item."

"Is it that wonderful?" Helen was skeptical.

"Einstein," lectured Nat, "is one of the greatest men in the world. You would treasure a letter you received from Abraham Lincoln or George Washington, wouldn't you? Or Leonardo Da Vinci? If you lived in Da Vinci's time. Well, Einstein is in their class, as great as any one of them. He'll go down in history as one of the greatest men of all time. His discoveries in the field of physics and mathematics have revolutionized the world."

At this point, feeling guilty, Danny told Nat about Einstein's subsequent statement which criticized him for releasing his letter to the press without express permission. Nat dismissed that with a brief gesture.

"A reporter I know very well who works on one of the metropolitan newspapers told me all about that. It was someone at the university, not Einstein himself, who gave out that statement. They didn't like Einstein getting himself all mixed up so much with attacks on the Un-American Activities Committee."

Danny put the letter away.

Nat called over the waitress and ordered another round of drinks. When she returned with the order he lifted his glass for another toast. "Here's hoping," he declaimed with a nervous flourish, "I'm able to help you solve your problems." He laughed and added, "Although that's extremely improbable — I mean that I'll be of any real help to you — although I'm sure you'll find a way to solve your problems without my help. Hell, you know what I mean. Let's drink to it and get it over with."

They drank to his toast.

"Of course," resumed Nat, as he set down his empty glass, "the whole world's got problems. It's a lousy schizophrenic world in which we're living." He saw the puzzled look on Helen's face and he explained. "We're taught one set of values when we're children, at home and in our school system. But if we try to live according to that set of values when we grow up we become abject failures in the business world. Anyone who tries to practice public school values in business is called a stupid *schmoe*, and rightly so." He gripped Danny's shoulder and laughed out loud. "Isn't that right?"

Danny shrugged his head and shoulders.

But Nat had not waited for any reply — he was already rushing on. "Of course, I don't see how the two of you can stand living here in Buffalo, with mother and Bob breathing down your necks all the time, putting on the pressure constantly to try to make you conform to their idea of what is a proper life for someone married to our dear sweet youngest sister, Helen." He leaned over and kissed Helen's cheek and cooed, "Hello, sweety pie, you brat, you!" — and he continued, "You know, of course, that their idea of what's proper and my idea of what's proper don't quite jibe. I know they don't approve of the life I lead. Mother and Bob would like me to find some nice sweet girl. Preferably here in Buffalo so I would marry and settle down here where they could watch over me. Some nice proper girl from a nice family who would help me find myself. Of course, by *find myself* they mean — help me to go into business and become a sober, well-mannered, industrious businessman, with a home in the staid suburban community, where I would belong to the country club and have the prescribed number of properly behaved children who will be given a proper upbringing; where I would be a real asset — and I do mean *ass*-et — to the community at large; and where I would not be a disturbing factor to any of the more proper members of the Stack family or to the dear old status quo in general, but would — by the very example of my quiet success, financial success, that is! — help to reinforce the way things are and always should be, God willing, merry gentlemen — where my example would serve to help shore up the sagging good old American ideal of grab hold of your own bootstraps, son, and lift yourself up out of that mire so you really get somewhere that really counts like getting somewhere and accomplishing things that really count in this world for something worthwhile with people who really count — "

He interrupted himself with his nervous chuckling which had become louder and louder as he went on. Then the chuckling died in his throat. And he became completely silent for a moment, his eyes staring down at his empty glass, not seeing anything. His mind seemed to have unexpectedly shifted its attention to something a million miles away from the cocktail lounge and his sister and his brother-in-law.

Haunted, thought Danny — haunted by ghosts he can't talk about, a lost boy — no, a lost man, hiding inside the protective shell of an irresponsible boy, afraid to grow up. Poor Nat. And poor Helen. He knew how Helen felt when Nat acted this way. At times like this she wanted to enfold Nat in her arms as if he were a little child and cry over him and shield him from the whole raw world.

Nat looked up. His face beamed again and he laughed nervously as he started to talk again, picking up speed as he went on. "The truth is I might not mind doing what they want me to do. — Sometimes I wish I could. — But it isn't in me — for some reason or other I got ants in my pants — I don't know where I'm going but I'm running goddamn hard to get there." He laughed out loud at himself. "I'm running so hard I'm all bushed out, and for all I know maybe I got to where I'm going but I just don't know it — maybe I don't recognize the place because I don't know where I'm trying to get to — and I'm still running hard." He laughed even louder. "That's damn silly, isn't it? Isn't it? Don't you think it is?"

Both Helen and Danny nodded, humoring Nat.

"That's so damn silly," Nat repeated, still laughing down in his throat — and breathing hard, as if he had been running.

And then again there was an abrupt change.

He became very serious and logical.

"You both realize, of course," he said, with an air of professorial importance, "that your problem is entirely different from mine. After all, I'm divorced and I'm almost like a single man again after living alone for five years. But you two are still married. And that in itself is quite an accomplishment in these times, especially when you come from such different backgrounds. This is no horseshit — you two are the happiest married couple I know, despite your problems, and I'd hate to even think of the two of you breaking up your marriage. But, Danny, you understand that Helen is my sister, and much as I like you as a person I must be concerned first with my sister's happiness. — I think the best thing she could do, what she has to do for her happiness, is to get away from this town like I've done — so she can get away from the constant influence of her mother — our dear, sweet, innocent mother who means so well — and away from our dear brother Bob who aspires to be the new father of the family, replacing Dad as the benevolent boss in the family — "

He put his hand on Danny's arm. "Don't misunderstand what I'm saying. Mother and Bob really do mean well. The trouble is that they have a set of values which is totally different from yours and mine and most people's. They have a perfect set of values for the small group they go with here — *if* you want to go with that group. — But if you don't want to go with that group, Danny, you shouldn't blame them for your situation — don't blame Mother and Bob — blame yourself — you should get the hell out of Buffalo — "

"I don't agree with that," injected Danny, not wanting to get into an argument with his brother-in-law but thinking that he had to say something because of the effect what his brother-in-law was saying might have on Helen.

"What don't you agree with?"

"Why can't we stay here and mix with all kinds of people here — why must we go somewhere else?"

"Because your union and The Park Lane can't sleep in the same bed."

"Nothing requires them to sleep together — "

"I mean you can't associate with all kinds of groups, you can't be all things to all people in Buffalo."

"That's a cliché, Nat, which doesn't mean much."

"You can't mix your union life and The Park Lane life — they don't go together."

"I don't think we have to run away from your mother and Bob and their segment of society. Why shouldn't we stay here and argue it out with them, on as friendly a basis as possible — especially when, if it's possible on an honorable basis, we'd like to be friends with them — on the basis of mutual respect for each one's right to his own opinions. Why run away? That won't help us and it won't help them! We have as much right to live here with our set of values as they have to live here with their set of values. And let that set of values which is best and most true for our time prevail. Or both co-exist."

Danny saw that Helen's face was screwed up with the intense effort she was making to catch every detail in this clash of ideas. "I don't believe," he continued, speaking to Nat, but directing the thought at Helen, "I don't believe in running away in a burst of glorious personal revolt which is really nothing but pellmell retreat from a face-to-face difficult struggle with the reality of the present, as it is here and now in Buffalo. You don't change anything in Buffalo by running away from the reality here to a side pocket in Greenwich Village."

"Crap!" Nat spat at Danny. "That's a lot of crap!"

He vehemently rapped his knuckles on the table and launched into a violent defense of himself. "I haven't run away!" he hissed across the table. "I haven't retreated! I've broken out of prison! I've revolted against the stultifying conventions of a dying segment of our society into which, without any choice on my part, I had the lousy luck to be born!"

He simmered down. "But your situation isn't the same as mine. — In your case you might be free here if you weren't married to Helen. But as long as you two are married you'll never be free here in Buffalo. Because Helen is still in prison and she holds you in prison with her. Your only solution is either to get a divorce and leave Helen remain in her prison, which she may not see as a prison as you and I do, while you go your way here, completely free, or else take her with you and go somewhere else where you'll both be free."

Realizing that Nat was creating problems for him with Helen, Danny could not contain his exasperation. "Nat, that's a lot of nonsense! Words with no intelligent meaning! That's the kind of revolt you've indulged in! A form of masturbation to avoid facing the reality outside of self!" He saw that Nat was stung by that — Nat wanted to interrupt — but Danny rushed on with intensified energy to keep his brother-in-law from breaking in. "Sure, you've revolted, Nat, but it's an anarchistic revolt, yourself against the world! You declared that you disagree with the values of the segment of society into which you were born, the segment of society here in which you grew up! So what did you do? You packed your bags and rushed off to the bohemian life in the big city, hiding away from the realities you should have faced and dealt with! Wouldn't it have been better to stay here and constructively attempt to change the situation, change these people you know, these people you grew up with — change their values?"

"Impossible! The odds are too great!"

"But it's better than running away! You think you're free because you took off for Greenwich Village. But in your mind and on your back you're carrying all the values you thought you left behind you. It's with you every minute, eating you, controlling you. — Look, you don't even dare to face your mother and your brother on this trip because it upsets you so much even to think of meeting them. You're not free. You're carrying this life here more vividly with you than the reality you would meet if you were still living here! You're a refugee from reality, carrying your prison with you wherever you go — "

"Why can't you keep your big mouth shut?" Helen snapped, interrupting him. "You're not so brilliant! You don't know everything!"

Danny realized he had gone too far. "I'm sorry," he apologized, reminding himself that Nat was in no condition to be talked to that sharply. "Nat, I'm sorry. Don't mind me. I shoot my mouth off and the words come out. I've got so many things on my mind right now I say things without thinking them through, things I don't really mean — "

"You didn't say anything too terrible, Danny." Nat was very magnanimous about it. "I often say worse of myself." He laughed at that, and then became serious, adding, "Besides, we all have our prisons, haven't we?"

"What do you mean by that?" Helen turned to Nat.

"Well, Danny's right. I do take my prison with me wherever I go. I'm much too concerned about what mother and Bob and the whole group of which they're a part here think about me and whatever I'm doing. And that *is* why I have to live somewhere else, away from them. I can't do what I would really like to do if I live here, not without such terrible guilt feelings that it's impossible to face that group — and you have a touch of the same ailment, Helen. In that respect it's a prison here for you too. You find it difficult to live here with a person like Danny because mother and Bob and their group are so sharply critical of everything Danny stands for. You've got the same prison I've got. What's the great difference whether I carry my prison with me in my mind or if like you, Helen, I stay right here in the middle of my prison in Buffalo? — I think I'm better off this way, better off than you — at least, I'm not continually emotionally involved, with all kinds of arguments and all kinds of pressures constantly exerted against me. At least I'm physically free from that kind of stuff."

Danny saw that this affected Helen. Her forehead wrinkled with the effort to grasp what was the right thing to do. He didn't want to argue with Nat but he had to counteract what had just been said.

He tried to be very pleasant about his disagreement. "Nat, I don't think I quite fully agree with you."

"Why?"

"Personally, Nat — and this is my own personal viewpoint with which you may disagree — and who am I to say finally that you're right or that I'm right? Personally, I think there *is* a difference, a great difference. Oh, I'll agree that you don't get into arguments with people in Buffalo because you're not living here. But you're always having a helluva argument with the ghosts you're carrying with you. They're with you all the time. The people you leave behind in Buffalo when you run away because you can't face them and live the life you want to live. — But if you stay here and argue for your right to live your life here as you want to live it, for your right to believe in what you believe — *then there would be a real difference, wouldn't there?"*

Nat shook his head but Danny wouldn't let him interrupt.

"Yes, Nat! The minute you face the reality here, as it is, and start trying to change it — that minute you'll no longer be in prison! You'll lose the feeling that you're rotting along with that segment of society you instinctively oppose and revolt against. You'll have importance in your own eyes! You won't have to run away any more in a futile effort to get away from the ghosts who are haunting you!"

"Give up." Nat leaned across the table and patted Danny gently on the shoulder. "Danny, give up. You sound like a Marxian psychiatrist I know who has been working on me for years without any luck. I appreciate your trying to help me, but that kind of pollyanna medicine won't do any good. My problems are much more complicated than that."

"Sorry," Danny apologized.

"Don't apologize. Thanks for trying to help."

There was a self-conscious schoolboy grin on Nat's face while he looked from Danny to Helen and back again. He laughed out loud at their solemn faces.

"Who's supposed to be advising who here? I'm the one who came up here to give you the benefit of my objective viewpoint. Be careful, Danny. My psychiatrist will throw a picket line around you — you're invading his jurisdiction." He laughed again, a shrill note. "The hell with all this psychoanalyzing — let's have a few more drinks and get stinko and forget all our problems for a little while. We're all handing out free advice and none of us are qualified psychiatrists."

He raised his hands to put a stop to any further talk. "I've got a good idea." He paused for dramatic effect. "You know what I think would be the correct solution for all three of us?"

Danny and Helen waited while Nat permitted the suspense to deepen. And then Nat delivered his pearl of wisdom.

"You two solve your problem in your own way. And I'll solve my problem in my own way. And you know what?"

They solemnly waited.

And Nat told them:

"A hundred years from now it won't make one bit of

difference what the hell we decide tonight! So why worry?"
He grabbed his sister and Danny by the arm, holding on to
both of them while he laughed out loud again. "So I say the
hell with it. Drink and be merry — and after us, the deluge!
Meanwhile, let's have more sex, blondes, millions of them,
with jumbo-sized tits flopping out of their brassieres — "

They ordered another round of drinks.

And another round.

And another round.

Nat was very happy and slightly incoherent when they
escorted him out to his plane and asked the airline
stewardess to look after him. He shook hands with Danny,
kissed Helen and offered to kiss the stewardess if she was
interested — the stewardess smiled politely but coolly and
looked the other way.

The plane taxied out onto the runway. Helen and Danny
watched it take off. Then they silently started back to their
car. As they walked, Helen took his right hand and slipped it
under her left arm so that he was holding her and guiding
her between cars in the parking lot.

They were only a few steps away from their car when
Helen suddenly threw her arms around him, clinging to him
so desperately that she scared him. Her body was shivering.
He held her close, waiting for her to speak.

"Danny — "

"Yes?"

"I'm so afraid."

"Of what?"

"Everything."

A man and woman came walking toward them. Helen
pulled away from Danny. He opened the door of the car for
her. She got in.

They drove home without a word between them all the
way.

He knew she would get around to talking after they got
into bed.

Chapter 59

They sat up in bed, in the dark, with pillows propped behind their backs. The children were asleep. Helen smoked a cigarette and Danny waited for her to start off the showdown scene. He sensed that she had made her decision but wanted to tell him in a way that could not possibly be interpreted either by him, herself, or anyone else, as submission by the female to the male.

Helen methodically smoked her way through one full cigarette, the end of the cigarette glowing a fiery red in the darkness each time she sucked in a breath of smoke. She lit another cigarette and the flare of the flame from the match illuminated the whole bedroom and then darkness swallowed up the room again.

"Danny — "

"Yes."

"You're a very sensitive person." — She spoke quietly as though she were continuing a conversation which had been going on for some time. "You seem to know many things about what I'm thinking before I even say them."

"Sometimes — "

"You know I've been thinking about us — "

"I know."

"About us — and where we stand with one another."

"I know."

Her cigarette's end glowed red as she slowly pulled in a deep breath — then she took the cigarette away from her lips, and he could see the glowing end of the cigarette describe an arc through the darkness as she brought her hand back to where it rested on the edge of the ash tray in her lap.

"I'm very confused."

"Aren't we all, to one degree or another."

"I don't think you're as confused as I am. If you were, you would be as uncertain as I am about what's right or wrong for us." She stopped to allow him to interrupt with some comment, but he remained silent. And she resumed. "You're

513

quite definite, aren't you — about what you want to do?"

"I'm not always certain." He thought she would resent it if he were too cocksure of himself. But he didn't want to give her any false impression that he had weakened in his conviction to stay and fight out the situation. "It's always possible I may find out later that I'm wrong. But right now I don't think we should run away from here to your sister's Shangri-La in Florida."

"Why?" She was not arguing.

"Because we carry the problem with us wherever we go. We have to solve it first and then we can go anywhere we want to go, *if we want to go anywhere else after we solve it here.*"

Helen puffed her cigarette and he watched the red glow flare up and die away again. There was the movement of the burning end of the cigarette, an arc back to the ash tray on her lap.

"You think we can solve our problem here?"

"I think this is the only place where we can solve it in a satisfying way."

There was along pause before he heard her say, "I'm not so sure." Another long pause. "Do you think you'll be a union organizer all your life?"

"For the immediate present, yes. But the future? I don't know. I doubt I'll be an organizer all my life until I die."

"What kind of work would you go into in the future if you weren't a union organizer?"

"I don't know. But right now it would be wrong for me to run away — to go into some other work right now."

"I'm not talking about right now."

"The future? Who knows? Years ago who dreamed that I would become a union organizer? It developed naturally and logically out of the circumstances of my life. In the same way I may end up sometime in the future in some other kind of work where I can use my background and training in a worthwhile and satisfying way. At least I hope I'll end that way."

"Not union organizing."

"I don't know. Union organizing is a tough game, usually a young man's occupation. Very few old men make good union organizers. The pace is too fast, too demanding."

"Must I wait until you're old and burned out before you'll change to something else?"

"Not necessarily. I don't know any more than you exactly what the future is going to bring."

"Would you make an effort to get into something else? Not right now, not right away. But before you're too old. To make me happy?"

He hesitated. "Something where I'll still be on the side of labor and the progressive forces in the community?"

"Yes," she said, after a moment's thought. "I know you would never be completely happy in anything else, and it would be wrong to force you to do anything else against your will, even if I could. We wouldn't have a very happy marriage. But you should be able to find some kind of work that isn't such a sharp contrast to my background. Some compromise area in between. Will you try to find something like that?"

"Helen, are you sure you're not kidding yourself?"

"Why?"

"Aren't you really trying to find a very subtle way to swing me over to the same side where your mother and Bob stand?"

She quickly objected. "No. I don't like where they stand any more than I like where you stand. I'm trying to find a middle ground — if there is one."

"It depends on what you mean by 'middle ground.'"

"Well" — she hesitated and then spoke slowly, feeling her way —"there must be some kind of work, Danny, some work where you can feel you're doing something worthwhile, not wasting your life on nothing. Some work where you feel you're using yourself to the fullest extent of which you're capable so you won't have regrets later that you wasted your life. Isn't that what you feel union organizer work is doing for you? I don't mean you're being selfish. But you need something that completely fulfills you that way—I'm not putting it exactly right. But you know what I mean, don't you?"

"I think so — "

"Don't you think you can find something like that, something out of the area where you're presently working, which will still fulfill what you need in exactly the same way, just as strongly? Maybe there isn't anything like that around for you right now — but maybe there will be some time in the future. Isn't that possible?"

"Anything's possible. Anything. There's still a lot of pressure to drive me out of the labor movement. If that happens I might be out of union organizing work much quicker than either of us realize, though I hope not. But I'd prefer it not to happen that way."

"I hope it doesn't happen that way, either. It wouldn't be good for either of us if you were forced out of your present work against your will. But at the same time, to be honest, I wouldn't cry too much if it did happen that way."

He had no answer to that. They were silent for a while.

"Do you know that I'm proud of you?"

"Are you, honestly?"

"Yes. But I'm also terrified by fear of what may happen. I'm so afraid."

He found her left hand and held it. Her palm was moist and hot. He felt her nails gripping into him.

"Baby, don't be afraid. The things we worry about usually don't happen. But even if they do they're rarely as bad as we imagined they would be."

"I know."

They were silent a while, squeezing hands. Then he felt her hand relax.

"Danny — "

"Yes?"

"I don't want to go to Florida without you."

"Don't you?"

"No. If we had the money and could afford it, I'd like to take you and the children off with me to Florida — or anywhere else away from here — for a long vacation before we come back and face my family and all those people again."

"We can't afford it, Helen."

"I know. I could get the money from Mother or Bob if I were going to Florida without you, but I can't ask them for the money to take off with you on vacation."

"I'm quite a liability."

She squeezed his hand. "Do you think we'll be able to afford to take a week off during the summer and go somewhere else without the kids and just be alone together and relax?"

"Why not?"

She took another puff from the cigarette she was still holding in her other hand and then ground the burning end of the cigarette into the ash tray until all the sparks had been extinguished. She put the ash tray over on the night table. His eyes were used to the darkness and he could see her straighten up and lean her head back. She stared up toward the ceiling. He waited for her to speak.

"We'll be starting off with a clean slate," she said.

He waited for her to explain.

"I'm talking about friends. One thing we can be sure of —"

"What's that?"

"We'll never have any less friends than we got right now. Things will have to get better because they can't get any worse."

"We've got a lot of friends, Helen. People I know and work with in the union."

"I wasn't talking about them. I'd like to know them better and get to be friends with them. But it's hard for me to get over being very self-conscious when I'm with your labor people."

"They're no different from any other people."

"I know. But I wasn't talking or thinking about them. I was thinking about the people who won't associate with you, the people who once were my friends. They're gone, probably forever, and it's a very sad thing for me to think about. They're just as much a part of me as you are, and I know I'll never again be friends with them like we used to be."

"We'll have a lot more, Helen. On a much sounder basis than before. Including a lot of the old friends who are temporarily afraid of us on account of the heat the newspapers poured on me."

"If we don't — we're liable to be awfully lonesome in this house."

"Oh, I think we'll do all right, Helen."

She stopped staring at the ceiling and she took both his hands into hers. "Well, I think we'll do all right too," she said, surprising him by her calm optimism. "They won't be chasing after me like they used to do at one time, seeking out the glamorous Miss Park Lane. But it probably will be much better this way. I'll have to exert myself to make friends, to make them like me because of myself, which will be very good for me because I've been spoiled. I always pushed people around and they came back for more only because I was Miss Park Lane. You were the only one I couldn't push around. When I stop to think and look back at how I used to act, I must have been a real bitch."

"You're still essentially sound."

"Oh, thank you."

"You're welcome."

She squeezed his hands and he returned the squeeze. She took a deep breath.

"You know I've been thinking — "

"Be careful," he kidded her.

She went right on, ignoring his attempt at humor. "I think I should be active in something. Isn't there some kind of organization in this town which fights for women's rights? One that's not too far to the left."

"Sure, there must be. If there isn't, get some people together and start one."

"You want another organizer in the family?"

"It'll do you good to be active that way, where you can express your opinions and help to shape things into what you think they should be. Every person should be active in some way, trying to affect the direction of the entire community. That's how a community begins to reflect the people in it — "

"Don't push me, Danny."

"Sorry, I was only trying to help."

"Let me work it out myself."

"Okay, kid."

She was quiet a long while. Then he felt her hands tighten and she pulled him toward her.

"As long as we're going to stay married," she whispered, "let's try to act like it."

Later, she lay in his arms as he wondered how many times they would go through a similar crisis in their relationship before the world situation might change sufficiently to permit them to happily integrate their lives completely.

Afterword by the author

Having read my account of what happened back in that "bad time" you may ask, "Well, were you ever a member of the Communist Party?" — I answer, "Yes, over forty years ago."

When I was a member of the Theatre of Action in New York City — in the latter Thirties — another member of the cast of *The Young Go First*, directed by Elia Kazan, a play in which I had the lead role — asked me to join with other theatre people in the Communist Party. And I did. That was still deep depression time, and we tried to improve the lot of the unemployed and the underpaid.

I was still a member of the Communist Party in 1941 when I went to work for the United Electrical, Radio & Machine Workers of America (UE) as a union organizer whose job it was to organize the unorganized, which I did quite well, helping to bring improved wages and working conditions to approximately 30,000 Western New York men and women we represented in a democratically controlled union run by its members.

Just prior to April, 1944, I formally severed my membership in the Communist Party — just prior to the date I enlisted in the Army of the United States during the Second World War, as a private in the infantry — where, primarily because of my union experience, I very quickly was commissioned an officer, a second lieutenant, later promoted to first lieutenant.

Returning to civilian life in November, 1946, I returned to my job as a union organizer with the UE union. While I did maintain a friendly working relationship with members of the Communist Party, not hesitating to work with them on matters intended to improve the wages and working conditions of the people we represented, in the next four years I allowed my formal membership in the Party to just fade away; when I appeared before the House Committee on Un-American Activities in 1954 I was not a member of the Party. To be honest, the primary reason for letting my Party membership fade away was that I was afraid of the hell it might bring down on me and my family.   Yet I was determined not to let that fear cause me to cut and run from what I believed in — the fight to improve the lives of the people who have to work for a living — the working people of our country.

THE UN-AMERICAN

April 16,1954

Mr.Emanuel Fried
360 Delaware Ave.
Buffalo 2,N.Y.

Dear Mr.Fried:

        I am convinced that you did the *under difficult circumstances.* right thing and fulfilled your duty as a citizen.

    My respect,

A. Einstein

Albert Einstein.

"Letter received from Albert Einstein after I refused to answer any questions before the House Committee on Un-American Activities without basing that refusal on protection afforded by amendments in the Bill of Rights, but instead — seeking to be indicted for a court test — challenged the right of the Committee to exist, on grounds that the enabling resolution establishing the Committee was unconstitutional."

"From left to right, actors Frank McCarthy, David Groh and Edward Power in my play *DROP HAMMER* at Los Angeles Actors Theatre (now renamed Los Angeles Theatre Center) in 1980. Excellent reviews prompted Buffalo drama critic Doug Smith to liken situation with my plays and Buffalo to rum produced in a Caribbean island that could not be bought by inhabitants there, but sold only elsewhere. This resulted in Buffalo production of my play *ELEGY FOR STANLEY GORSKI*, followed by production there of four more of my plays. However, the artistic director at leading regional theatre there, Studio Arena, told me he could not do my plays because two leading members of his board, headed by chairman Franz Stone and vice-chairman Robert Swados, objected. As a union organizer I'd organized employees of Stone's Columbus McKinnon Chain Corporation and struck it three times. Swados had been a best friend who, when I refused his demand that I publicly condemn my union and become a stoolpigeon for the FBI, publicly repudiated his friendship with me."

"Mindy and Lorrie. Photo, circa 1983."

THE UN-AMERICAN

JANUARY 28, 1980

Theater/William Murray

INDUSTRIAL REVELATION

"... The strength of *Drop Hammer* lies not so much in its plot turns, but in its commitment to getting the blue-collar life just right ..."

NO IMPORTANT American playwright I can think of has ever dealt realistically with the lives and aspirations of blue-collar workers. Our mainly middle-class writers have tended either to idealize the category, usually in the pseudopoetic tradition of Clifford Odets, or poke fun at it. This is strange, because we are not only a nation of dying salesmen, money-hungry little foxes and fading aristocrats dependent on the kindness of strangers, but flesh-and-blood plodders on the assembly lines. Most of the important plays of the past half-century have enlightened us as to where the money came from, who got it and/or how it got used, but almost none have dealt with the daily problems of how people earn it hour by hour, day after day, and what price they pay for it spiritually.

Emanuel Fried's **Drop Hammer,** currently being given a splendid production at the Los Angeles Actors' Theatre, helps to fill this void. Crudely eloquent and powerful, unfailingly honest in its observations, it is exactly the sort of play Odets might have written if, like Fried, he had ever actually worked in a factory. *Drop Hammer* is to *Waiting for Lefty* as *Das Kapital* is to the works of Horatio Alger. Unlike Odets, Fried knows his people too well to sentimentalize them. His workers are really dirty, they sweat real sweat; they also lie, cheat and betray each other just like the rest of us.

The strength of the piece lies not so much in its plot turns, which are ordinary enough and occasionally clumsy, but in its ferocious commitment to getting it right. The action, all of which takes place in a northeastern saloon during the course of an afternoon and following morning in the mid-1950s, turns largely on which union officer looted the local's treasury of about $1,400 and why, but the reverberations are far more profound. They compel us to examine how, even with the best of intentions, we are all capable of betraying not only each other, but our own most cherished ideals, while, blinded by our intramural pettifoggery, we are in turn betrayed. Even as the men squabble and accuse each other, their employers are preparing to move the machine shop they work in to Kentucky, where they won't have a union to contend with. The omnipresent booming of the nearby factory's drop hammer tolls a death knell, but they have grown too used to it to hear it.

One of the pleasures of attending any production at LAAT is the prospect of being confronted by a strong cast of professional actors. There are no weak performances from anyone in this huge cast of 30 men and one woman. Outstanding, however, are David Groh, as the harassed union trouble-shooter who knows what is really at stake but can't seem to make it

clear to anyone, and Edward Power, all phony Irish charm masking an anger and bitterness that will eventually mortally wound those he loves best.

Al Rossi has directed with a sure hand and helped also to clarify several muddy points in the text, though the writer still has some work to do in this area. The play needs pruning here and there and a stronger plot line.

Joy Barrett-Densmore's costumes looked about as blue in the collar as they could get; the sound design by Gregory E. Clark was exactly right; and D. Martyn Bookwalter's gloriously dingy set made me want to step right up to the bar, which was ably tended by Charles Hutchins. Emanuel Fried, the playwright, was born in 1913 and has written ten plays. He may not be a polished writer, but he's a very truthful one.

"*NEW WEST* magazine's William Murray joined other drama critics with praise for dealing 'realistically with lives and aspirations of blue-collar workers' when my play *DROP HAMMER* was produced in 1980 at Los Angeles Actors Theatre, now renamed Los Angeles Theatre Center."

"American actors, musicians and writers who met with counterparts in Leipzig in what was then, in 1981, East Germany. That's Tony Award winnng actor John Randolph center, flanked in first row by actresses Audra Lindley and Susan Franklin-Tanner, in second row by his actress wife Sara and choreographer Gemze De Lapp. That's actor James Whitmore behind Lindley, and I'm behind him, invited because of plays I'd written, including *THE DODO BIRD* which Leipzig dramaturg Hans Michael Richter translated into German."

"That's Rhoda, second from left, outside London's National Theatre, with some members of tour group sponsored by Theatre Department of State University of New York at Buffalo. You don't see me — I'm taking the picture. Photo, 1982."

"Noted writer Meridel LeSueur and I read from our work at Moushy's Pub in Pittsburgh, a fund raiser for Mill Hunk Herald, a cultural newspaper put out by rank-and-file workers, most of whom had been employed in steel plants in the area. Photo, 1983."

"Teaching delegates to Labour Education Conference of Metropolitan Toronto's Labour Council how to embody their union and work experience in plays and short stories. May, 1985."

"Lorrie, in 1990, heads Counseling Center, Carnegie-Mellon University, Pittsburgh."

"Mindy (Melinda), in 1990, reading to children of Elizabeth Hay and Mark Fried. Her cousin Mark edits NACLA, international magazine dealing with economic and political situation in Central and South America. Mindy, doing free lance work with child care and other family care organizations, is in doctoral program, seeking her Ph.D. at Brandeis University. Photo taken at home of my sister-in-law Ruth Fried, widow of my brother, David, in Swampscott, Massachusetts."

"Receiving Joe Hill Award for lifetime contribution to cause of labor through the arts, from Joe Glazer, Chairman, and Joe Uehlein, President, of Labor Heritage Association, June 25, 1990."

Buffalo playwright to get award from AFL-CIO

Emanuel Fried, once blackballed by labor groups, now is honored by them

EMANUEL (Manny) Fried, Buffalo playwright, actor and longtime labor activist and gadfly on the left, has been chosen to receive the Joe Hill Award for Lifetime Achievement by the Labor Heritage Foundation.

The award for the 77-year-old Fried comes at the end of a turbulent labor career, which saw him blackballed by much of organized labor during the height of the Cold War in the 1950s.

The award celebrates Fried's contribution in telling labor's message through the arts during most of his adult life. It will be presented Monday at the annual Labor Arts Exchange Conference at the George Meany Labor Center outside Washington, D.C.

Of Fried's work, which includes 15 plays, the drama critic of the Los Angeles Times wrote that "no American playwright writes so knowledgeably and

On The Job
By JOSEPH P. RITZ

sensitively of labor's rank and file as Emanuel Fried."

His one-act play, "The Dodo Bird," set in a workingman's bar near a Buffalo factory, has been performed several times in various theaters throughout the United States and Canada since it

was first staged off-Broadway in 1967. At the time it was hailed by Richard P. Cooke of the Wall Street Journal as "compelling theater, entirely convincing."

At one time, Fried wrote a short story a week for the now-departed Buffalo Union Leader. He began his acting as a youngster, playing juvenile parts in 13 Broadway plays during the 1930s. Returning to Buffalo in 1939, he organized the short-lived Buffalo Contemporary Theater.

Fried has self-published an autobiographical novel, "Big Ben Hood." His short story "The Junkman Sings in Spring" won the Pushcart Press "Outstanding Story of the Year" award.

Seven years ago, he founded the Just Buffalo Literary Center's Western New

See Fried Page B9

Emanuel Fried: Cold War victim.

Continued from Page B7

York playwright's workshop in residence at the Alleyway Theatre. Last year, he was instrumental in establishing the annual Labor in Literature competition, co-sponsored by Just Buffalo and the Buffalo AFL-CIO Council, to encourage workers to write about their lives.

The competition currently is being held again this year with additional sponsorship by the United Steelworkers of America.

Fried, a former union organizer for the United Electrical Union, came under fire from the House Un-American Affairs Committee and from many area union leaders in the 1950s and early 1960s. During the period, the UE was expelled from the CIO for pro-communist activities and Fried later was forced out of the International Association of Machinists on simi-

A yellowed newspaper clipping names him as one of the escorts of Earl Browder, then general secretary of the Communist Party U.S.A., at a communist rally here in 1943. He was denounced by Unionists Against Communism and, at one time, was unwelcome at Buffalo AFL-CIO Council meetings.

But that was more than a generation ago. Fried had red hair then, and passions were higher on both sides of the Cold War struggle.

Today, he chairs the Buffalo AFL-CIO Council's Labor Arts Committee and is a member of the advisory board of the Arts Council in Buffalo and Erie County.

THE BUFFALO NEWS

Business

June 23, 1990

"Labor reporter Joseph Ritz may have had a little difficulty reporting that I got the 1990 Joe Hill Award for Lifetime Achievement from the Labor Heritage Association. Any time he mentioned my name before that, he always added a little redbaiting touch: that I had been an organizer for the allegedly communist-dominated United Electrical Workers (UE). The Buffalo News, June 23, 1990."

"Recipient of Individual Artist Award for lifetime contribution to the arts, along with other awardees: Charles Mitschow, Regional President of Marine Midland Bank, Business Contributor; Renee Perez, Patron of the Arts; Margaret Foster, Executive Director, and Roger Simon, Board President of The Arts in Education Institute of Western New York, Inc., Nonprofit Arts Organization Award — Annual Arts Awards by Arts Council in Buffalo and Erie County and Greater Buffalo Chamber of Commerce, March 6, 1991."

THE UN-AMERICAN

City of Buffalo
Common Council

At the regular meeting of the Common Council of the City of Buffalo, which was held on Tuesday, July 17, 1990, the following resolution was unanimously adopted, sponsored by Eugene M. Fahey:

WHEREAS: The Labor Heritage Foundation has chosen Emanuel Fried to receive the Joe Hill Award for Lifetime Achievement; and

WHEREAS: Manny Fried, who came to Buffalo 71 years ago from Brooklyn, began his career in union organizing in 1939 when he brought fellow employees at Curtiss Wright Aircraft into the United Auto Workers; and

WHEREAS: An outspoken union leader, Manny Fried continued his organizing activities after he returned from serving in World War II; and

WHEREAS: As a young man, Manny acted in many Broadway plays before he returned to Buffalo where he organized the Buffalo Contemporary Theatre; and

WHEREAS: Manny is a prolific writer whose works include plays, short stories, and an autobiographical novel. His short story "The Junkman Sings in Spring" won the Pushcart Press "Outstanding Story of the Year" award. His play "The Dodo Bird" has been performed in theatres across the country and Canada since first being performed off-Broadway in 1967; and

WHEREAS: Manny Fried founded the Just Buffalo Literary Center in 1983 and was instrumental in establishing the Labor in Literature contest which gets union members to write about their experiences; and

WHEREAS: His greatest impact on Western New York may be seen in the admiration of the many students he taught at Buffalo State College from 1971 until his 1983 retirement; and

WHEREAS: In retirement, Manny chairs the Buffalo AFL-CIO Council's Labor Arts Committee and is a member of the advisory board of the Arts Council in Buffalo and Erie County;

NOW, THEREFORE BE IT RESOLVED:

That this Common Council extends its congratulations to Emanuel Fried for being the 1990 recipient of the Joe Hill Award; and

BE IT FURTHER RESOLVED:

That this Honorable Body expresses its deep appreciation to Manny Fried for his lasting contributions to the labor movement, literature and Western New York; and

BE IT FINALLY RESOLVED:

That this Common Council extends its best wishes to Manny Fried for continued good health, happiness and prosperity.

GEORGE K. ARTHUR-COUNCIL PRESIDENT

EUGENE M. FAHEY-MAJORITY LEADER

CHARLES L. MICHAUX, III-CITY CLERK

"Resolution adopted by City of Buffalo Common Council, July 17, 1990. It came as completely unexpected but welcome surprise. I thanked the Council for their decency in doing this for someone they know is on the Left."

"After my acceptance speech, thanking the Arts Council in Buffalo and Erie County and the Greater Buffalo Chamber of Commerce people for their decency and sense of perspective — taking the long view — in giving the 1991 Individual Artist Award for lifetime achievement in the arts to a man they know is on the Left and a dedicated labor man. County Executive Dennis Gorski jocularly congratulated me, 'I'm glad we've got at least one Leftist left in town.' I thought he was taking an oblique swipe at some local politicians who were hastily distancing themselves from the Left because of the changes in Europe. Photo, March 6, 1991."

"Lorrie, myself and Mindy, at Hyatt Hotel, immediately following my receipt of 1991 Individual Artist Award from Arts Council in Buffalo and Erie County and the Greater Buffalo Chamber of Commerce."